Contents at a Glance

PART III
Using RMAN Effectively

Oracle Press™

Oracle9*i* RMAN
Backup & Recovery

Robert G. Freeman
Matthew Hart

McGraw-Hill/Osborne

New York   Chicago   San Francisco
Lisbon   London   Madrid   Mexico City
Milan   New Delhi   San Juan
Seoul   Singapore   Sydney   Toronto

The McGraw·Hill Companies

McGraw-Hill/Osborne
2600 Tenth Street
Berkeley, California 94710
U.S.A.

To arrange bulk purchase discounts for sales promotions, premiums, or fund-raisers, please
contact **McGraw-Hill**/Osborne at the above address. For information on translations or book
distributors outside the U.S.A., please see the International Contact Information page
immediately following the index of this book.

Oracle9*i* RMAN Backup & Recovery

Oracle is a registered trademark and Oracle9*i* is a trademark or registered trademark of Oracle
Corporation.

1234567890 FGR FGR 0198765432
ISBN 0-07-222662-5

Publisher
  Brandon A. Nordin

Vice President & Associate Publisher
  Scott Rogers

Acquisitions Editor
  Jeremy Judson

Editorial Director
  Wendy Rinaldi

Senior Project Editors
  Betsy Manini, Jody McKenzie

Project Editors
  Patty Mon, Jennifer Malnick

Acquisitions Coordinator
  Athena Honore

Technical Editor
  Matthew Arrocha

Copy Editor
  Bill McManus

Proofreader
  Linda Medoff

Indexer
  Valerie Perry

Computer Designers
  Tabitha M. Cagan, Tara A. Davis

Illustrators
  Michael Mueller, Lyssa Wald

Series Design
  Jani Beckwith

Cover Series Design
  Damore Johann Design, Inc.

This book was composed with Corel VENTURA™ Publisher.

To the great explorers who found this place,
To the founding fathers who made it great.
To the pioneers who moved out west,
To my parents with whom I was blessed.
To my wife, who supports me through it all,
To my kids, who are getting way to tall
I dedicate this work to you,
and, I'm really thankful that it is through.
Robert Freeman

This book is dedicated to Lily's grandparents.
Matthew Hart

About the Authors

Robert G. Freeman lives somewhere in Florida where he works as a database architect and author. He is the husband of one, and father of five. Robert has been working with Oracle databases for more than ten years, and has written several Oracle database-related books, such as the Oracle Press title *Oracle9i New Features* (McGraw-Hill/Osborne, 2002). In his off time, he does karate and Krav Maga, and hopes someday to find time to start flying again. If you would like to write to Robert and provide constructive feedback, his e-mail address is dbaoracle@aol.com. You can also find Robert on the Quest DBA Pipelines, http://quest-pipelines.com/ where he tends to SYSOP duties.

Matthew Hart is currently surviving the economy and living in Kansas City, Missouri, where his wife and daughter patiently wait for him to get the writing bug "out of his system for good." Mr. Hart is currently in his fifth year at Oracle. He is also the co-author of the Oracle Press title *Oracle9i for Windows 2000: Tips and Techniques* (McGraw-Hill/Osborne, 2002).

PART IV

RMAN: Beyond Backup and Recovery

PART V

Appendixes

Contents

PART I
Starting Out

PART II
Setup Principles and Practices

PART IV
RMAN: Beyond Backup and Recovery

PART V
Appendixes

Acknowledgments

irst of all, thanks to Matthew Hart, my co-author. Matthew is an RMAN guru, and this book is made much better with his co-authorship. The RMAN Workshops were his brilliant stroke of genius. Matthew (like the rest of us) moved mountains to get this book out on time. Thanks Matthew!

Thanks to all of those at McGraw-Hill/Osborne who helped put this Oracle Press book together. Jeremy Judson got this book off the ground. Athena Honore kept it in the air and put up with my constant financial questions. Special mention goes to senior project editor Betsy Manini. When others might have thrown up their hands in disgust, she pushed this thing along in the end so we could get this out when we needed to. She took on a pile of work and moved that pile well! Thanks also to Jody McKenzie who did some editing for us, and our copy editor Bill McManus was just terrific! Our technical editor, Matthew Arrocha, was spot on with his comments. Thanks to you all.

When we started this book, our goal was to provide coverage of all things RMAN. However, we recognized that we lacked expertise with regard to some of the vendor-supplied products that interfaced with RMAN. Thus, the call went out for contributors to provide this content—and provide they did! So, thanks to Radhakrishnan Ramamurthi, Sujatha Madan, Rob O'Brien, Marc Palen, and Sue Sieger, each of whom authored or co-authored one chapter of this text, and made it much more complete than it otherwise would have been. They went out of their way to provide these chapters, with no more thanks or remuneration than what you are seeing here.

My life has been full of great people who have mentored me, or who are just great personal friends. Thanks to those people. Thanks to Gary Chancellor, my Oracle mentor; Glen Webster, my friend and early IT mentor; Don Faur, another friend and early IT mentor; Mark Blomberg, who has long been a friend and who co-authored another book with me; Jeff Kellum, who got me my first writing job; and Paul Winterstein, another of my Oracle mentors from long ago. Thanks also to Mike Ault, John B., K. Gopalakrishnan, Marlene Theriault, Pete Sharman, Steve

Adams, Steve Hilker, and many more good people who have helped me out a great deal over the years of my Oracle life (and probably don't even know it!).

When you go to write a book, your life changes. You have even less free time than you had before. The people around you can really make this either a good or bad experience and the people around me have helped to make it great. Thus, this book is, as always, dedicated to the special people in my life who keep me going, or who set me on this path. It is dedicated to Master Clark, Ms. Skutnik and Mr. Cossa who give me the stress relief I need by making me kick, punch, and yell until I can't do it anymore. Thanks to everyone at work who put up with me as I churned through this writing process. Thanks to Tim, Charles, Nancy, Stephanie, Yang, Rich, Bob, Ronald, John, Bill B., Bill S., Don, Maritza, Gunjan, Nirupaum, Wendy, Barbara, Cindy, Caroline… You are all great. If I have left someone out of my acknowledgments, please know that I am inexpressibly grateful for your help and forbearance!

I'd have never finished my first book, let alone six now, if it had not been for the way my folks raised me. Because they have made this book possible, I thank my parents who always pushed me to work harder and never be satisfied with second best.

Finally, and most of all, the people who suffer the most when you write are those closest to you. That would be my wife and my five kids. I couldn't do much of anything without them in my life, and they enable me to write away as I do.

Robert G. Freeman

Who reads the acknowledgments? I posed this question in my last book. Talk about a rookie mistake. As it turns out, *everyone you know* reads the acknowledgments, but usually not the people who actually read the rest of the book. Barring a few exceptions, the two groups are mutually exclusive. I have decided that this is the unusual fate of writing technical books when most of your friends and family are not very technical.

With that in mind, I must first thank those at McGraw-Hill/Osborne who made this book a reality. Jeremy Judson put this book on the shelf, first and foremost, and we owe its existence to him. We won't forget you, Jeremy. Then there is the ever-present task-master, Athena Honore, without whom no deadline would ever be met. She deserves all the credit for keeping me moving along what seemed like a draconian timeline for completion. Finally, thanks and praise must go out to our senior project editor Betsy Manini, who struggled through personal hardship unlike any other just in time for this entire project to fall into her lap. Her last-minute struggle to get this thing out on time, in good fashion, and in working order, is a testament to her own resilience and fortitude. I must also thank Bill McManus for a great copyedit, and Jody McKenzie for taking up the slack during Betsy's absence and not missing a beat.

Beyond the McGraw-Hill/Osborne gang, I must convey my thanks to our contributing authors, without whom this book would have suffered the myopic fate of containing only the most rudimentary media management coverage. Radhakrishnan Ramamurthi, Sujatha Madan, Rob O'Brien, Marc Palen, and Sue Sieger: Thank you.

The energy you devoted to this project enabled us to provide a complete product, and our readers will benefit immensely. The world of technical writing is by its very nature collaborative, and you have raised the level of this book above my highest expectations.

I owe my deepest gratitude to Matt Arrocha, our fearless technical editor, for reading through this entire book when it was at its most ugly, and seeing through the lousy prose long enough to fix our technical inconsistencies and make excellent suggestions for inclusion. I've had the pleasure of working with Matt for sometime now, and have never found a person more willing to teach you what he knows.

Working with Robert Freeman has been a pleasure, from the beginning of the project to its hectic finale. We had very little time to waste getting this book to press, and Robert's light-heartedness combined with his hard work was a continual inspiration. I hope the opportunity will arise in the future for more collaboration.

Throughout the duration of the writing of this book, my colleagues at Oracle have been patient with my yawns and occasional late mornings. In particular, I must thank Tim Floyde, Thom Walker, Kevin Smith, Todd Dekam, Kevin Cook, Svetlana Grove, and Tracey Tilton. The team we put together and the work we accomplished was amazing to witness. It is not often you can get eight people each with a raging work ethic all lined up for a common goal. What it took was the type of solid leadership we had from Steve Israel, my boss and agent. Steve, I promise, the minute I sell the rights to Hollywood for the movie, you'll get your 10 percent. It's an oath I will not break.

My good friend and colleague, Martin Ingram, played a crucial role in getting me through my last book and this book, and I'm sure he will be there for all future books as well. He's also been integral in getting me through two mediocre years of Broncos football by helping me drown it in pitchers of Old Style down at Tony's. Martin is the kind of friend who always comes through, especially when you need it most. Oh, and for a manager, he's a pretty good techie—I would not have survived the EM chapter without him. Or maybe I should say, for a techie, he's a pretty good manager....

I had the opportunity to spend a month of the summer while working on this book with my parents and two of my brothers, and the support and advice I received meant the world to me. The experience changed my priorities forever, and I can't thank them enough. This book is for my mom, who is tougher than any other person I've ever met, except maybe my father, who fought all odds to be who he is today. I try to be as good as they are every day of my life. To my brothers: here's to long games of cross-country bocce in city parks from the Rockies to the East Coast.

This book could not have happened had Beth and I not had the continual support of her family. My thanks must go out to Anne and Mark, for giving us nights out when we needed them most; to Clare, for giving Beth the help she needed while I disappeared into the office, or onto a plane; and to Alex, for judicious use of his pool, for cold beer, and for great family get-togethers.

Finally, my contribution to this book is merely a testament to the love and dedication I have received from my wife. Beth, thank you for everything. For putting my office together first after the move. For watching Lily every day while I sat in this little side-room, hour after hour, plinking away at a keyboard. For going to Idaho Falls with me. For being supportive even when I walked bleary-eyed into the bedroom at all hours of the morning. For helping me laugh at myself and the whole project when it deserved to be laughed at. Thanks. You and Lily are at the very center of this, your names written into the white space between words, your love imprinted on every page.

Matthew Hart

Introduction

*In order to live free and happily you must
sacrifice boredom. It is not always an easy sacrifice.*

—Richard Bach

Answering the Question

You are holding in your hot little hands the answer to a question. It may be the question that prompted you to pick this book up; it may be a question you are wrestling with every day at your job. It is the question that drives you to utilize more and more complex software and hardware configurations every day, striving to answer the one big fat burning question. How can I balance availability with recoverability?

Okay, it may seem a simple question. And maybe this in particular is not what keeps you up at night. But if you dig deeper, past all the hard work you put into your backups, and think about backups, writing scripts, configuring software and hardware, and furnishing your server room with all kinds of lavish robotic tape jukeboxes, you may find that this fundamental question sits alone, patiently waiting for you:

How can I keep my database up and available, free from performance-sucking monsters, but still make that database disaster-proof?

Oracle, as you might imagine, would like to outfit you with the answer to this question. In fact, Oracle has a litany of high availability solution packages to meet every business need you might think up. And if you can stump them, trust me, the next version will catch up to your need. Availability is the siren call of every self-respecting database developer in the world, and Oracle hears that call ring out crisp in the night air.

This book, sadly, cannot cover the entirety of the high-availability software offerings from Oracle. That is a topic for a different volume than this. Instead, this book looks to answer the second part of the question: recoverability. Thus, this book helps you to ensure that you have a secure, unbreakable, reliable backup of your database, one that performs without interference with production work. This book, then, is about RMAN. But you probably already knew that.

Bundled tightly with every copy of its flagship database software comes Oracle Recovery Manager, or RMAN for short. RMAN provides an interface for backing up and recovering your database. Of course, if it were only that simple, you wouldn't need our help. But with complex demands come complex solutions, and RMAN is no different. Sure, at its core, you can perform basic backup and recovery operations with little or no training, nor even the most basic understanding of how it works. If that's what you need, put this book next to your database server and dog-ear the table of contents; when you need to do something, we'll give you the steps and reference you need.

But RMAN also provides a number of extremely useful features for those who need to take their backup and recovery strategies to the next level. You need to be able to recover a single block, and avoid work stoppage on anything but a single table. You need to clone your database to another server for new application testing. You need to create a standby database for protecting your system from disaster-related outages. You need to backup directly to tape to ease the load on your disk storage system. You are required to manage the backup and recovery work for a number of enterprise-wide databases. For all of this work, and more, we have written a complete guide to everything there is to know about RMAN. From the simplest of backups to the most complex recovery scenarios, this book is at your service.

A Book for the DBA and the System Administrator

Perhaps the most frustrating aspect of choosing a solid, reliable backup strategy for an Oracle database is that such a strategy usually overlaps the duties of two different kinds of people: the database administrator, and the system administrator. Choosing RMAN as your backup strategy is no different. Its tight integration with the Oracle RDBMS means a working knowledge of an Oracle database must be established. But, the reliance on external tape storage systems and the network topology makes the ability to administer networked computer systems critical. This leads to an interesting separation of duties, and headaches on each side.

This book is written to be as inclusive as possible. If you come from a database background, we provide the detail needed to get you up to speed with the role the system administrator must play in the backup system. If you come from the sys admin world, we spell out clearly the steps that must be taken in the database, and why. This book will help you implement the backup system from the database internals to the tape storage software.

RMAN: An Evolution into Excellence

RMAN was introduced in version 8.0.3, the first production release of Oracle8. Prior to this, the Oracle-provided interface for streaming backups directly to tape involved logical backups using the Export utility, or use of the Enterprise Backup Utility (EBU). Ah, EBU. May it rest it peace, and we promise this is the last time we will ever mention it. *Ever.*

As an initial release, RMAN had its pratfalls and quirks. But with every release since its rollout, new features have been added, bugs have been fixed, and the interface has been polished. The best way to visualize the progress is to think of the traditional poster showing the evolution of humans. On the left, you see a monkey, walking on all fours. Then, moving to the right, you see increasingly upright versions of a human, until you arrive at the left, with a fully upright, modern homo sapiens.

With the release of Oracle9i, RMAN has finally reached a full, upright walking position. It has truly become a necessary component in any serious strategy for a highly available database system.

What this Book Covers

This handbook was written to utilize the latest features included in Oracle9i, Release 2 (version 9.2.0.0.0). It therefore takes advantage of the latest enhancements to the RMAN interface and explains the newest features available. If a particular topic is not available in Oracle9i, Release 1, we point this out in the text. But all code examples and architectural explanations are based on the Oracle9i release of RMAN.

If you are still using Oracle8i, you should know that the command interface for operating RMAN took a fundamental turn for the better in version 9i, and there are some explicit differences. But fear not, we shall not leave you behind. At the end of this book, Appendix C discusses each specific difference between how the product is explained in the book and Oracle8i. In addition, we mark explicitly in the text those features that are not available in 8i.

In addition to differences between 8i and 9i, the product even changed significantly between 8.1.6 and 8.1.7. These differences are explained Appendix C as well, along with a brief discussion of Oracle8 limitations.

Using this Book Effectively

Like all technical manuals worth their weight, this book is meant to be readable, cover to cover, as a way to familiarize yourself with RMAN and its role in any high-availability or disaster-recovery solution. The topics are approached in a format that allows each complex subject to build on previous chapters, slowly working forward from principles, to setup, to backups, and then beyond backups to advanced functionality and practices.

As such, **Part I** is dedicated to an introduction to backup and recovery principles in the Oracle RDBMS. It gives you an important conceptual understanding of RMAN and how it does that mojo that it does. These two chapters lay the foundation for all future chapters, and we encourage you to read them carefully and understand the concepts being discussed. If you can understand the concepts and internal workings presented in Part I, then the rest of the book will be a breeze.

Part II is dedicated to setting up RMAN for initial usage. We cover all possible RMAN configuration options. Then, we discuss the integration with a media manager. The media manager is the layer that allows you to write your backups directly to a tape device, and is not provided by Oracle. While there are many products on the market, we discuss only the three most popular products: Veritas NetBackup, Legato Networker, and IBM's Tivoli Storage Manager.

In **Part III**, we provide the basics for RMAN usage, from the most basic backup operation to the most advanced recovery option. We discuss catalog maintenance and how to keep and eye on the catalog so that you can effectively manage the backups that are accumulating. Finally, there is a discussion on tuning RMAN backups and restores for optimal performance when it counts.

Part IV jumps into the thick of it, discussing how RMAN can assist you in tasks other than just simple backups. It runs through how to use the RMAN backups to make a cloned copy of your database, as well as how to use the backups to create a standby database. Then it discusses using RMAN in a Real Application Clusters (RAC) environment, with its special needs and requirements. Part IV ends with a series of RMAN Case Studies, which delve into common (and not so common) situations that require RMAN.

There are four **Appendixes**. Appendix A is an RMAN syntax reference, for building a successful RMAN command. Appendix B explores the RMAN catalog, both in V$ views in the database and rc_* views in the recovery catalog. Appendix C, as mentioned, covers the syntactical differences between Oracle8i and Oracle9i. Finally, Appendix D gives a short guide to setting up a good test environment for putting RMAN functionality through the ringers prior to implementing a production backup and recovery strategy.

RMAN Workshops

Not everyone reads a book cover to cover. We know this. Sometimes that's not the higher calling of a good technical book. A good book lives next to the computer, with pages dog-eared, sections highlighted, and little yellow post-its hanging off the side.

This book is meant to be a reference guide in addition to a conceptual explanation. We've packed this thing with useful techniques and timesaving practices that you can implement now, even if you're a little spotty on the architecture. Sometimes you just need to *know how to do it*, right? This applies especially when it comes to backup and recovery. No one wants to get stuck in the middle of a weekend recovery binge, trying to figure out the exact syntax for a particular restore operation while the production database sits idly by, bleeding revenue at a spectacular rate.

So, to help with the highlighting and dog-earing of pages, we are introducing the RMAN Workshop sections of the book. Whenever we provide useful code for performing a specific operation, or a series of steps to complete a certain project, we mark it in a larger font and gray box. When you see this box, you know the following pages will be filled with the actual steps you need to follow to get your job done fast. Think of RMAN Workshops as recipes, providing the ingredients and the mixing instructions for a quick and easy meal.

To make your life even easier, we've compiled a separate Contents listing for every RMAN Workshop in this book, with its descriptive title and the page number. You'll find this RMAN Workshop reference as part of the Contents at a Glance at the beginning of the book as well as in the main Contents. Using the Contents at a Glance, you can skip directly to the one you need and get right to work That way, if you find our prose boring and concepts overblown, you can still get lots of specific use from this book.

In addition to the RMAN Workshops, the final chapter of this book is a series of case studies that discuss actual backup and recovery scenarios, along with the best means of dealing with those scenarios. These scenarios are as simple as preserving backup metadata while recreating the control file, or as complex as recovering a database through a resetlogs.

Again, we encourage you to read the book chapter for chapter. Nothing can replace a conceptual understanding of a product, especially when that product is protecting your most valuable asset: the database. But if you skip around for the stuff you need, as you need it, don't worry. We have you covered.

So, enjoy the book! RMAN is a challenging and rewarding product to dig into and utilize. It can save you time and energy, and help you to avoid health problems related to insomnia, outage stress, and paranoia.

PART
I

Starting Out

CHAPTER
1

Oracle9i Backup and Recovery Architecture Tour

o, you bought this book to learn about RMAN. Great choice! Before we get deep into RMAN, though, we thought you would like to take a tour of the Oracle backup and recovery landscape. For some of you, this might be old hat, and if so, just enjoy the ride. If you are new to Oracle, this tour will really help you to be prepared for the onslaught of RMAN information you will be getting down the road. So, jump on the bus, keep your feet and hands inside at all times, and we will be off.

In this tour of the Oracle database backup and recovery architecture, you will encounter the following:

- Backup and recovery essentials

- A few Oracle terms to know

- Oracle database physical architecture

- Oracle operational internals

- ARCHIVELOG vs. NOARCHIVELOG mode operations

- Oracle recovery modes

- Manual backup operations in Oracle

- Manual recovery operations in Oracle

As we proceed through this tour of Oracle, you will learn that it is important to understand how the Oracle product works so that you can properly apply the techniques that will be documented in this book to bring your wayward database back to life. You will also see that there is more to backing up and recovering a database than just entering a few commands and putting tapes in the tape drive.

The direct results of misapplying a technique, or not understanding a principle of the architecture, may be an extended outage or even loss of data. The old adage that you must walk before you can run applies with this topic. Finally, we are only going to cover basics and any additional information that you will need to know with regard to RMAN and recovering your database. If you need more information on these subject areas, there are several good Oracle Press titles that can help you.

Backup and Recovery Essentials

Okay, getting on our way, our first stop is in the area of backup and recovery essentials. There are generally two different areas that need to be dealt with when crafting plans to execute in the event your database goes bottom up. The first architectural question is one of high availability, which is loosely coupled with the second question, which is one of backup and recovery. Let's look at these questions of high availability and backup and recovery in more detail.

High Availability

High availability (HA) implies an architecture that prevents the users from being aware of partial or total system (database, network, hardware, and so forth) failure. HA solutions can include such elements as mirrored drives, RAID architectures, database clustering, database failover schemes, and, of course, backup and recovery. HA adds additional costs to the overall database architectural solution, over and above the costs of the backup and recovery solution selected. RMAN is really not an HA solution, but it is part of an overall database solution that can include HA. Be clear that you need a backup and recovery solution, regardless of whether or not you decide to implement an HA solution.

If you are interested in looking at HA solutions, there are a number of them out there, including these:

- Oracle9i Data Guard

- Oracle9i Real Application Clusters

- Oracle Replication

- RAID and mirrored drives

Various other vendors provide HA solutions as well. Because HA options are really a separate topic from RMAN, we do not cover them in this book.

Backup and Recovery

As we continue our tour (anyone want to stop at the snack bar?), we move to backup and recovery, which is getting us close to the main topic of this book, RMAN. We will talk in detail throughout this chapter about the different kinds of backups that can be done in Oracle, but for now, let's talk about the primary types of backups: offline (cold) and online (hot).

Offline backups are done with the database down, which means that it is also unavailable to users. Online backups, on the other hand, are done with the database up and running, so users can continue with their business. RMAN supports both types of backups. In fact, as you will see in later chapters, some of the features of RMAN make it the preferable method for performing online database backups.

You shouldn't just "decide" that it's time to back up your database. This is particularly true in the case of production databases, where the users have certain levels of expectations for protection of their data. Before you just decide when and how to back up your database, you should gather some of your users' requirements and consider your company's general backup policy. Only after you have gathered those requirements can you craft that backup plan. Let's look in some more detail at how you gather those requirements.

Backup and Recovery Strategy Requirements Gathering

In gathering user requirements, we really want to find out from them what their needs are. A number of questions need to be asked, and as the database administrator (DBA), you should take the lead in asking them. To collect backup and recovery requirements, we need to ask our customers a few questions like the following:

- How much data loss can you afford in the event of a database failure?

- What is the maximum length of time you are able to allow for recovery of your database?

- How much are you willing to spend to ensure your data is recoverable?

- Can the system be down during the backup?

Quickly, let's look at each of these questions in more detail.

How Much Data Loss Can You Afford?   This is probably the most important question of all. All backup and recovery plans have some risk of data loss associated with them, and as you move closer to a zero data loss solution, the costs of the backup and recovery plan can skyrocket. Just as was the case with HA, the organization needs to quantify the cost of data loss and, based on that cost, craft a cost-effective backup and recovery plan. It is critical that the customer understand how much data loss risk they are taking with the chosen backup and recovery plan. Of course, each database has an allowable amount of loss too, one database may be much more tolerant of data loss than another.

What Is the Maximum Length of Time You Are Able to Allow for Recovery?   Different technologies perform in different ways, and vary widely in price. Generally, the faster you wish your recovery to go, the more expensive it ends up being. For example, recoveries direct from disk tend to be a bit more expensive than recoveries from tape, but also tend to be faster. It is important that the customer understand how long recovery of the database will take in the event of a complete outage.

How Much Can You Spend on Recovery?   There is a direct relationship between how much data loss you can tolerate, how long it will take to actually recover the database, and how much it will cost to provide a given level of protection. It is important, early on, to understand just how much the customer is willing to spend on architecture to support your proposed backup and recovery plan. Nothing is more embarrassing than proposing a massive architecture with a high dollar cost, and having the customer look at you and laugh at the projected expense.

Can the System Be Down During the Backup?   Another key piece of information to determine is what the state of the database needs to be during the backup. Can an outage be afforded to do backups, or do those backups need to be done online? The answer to this question impacts your total overall cost and your decisions in backup strategy.

Backup and Recovery—Crafting the Plan

Now that you have gathered your requirements, you can begin to craft your backup and recovery plan. You need to make a number of decisions, including

- Based on the user (and business) requirements, do you need to do offline or online backups of the database?

- If you are going to use online backups, how often do you need to back up archived redo logs? How will you protect the archived redo logs from loss between backup sessions?

- What are the company policies and standards with regard to recoverability?

- How are you going to ensure your system is recoverable in the event of a disaster?

Each of these questions is important. Disasters are important to plan for, and they do happen. Company policies may well supercede the needs of the users. Backup policies and standards are important to implement and enforce. Managing one database backup and recovery policy is easy. Managing many different databases with different methods of doing backup and recovery becomes cumbersome and dangerous.

Managing archived redo logs is important because they are critical to recovery, and you want to be able to support your users as much as you can. After all, the users are the reason you are there! To really be able to determine how to craft our backup strategy, you need to understand how Oracle works and how Oracle backup and recovery works; we will talk about that shortly. First, just to make sure we are all on the same page, let's discuss some basic Oracle terms.

Oracle: A Few Oracle Terms to Know

It is always a bit hard to decide where to start when discussing the Oracle architecture because so many of the different components are interrelated. This makes it hard to talk about one without making reference to the other. So that we can have a common point of reference for some basic terms, in this section, we quickly define those terms. We will be using these terms throughout the rest of this book, so it is really important that you clearly understand them (we also define them in more depth as this chapter progresses). So, if you are a bit hazy on Oracle internal terms, please review the following until you know what they are without hesitation:

- **Alert log**   A text log file in which the database maintains error and status messages. The alert log can be a critical structure when trying to determine the nature of a database failure. Typically, the alert log is in the background dump destination directory, as defined by the database parameter BACKGROUND_DUMP_DEST, and is called alert<sid>.log.

- **Archived redo logs**   When the database is in ARCHIVELOG mode, archived redo logs are generated each time Oracle switches online redo logs by the LGWR process. Archived redo logs are used during database recovery. Copies of the archived redo logs can be written to as many as ten different directories, defined by the Oracle parameter LOG_ARCHIVE_DEST_n in the database parameter file.

- **Backup control file**   A backup of the control file generated as the result of the **alter database backup control file to *filename*** or **alter database backup controlfile to trace** commands.

- **Block**   The most atomic unit of storage in Oracle. The default block size is determined by the parameter DB_BLOCK_SIZE in the database parameter file, and it is set permanently when a database is created. Oracle9i allows tablespaces to be different block sizes than the default.

- **Checkpoint**   A database event that causes the database to flush dirty (used) blocks from memory and write them to disk.

- **Database**   Consists of the different components that make up an Oracle database (tablespaces, redo logs, and so forth). A database is much different than an instance. A database is where the data lives, and what you will be backing up and recovering with RMAN.

- **Database consistency**   Implies that each object in the database is consistent to the same point in time.

- **Database datafile**   A physical entity that is related to a tablespace. A database consists of at least one database datafile (which would be assigned to the SYSTEM tablespace), and most databases consist of many different database datafiles. Whereas a tablespace can have many different database datafiles associated with it, a given database datafile can have only one tablespace associated with it.

■ **Database parameter file**   Contains instance and database configuration information (also known as the init.ora file). The database parameter file comes in two flavors (each are mutually exclusive). There is the init.ora, which is a text file, and the spfile.ora file, which allows for persistent settings of database parameters via the **alter system** command.

■ **Granule**   A unit of Oracle memory measurement introduced in Oracle9*i*. All SGA memory allocations are rounded to the nearest granule units. The size of a granule is dependent on the overall expected size of the SGA, and it may be 4MB or 16MB.

■ **Instance**   An instance is the collection of Oracle memory and processes. When the SGA (memory) is allocated and each of the required Oracle processes is up and running successfully, then the Oracle instance is said to be started. Note that just because the Oracle instance is running, this does not mean that the database itself is open. An instance is associated with one, and only one, database at any given time.

■ **Online redo logs**   When redo is generated, it is physically stored in the online redo logs of the database. Oracle requires that at least two online redo logs be created for a database to operate. These online redo logs can have multiple mirrored copies for protection of the redo. This is known as *multiplexing* the redo log. As an online redo log fills with redo, Oracle switches to the next online redo log, which is known as a *log switch* operation.

Each online redo log file has a unique *log sequence number* associated with it. This log sequence number uniquely identifies an online redo log file and, if it's archived, its associated archived redo log file. You can find the log sequence number of the online redo logs by querying the V$LOG view. The sequence number of a given archived redo log can be found in the V$ARCHIVED_LOG view.

Additionally, an Online redo log (and an archived redo log) contains a range of database SCNs that is unique to that redo log. During recovery, Oracle applies the undo in the archived/online redo logs in order of log sequence number.

■ **Database parameter file**   Also called the init.ora file, this parameter file provides configuration information for the Oracle database instance and its related database. This file defines such things as memory requirements, directories for log files and trace files, and database network configuration information.

- **Processes** The programs that do the actual work of the Oracle database. There are five required processes in Oracle9i, and there are a number of others.

- **Redo** A record of all changes made to a given database. For almost any change in the database, an associated redo record is generated.

- **Schema** Owns the various logical objects in Oracle, such as tables and indexes, and is really synonymous with the user.

- **SGA (system global area)** An area of shared memory that is allocated by Oracle as it is started. This memory can be shared by all Oracle processes.

- **System change number (SCN)** A counter that represents the current state of the database at a given point in time. Like the counter on your VCR, as time progresses, the SCN increases. Each SCN atomically represents a point in the life of the database. Thus, at 11 A.M., the database SCN might be 10ffx0 (4351 decimal), and at 12 P.M., it might be 11f0x0 (4592 decimal).

- **Tablespace** A physi-logical entity. It is a logical entity because it is the place that Oracle logical objects (such as tables and indexes) are stored. It is a physical entity because it is made up of one or more database datafiles. A database must contain at least one tablespace, the SYSTEM tablespace, but most databases consist of many different tablespaces.

- **Trace files** Generated by the database in a number of different situations, including process errors. Each database process also generates its own trace file. Trace files can be important when trying to resolve the nature of a database failure.

Controlling the Database Software

During various recovery operations, you need to control the state of the Oracle database and its associated instance. Let's quickly review how to start and stop Oracle databases.

To start the Oracle9*i* database, you use the SQL*Plus Oracle utility. Log in as the user system using the SYSDBA login ID. At the SQL*Plus prompt, issue the **startup** command, as you can see in this example:

```
C:\>sqlplus "sys as sysdba"
D:\oracle\admin\robt\pfile>sqlplus "sys as sysdba"
SQL*Plus: Release 9.2.0.1.0 - Production on Fri May 31 21:04:57 2002
Copyright (c) 1982, 2002, Oracle Corporation.  All rights reserved.
Enter password:
```

```
Connected to:
Oracle9i Enterprise Edition Release 9.2.0.1.0 - Production
Connected to an idle instance.
SQL> startup
```

When you start an Oracle database with the **startup** command, the operation goes through three different phases:

- **Instance startup**   The Oracle database instance is started.

- **Database mount**   The Oracle database is mounted.

- **Database open**   The Oracle database is opened for user activity.

The **startup** command has several different variations (which is important to know for several different RMAN operations), some of which include the following:

- **startup**   Causes Oracle to go through each of the three startup phases, and open to the user community.

- **startup restrict**   Causes Oracle to go through each of the three startup phases, and open in restricted mode. Only those users with restricted privileges can access the database.

- **startup nomount**   Causes the startup process to stop after it has successfully started the database instance. You will often use this command to start the database instance prior to actually creating a database. This command is also handy to have if you need to re-create the control file. Note that in order to be able to use RMAN with a given database, you must be able to successfully start the instance with the **startup nomount** command.

- **startup mount**   Causes the startup process to stop after it has successfully started the database instance and then mounted it. This command is helpful if you need to recover the SYSTEM tablespace.

- **startup force**   Causes the database to be shut down with a **shutdown abort** (discussed in the next list). This command can be followed by the mode you wish the database to be opened in again. Examples include

  - **startup force restrict**

  - **startup force mount**

  - **startup force nomount**

Of course, now that we know how to start up the database, how do we shut it down? Again, from SQL*Plus, we can use the **shutdown** command, which comes in these flavors:

- **shutdown** (also **shutdown normal**)   Causes Oracle to wait for all user processes to disconnect from the database. Once this has occurred, the database will be completely shut down. Use of this option avoids instance recovery. After the **shutdown** command is executed, no new user processes are able to connect to the database.

- **shutdown immediate**   Kills all existing user sessions and rolls back all uncommitted transactions. Use of this option avoids instance recovery. After the **shutdown immediate** is executed, no new user processes are able to connect to the database.

- **shutdown abort**   Basically, crashes the database. Use of this option requires instance (but not media) recovery. After a **shutdown abort** is executed, no new user processes are able to connect to the database.

- **shutdown transactional**   Causes Oracle to wait for all user processes to commit their current transactions and then disconnects the user processes and shuts down the database. While it is waiting for these transactions to complete, no new user sessions are allowed to connect to the database.

As we proceed through this book, we use many of these commands, and it is important to understand what state the database and its associated instance are in when the command has completed.

Oracle Architecture

Our tour continues now as we begin looking at the physical components of Oracle. First, we take a look at the processes that make up an Oracle database. Then, we look at Oracle memory structures and the different logical, physical, and physi-logical structures that make up an Oracle database. Finally, we discuss the differences between an instance and an Oracle database.

The Oracle Processes

When the **startup nomount** command is issued, Oracle attempts to start an Oracle *instance*. An Oracle instance is started after several required operating system processes (programs) are started, and a memory area known as the System Global Area (SGA) is allocated. In this section, we are going to take a look at the processes that get Oracle started. First, we look at the basic five Oracle processes required for any Oracle database to be functional. Next, we look at user and server processes. Finally, we look at other, optional Oracle processes that you might see from time to time.

NOTE
This is just a basic introduction to the Oracle processes. If you want more in-depth detail on them, please refer to the Oracle documentation.

The Five Required Oracle Processes

If an Oracle9i instance has successfully started, there will be a minimum of five different processes started. Of course, on certain systems (such as Microsoft-based OSs), the five different processes are really just threads of a single Oracle process, but the basic idea is still the same. These required processes are as follows:

- **PMON**   Also known as the process monitor process (and one of what I call the "Jamaican processes").

- **SMON**   Also known as the system monitor process (and the other "Jamaican process").

- **DBWn**   Known as the database writer processes. An instance can be configured with up to nine of these processes in Oracle9i (but generally no more than one is required). DBWn is responsible for writing information to the database datafiles from the database buffer cache structure in the SGA.

- **LGWR**   The log writer process is responsible for writing generated redo to the database online redo logs from the log buffer. LGWR is signaled to do these writes when a user session is committed, when the redo log buffer is nearly full, and at other times as required.

- **CKPT**   During a checkpoint operation, the CKPT process notifies DBWn of the checkpoint. The CKPT process also updates database datafile headers with current checkpoint information.

The User and Server Processes

When a user connects to the database, a user process is spawned (or a new thread is started on NT) that connects to a separately spawned server process. These processes communicate with each other using various protocols, such as bequeath or TCP/IP.

Other Optional Oracle Processes

A number of other Oracle processes may be launched as well when the Oracle instance is started (and in some cases, optional processes may actually be started much later on demand), depending on the configuration of the Oracle database parameter file. Most of these processes have little bearing on RMAN and database backup and recovery (unless it's the failure of that process that caused the database to crash), so we won't spend much time on them. All of the optional processes are documented in the Oracle documentation as well as in several Oracle Press books.

One optional process that does have some bearing on RMAN and backup and recovery are the ARCHn processes. These processes (and, in reality, there may be one or many of them) are critical to the backup and recovery process if you are doing online backups. See the section titled "ARCHIVELOG Mode vs. NOARCHIVELOG Mode," later in the chapter, for more on the ARCHn process(es).

Oracle Memory and RMAN

In this section, we look at the memory areas that we need to be concerned with in relationship to RMAN. As with any process, RMAN does require memory for its own operations and as a part of its database interactions. First, we look at the Oracle SGA, and then we look at private memory areas.

The Oracle System Global Area

The principal memory structure that we are concerned with in terms of RMAN and backup and recovery is called the system global area (SGA). The SGA consists of one large allocation of shared memory that can be broken down into several memory substructures:

- The database buffer cache

- The shared pool

- The redo log buffer

- The large pool

- The Java pool

Of particular interest to the RMAN user are the shared pool and the large pool. RMAN uses several Oracle PL/SQL packages as it goes through its paces (as you will see in Chapter 2). These packages are like any other Oracle PL/SQL packages in that they must be loaded into the shared pool. If the shared pool is not large enough, or if it becomes fragmented, it is possible that the RMAN packages will not be able to execute. Thus, it is important to allocate enough memory to the shared pool for RMAN operations.

The large pool is used by RMAN in specific cases and is not used by default, even if it is configured. RMAN allows you to duplex RMAN backups (or make concurrent copies of the same backup in different places) if either of the database parameters, BACKUP_TAPE_IO_SLAVES or DBWR_IO_SLAVES, is set to TRUE. In this case, Oracle can use the large pool memory rather than local memory (PGA). The use of the PGA is the default.

Defining Memory Allocations in the SGA   The individual size of the SGA components are allocated based on the settings of parameters in the database parameter file. Several parameters have no real direct bearing on RMAN operations (although they have some indirect bearing in terms of overall database performance). These parameters include DB_CACHE_SIZE, DB_nK_CACHE_SIZE, LOG_BUFFER, SGA_MAX_SIZE, LARGE_POOL_SIZE, and JAVA_POOL_SIZE.

Each of these is defined in the Oracle documentation, so refer to it if you need more information on them. The main parameters that have some bearing in terms of RMAN usage are SHARED_POOL_SIZE and LARGE_POOL_SIZE, which we will cover in detail in Chapter 2.

To recap quickly, we have discussed the makings of an Oracle instance in the last several pages. We have talked about the different Oracle processes and the different Oracle memory structures. When the processes and the memory all come together, an Oracle instance is formed. Now that we have an instance, we are ready for a database. In the next section, we discuss the various structures that make up an Oracle database.

The Oracle Database

Our tour now moves its attention to the Oracle database architecture itself. An Oracle database is made up of a number of different structures—some physical, some logical, and some physi-logical. In this section, we look at each of these types of structures and discuss each of the individual components of the Oracle database.

Oracle Physical Structures

Oracle physical structures are structures such as the following:

- Database datafiles

- Online redo logs

- Archived redo logs

- Database control files

Each of these structures is physically located on a storage device that is connected to your computer. These objects make up the physical existence of your Oracle database, and to recover your database, you may need to restore and recover one or more of these objects from a backup. Let's look at each of these objects in a bit more detail.

Database Datafiles   The database datafiles are the data storage medium of the database and are related to tablespaces, as you will see shortly. When information is stored in the database, it ultimately gets stored in these physical files. Each database datafile contains a *datafile header* that contains information to help track the current state of that datafile. This datafile header is updated during checkpoint operations to reflect the current state of the datafile.

Database datafiles can have a number of different statuses assigned to them. The primary statuses we are interested in are ONLINE, which is the normal status, and OFFLINE, which is an abnormal status. A database datafile might take on the RECOVER status, as well, indicating that there is a problem with it and that recovery is required.

If the database is in ARCHIVELOG mode, you can take a datafile offline, which may be required for certain recovery operations. If the database is in NOARCHIVELOG mode, then you can only take the database datafile offline by dropping it. Offline dropping a datafile can have some nasty effects on your database (such as loss of data), so do so with care.

Online Redo Logs   If the Oracle SCN can be likened to the counter on your VCR, then the redo logs can be likened to the videotape. The online redo logs are responsible for recording every single atomic change that occurs in the database. Each Oracle database must have a minimum of two different online redo log groups, and most databases generally have many more than that, for performance reasons.

Each online redo log group can have multiple members located on different disk drives for protection purposes. Oracle writes to the different members in parallel, making the write process more efficient. Oracle writes to one redo log group at a time, in round-robin fashion. When the group has been filled, the LGWR process closes those redo logs and then opens the next online redo log for processing.

Within redo logs are records called *change vectors.* Each change vector represents on atomic database change, in SCN order. During recovery (RMAN or manual), Oracle applies those change vectors to the database. This has the effect of applying all change records to the database in order, thus recovering it to the time in point of the failure (or another, earlier time if required). The LGWR process is responsible for writing the change vectors (cumulatively known as redo) to the online redo logs from the redo log buffer. We discuss this in more detail shortly in the "The Combined Picture" section of this chapter.

Archived Redo Logs   A *log switch* occurs when Oracle stops writing to one online redo log and begins to write to another. As the result of a log switch, if the database is in ARCHIVELOG mode and the ARCH process is running, a copy of the online redo log will be made. This copy of the online redo log is called an archived redo log. Oracle can actually copy the archived redo log files to up to ten different destinations. During media recovery, the archived redo logs are applied to the database to recover it. We discuss this in more detail shortly, in "The Combined Picture."

Database Control Files   Each Oracle database has one or more database control files. The control file contains various database information, such as the current SCN, the state of the database datafiles, and the status of the database. Of interest to the RMAN DBA is the fact that the control file also stores critical information on various RMAN operations, such as the backup status of each database datafile.

Oracle Tablespaces   Oracle tablespaces are kind of the metaphysical part of Oracle. They are the link between the physical world of Oracle, in the form of the database datafiles, and the logical link, in the form of the Oracle tablespace. Often, we refer to a tablespace as a physi-logical structure. Oracle stores objects within tablespaces, such as tables and indexes.

A tablespace is physically made up of one or more Oracle database datafiles. Thus, the overall space allocation available in a tablespace is dependent on the overall allocated size of these database datafiles. A tablespace can be OFFLINE or ONLINE, and may also be in either READ WRITE or READ ONLY mode. If a tablespace is in READ ONLY mode, the contents of the tablespace will not change. Because the contents of a READ ONLY tablespace do not change, DBAs often only back up READ ONLY tablespace database datafiles once, immediately after they are made read only. Of course, if the tablespace is ever taken out of READ ONLY mode, you need to start backing up the tablespace again.

ARCHIVELOG Mode vs. NOARCHIVELOG Mode

An Oracle database can run in one of two modes. By default, the database is created in NOARCHIVELOG mode. This mode permits normal database operations, but does not provide the capability to perform point-in-time recovery operations or online backups. If you want to do online (or hot) backups, then run the database in ARCHIVELOG mode. In ARCHIVELOG mode, the database makes copies of all online redo logs via the ARCH process, to one or more archive log destination directories.

The use of ARCHIVELOG mode requires some configuration of the database beyond simply putting it in ARCHIVELOG mode. You must also configure the ARCH process and prepare the archived redo log destination directories. Note that once an Oracle database is in ARCHIVELOG mode, that database activity will be suspended once all available online redo logs have been used. The database will remain suspended until those online redo logs have been archived. Thus, incorrect configuration of the database when it is in ARCHIVELOG mode can eventually lead to the database suspending operations because it cannot archive the current online redo logs.

More coverage on the implications of ARCHIVELOG mode, how to implement it (and take it out), and configuration for ARCHIVELOG operations can be found in Chapter 3.

Oracle Logical Structures

There are several different logical structures within Oracle. These structures include tables, indexes, views, clusters, user-defined objects, and other objects within the database. Schemas own these objects, and if storage is required for the objects, that storage is allocated from a tablespace.

It is the ultimate goal of an Oracle backup and recovery strategy to be able to recover these logical structures to a given point in time. Also, it is important to recover the data in these different objects in such a way that the state of the data is consistent to a given point in time. Consider the impact, for example, if I recover a table as it looked at 10 A.M., but only recovered its associated index as it looked at 9 A.M. The impact of such an inconsistent recovery could be awful. It is this idea of a consistent recovery that really drives Oracle's backup and recovery mechanism, and RMAN fits nicely into this backup and recovery architectural framework.

The Combined Picture

Now that we have introduced you to the various components of the Oracle database—and there are a number of them—let's quickly put together a couple of narratives that demonstrate how they all work together. First, we look at the overall database startup process, which is followed by a narrative of the basic operational use of the database.

Startup and Shutdown of the Database

Our DBA, Eliza, has just finished some work on the database, and it's time to restart it. She starts SQL*Plus and connects as sys using the sysdba account. At the SQL prompt, Eliza issues the **startup** command to open the database. The following shows an example of the results of this command:

```
SQL> startup
ORACLE instance started.
Total System Global Area    84700976 bytes
Fixed Size                    282416 bytes
Variable Size               71303168 bytes
Database Buffers            12582912 bytes
Redo Buffers                  532480 bytes
Database mounted.
Database opened.
```

Recall the different phases that occur after the **startup** command is issued: instance startup, database mount, and then database open. Let's look at each of these stages now in a bit more detail.

Instance Startup (startup nomount)

The first thing that occurs when starting the database is instance startup. It is here that Oracle parses the database parameter file, and makes sure that the instance is not already running by trying to acquire an instance lock. Then, the various database processes (as described in "The Oracle Processes," earlier in this chapter), such as DBWn and LGWR, are started. Also, Oracle allocates memory needed for the SGA. Once the instance has been started, Oracle reports to the user who has started it that the instance has been started back, and how much memory has been allocated to the SGA.

Had Eliza issued the command **startup nomount**, then Oracle would have stopped the database startup process after the instance was started. She might have started the instance in order to perform certain types of recovery, such as control file re-creation.

Mounting the Database (startup mount)

The next stage in the startup process is the mount stage. As Oracle passes through the mount stage, it opens the database control file. Having done that successfully, Oracle extracts the database datafile names from the control file in preparation for opening them. Note that Oracle does not actually check for the existence of the datafiles at this point, but only identifies their location from the control file. Having completed this step, Oracle reports back that it has mounted the database.

At this point, had Eliza issued the command **startup mount**, Oracle would have stopped opening the database and waited for further direction. When the Oracle instance is started and the database is mounted but not open, certain types of recovery operations may be performed, including renaming the location of database datafiles and recovery of recovered system tablespace datafiles.

Opening the Database

Eliza issued the **startup** command, however, so Oracle moves on and tries to open the database. During this stage, Oracle verifies the presence of the database datafiles and opens them. As it opens them, it checks the datafile headers and compares the SCN information contained in those headers with the SCN stored in the control files. Let's talk about these SCNs for a second.

SCNs are Oracle's method of tracking the state of the database. As changes occur in the database, they are associated with a given SCN. As these changes are flushed to the database datafiles (which occurs during a *checkpoint* operation, the headers of the datafiles are updated with the current SCN. The current SCN is also recorded in the database control file.

When Oracle tries to open a database, it checks the SCNs in each datafile and in the database control file. If the SCNs are the same and the bitmapped flags are set correctly, then the database is considered to be consistent, and the database is opened for use.

NOTE
Think of SCNs as being kind of like the counter on your VCR. As time goes on, the counter continues to increment, indicating a temporal point in time that the tape is currently at. So, if you want to watch a program on the tape, you can simply rewind (or fast forward) the tape to the counter number, and there is the beginning of the program. SCNs are the same way. When Oracle needs to recover a database, it "rewinds" to the SCN it needs to start with and then replays all of the transactions after that SCN until the database is recovered.

If the SCNs are different, then Oracle automatically performs *crash or instance recovery*, if possible. Crash or instance recovery occurs if the redo needed to generate a consistent image is in the online redo log files. If crash or instance recovery is not possible, because of a corrupted datafile or because the redo required to recover is not in the online redo logs, then Oracle requests that the DBA perform *media recovery*. Media recovery involves recovering one or more database datafiles from a backup taken of the database, and is a manual process, unlike instance recovery. Assisting in media recovery is where RMAN comes in, as you will see in later chapters. Once the database open process is completed successfully (with no recovery, crash recovery, or media recovery), then the database is open for business.

Shutting Down the Database

Of course, Eliza will probably want to shut down the database at some point in time. To do so, she could issue the **shutdown** command. This command closes the database, unmounts it, and then shuts down the instance in almost the reverse order as the startup process we have already discussed. There are several options to the **shutdown** command.

Note in particular that a **shutdown abort** of a database is basically like simulating a database crash. This is a command that is often used, and it rarely causes problems. There are, however, some rather unique situations that can arise from the use of the **shutdown abort** command, and care should be used before deciding to use it. Oracle generally recommends that your database be shut down in a consistent manner, if at all possible.

If you must use the **shutdown abort** command to shut down the database (and in the real world, this does happen with frequency because of outage constraints), then you should reopen the database with the **startup** command (or perhaps **startup restrict**). Following this, do the final shutdown on the database using the **shutdown immediate** command before performing any offline backup operations. Note that even this method may result in delays shutting down the database because of the length of time it takes to roll back transactions during the shutdown process.

NOTE
*As long as your backup/recovery strategy is correct, it really doesn't matter whether the database is in a consistent state (as with a normal **shutdown**) or inconsistent state (as with a **shutdown abort**) when an offline backup occurs. Oracle does recommend that you do cold backups with the database in a consistent state, and we recommend that, too (because the online redo logs will not be getting backed up by RMAN). Finally, note that online backups eliminate this issue completely!*

Using the Database and Internals

In this section, we are going to follow some users performing some different transactions in an Oracle database. First, we provide you with a graphical road map that puts all the processes, memory structures, and other components of the database together for you. Then, we follow a user as changes are made to the database. We then look at commits and how they operate. Finally, we look at database checkpoints and how they work.

Process and Database Relationships

We have discussed a number of different processes, memory structures, and other objects that make up the whole of the Oracle database. Figure 1-1 provides a graphic that might help you better understand the interrelationships between the different components in Oracle.

Changing Data in the Database

Now, assume the database is open. Let's say that Fred needs to add a new record to the DEPT table for the janitorial department. So, Fred might issue a SQL statement like this:

```
INSERT INTO DEPT VALUES (60, 'JANITOR','DALLAS');
```

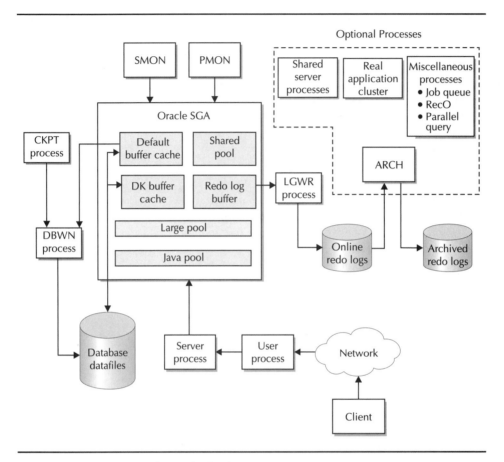

FIGURE 1-1. *A typical Oracle database*

The **insert** statements (as well as **update** and **delete** commands) are collectively known as Data Manipulation Language (DML). As a statement is executed, redo is generated and stored in the redo log buffer in the Oracle SGA. Note that redo is generated by this command, regardless of the presence of the **commit** command. The **delete** and **update** commands work generally the same way.

One of the results of DML is that undo is generated and stored in *rollback segments.* **UNDO** consists of instructions that allow Oracle to undo (or roll back) the statement being executed. Using undo, Oracle can roll back the database changes and provide *read consistent images* (also known as read consistency) to other users. Let's look a bit more at the **commit** command and read consistency.

Committing the Change

Having issued the **insert** command, Fred wants to ensure that this change is committed to the database, so he issues the **commit** command:

 COMMIT;

The effects of issuing the **commit** command include the following:

- The change becomes visible to all users who query the table at a point in time after the commit occurs. If Eliza queries the DEPT table after the commit occurs, then she will see department 60. However, if Eliza had already started a query before the commit, then this query would not see the changes to the table.

- The change is recoverable if the database is in NOARCHIVELOG mode and crash or instance recovery is required.

- The change is recoverable if the database is in ARCHIVELOG mode (assuming a valid backup and recovery strategy) and media recovery is required and all archived and online redo logs are available.

The **commit** command causes the Oracle LGWR process to flush the online redo log buffer to the online redo logs. Uncommitted redo is flushed to the online redo logs regardless of a commit (in fact, uncommitted changes can be written to the datafiles, too). When a commit is issued, Oracle writes a *commit vector* to the redo log buffer, and the buffer is flushed to disk before the commit returns. It is this commit vector, and the fact that the commit issued by Fred's session will not return until his redo has been flushed to the online redo logs successfully, that will ensure that Fred's changes will be recoverable.

The commit Command and Read Consistency   Did you notice that Ellie was not able to see Fred's change until he issued the **commit** command? This is known as *read consistency.* Another example of read consistency would be a case where Ellie started a report before Fred committed his change. Assume that Fred committed the change during Ellie's report. In this case, it would be inconsistent for department 60 to show up in Ellie's report, since it did not exist at the time that her report started. As Ellie's report continues to run, Oracle checks the start SCN of the report query against the SCNs of the blocks being read in Oracle to produce the report output. If the time of the report is earlier than the current SCN on the data block, then Oracle goes to the rollback segments and finds undo for that block that will allow Oracle to construct an image consistent to the time that the report started.

As Fred continues other work on the database, the LGWR process writes to the online redo logs on a regular basis. At some point in time, an online redo log will fill up, and LGWR will close that log file, open the next log file, and begin writing to it. During this transition period, LGWR also signals the ARCH process to begin copying the log file that it just finished using to the archive log backup directories.

Checkpoints

Now, you might be wondering, when does this data actually get written out to the database datafiles? Recall that a checkpoint is an event in which Oracle (through DBWR) writes data out to the datafiles. There are several different kinds of checkpoints. Some of the events that result in a checkpoint are the following:

- A redo log switch

- Normal database shutdowns

- When a tablespace is taken in or out of online backup mode (see "Oracle Physical Backup and Recovery" later in this section).

Note that ongoing incremental checkpoints occur throughout the lifetime of the database, providing a method for Oracle to decrease the overall time required when performing crash recovery. As the database operates, Oracle is constantly writing out streams of data to the database datafiles. These writes occur in such a way as to not impede performance of the database. Oracle provides certain database parameters to assist in determining how frequently Oracle must process incremental checkpoints.

Oracle Backup and Recovery Primer

Before you use RMAN, you should understand some general backup and recovery concepts in Oracle. Backups in Oracle come in two general categories, logical and physical. In the following sections, we quickly look at logical backup and recovery. Then we will do a full treatment of Oracle physical backup and recovery.

Logical Backup and Recovery

Logical backup and recovery of Oracle databases are handled by the Oracle-supplied utilities, **exp** and **imp**. The Oracle **exp** utility handles the logical backups, and the **imp** utility is responsible for recovering them. With logical backups, point-in-time recovery is not possible. Logical backups are generally not used as a part of a production database backup and recovery plan, and thus are beyond the scope of this book.

Oracle Physical Backup and Recovery

Physical backups are what RMAN is all about. Before we really delve into RMAN in the remaining chapters of this book, let's first look at what is required to manually do physical backups and recoveries of an Oracle database. While RMAN removes you from much of the work involved in backup and recovery, some of the principles remain the same. Understanding the basics of manual backup and recovery will help you understand what is going on with RMAN and will help us contrast the benefits of RMAN versus previous methods of backing up Oracle.

We have already discussed ARCHIVELOG mode and NOARCHIVELOG mode in Oracle. In either mode, Oracle can do an offline backup. Further, if the database is in ARCHIVELOG mode, then Oracle can do offline or online backups. We will cover the specifics of these operations with RMAN in later chapters of this book.

Of course, if you back up a database, it would be nice to be able to recover it. Following our sections on online and offline backups, we will discuss the different Oracle recovery options available. Finally, in these sections, we take a very quick, cursory look at Oracle manual backup and recovery. For a fuller treatment of manual backup and recovery in Oracle, see the other Oracle Press books on this subject, such as *Oracle Backup and Recovery 101* (by Kenny Smith and Stephan Haisley, McGraw-Hill/Osborne, Oracle Press, 2002).

NOARCHIVELOG Mode Physical Backups

We have already discussed NOARCHIVELOG mode in the Oracle database. This mode of database operations only supports backups of the database when the database is shut down. Also, only full recovery of the database up to the point of the backup is possible in NOARCHIVELOG mode. To perform a manual backup of a database in NOARCHIVELOG mode, follow these steps (note that these steps are different if you are using RMAN, which we will cover in later chapters):

1. Shut down the database completely.

2. Back up all database datafiles, the control files, and the online redo logs.

3. Restart the database.

ARCHIVELOG Mode Physical Backups

If you are running your database in ARCHIVELOG mode, you can continue to perform full backups of your database with the database either running or shut down.

Even if you perform the backup with the database shut down, you will want to use a slightly different cold backup procedure:

1. Shut down the database completely.

2. Back up all database datafiles.

3. Restart the database.

4. Force an online redo log switch with the **alter system switch logfile** command. Once the online redo logs have been archived, back up all archive redo logs.

5. Create a backup of the control file using the **alter database backup control file to trace** and **alter database backup controlfile to 'filename'** commands.

Of course, with your database in ARCHIVELOG mode, you may well want to do online, or hot, backups of your database. With the database in ARCHIVELOG mode, Oracle allows you to back up each individual tablespace and its datafiles while the database is up and running. The nice thing about this is that you can back up selective parts of your database at different times. To do an online backup of your tablespaces, follow this procedure:

1. Use the **alter tablespace begin backup** command to put the tablespaces and datafiles that you wish to back up in online backup mode.

2. Back up the datafiles associated with the tablespace you have just put in hot backup mode. (You can opt to just back up specific datafiles.)

3. Take the tablespaces out of hot backup mode by issuing the **alter tablespace end backup** command for each tablespace you put in online backup mode in Step 1.

4. Force an online redo log switch with the **alter system switch logfile** command.

5. Once the log switch has completed and the current online redo log has been archived, back up all the archived redo logs.

Note the log switch and backup of archived redo logs in Step 5. This is required, because all redo generated during the backup must be available to apply should a recovery be required. While Oracle continues to physically update the datafiles during the online backup (except for the datafile headers), there is a possibility of block splitting during backup operations, which will make the backed up datafile inconsistent. Further, since a database datafile might be written after it has been backed up but before the end of the overall backup process, it is important to have the redo generated during the backup to apply during recovery because each datafile on the backup might well be current as of a different SCN, and thus the datafile backup images will be inconsistent.

Also note that when you issue the **alter tablespace begin backup** command, Oracle records entire block changes to the database datafiles in the online redo logs rather than just the change vectors. This means total redo generation during online backups can increase significantly. This can impact disk space requirements and CPU overhead during the hot backup process. RMAN offers you the ability to perform hot backups without having to put a tablespace in hot backup mode, thus eliminating the additional I/O you would otherwise experience.

Note that in both backups in ARCHIVELOG mode (online and offline), we do not back up the online redo logs, and instead back up the archived redo logs of the database. In addition, we do not back up the control file, but rather create backup control files. We do this because we never want to run the risk of overwriting the online redo logs or control files during a recovery.

You might wonder why we don't want to recover the online redo logs. During a recovery in ARCHIVELOG mode, the most current redo is likely to be available in the online redo logs, and thus the current online redo log will be required for full point-in-time recovery. Because of this, we do not overwrite the online redo logs during a recovery of a database that is in ARCHIVELOG mode. If the online redo logs are lost as a result of the loss of the database (and hopefully this will not be the case), then you will have to do point-in-time recovery with all available archived redo logs.

For much the same reason that we don't back up the online redo logs, we don't back up the control files. Because the current control file contains the latest online and archived redo log information, we do not want to overwrite that information with earlier information on these objects. In the case that we lose all of our control files, you will use a backup control file to recover the database.

Finally, consider supplemental backups of archived redo log files and other means of protecting the archived redo logs from loss. Loss of an archived redo log directly impacts your ability to recover your database to the point of failure. If you lose an archived redo log and that log sequence number is no longer part of the online redo log groups, then you will not be able to recover your database beyond the archived redo log sequence prior to the sequence number of the lost archived redo log.

NOARCHIVELOG Mode Recoveries

If you need to recover a backup taken in NOARCHIVELOG mode, doing so is as simple as recovering all the database datafiles, the control files, and the online redo logs and starting the database. Of course, a total recovery may require such things as recovering the Oracle RDBMS software, the parameter file, and other required Oracle items, which we will discuss in the last section in this chapter.

Note that a recovery in NOARCHIVELOG mode is only possible to the point in time that you took your last backup. If you are recovering a database backed up in NOARCHIVELOG mode, you can only recover the database to the point of the backup. No database changes after the point of the backup can be recovered if your database is in NOARCHIVELOG mode.

ARCHIVELOG Mode Recoveries

A database that is in ARCHIVELOG mode can be backed up using online or offline backups. The fortunate thing about ARCHIVELOG mode, as opposed to NOARCHIVELOG mode, is that you can recover the database to the point of the failure that occurred. In addition, you can choose to recover the database to a specific point in time, or to a specific point in time based on the change number.

ARCHIVELOG mode recoveries also allow you to do specific recoveries on datafiles, tablespaces, or the entire database. In addition, you can do point-in-time recovery or recovery to a specific SCN. Let's quickly look at each of these options. More detail on each of these options is available in Oracle Press's *Oracle Backup and Recovery 101* (McGraw-Hill/Osborne, 2002).

In this section, we briefly cover full database recoveries in ARCHIVELOG mode. We then look at tablespace and datafile recoveries, followed by point-in-time recoveries.

ARCHIVELOG Mode Full Recovery   You can recover a database backup in ARCHIVELOG mode up to the point of failure, assuming that the failure of the database did not compromise at least one member of each of your current online redo logs groups and any archived redo logs that were not backed up. If you have lost your archived redo logs or online redo logs, then you will need to perform some form of point-in-time recovery, as discussed later in this section. Also, if you have lost all copies of your current control file, you will need to recover it and perform incomplete recovery.

To perform full database recovery from a backup of a database in ARCHIVELOG mode, follow this procedure:

1. Restore all the database datafiles from your backup.

2. Restore all backed up archived redo logs.

3. Mount the database (**startup mount**).

4. Recover the database (**recover database**).

5. Oracle prompts you to apply redo from the archived redo logs. Simply enter **AUTO** at the prompt and Oracle will automatically apply all redo logs.

6. Once all redos have been applied, open the recovered database (**alter database open**).

ARCHIVELOG Tablespace and Datafile Recovery   Tablespace and datafile recovery can be performed with the database mounted or open. To perform a recovery of a tablespace in Oracle with the database open, follow these steps:

1. Take the tablespace offline (**alter tablespace offline**).

2. Restore all datafiles associated with the tablespace to be recovered.

3. Recover the tablespace (**recover tablespace**) online.

4. Once recovery has completed, bring the tablespace online (**alter tablespace online**).

Just as you can recover a tablespace, you can also recover specific datafiles. This has the benefit of leaving the tablespace online. Only data that resides in the offline datafiles will be unavailable during the recovery process. The rest of the database will remain available during the recovery. Here is a basic outline of a datafile recovery:

1. Take the datafile offline (**alter database datafile 'file_name' offline**).

2. Restore all datafiles to be recovered.

3. Recover the tablespace (**recover datafile**) online.

4. Once recovery has completed, bring the datafile online (**alter database datafile 'file_name' online**).

ARCHIVELOG Point-in-Time Recoveries   Another benefit of ARCHIVELOG mode is the ability to recover a database to a given point in time rather than to the point of failure. This ability is used often when creating a clone database (perhaps for testing or reporting purposes) or in the event of major application or user error. You can recover a database to either a specific point in time or a specific database SCN.

If you want to recover a tablespace to a point in time, you need to recover the entire database to the same point in time (unless you perform tablespace point-in-time recovery, which is a different topic). For example, assume that you have an accounting database, that most of your data is in the ACCT tablespace, and that you wish to recover the database back in time two days. You cannot just restore the ACCT tablespace and recover it to a point in time two days ago, because the remaining tablespaces (SYSTEM, TEMP, and RBS, for example) will still be consistent to the current point in time, and the database will fail to open because it will be inconsistent.

To recover a database to a point in time, follow these steps:

1. Recover all database datafiles from a backup that ended before the point in time that you want to recover the database to.

2. Recover the database to the point in time that you wish it to be recovered to. Use the command **recover database until time '01-01-2002 21:00:00'** and apply the redo logs as required.

3. Once the recovery is complete, open the database.

You can also choose to recover the database using an SCN number:

1. Recover all database datafiles from a backup that ended before the point in time that you want to recover the database to.

2. Recover the database to the system change number (SCN) that you wish it to be recovered to. Use the command **recover database until change '221122'** and apply the redo logs as required.

3. Once the recovery is complete, open the database.

Further, you can apply changes to the database and manually cancel the process after a specific archived redo log has been applied:

1. Recover all database datafiles from a backup that ended before the point in time that you want to recover the database to.

2. Recover the database to the point in time that you wish it to be recovered to. Use the command **recover database until cancel** and apply the redo logs as required. When you have applied the last archived redo log, simply issue the **cancel** command to finish applying redo.

3. Once the recovery is complete, open the database.

Keep in mind the concept of database consistency when doing point-in-time recovery (or any recovery, for that matter). If you are going to recover a database to a given point in time, you must do so with a backup that finished before the point in time that you wish to recover to. Also, you must have all the archived redo logs (and possibly the remaining online redo logs) available to complete recovery.

A Final Word on Backups

We have quickly covered the essentials of backup and recovery for Oracle. One last issue that remains to be covered are the things that need to be backed up. These are items that generally are backed up with less frequency because they change rarely. These items include

- The Oracle RDBMS software (Oracle home and the Oracle Inventory).

- Network parameter files (names.ora, sqlnet.ora, and tnsnames.ora).

- Database parameter files (init.ora, INI files, and so forth). Note that RMAN in 9iR2 has a nice new feature that allows you to back up the database parameter file along with the control file!

- The system oratab file and other system Oracle-related files (for example, all rc startup scripts for Oracle).

It is important that these items be backed up on a regular basis as a part of your backup and recovery processes. You need to plan to back up these items regardless of whether you do manual backups or RMAN backups, because RMAN does not back up these items either.

As you can see, the process of backup and recovery of an Oracle database can involve a number of steps. Since DBAs want to make sure they do backups correctly every time, they generally write a number of scripts for this purpose. There are a few problems with this. First of all, scripts can break. When the script breaks, who is going to support it, particularly when the DBA who wrote it moves to a new position somewhere in the inaccessible tundra in northern Alaska? Second, either you have to write the script to keep track of when you add or remove datafiles, or you have to manually add or remove datafiles from the script as required.

With RMAN, you get a backup and recovery product that is included with the base database product for free, and that reduces the complexity of the backup and recovery process. Also, you get the benefit of Oracle support when you run into a problem. Finally, with RMAN, you get additional features that no other backup and recovery process can match. We will look at those in coming chapters.

RMAN solves all of these problems and adds additional features that make its use even more beneficial for the DBA. In this book, we will look at these features, and how they can help make your life easier, and make your database backups more reliable.

Summary

We didn't discuss RMAN much in this chapter, but we laid some important groundwork for future discussions on RMAN that you will find in later chapters. As promised, we covered some essential backup and recovery concepts, such as high availability and backup and recovery planning, that are central to the purpose of RMAN. We then defined several Oracle terms that you will need to be familiar with later in this text. We then reviewed the Oracle database architecture and internal operations. It can not be stressed enough how important it is to have an understanding of how Oracle works inside when it comes time to actually recover your database in an emergency situation. Finally, we discussed manual backup and recovery operations in Oracle. Contrast these to the same RMAN operations that you will find in later chapters, and you will find that RMAN is ultimately an easy solution to backup and recovery of your Oracle database.

CHAPTER
2

Introduction to the
RMAN Architecture

eaching a person to understand the world conceptually can be quite challenging, but ultimately it rewards the teacher and the taught. For example, my mother teaches nursing to college students. Nursing, as it turns out, is a pretty important part of everyone's life (you learn this when you or your wife goes into labor, or earlier, it seems, if your mother happens to be a nurse), and you pretty much always want a well-trained nurse next to your bed when the going gets tough. One of the most common tasks for a nurse is the preparation of a sterile environment for surgeries, births, examinations, and so forth, so that no possible disease can be spread during the procedure itself. When you are training a nurse to always create a sterile environment, it tends to boil down to a series of specific actions taken in a certain order. My mother noticed that her students would memorize the procedure list for one sterile environment or the other, but not necessarily learn the fundamental concepts of how to make any situation sterile. This was distressing to her, as it has been her experience in 35 years of nursing that there always comes a time when you have to sterilize an environment for which there are no documented steps.

So how could she get her students to stop thinking about the steps and start learning the concepts? Well, she took a somewhat unorthodox approach during oral examinations. When the student entered the examination room, instead of a known set of operating room utensils, what they found were the ingredients for making a cookie. My mom looked them in the eye and said, "Make me a sterile cookie." When the student realized that my straight-faced mother was not joking, they had to check everything they thought they knew, and actually dig deep for what they needed to know to sterilize the lip of a chocolate container, and a stirring spoon, and a sugar canister.

When they emerged victorious, the students knew two things: that if they understand the concepts, then everything else is just details that can be figured out; and that they could face even the most unexpected situations and still be able to do what is necessary to protect the life of the patient.

Why are we killing your time with this? Because we've spent the last five years recovering databases for all kinds of companies throughout the world, and the one most important thing we can give you is the conceptual understanding and confidence to know that any recovery situation is understandable and fixable. If you know how RMAN operates, then you will not fear the unexpected situation that you inevitably will find yourself in. We cannot give you a case study for every possible recovery scenario, but we can equip you with the understanding that it will take to attack any possible scenario and get through it successfully, with minimal downtime.

So are you ready to make sterile cookies? Find a nice chair, grab a highlighter, and get comfortable. Here we go.

This chapter will take you through each of the components in the RMAN architecture one by one, explaining the role each plays in the backup and recovery. Most of this relies heavily on a knowledge of the Oracle RDBMS architecture. If you are not familiar at a basic level with the different components of an Oracle database, you might want to pick up a beginner's guide to database administration before continuing. We do little to explain Oracle, just the role that RMAN has within it. After we discuss the different components, we walk through a simple backup procedure to disk and talk about each component in action.

Server-Managed Recovery

In the previous chapter, you learned the principles and practices of backup and recovery in the old world. It involved creating and running scripts to capture the filenames, associate them with tablespaces, get the tablespaces into backup mode, get an OS utility to perform the copy, and then stop backup mode.

But this book is really about using Recovery Manager, or RMAN for short. Recovery Manager implements a type of *server managed recovery*, or SMR. SMR refers to the ability of the database to perform the operations required to keep itself backed up successfully. It does so by relying on built-in code in the Oracle RDBMS kernel. Who knows more about the schematics of the database than the database itself?

The power of SMR comes from what details it can eliminate on your behalf. As you may have already experienced as a DBA, the legwork that goes into the upkeep of backup and recovery scripting can be the source of regrettable time erosion: hours lost that you will never get back. But when the database is responsible for the backup process, we can take a step back from the day-to-day upkeep and concentrate on more important things. Granted, the utilization of RMAN introduces certain complexities that overshadow the complete level of ease that might be promised by SMR—why else would you be reading this book? But the blood, sweat, and tears you pour into RMAN will give you huge payoffs. You'll see.

The RMAN Utility

RMAN is the specific implementation of SMR provided by Oracle. RMAN is a stand-alone application that makes a client connection to the Oracle database to access internal backup and recovery packages. It is, at its very core, nothing more than a command interpreter that takes simplified commands you type and turns those commands into remote procedure calls (RPCs) that are executed at the database.

We point this out primarily to make one thing very clear: RMAN does very little work. Sure, the coordination of events is important, but the real work of actually backing up and recovering a database is performed by processes at the target database itself. The *target database* refers to the database that is being backed up. The Oracle database has internal packages that actually take the pl/sql blocks passed from RMAN and turn them into system calls to read from, and write to, the disk subsystem of your database server.

The RMAN utility is installed as part of the Database Utilities suite of command-line utilities. This suite includes import, export, sql*loader, and dbverify. During a typical Oracle installation, RMAN will be installed. It is included with Enterprise Edition and Standard Edition, although there are restrictions if you only have a license for Standard Edition: without Enterprise Edition, RMAN can only allocate a single channel for backups. If you are performing a client installation, it will be installed if you choose the Administrator option instead of the Runtime client option.

The RMAN utility is made up of two pieces: the executable file and the recover.bsq file. The recover.bsq file is essentially the library file, from which the executable file extracts code for creating pl/sql calls to the target. The recover.bsq file is the brains of the whole operation. These two files are invariably linked, and logically make up the RMAN client utility. It is worth pointing out that the recover.bsq and the rman executable must be the same version or nothing will work.

The RMAN utility serves a distinct, orderly, and predictable purpose: it interprets commands you provide into pl/sql calls that are remotely executed at the target database. The command language is unique to RMAN, and takes a little practice (although it simplified itself nicely in the 9i releases). It is essentially a stripped-down list of all the things you need to do to back up, restore, recover, or manipulate those backups in some way. These commands are interpreted by the executable translator, and then matched to pl/sql blocks in the recover.bsq file. RMAN then passes these RPCs to the database to gather information based on what you have requested. If your command requires an I/O operation (in other words, a backup command or a restore command), then when this information is returned, RMAN prepares another block of procedures and passes it back to the target database. These blocks are responsible for engaging the system calls to the OS for specific read or write operations.

RMAN and Database Privileges

RMAN needs to access packages at the target database that exist in the SYS schema. In addition, RMAN requires the privileges necessary to start up and shut down the target database. Therefore, RMAN always connects to the target database as a SYSDBA user. Don't worry, you do not need to specify this as you would from SQL Plus; because RMAN requires it for every target database connection, it is assumed. Therefore, when you connect to the target, RMAN automatically supplies the as sysdba to the connection.

```
RMAN> connect target sys/password
connected to target database: PROD (DBID=4159396170)
```

If you try to connect as someone who does not have sysdba privileges, RMAN will give you an error:

```
RMAN> connect target /
RMAN-00571: ===========================================================
RMAN-00569: =============== ERROR MESSAGE STACK FOLLOWS =============
RMAN-00571: ===========================================================
ORA-01031: insufficient privileges
```

This is a common error during the setup and configuration phase of RMAN. It is encountered when you are not logged in on your server as a member of the dba group. This OS group controls the authentication of sysdba privileges to all Oracle databases on the server. (The name dba is a default, and is not required. Some OS installs use a different name, and you are by no means obligated to use dba. But it's the default, usually.) Typically, most Unix systems have a user named oracle that is a member of the group dba. This is the user that installs the Oracle software to begin with, and if you are logged in as oracle, it doesn't matter who you connect as within RMAN—you will always be connected as a sysdba user, with access to the SYS schema and the ability to start up/shut down the database. On Windows platforms, Oracle creates a local group called ORA_DBA, and adds the installing user to the group.

If you are logged in as a user who does not have dba group membership, and you will need to use RMAN, then you have to create and use a password file for your target database. If you will be connecting RMAN from a client system across the network, you need to create and use a password file. The configuration steps for this can be found in Chapter 3.

The Network Topology of RMAN Backups

The client/server architecture of RMAN inevitably leads to hours of confusion. The reasons have to do with how the human mind stores spatial information; if you're good at spatial puzzles, RMAN will seem simple. If those tests in grade school were always baffling, read carefully.

This confusion is based entirely on where RMAN is being executed, versus where the backup work is actually being done. RMAN is a client application that attaches to the target database via an Oracle NET connection. If you are running the RMAN executable in the same ORACLE_HOME as your target database, then this Oracle NET connection can be a bequeath, or local connection, and won't require you to provide a NET alias—as long as you have the appropriate ORACLE_SID variable set in your environment. Otherwise, you will need to configure your tnsnames.ora file with an entry for your target database, and you will need to do this from the location where you will be running RMAN. Figure 2-1 provides an illustration of the network topology of different RMAN locations.

TIP
Decide where you will run your RMAN executable, and stick with it. You can run it from a client-management system (typically a Windows system running Oracle Enterprise Manager or your third-party equivalent), so that you have a centralized location for your RMAN scripts and tasks. Or you can always run it from the target database's ORACLE_HOME, meaning that you forego the possibility of running into compatibility headaches when you start upgrading databases.

Running RMAN Remotely

If you are responsible for many databases spread over the enterprise, it makes sense to consolidate your application at a single client system, where you can better manage your tnsnames.ora entries. All your RMAN scripts can be consolidated, and you have no confusion later on where RMAN is running. You know exactly where it is running: on your laptop, your desktop, or your Linux workstation. This client/server model makes sense, as well, if you will be using a Recovery Catalog in your RMAN

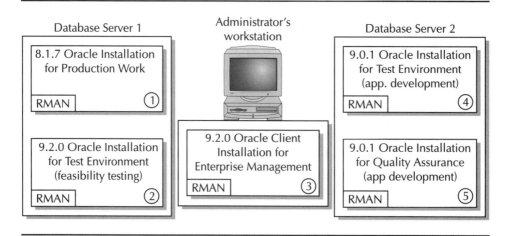

FIGURE 2-1. *Five different locations (and versions) for the RMAN executable*

> ## Who Uses a Recovery Catalog?
>
> A Recovery Catalog is a repository for RMAN's backup history, with metadata about when the backups were taken, what was backed up, and how big they are. It includes crucial information about these backups that is necessary for recovery. This metadata is extracted from the default location, the target database controlfile, and held in database tables within a user's schema. Do you need a recovery catalog? No. Does a recovery catalog come in handy? Yes. Chapter 3, which discusses the creation and setup of a recovery catalog, goes into greater depth about why you should or should not use a recovery catalog. We provide a discussion of the Recovery Catalog architecture later in this chapter.

configuration, since you will be making more than one NET connection each time you operate RMAN. On the other hand, running RMAN from a different system (or even a different ORACLE_HOME) than the target database means you will be required to set up a password file, leading to more configuration and management at each of your target databases.

If you will be making a remote connection from RMAN to the target database, you need to create a tnsnames.ora entry that can connect you to the target database with a dedicated server process. RMAN cannot use Shared Servers (formerly known as Multi-Threaded Server) to make a database connection. So, if you use Shared Servers, which is the default setup on all new 9iR2 installations, then you need to create a separate NET alias that uses a dedicated server process. The difference between the two can be seen in the following sample tsnames.ora file. Note that the first tns entry is for dedicated server processes, and the second uses the Shared Server architecture.

```
PROD_RMAN =
  (DESCRIPTION =
    (ADDRESS_LIST =
      (ADDRESS = (PROTOCOL = TCP)(HOST = cervantes)(PORT = 1521))
    )
    (CONNECT_DATA =
      (SERVER = DEDICATED)
      (SERVICE_NAME = prod)
    )
  )
PROD =
  (DESCRIPTION =
    (ADDRESS_LIST =
```

```
         (ADDRESS = (PROTOCOL = TCP)(HOST = cervantes)(PORT = 1521))
      )
      (CONNECT_DATA =
        (SERVER = SHARED)
        (SERVICE_NAME = prod)
      )
   )
```

Running RMAN Local to the Target Database

Always running RMAN from the target database's ORACLE_HOME is preferable if you intend to be using RMAN for very simply operations, if you will not be using the Recovery Catalog, and if you have few databases to manage. It means you can always connect locally to the database, requiring no password file setup and no tnsnames.ora configuration. Bear in mind that the simplicity of this option is also its drawback: as soon as you want to introduce a Recovery Catalog, or perform a DUPLICATION, you introduce all the elements that you are trying to avoid in the first place. This option can also lead to confusion during usage: because you always make a local connection to the database, it is easy to connect to the wrong target database. It can also be confusing to know which environment you are connecting from—if you have more than one Oracle software installation on your system (and who doesn't?), then you can go down a time-sucking rat hole if you assume you are connecting to your PROD database, when in fact you set up your ORACLE_HOME and ORACLE_SID environment variables for the TEST instance.

So, choose your option wisely. As Figure 2-2 depicts, even our simplification into two options—client RMAN or server RMAN—can be tinkered with, giving you a hybrid model that fits your needs. In Figure 2-2, there are four different scenarios:

1. RMAN runs from the 8.1.7 client installation at the DBA's workstation so that he can schedule jobs from Enterprise Manager. The PRODWB instance is also running 8.1.7.

2. RMAN backs up the DW_PROD database remotely from the 8.1.7 client installation at the DBA's workstation. This is mainly to consolidate administration.

3. The REPO_1 database is in a separate ORACLE_HOME on the Database Server 1, a 9.2 installation. Due to new functionality, the DBA has opted to run the backups here using the local 9.2 RMAN executable.

4. The TEST database that exists on the DBA workstation uses the local copy of RMAN to back itself up. This is due to the version being different from other instances, and because it is a test database used solely by the DBA for functionality testing.

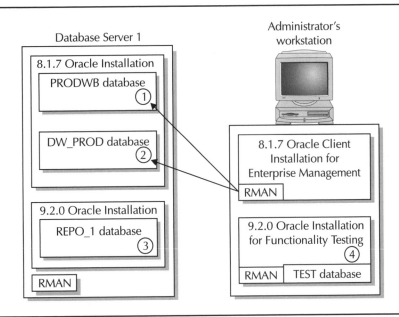

FIGURE 2-2.   *Running different versions of the RMAN executable in Enterprise Manager*

Remember to remain flexible in your RMAN topology. There will be times when you will need to run your backups in nocatalog mode, using the local RMAN executable. And there may come a time when you need to run a remote RMAN job as well.

The Database Controlfile

So far, we have discussed the RMAN executable and its role in the process of using server managed recovery with Oracle9i. As we said, though, the real work is being done at the target database—it's backing itself up. Next, then, we must discuss the role of the controlfile in an RMAN backup or recovery process.

The controlfile has a day job already; it is responsible for the physical schematics of the database. The name says it all: the controlfile controls where the physical files of a database can be found, and what header information each file currently contains (or should contain). Its contents include datafile information, redo log information, and archive log information. It has a snapshot of each file header for the critical files associated with the database. Because of this wealth of information, the controlfile has been the primary component of any recovery operation prior to RMAN (Chapter 1 discusses this in greater detail).

Because of its role as the repository of database file information, it makes sense that RMAN would utilize the controlfile to pull information about what needs to be backed up. And that's just what it does: RMAN uses the controlfile to compile file lists, obtain checkpoint information, and determine recoverability. By accessing the controlfile directly, RMAN can compile file lists without a user having to create the list herself, eliminating one of the most tiresome steps of backup scripting. And it does not require that the script be modified when a new file is added. It already knows about your new file. RMAN knows this because the controlfile knows this.

The controlfile also moonlights as an RMAN catalog. After RMAN completes a backup of any portion of the database, it writes a record of that backup to the controlfile, along with checkpoint information about when the backup was started and completed. This is one of the primary reasons that the controlfile grew exponentially in size between Oracle version 7 and Oracle version 8—RMAN tables in the controlfile. These records are often referred to as *metadata*—data about the data recorded in the actual backup. This metadata can also be stored in a Recovery Catalog (see Chapter 3).

Record Reuse in the Controlfile

The controlfile can grow to meet space demands. When a new record is added for a new datafile, a new logfile, or a new RMAN backup, it can expand to meet these demands. However, there are limitations. As most databases live a life that spans years, in which thousands of redo logs switch and thousands of checkpoints occur, the controlfile has to be able to eliminate some data that is no longer necessary. So, it ages information out as it needs space, and reuses certain "slots" in tables in round-robin fashion. However, there is some information that cannot be eliminated—for instance, the list of datafiles. This information is critical for the minute-to-minute database operation, and new space *must* be made available for these records.

The controlfile thus separates its internal data into two types of records: circular reuse records and noncircular reuse records. *Circular reuse records* are records that include information that can be aged out of the controlfile, if push comes to shove. This includes, for instance, archive log history information, which can be removed without affecting the production database. *Noncircular reuse records* are those records that cannot be sacrificed. If the controlfile runs out of space for these records, the file expands to make more room. This includes datafile and logfile lists.

The record of RMAN backups in the controlfile falls into the category of circular reuse records, meaning that the records will get aged out if the controlfile section that contains them becomes full. This can be catastrophic to a recovery situation: without the record of the backups in the controlfile, it is as though the backups never took place. Remember this: if the controlfile does not have a record of your RMAN backup, the backup cannot be used by RMAN for recovery (we'll show you a way out of this in Chapter 12). This makes the controlfile a critical piece in the

RMAN equation. Without one, we have nothing. If records get aged out, then we can no longer utilize the backups that those records pointed to.

Fear not, though. Often, it is never that important when records get aged out; it takes so long for the controlfile to fill up, the backups that are removed are so old they are obsolete. You can also set a larger time frame for when the controlfile will age out records. This is controlled by the init.ora parameter CONTROLFILE_RECORD_KEEP_TIME. By default, this parameter is set to 7 (in days). This means that if a record is less than seven days old, it will not delete it, but rather expand the controlfile section. You can set this to a higher value, say, 30 days, so that it always expands, until only records older than a month will be overwritten when necessary. Setting this parameter to 0 means that the records are never reused, but we do not recommend this. The controlfile will continue to grow and grow, and become unmanageable.

In addition, if you will be implementing a recovery catalog, you need not worry about circular reuse records. As long as you resync your catalog at least once within the timeframe specified by the CONTROLFILE_RECORD_KEEP_TIME parameter and then let those records age out—the Recovery Catalog never ages records out.

Re-Creating the Controlfile: RMAN Users Beware!

It used to be that certain conditions required the occasional rebuild of the database controlfile, such as resetting the MAXLOGFILES parameter or the MAXLOGHISTORY parameter. Certain parameters cannot be set unless you rebuild the controlfile because these parameters define the size of the internal controlfile tables that hold noncircular reuse records. Therefore, if you need that section to be larger, you have to rebuild the controlfile.

If you use RMAN, and you do not use a recovery catalog, be very careful of the controlfile rebuild. When you issue the command

```
Alter database backup controlfile to trace;
```

the script that is generated does not include the information in the controlfile that identifies your backups. *Without these backup records, you cannot access the backups when they are needed for recovery.* All RMAN information is lost, and you cannot get it back. The only RMAN information that gets rebuilt when you rebuild the controlfile is any permanent configuration parameters you have set with RMAN. Therefore, we encourage you to avoid a controlfile rebuild at all costs.

If you back up the controlfile to a binary file, instead of to trace, then all backup information is preserved. This is discussed more completely in Chapter 9.

The Snapshot Controlfile

As you can tell, the controlfile is a busy little file. It's responsible for schematic information about the database, which includes checkpoint SCN information for recovery. This constant SCN and file management is critical to the livelihood of your database, so the controlfile must be available for usage by the RDBMS on a constant basis.

This poses a problem for RMAN. RMAN needs to get a consistent view of the controlfile when it sets out to make a backup of every datafile. It only needs to know the most recent checkpoint information and file schematic information at the time the backup begins. After the backup starts, it needs this information to stay consistent for the duration of the backup operation; in other words, it needs a *read consistent* view of the controlfile. With the constant updates from the database, this is nearly impossible—unless RMAN were to lock the controlfile for the duration of the backup. But that would mean the database could not advance the checkpoint or switch logs or produce new archive logs. Impossible.

To get around this, RMAN uses the *snapshot controlfile,* an exact copy of your controlfile that is only used by RMAN during backup and resync operations. At the beginning of these operations, RMAN refreshes the snapshot controlfile from the actual controlfile, thus putting a momentary lock on the controlfile. Then, RMAN switches to the snapshot and uses it for the duration of the backup; in this way, it has read consistency without holding up database activity.

By default, the snapshot controlfile exists in the ORACLE_HOME/dbs directory on Unix platforms, and in the ORACLE_HOME/database directory on Windows. It has a default name of SNCF<ORACLE_SID>.ORA. This can be modified or changed at any time by using the **configure snapshot controlfile** command:

```
Configure snapshot controlfile name to '<location\file_name>';
```

There are certain conditions that might lead to the following error on the snapshot controlfile, which is typically the first time a person ever notices the file even exists:

```
RMAN-08512: waiting for snapshot controlfile enqueue
```

This error happens when the snapshot controlfile header is locked by a process other than the one requesting the enqueue. If you have multiple backup jobs, it may be that you are trying to run two backup jobs simultaneously from two different RMAN sessions. To troubleshoot this error, open a SQL*Plus session and run the following SQL statement:

```
SELECT s.sid, username AS "User", program, module, action, logon_time"Logon", l.*
FROM v$session s, v$enqueue_lock l
WHERE l.sid = s.sid and l.type = 'CF' AND l.id1 = 0 and l.id2 = 2;
```

The RMAN Server Processes

RMAN makes a client connection to the target database, and two server processes
are spawned. The primary process is used to make calls to packages in the SYS
schema in order to perform the backup or recovery operations. This process
coordinates the work of the channel processes during backups and restores.

The secondary, or shadow, process polls any long-running transactions in RMAN
and logs the information internally. You can view the results of this polling in the
view V$session_longops:

```
SELECT SID, SERIAL#, CONTEXT, SOFAR, TOTALWORK,
       ROUND(SOFAR/TOTALWORK*100,2) "%_COMPLETE"
FROM V$SESSION_LONGOPS
WHERE OPNAME LIKE 'RMAN%'
AND OPNAME NOT LIKE '%aggregate%'
AND TOTALWORK != 0
AND SOFAR <> TOTALWORK
/
```

You can also view these processes in the v$session view. When RMAN allocates a
channel, it provides the session ID information in the output:

```
allocated channel: ORA_DISK_1
channel ORA_DISK_1: sid=16 devtype=DISK
```

The "sid" information corresponds to the SID column in V$session. So you could
construct a query such as this:

```
SQL> column client_info format a30
SQL> column program format a15
SQL> select sid, saddr, paddr, program, client_info
     from v$session where sid=16;
     SID SADDR    PADDR    PROGRAM         CLIENT_INFO
---------- -------- -------- --------------- ------------------------
     16 682144E8 681E82BC RMAN.EXE        rman channel=ORA_DISK_1
```

RMAN Channel Processes

In addition to the two default processes, an individual process is created for every
channel that you allocate during a backup or restore operation. RMAN refers to
a channel as the server process at the target database that coordinates the reads
from the datafiles and the writes to the specified location during backup. During a
restore, the channel coordinates reads from the backup location and the writing
of data blocks to the datafile locations. There are only two kinds of channels: disk
channels and tape channels. You cannot allocate both kinds of channels for a single

backup operation—you are writing the backup either to disk or to tape. Like the background RMAN process, the channel processes can be tracked from the data dictionary, and then correlated with a sid at the OS level. It is the activity of these channel processes that gets logged by the polling shadow process into the v$session_longops view.

RMAN and I/O Slaves

RMAN can utilize I/O slaves if they are configured on the target database. For the purposes of RMAN backups and restores, there are two kinds of slaves that are used: disk I/O slaves and tape I/O slaves.

Disk I/O slaves are configured using the parameter DBWR_IO_SLAVES. This parameter can be set to any number of values, and its primary use in life is to wake up extra DBWR slaves for disk writes when the dirty buffers are flushed to disk from the buffer cache. However, if this parameter is set to any non-zero value, be it 1 or 12 or 32, RMAN throws a switch that will automatically engage four I/O slaves per channel to assist with reading data blocks into RMAN memory buffers. This is a nice feature, but it changes considerably the way in which RMAN allocates memory. Using DBWR_IO_SLAVES is only important if your OS platform does not support native asynchronous I/O, or if you have disabled asynchronous I/O for the Oracle RDBMS. If you have asynchronous I/O enabled, then you do not need to use disk I/O slaves.

Tape I/O slaves assist with server process access to the tape device. If you have the parameter BACKUP_TAPE_IO_SLAVES set to TRUE, then RMAN will allocate a single I/O slave per tape channel process to assist with writes to the tape location. Unlike disk I/O slaves, this parameter affects no part of the database other than RMAN tape backups. Because there is no native asynchronous I/O to tape devices, we recommend you set this parameter to TRUE. It will help keep your tape drives streaming, meaning better performance on backups and restores. Chapter 15 discusses tape streaming in more depth.

The SYS Packages Used by RMAN

The RMAN server process that coordinates the work of the channels has access to two packages in the SYS schema: **dbms_rvcman** and **dbms_backup_restore**. These two packages comprise the entirety of the RMAN functionality in the target database.

SYS.DBMS_RCVMAN

The **dbms_rcvman** is the package that is used to access the tables in the controlfile and pass this information to RMAN so it can build backup and restore operations that accurately reflect the database schematics. This package is responsible for setting TIME operators and verifying checkpoint information in the datafile headers prior to running any operation. It also checks file locations and sizes, along with other information concerning node affinity (in a RAC environment) and disk affinity. This kind of information affects performance, and RMAN has automatic load-balancing and performance-enhancing algorithms that it runs through prior to building the actual backup/restore commands. Chapter 15 talks in depth about these performance gains. Stay tuned.

SYS.DBMS_BACKUP_RESTORE

The **sys.dbms_rcvman** accesses the controlfile and verifies all the requisite information. It passes this information back to the RMAN server process, which can then create pl/sql blocks based on code in the recover.bsq file. These pl/sql blocks are made up of calls to the package DBMS_BACKUP_RESTORE, the true workhorse of RMAN. DBMS_BACKUP_RESTORE is the actual package that creates system calls to back up datafiles, controlfiles, and archived redo logs. RMAN takes the information returned from **dbms_rcvman**, divvies out the work among the channels based on the load-balancing algorithm, and then creates a series of calls to DBMS_BACKUP_RESTORE.

It is the work of DBMS_BACKUP_RESTORE that you can track in V$session_longops. It performs the backup and restore operations. In addition, it accesses the controlfile, but only in a very limited way. It accesses it to back it up (actually, it backs up the snapshot controlfile), and to write backup information to it after backups have completed. Once it has completed a backup set, it writes the information about when the backup was taken, how long it took to complete, and the size and name of the backup to tables in the controlfile.

RMAN Packages in the Kernel

Both of these RMAN packages are installed by default by running the catproc.sql script when the database is created. There is no way to omit them during database creation, and therefore they exist in every Oracle database since version 8.0.3. What this means to you is that there is no configuration required by you for RMAN to work. You can run RMAN right now and start backing up your database.

These packages have another important trait: they are hard-coded into the Oracle software library files, so they can be called even when the database is not open. Most packages, as you know, would only be available when the database is open. However, RMAN can write calls to DBMS_BACKUP_RESTORE when the database instance is in nomount or mount mode. This is a critical element, and the reason is clear: we need to be able to back up and restore the database even when it is not open.

This brings us to an interesting point: what state must the target be in if we are to connect to it using RMAN? Does the instance need to be started, or do we need to mount it, or must it be open? The answer is that RMAN can connect to the target database in any of these three states, but it must at least be in nomount mode (otherwise, there's no *there* there!).

Backing Up the Data Block

As you learned in Chapter 1, even when you used advanced techniques for backups, the units you were backing up were datafiles. The OS utility that ultimately made the backup was looking at the entire file and backing it up, and because of this, we had to go to extraordinary lengths to protect the integrity of the Oracle data blocks. RMAN, however, is different. Because RMAN is integrated into the RDBMS, it has access to your data at the same level that the database itself uses: the data block.

Block-level access is what distinguishes RMAN from any other backup utility, and even if you didn't already know this, it's why you are reading this book and implementing an RMAN backup strategy. This is an extremely powerful level of access that provides nearly all the benefits that you will get from using RMAN. It is because of this access that we can utilize the data block for more efficient backup and recovery.

The Data Block Backup Overview

Here's how it works: RMAN compiles the list of files to be backed up, based on the backup algorithm rules. Based on the number of channels and the number of files being simultaneously backed up, RMAN creates memory buffers in the Oracle shared memory segment. This is typically in the PGA, but there are circumstances that push the memory buffers into the SGA. The channel server process then begins reading the datafiles and filling the RMAN buffers with these blocks. When a buffer is full, it pushes the blocks from an input buffer into an output buffer. This memory-to-memory write occurs for each individual data block in the datafile. If the block meets the criteria for being backed up, and the memory-to-memory write detected no corruption, then it remains in the output buffer until the output buffer is full. Once full, the output buffer is pushed to the backup location—a disk or a tape, whichever it may be.

Once the entire set of files has been filtered through the memory buffers, the backup piece is finished, and RMAN writes the completion time and name of the backup piece to the target database controlfile.

The Benefits of Block-Level Backups

Memory-to-memory writes occur for each block that is moved from disk into memory. During this operation, the block can be checked for corruption. Corruption checking is one of the nicest features of RMAN, and we discuss it in great length in Chapter 9. Be aware that block checking is not used if you are performing a proxy copy.

Null compression becomes an option when we have access to the data block. We can eliminate blocks that have never been used (have a zeroed header), and discard them during the memory-to-memory write. Therefore, we only back up blocks that have been used and have a more efficient backup.

Misconceptions about Null Compression

This is a good place to mention the different misconceptions related to null compression. The first misconception is that we eliminate empty blocks. This means discussing the two access points that RMAN has to the database: the file header and the block header. RMAN can only draw conclusions about the contents of a block from its header or the file header information. Why no space management information? Well, space management information is only available when the database is open, and RMAN cannot rely on the database being open. We must only rely on that information that we can get without an open database: namely, file headers and block headers. So, if you truncate a table, all the blocks that had information in them but are now empty will be backed up, because RMAN only knows that the block has been initialized by a segment. It does not know that the block is empty.

The second common misconception about null compression is that an incremental backup can save time during the backup, as less is being backed up. This is true, to a certain extent, but only if your backup device is an extremely bad bottleneck. If you stream very quickly to your disk or tape backup location, then the act of eliminating blocks in memory saves little time, because RMAN is still reading every block in the file into memory—it just is not writing every block to the output device. Even during incremental backups, which eliminate blocks based on an incremental checkpoint SCN, we still have to check the header of each block to discover if it has changed since the last incremental backup. Incremental backups, then, save space in our backup location, and they provide a faster form of recovery, but they are not meant to be a significant or reliable time-saver during the actual backup.

Finally, there is plenty of rumor that RMAN uses back image compression, such as that done by the pkzip utility. This is not the case. RMAN only compresses a datafile by eliminating unused blocks. There is no whitespace compression of any kind within those blocks.

Block-level backup also provides performance gains from the perspective of redo generation. As you learned in Chapter 1, if you use old-school hot backup methodology, the amount of redo that you generate while you are running with a tablespace in hot backup mode can sometimes grow exponentially. This causes excess redo log switching, checkpoint failure, and massive amounts of archive log generation that can further cascade into space management challenges in your log archive destination.

RMAN, on the other hand, does not require hot backup mode because it does not need to guarantee block consistency during a backup. RMAN's access to the data block allows it to coordinate with DBWR processes writing dirty buffers, and it can wait until the block is consistent before it reads the block into memory. So, blocks aren't being dumped to redo, and we always have consistent blocks in our backup.

RMAN does require ARCHIVELOG mode, of course. In fact, RMAN will not allow you to back up a datafile while the database is open unless you are in ARCHIVELOG mode. It gives you the following polite error:

```
ORA-19602: cannot backup or copy active file in NOARCHIVELOG mode
```

New in 9i, RMAN now uses block-level backups to provide the next revolutionary recovery option: block media recovery. Now, if you were to receive the stomach-turning "ora-1578: block corruption detected" error, instead of recovering the entire file and performing recovery, RMAN can simply recover the bad block and perform recovery, meaning the rest of the data in the datafile is available during the recovery. More information on this appears in Chapter 12.

This just touches the surface, but you get the point. The payoff is enormous when RMAN is utilized for block-level backups. The rest of this book is dedicated to utilizing this to your advantage.

RMAN in Memory

RMAN builds buffers in memory through which it streams data blocks for potential backup. This memory utilization counts against the total size of the PGA and, sometimes, the SGA. There are two kinds of memory buffers. *Input buffers* are the buffers that are filled with data blocks read from files that are being backed up. *Output buffers* are the buffers that are filled when the memory-to-memory write occurs to determine whether or not a particular block needs to be backed up. When the output buffer is filled, it is written to the backup location. There is a difference in the memory buffers depending on whether you are backing up to, or restoring from, disk or tape. Figure 2-3 illustrates input and output buffer allocation. It illustrates a backup of two datafiles being multiplexed into a single backup set.

Input Memory Buffers

When you are backing up the database, the size and number of input memory buffers depends on the exact backup command being executed. Primarily, it depends on the number of files being multiplexed into a single backup. *Multiplexing* refers to the number of files that will have their blocks backed up to the same backup piece. In order to keep the memory allocation within reason, the following rules are applied to the memory buffer sizes based on the number of files being backed up together.

■ If the number of files going into the backup set is four or less, then RMAN allocates four buffers per file at 1MB per buffer. The total will be 16MB or less.

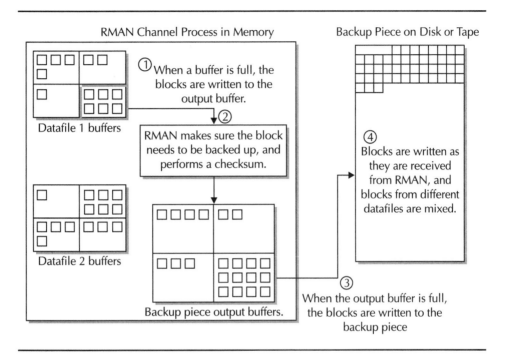

FIGURE 2-3. *Input and output buffers in memory*

■ If the number of files going into the backup set is greater than four, but no greater than eight, then each file gets four buffers, each of size 512KB. This will ensure the total remains at 16MB or less.

■ If the number of files being multiplexed is greater than eight, then RMAN allocates four buffers of size 128KB. This ensures that each file being backed up will account for 512KB of buffer memory.

Bear in mind that these memory amounts are on a per-channel basis. So, if you allocate two channels to back up a database with 32 datafiles, for instance, then RMAN will load-balance the files between the two channels and may not end up with 16 files per channel. If some files are significantly larger than others, we may end up with only 8 files going into one backup set, and 24 going into the other. If this were the case, then the buffers for the first channel with 8 files would allocate 16MB of memory for input buffers (4 buffers multiplied by 512KB each, multiplied by 8 files), and the second channel would allocate 12MB of memory buffers (512KB per file multiplied by 24 files).

Output Buffers When Backing Up to Disk

In addition to input buffers, RMAN allocates output buffers, depending on what the output source is. If you are backing up to disk, then RMAN allocates output buffers that must fill up with data blocks from the input buffers before being flushed to the backup piece on your file system. Per channel, there will be four output buffers, each of which is 1MB in size. So, the memory footprint per channel will always be 4MB.

Output Memory Buffers When Backing Up to Tape

Memory allocation is different when backing up to tape, to account for the slower I/O rates that we expect from tape devices. When you are backing up or restoring from tape, RMAN allocates four buffers per channel process, each of which is 256KB in size, so that the total memory footprint per channel is 1MB.

Memory Buffers on Restore

Memory utilization during restore operations is slightly different than during backups. This is due to the fact that the roles are reversed: instead of reading from the datafiles and writing to the backup location, we are reading from the backup location and writing to the datafiles. During a restore from a disk backup, the input buffers will be 1MB in size, and RMAN will allocate four buffers per channel. When restoring from tape, RMAN allocates four input buffers with a size of BLKSIZE, which defaults to 256KB. The output buffers on restore are always 128KB, and there will be four of them per channel.

There is further discussion about setting BKLSIZE in a backup, and tuning memory for RMAN backups, in Chapter 15.

RMAN Memory Utilization: PGA vs. SGA

Backups to disk use PGA memory space for backup buffers, which is allocated out of the memory space for the channel processes. If your operating system is not configured for native asynchronous I/O, then you can utilize the parameter DBWR_IO_SLAVES to use I/O slaves for filling up the input buffers in memory. If this parameter is set to any non-zero value, RMAN automatically allocates four I/O slaves to coordinate the load of blocks into the input memory buffer. To coordinate this work, RMAN must utilize a shared memory location. So, the memory buffers for disk backups are pushed into the shared pool, or the large pool if one exists.

Memory for tape output buffers is allocated in the PGA unless you are using tape I/O slaves. To enable tape I/O slaves, you set the init.ora parameter BACKUP_TAPE_IO_SLAVES=true. This can be done dynamically and set in the spfile if you desire. When this is set to TRUE, RMAN creates a single slave process per channel to assist with the backup workload. To coordinate this work, RMAN pushes the memory allocation into the SGA.

The Large Pool in the Oracle SGA

The large pool is a specific area in the Shared Global Area (SGA) of Oracle's memory space. It is configured using the LARGE_POOL_SIZE parameter in your init.ora or spfile, and the value is specified in bytes. The large pool is utilized for certain memory activities that require shared space but tend to walk all over the usual operations in the shared pool. Its occupants are primarily restricted to RMAN memory buffers, if I/O slaves are used, and Shared Servers for connection pooling. There are times that the large pool is used for java connections, and it will also house parallel query slaves if you set PARALLEL_AUTOMATIC_TUNING to TRUE.

Do you need a large pool? No. Without one, all of its potential occupants simply take up space in the shared pool. This is not the end of the world, but it's highly desirable to separate out RMAN buffers into their own space in the PGA. That way, sql and pl/sql parsing and other normal shared pool operations are not affected by RMAN backups, and vice versa. It also makes tuning for RMAN simpler and more straightforward.

If either of these I/O slave options is configured, memory will be pulled from the shared pool area in the SGA, unless you have a large pool configured. If you do not have a large pool configured, and you expect to use I/O slaves, we highly recommend that you create a large pool with a size based on the total number of channels you expect to allocate for your backups, plus 1MB for overhead. How many channels makes sense? Chapter 15 can help. If you already have a large pool for Shared Servers (MTS), JDBC connection pooling, or because you have PARALLEL_AUTOMATIC_TUNING set to TRUE, then increase the size of the pool to account for the RMAN memory buffers.

This introduction to the RMAN memory architecture does not include much information on tuning your system to cope with RMAN backups. Obviously, there is a resource hit that takes place while RMAN is running. In fact, you can tune RMAN to use more or less resources, depending on your needs. Chapter 15 discusses how to do this in greater detail.

One last note on memory utilization: If you are backing up to tape, you will be using a Media Management Server product. If you are running your Media Manager from the same system as your target database, there will be additional system resources needed for the tape subsystem. Be sure to factor this in when tuning for backups.

The Recovery Catalog

So far, we have discussed the two most important RMAN components: the RMAN client utility and the internal database packages. However, there is another component that is involved with RMAN backups, although its usage is entirely optional: the recovery catalog.

The recovery catalog is a repository for metadata about RMAN backups. In a sense, you can think of the catalog as merely a copy of the pertinent information out of the controlfile that RMAN requires for backup and recovery purposes. You create the recovery catalog in a user's schema in an Oracle database, and it is no more than a few packages, tables, indexes, and views. These tables contain data that is refreshed from the target database controlfile upon a resync command from within RMAN.

To use a recovery catalog, you first connect from RMAN to the target database. Then, you make a second NET connection to the recovery catalog from within RMAN, like this:

```
Rman>connect target /
rman>connect catalog rman/password@rcat
```

In the connect string to the catalog, you pass the username and password for the user that owns the RMAN catalog. Unlike the target, the connection to the catalog is not a SYSDBA connection and does not need this privilege granted to it.

Once connected, you can manually resync the catalog, or it will be implicitly resynchronized on any backup operation. A resync refers to the refreshing of the information from the target database controlfile to the tables in the recovery catalog.

A recovery catalog can serve as a repository for more than one target database, and as such can help centralize the administration of backups of many different databases. It has views that can be queried from sql*plus to determine the number, size, and range of backups for each target database that has been registered in that catalog.

In Oracle8i, there were a number of extremely useful operations that could only be performed if you used a recovery catalog. However, there is only one set of operations that now require the recovery catalog: using different database incarnations. This is discussed in detail in Chapter 12.

Figure 2-4 details the network topology when a catalog is used. Inside of the recovery catalog, there are two packages: DBMS_RCVMANand **dbms_rcvcat**. The first one, **dbms_rcvman**, is identical in form to that same package in the SYS schema. It is in this way that the RMAN utility can use either the recovery catalog or the target database controlfile for information about backup and recovery, and not worry about different implementations.

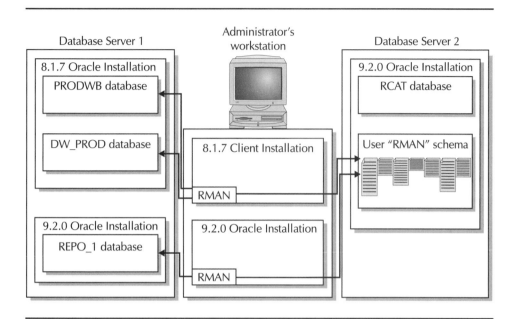

FIGURE 2-4. *Connecting to a recovery catalog*

The existence of the package name DBMS_RCVMAN in the recovery catalog can lead to some confusion on the database that houses the recovery catalog. This database is usually referred to as the catalog database. The catalog database is also a potential target database, and so it also has a package in the SYS schema called **dbms_rcvman**; thus, if you select from dba_objects on your catalog database, there are two packages with the same name, in two different schemas. This is not a mistake or a problem. One of them is built by catproc at the time of database creation (in the SYS schema), and the other is built when we create the recovery catalog (in a regular user schema).

The second package in the recovery catalog is DBMS_RCVCAT, and is only used to perform operations specific to the recovery catalog during RMAN operations. In essence, you can think of this package as being the recovery catalog implementation of **dbms_backup_restore**; whereas **dbms_backup_restore** writes backup completion information to the target database controlfile, **dbms_rcvcat** does this in the recovery catalog.

The base tables that contain information in the recovery catalog are unimportant, really, as you do not want to manually modify them. Instead, for the catalog's protection, Oracle created a series of views, all prefixed with RC_, that can be used to extract information from the catalog. Manually issuing any DML against catalog objects is a dangerous prospect, and we don't recommend it. The RC_* views, and what you can get from them, is outlined in Appendix B. As noted there, these views are different implementations of corresponding v$views in the database controlfile.

One final note on the recovery catalog: Starting in version 9.0.1, the default databases that get copied to your system when Oracle is installed all contain a user schema named RMAN. This is a prebuilt recovery catalog with no databases currently registered. By default, this account is locked. Once unlocked, you can utilize this schema for recovery catalog purposes, or you can build your own user.

The Auxiliary Database

The auxiliary database refers to the instance that will become host to restored files from the target database in the event of a Tablespace Point In Time Recovery (TSPITR), a DUPLICATION operation, or the creation of a standby database using RMAN backups. When you perform any of these tasks, you will be connecting to the target database and the auxiliary database at the same time from within RMAN. In this way, you can utilize the information about the backups in the target database controlfile to coordinate the restore of those backups to the auxiliary database location. The following shows the connection to both the target database (locally) and the auxiliary database (using an Oracle NET Connection):

```
Rman>connect target /
rman>connect auxiliary sys/pwd@aux1
```

RMAN makes a simultaneous connection to each database, and requires access to the **sys.dbms_backup_restore** and **sys.dbms_rcvman** packages in both the target database and the auxiliary database. As such, RMAN requires sysdba privileges at the auxiliary, just as it does at the target. Because RMAN must make a sysdba connection to two separate databases, it is required that you configure at least one of them with a passwordfile and make a NET connection to it—there is no way to connect locally to two different databases.

We discuss the exact auxiliary database setup in great detail in Chapter 16. Figure 2-5 shows the network topology of an RMAN configuration when an auxiliary database is used. In Oracle8i, a recovery catalog was required in order to perform any actions at the auxiliary database, so this figure shows the topology with a catalog, as well.

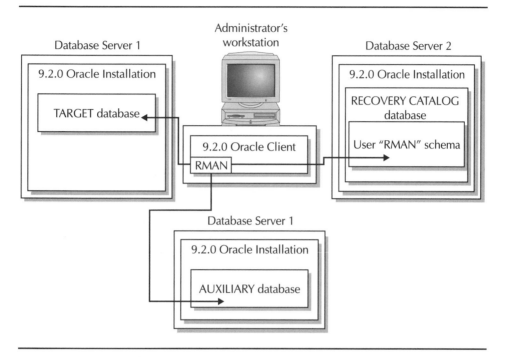

FIGURE 2-5.   *Network topology with an auxiliary database in the mix*

Compatibility Issues

Given the number of different components that we have to work with, there are database version restrictions that you must stick with when working with RMAN. There are five different pieces of the compatibility puzzle, each of which has a version number:

- The RMAN executable version (the client utility)
- The target database
- The recovery catalog schema
- The recovery catalog database
- The auxiliary database (for duplication, TSPITR, and standby creation)

The easiest answer, of course, is to make sure all of these components are on the latest version, 9.2. If they are all at the same level, then there is no problem, right? Of course, in the world where all of your databases are at the same level, everyone has his or her very own pony, fairies roam the earth, babies never cry, and no one ever has to take backups because failures never occur. But for the world we live in, there are some things to understand about RMAN version compatibility.

The Target and the RMAN Executable

The first general rule to stick with is to try and make sure that the target database and the RMAN executable are the same version. This is easy, if you will always be running RMAN from the target database environment. It gets trickier if you will be running all of your RMAN jobs from a centralized client interface. It means your client system will have to have an ORACLE_HOME client installation that corresponds in version to every database version that you will need to connect to and back up. The level of complexity is pretty high with this solution. This can also be avoided by using Oracle9i Enterprise Manager. This allows a centralized interface so you can use the remote RMAN executables from a single console, or more consoles if the backup tasks are divided among DBAs. We discuss the Enterprise Manager interface in Chapter 11.

The Catalog Database and Catalog Schema

There are essentially three tiers to worry about with compatibility: Oracle8, Oracle8i, and Oracle9i. From the perspective of the catalog database and the catalog schema, there's a simpler answer: If you create a 9.2 recovery catalog in a 9.2 database, all databases down to 8.0.4 can be registered in it. If that is not possible, then listen closely: All Oracle8 versions can be registered in an 8.1.x catalog. However, a 9.0.1 or 9.2.0 database cannot be registered in an 8i catalog. So, if you do not have an available database to use for the 9i recovery catalog, you will need to run it in nocatalog mode until one becomes available.

The Auxiliary Database

From a compatibility standpoint, the auxiliary database must be the same version as the target database that it will be cloned from. In fact, we would go so far as to encourage that you patch the ORACLE_HOME to which you will duplicate to the same level as the target database's ORACLE_HOME. In Chapter 16, we discuss in greater detail the use of an auxiliary database.

The RMAN Process:
From Start to Finish

So far, we have discussed the different architectural components of taking a backup using Recovery Manager. As you may have noticed, there are a number of pieces to keep straight. To put it into a little perspective, we will run through a typical backup operation and explain the underlying RMAN activity at every step that it takes. By doing so, you should be able to associate the lengthy expository in this chapter to the actual steps that you will take to perform a backup.

The following will illustrate a backup of a database called PROD. The backup will be going to a disk location; at this point in the book, the discussion of setting up and utilizing a Media Manager for backups to tape will be deferred to Chapters 4 through 8. The target database PROD has 20 datafiles, and is running in ARCHIVELOG mode. The database is up and running during this operation. Here is our backup command:

```
C$>rman
rman>connect target /
rman>backup database;
```

That's it. That's all it takes. The following discussion explains what happens.

RMAN makes the bequeath connection to the target database that we have set up on our environment. This means it checks the variable ORACLE_SID for an instance name, and then spawns a server process at that instance, logging in as a SYSDBA user. This connects us as the internal database user SYS. RMAN immediately spawns the channel processes that will be used to perform the backup. In this case, we are using default settings, so only one channel is allocated. We are not using I/O slaves, so the process allocates memory in the PGA.

Next, RMAN compiles a call to **sys.dbms_rcvman** to request database schematic information from the target database controlfile, starting with a determination of the target database version. It gathers version information from the controlfile, along with controlfile information itself: What type of controlfile is it? What is the sequence number current in it? When was it created?

Because we have specified a full database backup, RMAN requests information for each datafile in the database and determines if any files are offline. As part of this information, it gathers which disk each file is on and how to dole out the work. Because we are using default settings, there will be only one channel and only one backupset. Therefore, RMAN ignores all disk affinity information and concentrates on compiling the list of files for inclusion in the backupset.

After the list is compiled, RMAN is ready to begin the backup process itself. To guarantee consistency, it then builds the snapshot controlfile. If one already exists, it overwrites it with a new one. Then RMAN creates the call to the **dbms_backup_restore** package to create the backup piece. The backup piece will be built in the default file location; on Unix, this is ORACLE_HOME/dbs, and on Windows, it is ORACLE_HOME/database. RMAN has the file list, so it can allocate the memory buffers for performing the read from disk. With 20 files, RMAN allocates input buffers of size 128KB. There will be four per file, for a total memory utilization of 10MB for input buffers. RMAN will only allocate four output buffers, each of size 1MB. This brings our total memory utilization to 14MB for the backup.

After the memory is allocated, RMAN initializes the backup piece. The backup piece will be given a default name that guarantees uniqueness. RMAN then determines if there will be enough space for the backup to be successful. It does this by using a pessimistic algorithm that assumes the backup will be the same size as the sum of all the datafiles. Due to null compression, this will not be the case. But it checks to see if this much space exists prior to running the backup. Be aware that RMAN initializes the backup piece with this initial size and will not be shrunk to the actual size until the backup completes, so you will see an overly large backup piece. This only holds true on 9.0.1 and lower; in 9.2, the backup piece does not preallocate space for backups and is built incrementally as the buffers are filled.

Once the backup piece is initiated, then the channel process can begin the database backup process. In version 9.2, RMAN determines if you are using an spfile, and if so, it backs it up automatically as part of your backupset. Then RMAN will back up the current controlfile to the backupset. This controlfile backup is automatic whenever the SYSTEM tablespace is backed up; this behavior is changed if you have Controlfile Autobackup turned on (see Chapter 9).

So, we have the spfile and the controlfile backed up, and it is time to begin the datafile reads to pull data blocks into memory. The channel process does this by doing a read-ahead on the disk and pulling several blocks into memory at the same time. Then, the memory-to-memory write from input buffer to output buffer occurs. During this write, RMAN determines if the block has ever been initialized or if the block header information is still zeroed out. If it is an unused block, the write to the output buffer never occurs and the block is discarded. If the block has been used, RMAN performs a checksum on the block. If the header and footer of the block do not match, RMAN indicates a corrupt block and aborts the backup. If the block has been initialized and it passes the checksum, then that block is written to the output buffer.

Once the output buffer fills to capacity, we dump the buffer to the backup file location. The RMAN buffers are being filled up with blocks from all of the datafiles, so there is no order to the blocks in the dump file. The file is merely a bucket, and only RMAN will be able to restore the blocks to their proper location upon restore. While the blocks are being written out to the backup piece, the status of the backup is being polled by the RMAN shadow process. It checks in on the RPCs at the target and passes that information to V$session_longops for your review. Based on the information gathered at the beginning of the backup operation, RMAN has an

estimated completion percentage for each channel process. This can be viewed in
v$session_longops:

```
SELECT SID, SERIAL#, CONTEXT, SOFAR, TOTALWORK,
        ROUND(SOFAR/TOTALWORK*100,2) "%_COMPLETE"
FROM V$SESSION_LONGOPS
WHERE OPNAME LIKE 'RMAN%'
AND OPNAME NOT LIKE '%aggregate%'
AND TOTALWORK != 0
AND SOFAR <> TOTALWORK
/
       SID    SERIAL#    CONTEXT      SOFAR  TOTALWORK %_COMPLETE
---------- ---------- ---------- ---------- ---------- ----------
        17        167          1       4784     116328       4.11
```

You can reissue this query throughout the backup process to get an update on
the work still needing to be completed:

```
       SID    SERIAL#    CONTEXT      SOFAR  TOTALWORK %_COMPLETE
---------- ---------- ---------- ---------- ---------- ----------
        17        167          1      96999     116328      83.38
```

Once every block in a datafile has been read into an input buffer and its status
determined, then RMAN completes the file backup by writing the datafile header
out to the backup piece. After all the files have their file headers written to the backup
piece, RMAN makes a final call to **sys.dbms_backup_restore**, which writes backup
information to the controlfile. This information includes the name of the backup
piece, the checkpoint SCN at the time it started, and the time it completed.

And that is the entire process. Obviously, it gets more complex if we exercise
more backup options, such as using multiple channels, using the **filesperset**
parameter, and backing up to tape. But each of these configurations shares the
same fundamental process as previously described. If at any time during your study
or testing of RMAN you want a more intimate look at the internal steps RMAN
takes during backup, you can turn the debug option on for the backup and get a
complete list of the entire process:

```
Rman target / debug trace=/u02/oradata/trace/rmanbkup.out
```

Be warned, though, that this output is extremely verbose, and it can hamper backup
performance. Only use debug for learning purposes on test instances, unless otherwise
instructed to do so by Oracle Support Services when you are troubleshooting a
production backup problem.

Summary

In this chapter, we discussed the underlying architecture employed by RMAN to perform backups of an Oracle9i database. We covered the RMAN executable, the target database packages, and the controlfile. We discussed in detail the process architecture and how memory is allocated for RMAN backups. We discussed the usage of an RMAN recovery catalog, and how to connect to an auxiliary database. After discussing the different architectural components, we gave a brief run-through of a typical backup operation to show the different components in use.

PART
II

Setup Principles
and Practices

CHAPTER
3

RMAN Setup
and Configuration

ell, let's get started with this RMAN thing, shall we? I'll just reach down, pull on the handle…. I said pull on the handle…and, it doesn't start. Like many other things, we first need to set up RMAN and our database for backup and recovery operations before we can actually do anything. In this chapter, we look at initial RMAN setup requirements and options. First, we look at putting the database in ARCHIVELOG mode, in case you want to do online backups. We then look at the basic RMAN interface, so that you can get into RMAN itself. Next, we discuss configuring RMAN for database backup operations. Finally, we discuss the RMAN recovery catalog, including why you might want to use it and how to configure it for use.

Configuring to Operate in ARCHIVELOG Mode

The first thing you need to decide when setting up RMAN for backups is what mode you are going to run your database in, ARCHIVELOG mode or NOARCHIVELOG mode. Chapter 1 discussed the benefits of running in each of these modes. In this section, we address the configuration of ARCHIVELOG mode. First, we look at the process of putting the database in ARCHIVELOG mode and taking it out. Then, we examine the process of configuring the database ARCH process.

Preparing to Put the Database in ARCHIVELOG Mode

A very common mistake that new DBAs make is to fail to enable the ARCH process after putting the database in ARCHIVELOG mode. As discussed in Chapter 1, the ARCH process is responsible for making copies of online redo logs and making archive redo logs out of them.

The ARCH process is signaled by the Oracle LGWR process as soon as an online redo log fills up, and LGWR switches to another online redo log group. ARCH will respond to the log switch by making copies of the online redo log in the locations defined by the Oracle database parameter **log_archive_dest_n**. Until the ARCH process has completed the creation of the ARCHIVED redo log's copies, that online redo cannot be reused by Oracle.

The **log_archive_dest_n** parameter can be used to define up to ten different archive log destinations. These destinations can be local directories, network directories (for example, NT Folders), or even a defined database service name if you are using Oracle's standby database product. You can define each location as a mandatory or optional location.

In addition to the LOG_ARCHIVE_DEST_n parameter(s) to the location(s) you wish Oracle to create archived redo logs, you need to set the LOG_ARCHIVE_START parameter to TRUE. It is this parameter that actually tells Oracle to fire up the ARCH process when the database instance is started. Fortunately, this parameter is dynamic as well, so if you forget to set it, you can issue the command **alter database set log_archive_start=TRUE** and the ARCH process will start.

The following are other parameters that you need to consider with regard to the ARCH process:

- **LOG_ARCHIVE_STATE_n**   Defines one of two different states for each log archive destination. If set to ENABLE, the ARCH process will consider the destination associated with this state as a valid archive log destination. If set to DEFER, the ARCH process will not archive logs to the related LOG_ARCHIVE_DEST_n location.

- **LOG_ARCHIVE_FORMAT**   Provides a template for Oracle to use when naming archived redo logs. As Oracle creates the archived redo logs, it renames them in such a way that each of the archived redo logs has a unique name assigned to it. Using the LOG_ARCHIVE_FORMAT parameter, you can manipulate the default naming standard as you require.

- **LOG_ARCHIVE_MIN_SUCCEED_DEST**   Allows the DBA to define a minimum number of archive log destination copies that must succeed in order for Oracle to be able to reuse the associated online redo log again.

Each of the different parameters mentioned thus far is defined in the Oracle9i Database Reference manual (which is part of the overall Oracle documentation), should you need further information on them.

In the following example, we have a database in ARCHIVELOG mode. We will create three different archive log destination directories, including one to a service name that supports an Oracle standby database. We will also enforce the requirement that at least two of these destinations must be written to in order for the movement of the archived redo log to be considered complete, and that the standby database must be one of those two locations. Here is an example of the use of the various database parameter file parameters related to ARCHIVELOG mode operations:

```
log_archive_dest_1='location=d:\oracle\oraarc\robt mandatory'
log_archive_dest_2='location=z:\oracle\oraarc\robt optional'
log_archive_dest_3='service=recover1 mandatory'
log_archive_min_succeed_dest=2
log_archive_format="robt_%s_%t.arc"
log_archive_start=TRUE
```

In this example, our first archive log destination goes to d:\oracle\oraarc\robt. The second archive log destination is to a secondary location on the Z: drive. We have made this an optional archiving location because it is a networking device (which may not be all that reliable). The third destination is to an Oracle NET service (probably a standby database) called recover1. This will cause Oracle to send the archived redo logs through net8 as they are generated.

Proceeding through the example, we have indicated that the archived redo logs must be successfully copied to at least two different locations via the **log_archive_ min_succeed_dest** parameter. The format of the archived redo log is defined with the **log_archive_format** parameter and finally the ARCH process configured to start up at database startup with the **log_archive_start** parameter.

NOTE
*If you forget to set the ARCH process to start in the initialization parameter file, you can issue the command **alter system archive log start;** to dynamically start the process with the database running. This is true of most of the parameters that are associated with archive logs.*

Switching Between ARCHIVELOG Modes

To switch a database from NOARCHIVELOG mode to ARCHIVELOG mode, you must first shut down the database in a consistent state using one of these commands: **shutdown**, **shutdown immediate**, or **shutdown transactional**. Once the database has been cleanly shut down, restart the database instance by issuing the **startup mount** command. Finally, to put the database in ARCHIVELOG mode, issue the command **alter database archivelog**.

RMAN Workshop: *Put the Database in ARCHIVELOG Mode*

Workshop Notes
For this workshop, you will need an installation of the Oracle software, and a database that is up and running in NOARCHIVELOG mode.

Before starting the workshop, determine where you want Oracle to copy the archived redo logs to.

Putting the database in ARCHIVELOG mode will add some additional overhead onto the system in terms of CPU and disk I/O requirements on the system. This additional overhead should be minimal.

Step 1. Modify the database parameter file and set the **log_archive_dest_1** parameter so that it is pointing to the correct location. Also **set log_archive_start** to TRUE.

Step 2. Shut down the database:

```
SQL> shutdown immediate
Database closed.
Database dismounted.
ORACLE instance shut down.
```

Step 3. Mount the database:

```
SQL> startup mount
ORACLE instance started.
Total System Global Area    84700976 bytes
Fixed Size                    282416 bytes
Variable Size               71303168 bytes
Database Buffers            12582912 bytes
Redo Buffers                  532480 bytes
Database mounted.
```

Step 4. Put the database in ARCHIVELOG mode:

```
SQL> alter database archivelog ;
Database altered.
```

Step 5. Open the database:

```
SQL> alter database open;
Database altered.
```

Taking the database out of ARCHIVELOG mode is as simple as reversing the process. Shut down the database, restart the database instance by issuing the **startup mount** command, and put the database in NOARCHIVELOG mode by issuing the command **alter database noarchivelog**. Note that there is no requirement to shut down the database in a consistent manner when moving from ARCHIVELOG mode to NOARCHIVELOG mode. Here is an example of switching back into NOARCHIVELOG mode:

```
SQL> shutdown
ORACLE instance shut down.
SQL> startup mount
ORACLE instance started.
```

```
Total System Global Area    84700976 bytes
Fixed Size                    282416 bytes
Variable Size               71303168 bytes
Database Buffers            12582912 bytes
Redo Buffers                  532480 bytes
Database mounted.
SQL> alter database noarchivelog;
Database altered.
SQL> alter database open;
Database altered.
```

Finally, you should do a backup of the database once you have completed either task.

The RMAN Command Line

Now that the database is in ARCHIVELOG mode (if you are going to do online backups), we are ready to configure RMAN and our database for backups. Before we can do that, it would be nice to actually know how to use the RMAN executable. So, let's take a slight detour in our setup discussion to look at the RMAN command-line interface (CLI) and how to use it.

There are two different ways to get to RMAN. The first is from the command line and the second is by using OEM. We will deal with the OEM interface in more detail in Chapter 10. Most of the examples you will see in this book, however, will be done using the CLI. We figure that if you can do it from the command line, you can do it from anywhere.

You can start RMAN from the OS prompt simply by typing the command **RMAN**. Once you have started the RMAN command interpreter, you can perform whatever operations you might need to perform. Often, it's much easier to get some of the preliminary work done by using command-line parameters. Thus, when we start RMAN, we can pass several command-line parameters. You can use the command-line parameters to connect RMAN to the database you are going to back up (known as the *target database*), the recovery catalog, or a number of other tasks. Table 2-1 provides a list of the command-line parameters, the data type for the argument of the parameter (if there is one), and the purpose of the parameter.

Here are some examples of starting RMAN with some command-line parameters (and you will see others later):

```
RMAN target=system/manager@robt nocatalog
RMAN target='sys/robert as sysdba@robt' nocatalog
RMAN target=system/manager@robt catalog=system/manager@catalog log="RMAN.log"
RMAN target system/manager@robt nocatalog log "RMAN.log"
```

RMAN Command-Line Parameter	Parameter Argument Type	Purpose
target	Character string	Defines the username, password, and service name of the target database to connect to.
catalog	Character string	Defines the username, password, and service name of the recovery catalog.
nocatalog	No arguments	Indicates that no recovery catalog is going to be used by this session. This parameter is the default parameter in Oracle8i and Oracle9i.
cmdfile	Character string	Indicates the name of a command file script to execute.
log	Character string	Indicates that the RMAN session should be logged. The log file will take the name of the argument to this parameter. Also causes all RMAN messages to the screen to be suppressed (except the RMAN prompt).
trace	Character string	Indicates that the RMAN session should be traced. The trace file will take the name of the argument to this parameter.
append	No arguments	Indicates that the log file (defined by the log parameter) should be appended to.
debug	Various arguments	Indicates that RMAN should be started in debug mode.
msgno	No arguments	Indicates that the RMAN- prefix should be shown with each error message. If this option is not selected, then certain non-error messages will not include a message number with them.

TABLE 3-1. *RMAN Command-Line Parameters*

RMAN Command-Line Parameter	Parameter Argument Type	Purpose
send	Character string	Sends the character string message to the media management layer.
pipe	String	Invokes the RMAN pipe interface.
timeout	Integer	Indicates the number of seconds to wait for pipe input.
Auxiliary	Character string	Defines the username, password, and service name of the auxiliary database to connect to.

TABLE 3-1. *RMAN Command-Line Parameters* (continued)

NOTE
*The = sign between the command-line parameter
and the value of that parameter is optional. Also, if you
are running Oracle9i Real Application Clusters,
you can only connect to one instance of that cluster.*

If you forget the command-line arguments to RMAN (and somehow manage to leave this book and your documentation at home), then there is a way to get RMAN to display the valid command-line parameters. Simply start RMAN with an invalid parameter. As you can see in the following example, RMAN will return an error, but will also provide you with a list of valid command-line parameters (we removed some of the errors at the bottom of the listing for brevity):

```
D:\oracle\oradata\robt>RMAN help
Argument      Value          Description
----------------------------------------------------------------
target        quoted-string  connect-string for target database
catalog       quoted-string  connect-string for recovery catalog
nocatalog     none           if specified, then no recovery catalog
cmdfile       quoted-string  name of input command file
log           quoted-string  name of output message log file
trace         quoted-string  name of output debugging message log file
append        none           if specified, log is opened in append mode
debug         optional-args  activate debugging
msgno         none           show RMAN-nnnn prefix for all messages
```

```
send         quoted-string  send a command to the media manager
pipe         string         building block for pipe names
timeout      integer        number of seconds to wait for pipe input
--------------------------------------------------------------------
Both single and double quotes (' or ") are accepted for a quoted-string.
Quotes are not required unless the string contains embedded white-space.
RMAN-00571: ========================================================
RMAN-00569: =============== ERROR MESSAGE STACK FOLLOWS ==============
RMAN-00571: ========================================================
```

Using the RMAN connect Command

If you start RMAN and realize that you either have not connected to the correct database or wish to connect to a different database (target, catalog, or auxiliary), you can use the **connect** command to change which database RMAN is connected to. To change to another target database, use the **connect target** command. To change to a different recovery catalog, use the **connect catalog** command. To connect to a different auxiliary database, use the **connect auxiliary** command. Here are some examples of the use of the **connect** command:

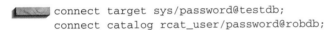

```
connect target sys/password@testdb;
connect catalog rcat_user/password@robdb;
```

Configuring the Database for RMAN Operations

Now that you know how to start RMAN, we need to deal with some configuration issues. While it is possible to just fire up RMAN and do a backup, it's a better idea to deal with some configuration questions before you do. First, you need to set up the database user that RMAN will be using. Next, you can configure RMAN to use several settings by default, so we will look at those settings as well.

Set Up the Database User

By default, you can use RMAN with the SYS account (as sysdba) without any configuration being required. Of course, that's probably not the best account to use when you are doing production backups. We recommend, before you use RMAN to do a backup, that you create a separate account setup that is designated for RMAN backups.

Property of M J Boyden

RMAN Workshop: *Create the Target Database RMAN Backup Account*

Workshop Notes
For this workshop, you will need an installation of the Oracle software, and a database that is up and running. You will need administrative privileges on this database.

Step 1. Determine the user account name that you want to use, and create it with the database **create user** command:

```
CREATE USER backup_admin IDENTIFIED BY backupuserpassword
DEFAULT TABLESPACE users;
```

Step 2. Grant the sysdba privilege to the backup_admin user. We need to grant this privlige because RMAN always connects to the database using the sysdba login. Here is an example of granting the sysdba privilege to the backup_admin account:

```
GRANT sysdba TO backup_admin;
```

So, what happens if you try to connect RMAN to an account that is not properly created? The following error will occur:

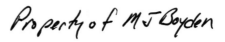

```
D:\oracle\oradata\robt>RMAN target=backup/backup@robt
Recovery Manager: Release 9.2.0.1.0 - Production
Copyright (c) 1995, 2002, Oracle Corporation.  All rights reserved.
RMAN-00571: ===========================================================
RMAN-00569: =============== ERROR MESSAGE STACK FOLLOWS ===============
RMAN-00571: ===========================================================
RMAN-00554: initialization of internal recovery manager package failed
RMAN-04005: error from target database:
ORA-01031: insufficient privileges
```

Now that we have created the user and granted it the privileges it will need, we are a step closer to being ready to use RMAN. Still, we have some RMAN default settings we need to configure, so let's look at those next.

Set Up Database Security

We need to discuss briefly the differences between connecting to RMAN on the local server and connecting to it via NET8. When you start RMAN, you might be logged on to the same server as the database. In this case, if you are logged on using a privileged OS user account, you will not need to do anything beyond the Steps 1 and 2 in the preceding RMAN Workshop. How do you know whether your user account is a privileged one? It depends on the OS you are using. If you are using Unix, there is generally a Unix group called dba (though it may be called something else) that is created when the Oracle owning account (usually called Oracle) is created. If your Unix user account is assigned to this group, then you will be able to connect to a target database without any additional work. If you are using Windows NT, then the privileged users are assigned to an NT group, generally called ORA_DBA.

If you are not logging on to the local server using a privileged account, or if you are connecting to the target database using NET8 from a client workstation (for example, you are connecting using system/manager@testdb), then you need to configure your database to use a password file. To do so, you first need to create the password file, and then configure the database so that it knows to use it. Let's look at each of these steps in detail.

Create the Password File

To create the database password file, you use the Oracle utility **orapwd**. This command takes three parameters:

- **file**   The password filename

- **password**   The password for the sys user

- **entries**   Any number of entries to reserve for additional privileged Oracle user accounts

By default, the Oracle database (on NT) will expect the password file to take on this naming standard, PWD*sid*.ora, where *sid* is your database name. Here is an example of the creation of a password file:

```
orapwd file=PWDrobt.ora password=robert entries=20
```

So, now that we have created the password file, we need to configure the database to use it, and thus allow us to do remote backups via NET8.

Configure the Database to Use the Password File

By default, an Oracle database is not configured to use the password file. To configure the database, edit the parameter file (init.ora) in your favorite editor. The parameter we are interested in is REMOTE_LOGIN_PASSWORDFILE. This parameter can be set to one of three values in Oracle9i:

- **none**   The default value. In this case, Oracle will ignore the password file, and only local privileged logins will be recognized for sysdba access.

- **shared**   This parameter indicates that multiple databases can use the same password file. When in this mode, only the SYS user account password can be stored.

- **exclusive**   This parameter indicates that the password file is used by only one database. In this mode, the password file can contain passwords for several privileged Oracle accounts.

If you are using Oracle9i's spfile instead of a text-based parameter file, then use the alter system command to modify this parameter setting:

```
alter system set REMOTE_LOGIN_PASSWORDFILE=NONE
scopes spfile;
```

Finally, the REMOTE_LOGIN_PASSWORDFILE parameter is not dynamic, so you cannot change it with the database up and running.

Setting the **CONTROL_FILE_RECORD_ KEEP_TIME Parameter**

When configuring your database for RMAN, you should consider how long you wish backup records to be stored in the control file. This includes records of full database backups, specific datafile, control file, parameter file, and archive log backups. The database parameter CONTROL_FILE_RECORD_KEEP_TIME is defined in days (the default is 7). Thus, by default, Oracle will maintain RMAN backup and recovery records for a period of seven days.

This parameter can have a number of operational database impacts. First, it directly impacts the size of the database control file because, as RMAN backups occur, records relating to these backups are stored in the control file. As records are saved in the control file, the control file might well run out of space. In this case, Oracle will expand the control file to accommodate the storage of the required number of backup records. Additionally, setting this parameter to 0 will disallow any control file growth. The result will be an uncertain RMAN backup history retention period.

We suggest that you set the CONTROL_FILE_RECORD_KEEP_TIME to a value no less than your selected database backup retention period. Otherwise, you risk having database backups available on your backup media without related backup records available in the control file. This can cause serious complications if you need to recover these older backups for some reason!

Configuring RMAN Default Settings

RMAN allows you to perform automated database backup and recovery, as you will see in later chapters. To support this feature, RMAN allows you to define default values for a number of settings, such as channel configuration. In this section, we look at the configuration of default RMAN settings. Of course, if you can configure something, you will want to be able to change that configuration, and even remove it completely if required. We will look at that, too. So, what will be the benefit of all of this configuration work? It will make the process of actually doing backups much easier in the end. First, we will quickly examine the **configure** command in RMAN and all that it provides us. Then, we will look at several of the different defaults you might want to configure using the **configure** command.

Throughout this section, we use a number of terms that you might not yet be familiar with, because they are covered in later chapters. Many of the terms were introduced in Chapter 2, though others may seem not quite clear to you yet. That's okay because, to use RMAN, none of the default configuration options are really required. We suggest you skim this section and get a feel for the various default values that you can set. Then, after you have read and applied later chapters, return here and reread this section. At that point, you will be ready to decide what defaults you want to apply to your Oracle database.

Introducing the configure Command

In Oracle9i and later, RMAN allows you to perform automated backup and recovery operations. Because of this, RMAN provides the **configure** command, which allows you to define default values to be applied when doing automated backup and recovery. Using the **configure** command, RMAN allows you to make changes to the default values of the various parameters that are persistent until cleared or changed again. The ability to customize default configuration settings allows you to execute automated RMAN operations. The following are several of the different settings that you can configure:

- A default device type, such as disk or sbt (tape), to use for RMAN jobs.

- The number of channels that are automatically allocated when performing automated backup and restore jobs.

- A tablespace exclusion policy to configure specific tablespaces to be excluded during full database backup operations.

- The maximum size for any given backup piece and the size of any backup set when doing an automated backup.

- Backup optimization to default to ON or OFF. Backup optimization eliminates duplicate backups of identical datafiles (for example, those associated with read-only tablespaces) and archived redo logs.

- The default filename for the snapshot control file (refer to Chapter 2 for more on the snapshot control file).

- The default for automated backups of the control file to ON or OFF, as well as the default format for the control file backup output files and the default device on which to create these backups.

- The default filenames for files of an auxiliary database.

- A default retention policy, which determines which backups and copies are eligible for deletion because they are no longer needed.

Each configurable setting has a default value assigned to it. The defaults are stored in the database control file (as are any configured values). This is true even if you are connecting to a recovery catalog. You can see what the current defaults are by using the **show** command. The **show** command also tells you if a specific configuration is using the default setting and the value for that default setting. Any nondefault RMAN configured settings are also listed in the V$RMAN_ CONFIGURATION database view. Here are some examples of the **show** command's use:

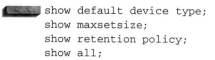

```
show default device type;
show maxsetsize;
show retention policy;
show all;
```

Configuring Various RMAN Default Settings

This section looks at setting RMAN defaults. First, let's look at configuration of channel default settings. You can configure channels in different ways. You can configure defaults for all channels with the **configure channel device type** command, or configure defaults for specific default channels with the **configure channel n device type** command.

You can clear channel defaults for all channels with the **configure channel device type clear** command, and clear channel defaults for specific default channels with the **configure channel n device type clear** command.

When you allocate a channel with the **allocate channel** command, you can specify the assigned names to the channels that you allocate. For example, the **allocate channel d1 device type disk** command will create a channel called d1. When automated channels are allocated, Oracle assigns default names to these channels. These default names depend on the type of default device used. The following table provides an example of the default name format that will be used.

Device Type	Default Name Format	Example
Disk	ORA_DISK_n	ORA_DISK_1, ORA_DISK_2
Tape	ORA_SBT_TAPE_n	ORA_SBT_TAPE_1, ORA_SBT_TAPE_2

The number of channels that are automatically allocated depends on the default level of parallelism defined (which we will discuss later in this chapter).

Now, let's look at some of the number of ways that you can use the **configure** command to automate the backup and restore process with RMAN.

Examples of the Use of the configure Command

This section presents some examples of using the **configure** command to define default values. Let's start with an example of configuring the default backup/restore device to tape or to disk. In this case, all channels assigned to backups will be allocated to disk:

```
configure default device type to sbt;
configure default device type to disk;
```

Now let's look at an example of configuring the number of channels to be allocated during an automated backup or recovery operation. Also in this example, we have set the default level of parallelism for disk operations to two. Thus, if you start an automated backup, two channels will be allocated to perform the backup in parallel.

```
CONFIGURE DEVICE TYPE DISK PARALLELISM 2;
CONFIGURE CHANNEL 1 DEVICE TYPE DISK FORMAT 'd:\backup\robt\backup_%U';
CONFIGURE CHANNEL 2 DEVICE TYPE DISK FORMAT 'e:\backup\robt\backup_%U';
```

NOTE
Generally, when setting the default level of parallelism, you should set it to the number of disks or tape drives attached to which you will be backing up.

Here is an example of controlling the size of a backup set piece or the entire backup itself. In this example, we are limiting channel 1 to create each individual backup piece at a maximum size of 100MB. Note that this command does not limit the overall size of the backup.

```
CONFIGURE CHANNEL 1 DEVICE TYPE DISK MAXPIECESIZE 100m;
```

If we had wished to limit all channels, we could have issued the command slightly differently:

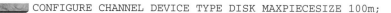

```
CONFIGURE CHANNEL DEVICE TYPE DISK MAXPIECESIZE 100m;
```

So, why might we want to change the maximum size a given backup set piece can be? First, we might have some specific file size limitations that we have to deal with. Tapes can only handle so much data, and some disk file systems have limits on how large a given datafile can be.

We might also want to set a tape device as the default device for all channels, along with some specific parameter settings. In this case, our **configure** command might look like this:

```
-- Note that we could have used the = sign after the PARMS clause if we preferred.
-- like this PARMS='ENV=(NB_ORA_CLASS=RMAN_rs100_tape). This is true with many parameters.
CONFIGURE CHANNEL DEVICE TYPE sbt MAXPIECESIZE 100m PARMS 'ENV=(NB_ORA_CLASS=RMAN_rs100_tape)';
```

You may wish to configure a default maximum size for an entire backup set, in which case you would use this slightly modified syntax (it is followed by an example of resetting this value back to the default, which is unlimited):

```
CONFIGURE MAXSETSIZE TO 7500K;
CONFIGURE MAXSETSIZE CLEAR;
```

CAUTION
Be careful when you are configuring the maxsetsize for the entire database. While your database might be smaller than the maxsetsize defined initially, it could quickly grow beyond the maxsetsize, causing your database backups to fail.

If you are going to be using the automated backup feature, you are going to want to clear a given configuration, so that you can use the default. To do this, use the **configure** command with the **clear** option. In this example, we are clearing out the default options set for default channel 1:

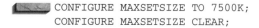

```
configure channel 1 device type disk clear;
```

As you will see in later chapters, you can configure the backup process to create duplexed backups; in other words, multiple copies of the backup can be created at different locations. You can also configure database default settings such that automatic backups will be duplexed using the **configure** command. Here is an example where we have defined that all backups to disk by default will be duplexed, with two copies:

```
configure datafile backup copies for device type disk to 2;
```

We discussed the snapshot control file in Chapter 2. This file is a point-in-time copy of the database control file that is taken during RMAN backup operations. This ensures that the backup is consistent to a given point in time. Thus, if you add a tablespace or datafile to a database after the backup has started (assuming an online backup, of course), that tablespace or datafile will not be included in the backup. Sometimes it is desirable to have RMAN create the backup control file in a location other than the default location. In this event, you can use the **configure** command to define a new default location for the snapshot control file:

```
configure snapshot control file name to 'd:\oracle\backup\scontrolf';
```

You may wish to exclude specific tablespaces during an automated backup, which Oracle allows you to do with the **configure** command. Here is an example of excluding a tablespace by default:

```
configure exclude for tablespace old_data;
```

The **configure** command allows you to enable or disable backup optimization. When enabled, *backup optimization* will cause Oracle to skip backups of files that already have identical backups on the device being backed up to. Here is an example of configuring backup optimization:

```
configure backup optimization on;
```

Note that for optimization to occur, you must have enabled it. In addition, you must issue the **backup database** or **backup archivelog** command with the **like** or **all** option. Alternatively, you can use the **backup backupset all** command (more information on these types of backups is provided in later chapters). Finally, you can disable the setting for backup optimization by using the **force** parameter of the **backup** command.

Automated Backups of the Control File and the Database Parameter File

RMAN in Oracle9i offers the ability to back up the control file and the database parameter file, and you can configure these backups to take place by default. Again, the **configure** command can be used to configure this automated backup process to happen automatically during a backup. Here is an example of configuring automated backups of these important database files and turning the default configuration off:

```
configure controlfile autobackup on;
configure controlfile autobackup off;
```

When autobackup of the control and parameter files is configured, the following rules apply:

- The control file and the server parameter file will be automatically backed up with each RMAN **backup** or **copy** command issued that is not included in a **run** block.

- If a **run** block is used, then the control files and parameter files will be backed up at the end of the **run** block if the last command is not **backup** or **copy**.

In addition to the last two types of automated control file backups, a special type of control file backup can be configured to occur as a direct result of database changes such as adding new tablespaces, adding datafiles, adding online redo logs, and so on. This type of automatic backup can only happen to disk. A special option of the **configure controlfile autobackup** command can be used to facilitate this backup. Here is an example:

```
RMAN> configure controlfile autobackup format for device type disk to
'd:\backup\contf\robt_%F'
```

When this option is used, the Oracle RDBMS will automatically back up the control file during database structure changes that impact the control file. These changes might include adding a new tablespace, altering the state of a tablespace or datafile (for example, bringing it online), adding a new online redo log, renaming a file, adding a new redo thread, and so forth. Note that this automated backup can only be to disk, as tape is not supported. These backups can get a bit large (since the control file contains a history of many of the past backups), so make sure you allocate enough disk space to the backup directory. In spite of the additional space that will be required, these backups can be incredibly handy to have for recovery. Finally, be aware that if the backup fails for any reason, the database operation itself will not fail.

NOTE
If you are not going to use a recovery catalog, and you wish to be able to recover your control file after an automated control file backup, you must know the database ID (DBID) of the database. You should, as a part of your initial setup and configuration of RMAN, note the DBID of the databases that you will be backing up and save that list somewhere safe.

Backup Retention Policy

So, how long do you want to keep your database backups? RMAN gives you the ability to configure a backup retention policy, using the **configure retention policy** command. Configuring a retention policy will not cause backups to be deleted automatically, but will cause expired backup sets to appear when the **report obsolete** command is executed (see Chapter 13 for more details on the RMAN **report** command).

Let's look at an example. First, let's configure a retention policy of three days:

```
RMAN> configure retention policy to recovery window of 3 days;
new RMAN configuration parameters:
CONFIGURE RETENTION POLICY TO RECOVERY WINDOW OF 3 DAYS;
new RMAN configuration parameters are successfully stored
```

Now that we have configured our retention policy, let's see which backups that we might have already done show up to be obsolete:

```
RMAN> report obsolete;
RMAN retention policy will be applied to the command
RMAN retention policy is set to recovery window of 3 days
Report of obsolete backups and copies
Type                    Key    Completion Time      Filename/Handle
-------------------     ------ ------------------   --------------------
Backup Set              4      02-JUN-02
Backup Piece            4      02-JUN-02
D:\ORACLE\ORA912\DATABASE\0ADQ1RV0_1_1
Backup Piece            5      02-JUN-02
D:\ORACLE\ORA912\DATABASE\0ADQ1RV0_1_2
Backup Set              5      02-JUN-02
Backup Piece            6      02-JUN-02
D:\BACKUP\ROBT\BACKUP_0BDQ1SA2_1_1
Backup Piece            7      02-JUN-02
D:\BACKUP\ROBT\BACKUP_0BDQ1SA2_1_2
Archive Log             4      02-JUN-02
D:\ORACLE\ADMIN\ROBT\ARCH\ROBT_201.ARC
Archive Log             3      02-JUN-02
D:\ORACLE\ADMIN\ROBT\ARCH\ROBT_200.ARC
Archive Log             2      02-JUN-02
D:\ORACLE\ADMIN\ROBT\ARCH\ROBT_199.ARC
```

In this example, we have two backup sets, and four related backup pieces that are obsolete based on our backup retention policy. Additionally, we have three archived redo logs that are ready to be removed as well. You can easily remove the backup sets using the **delete obsolete** command:

```
RMAN> delete obsolete;
RMAN retention policy will be applied to the command
RMAN retention policy is set to recovery window of 3 days
using channel ORA_DISK_1
using channel ORA_DISK_2
Deleting the following obsolete backups and copies:
Type                 Key    Completion Time    Filename/Handle
-------------------- ------ ------------------ --------------------
Backup Set           4      02-JUN-02
Backup Piece         4      02-JUN-02          D:\ORACLE\ORA912\DATABASE\0ADQ1RV0_1_1
Backup Piece         5      02-JUN-02          D:\ORACLE\ORA912\DATABASE\0ADQ1RV0_1_2
Backup Set           5      02-JUN-02
Backup Piece         6      02-JUN-02          D:\BACKUP\ROBT\BACKUP_0BDQ1SA2_1_1
Backup Piece         7      02-JUN-02          D:\BACKUP\ROBT\BACKUP_0BDQ1SA2_1_2
Archive Log          4      02-JUN-02          D:\ORACLE\ADMIN\ROBT\ARCH\ROBT_201.ARC
Archive Log          3      02-JUN-02          D:\ORACLE\ADMIN\ROBT\ARCH\ROBT_200.ARC
Archive Log          2      02-JUN-02          D:\ORACLE\ADMIN\ROBT\ARCH\ROBT_199.ARC
Do you really want to delete the above objects (enter YES or NO)? yes
deleted backup piece
backup piece handle=D:\BACKUP\ROBT\BACKUP_05DQ1NJ7_1_1 recid=1 stamp=463527534
deleted backup piece
backup piece handle=D:\ORACLE\ORA912\DATABASE\08DQ1P0T_1_1 recid=2 stamp=463529047
deleted backup piece
backup piece handle=D:\ORACLE\ORA912\DATABASE\07DQ1P0R_1_1 recid=3 stamp=463528990
deleted backup piece
backup piece handle=D:\ORACLE\ORA912\DATABASE\0ADQ1RV0_1_1 recid=4 stamp=463532002
<additional output removed for brevity>
deleted backup piece
backup piece handle=D:\ORACLE\ORA912\DATABASE\0ADQ1RV0_1_2 recid=5 stamp=463532002
deleted archive log
archive log filename=D:\ORACLE\ADMIN\ROBT\ARCH\ROBT_349.ARC recid=11 stamp=463524691
Deleted 11 objects
```

Note in the preceding example that the system will ask you to confirm that you really want to remove the objects that are slated to be removed. If any of the listed objects are not available to be removed, then you will need to run the **crosscheck** command (discussed in Chapter 12). Otherwise, each item listed as deleted in the **delete obsolete** output will be deleted by Oracle.

If you back up your database infrequently, you probably will prefer a redundancy policy that is stated in terms of number of backups rather than backups later than *x* days old. In this case, you can use the **configure** command again, this time using the **redundancy** parameter:

```
RMAN> configure retention policy to redundancy 3;
old RMAN configuration parameters:
CONFIGURE RETENTION POLICY TO RECOVERY WINDOW OF 2 DAYS;
new RMAN configuration parameters:
```

```
CONFIGURE RETENTION POLICY TO REDUNDANCY 3;
new RMAN configuration parameters are successfully stored
```

The **report obsolete** and **delete obsolete** commands work just the same when using this retention policy.

Finally, if you want to disable the retention policy, you use the command **configure retention policy to none**, and no retention policy will be applicable. Use the **configure retention policy clear** command to reset the retention policy to the default value (three days in 9iR2).

 NOTE
If you are using a tape management system, it may have its own retention policy. If the tape management system's retention policy is in conflict with the backup retention policy that you have defined in RMAN, the tape management system's retention policy will take precedence and your ability to recover a backup will be in jeopardy.

If You Are Using Shared Servers

If you are using Oracle's shared servers option (known as Multi-Threaded Server, or MTS, in previous Oracle versions), then you have to configure a dedicated server for use with RMAN because RMAN cannot use a shared server session to connect to the database. If you are using a shared server architecture, refer to the *Oracle9i Recovery Manager Reference* manual (see Chapter 8) for more information on how to configure RMAN for use with the Oracle9i shared server option.

Summary of RMAN Configuration Tasks

We have thrown a great deal of information at you in this chapter. Let's summarize some of the tasks that we suggest you perform on any database that you intend to install RMAN on. Here is a summary list of tasks:

1. Determine whether you wish to run the database in ARCHIVELOG mode or NOARCHIVELOG mode. Configure the database accordingly.

2. Set up a separate database user account (not sys) for use with RMAN.

3. In the database parameter file, set the CONTROL_FILE_RECORD_KEEP_TIME to a number of days equivalent to or greater than the number of days you wish to retain database backups.

4. If you are using shared servers, set up a dedicated server address for RMAN to connect to.

5. Using RMAN, connect to the target database to ensure the database is set up correctly.

6. If you intend to use automated backups, configure your default RMAN values. In particular, consider configuring the following:

   ■ The default degree of parallelism for tape or disk backups. Set to a default value equivalent to the number of disks or tape drives that you will be backing up to.

   ■ Automatic channels and device types. Configure as many channels as you have individual devices.

   ■ Automated control file/database parameter file auto backups.

7. Configure the retention policy as required. Make sure this retention policy is in sync with any other retention policies, such as those associated with tape management systems.

8. Configure RMAN such that it will use the new feature that causes the control file to be backed up after database changes.

9. Before you use it for production database backups, test your RMAN configuration using the methods you will find in later chapters.

The Recovery Catalog

When configuring and using RMAN, one of the initial things you need to decide is whether you are going to use a recovery catalog. In RMAN9i, RMAN defaults to the NOCATALOG connect option (previous versions expected you to connect to a recovery catalog unless you used the NOCATALOG parameter). In this section, first we look at what the recovery catalog is and when you need to use it. Then, we look at how you create a recovery catalog, and discuss backup and recovery of the recovery catalog.

What Is the Recovery Catalog?

The *recovery catalog* is an optional component of RMAN that stores historical backup information from RMAN backups. Unlike the database control file's RMAN information, the recovery catalog data is not purged on a regular basis. Thus, the historical information in the recovery catalog tends to retain more historical information than the control file. Using a recovery catalog does have a few additional benefits over just using the database control file. Some of these benefits include

- You must use a recovery catalog if you wish to use stored RMAN scripts.

- A recovery catalog allows you to restore a database from any previous incarnation that might be stored in the recovery catalog. An incarnation of a database is the logical lifespan of a given database. An incarnation of one database is the period of time between when the database is created and the execution of RESETLOGS on that database. Subsequent incarnations are created with each use of the RESETLOGS parameter.

- A recovery catalog offers a single, enterprise-wide repository of RMAN information. This provides an easier and more flexible central repository of enterprise backup information.

- The loss of a control file can be mitigated in several ways with the presence of a recovery catalog.

- A recovery catalog allows more flexibility when doing reporting, since you can report on the target database at a time other than the current time.

- With a recovery catalog, certain default database RMAN channel configuration information will still be maintained.

With the added benefits of using a recovery catalog, we recommend that if you have a database environment with many databases in it, you should consider using a recovery catalog. Generally, the added flexibility and centralized enterprise-wide reporting benefits of the recovery catalog outweigh the additional maintenance and administrative requirements that are added with the use of a recovery catalog.

When connecting to RMAN, you must use the CATALOG command-line parameter to indicate that you want RMAN to connect to a recovery catalog. By default, RMAN uses the NOCATALOG option, which indicates that a recovery catalog will not be used. After using the CATALOG parameter, indicate the userid and password of the recovery catalog schema that contains the recovery catalog objects. Here is an example of connecting to the recovery catalog using the RMAN command line:

```
RMAN target='sys/robert as sysdba@robt'
catalog='cataloguser/password@bcatalog'
```

Creating the Recovery Catalog

As you might expect, some setup is required before we can actually connect to the recovery catalog. First, we need to create the recovery catalog user and grant it the appropriate privileges. Then, we need to connect to it and create the recovery catalog schema objects. Let's look at each of these steps next.

Creating the Recovery Catalog User

Generally, the recovery catalog should reside in its own database, because the recovery catalog is pretty useless if it is in the same database that you are trying to recover. The next RMAN Workshop section provides a set of detailed instructions on creating the recovery catalog user account.

RMAN Workshop: *Create the Recovery Catalog User Account*

Workshop Notes
For this workshop, you will need an installation of the Oracle software. You will need to identify a database to create the recovery catalog schema in. You will need administrative privileges in this database to create the recovery catalog user account. Finally, determine the name and password you will assign to the recovery catalog user account.

You should create a tablespace for the recovery catalog schema objects. We suggest that you size the tablespace at about 15MB to start.

Step 1. Create the recovery catalog user. Make sure you do not use the SYSTEM tablespace as the temporary tablespace (check out the new Oracle9i default temporary tablespace feature!). Assign the recovery catalog tablespace that you have created (as suggested in the Workshop Notes) to this schema as its default tablespace. Also, assign the recovery catalog user to an **unlimited quota** on the recovery catalog tablespace. Here is an example of this operation:

```
CREATE USER rcat_user IDENTIFIED BY rcat_password
DEFAULT TABLESPACE catalog;
```

Step 2. Grant the following roles to the recovery catalog user:

- connect

- resource

- recovery_catalog_owner

Here is an example of granting the RCAT_USER user we created earlier the roles it requires:

```
GRANT connect, resource, recovery_catalog_owner TO rcat_user;
```

NOTE
The recovery catalog user account is somewhat of a privileged database account. Secure it as you would sys or system.

Creating the Recovery Catalog Schema Objects

Now that you have created the recovery catalog database and user, it's time to actually create the recovery catalog. This is a pretty simple process in Oracle9i. All you need to do is use RMAN. When you start RMAN, use the **target** parameter to connect to the target database, and use the **catalog** parameter to connect to the recovery catalog database schema (which you just created).

At the RMAN prompt, you then issue the **create catalog** command. Optionally, you can use the **tablespace** parameter to define a tablespace in which to create the RMAN schema objects in. The next RMAN Workshop section provides an example of using the **create catalog** command to create the recovery catalog schema.

RMAN Workshop: *Create the Recovery Catalog*

Workshop Notes

For this workshop, you should have completed the previous RMAN Workshop ("Create the Recover Catalog User Account"). Also, we assume that you have created a tablespace called catalog_tbs, and we will be creating the RMAN schema objects in that tablespace.

Step 1. Connect to the recovery catalog with RMAN:

```
RMAN catalog=rcat_user/rcat_password
```

Step 2. Issue the **create catalog** command from the RMAN prompt:

```
create catalog tablespace catalog_tbs;
```

Register the Database with the Recovery Catalog

Now that you have prepared the recovery catalog for use, you need to register databases with it. This is required before you can perform a RMAN backup of a database using the recovery catalog. This is a rather simple process, as you can see in the associated DO IT NOW section.

RMAN Workshop: *Register Your Database in the Recovery Catalog*

Workshop Notes

For this workshop, you should have completed the previous RMAN Workshop ("Create the Recover Catalog").

Step 1. Using RMAN, sign into the database and the recovery catalog at the same time:

```
set ORACLE_SID=main_db
RMAN target=backup_admin/backupuserpassword
CATALOG=rcat_user/rcat_password@recover
```

Step 2. Register the database with the recovery catalog:

```
RMAN> Register database;
```

Backing Up and Recovering the Recovery Catalog

We will look at how to actually use the recovery catalog in later chapters as we discuss RMAN backups in general. Since RMAN can back up databases without a recovery catalog, it makes sense that you can use RMAN to actually back up the recovery catalog itself. If you choose to use RMAN to back up your recovery catalog, it would be a very good idea to create backups of your control file and store them in a separate location from your RMAN backups of the recovery catalog. Since recovering the control file can be a time-consuming process during a non–recovery catalog restore of your database, a separate backup of the control file is something to consider.

Other Backup and Recovery Setup and Configuration Considerations

Finally, let's consider the other backup and recovery implications of your database. There are certain things that RMAN will not back up that you need to consider as a part of your overall backup and recovery strategy planning. These include such things as the base Oracle RDBMS software and the parameter files (tnsnames.ora, names.ora, sqlnet.ora, and so on). You need to make plans to back up and recover these files as a part of your overall backup and recovery planning.

You also need to consider your disaster planning with regard to RMAN and non-RMAN backups. How will you protect these backups from flood, fire, and earthquake? The beginning is a very good time to consider these questions, not when the fire is burning two flights below!

Summary

Whew! We have covered a great deal of ground in this chapter, and indeed there are several things you need to do before you start using RMAN. First, we looked at how to set up the database in ARCHIVELOG mode, if that is what you wish to do. Next, we looked at the RMAN command line and then at how to configure your database for use with RMAN, including setup of the password file and configuring a user account for use with RMAN. We also looked at configuring RMAN default settings. We strongly suggest you take advantage of this feature in RMAN, as it can make your life much easier. We then provided you with a summary of RMAN configuration tasks. Finally, we discussed the recovery catalog, including configuration and backup issues.

CHAPTER
4

Media Management
Considerations

s we have made redundantly clear, RMAN cannot write to a tape device without a little help from its friends. Writing to disk is no problem—the Oracle RDBMS has been doing that for years. But tape backups require outside assistance. This is primarily due to the disparate nature of the different sequential media subsystems that are on the market and put to use every day. Instead of trying to employ different system calls for each of these different types of tape devices, RMAN's developers decided to employ those software vendors that already earn a living by selling products that can read and write from tape.

This chapter covers the conceptual architecture of employing a media manager to back up your database directly to disk. It does so from a generic standpoint, by staying focused on the RMAN side of the equation and speaking in grand sweeping generalizations about the media management products themselves. We will talk about the setup from the RMAN side, including how it all works and what changes when you use tape for your output device. Chapters 5, 6, 7, and 8 go into detail about four of the most popular media management products on the market, and talk about configuring and using them specifically. The one media manager that we will discuss in this chapter is Legato Single Server Version (LSSV), which is a stripped-down version of Legato NetWorker and is shipped free of charge with each copy of Oracle9i Release 2.

Tape Backups: Who Backs Up to Disk, Anyway?

In the world of Oracle databases, size does matter. In fact, just five years ago, a very large database was a few gigabytes in size; now, databases range upward into the terabytes, and the average database is 50GB and growing. So, when it comes to backups, the idea of trying to find enough contiguous space on disk to back up a database is usually ludicrous. There's simply too much data to back up.

Thus, the first reason for tape backups is the size of the database. The size of a database determines whether you need to back up to tape: buying more hard drives can get pricey, but tapes? Well, they are cheap by comparison, and reliable, considering their purpose is to hold copies of data—copies that by the law of averages will rarely ever get used. Of course, there are times when disk backups become a critical piece of a strategy that stresses quick recovery—tape backups are much slower than disk backups on both the backup and the restore. We discuss this in greater detail in Chapter 15.

The second reason to use tape backups is manageability. Typically, enterprise-wide backup strategies are implemented and executed by a centralized person on a centralized system. And this is a good thing—economy of scale and all that. It allows your company to invest in large tape-storage jukeboxes that can stream data from multiple different sources. Then the data backups can be cataloged and removed without having someone trek all over the enterprise distributing tapes, troubleshooting individual tape devices, or training users on new software rollouts.

Centralization at a Price

The drawback to pooling backup resources is that it leads to complications, especially in regard to Oracle databases. The tricky nature of Oracle datafiles, log files, and control files means that we cannot simply let an OS job step in and copy the files at its leisure. Instead, we have to prepare the database for the backup job, signal the copy to begin, and then reconfigure the database afterward—or so it was in the old-school world (refer to Chapter 1).

Using RMAN means this database configuration is eliminated and that backups can occur anytime, under any circumstances. However, to get the backups to stream to your centralized tape backup location, you have to do some RMAN-specific configuration.

RMAN and the Media Manager: An Overview

RMAN streams backups to tape by engaging a media manager. The *media manager* is the software provided by a third-party vendor that takes the data stream of blocks passed from the RMAN channel process and redirects it to the appropriate tape. Most often, a media management server exists in an enterprise network. The *media management server* is a centralized system that handles all enterprise-wide backup operations to tape devices that are managed there.

To engage the media manager, a computer system must have the media management (MM) client software installed on it. This is the software that makes the connection to the MM server and passes the data to it over the network. For RMAN to engage the MM server, an additional software component is needed. After you install the client software, you must also install the Oracle module for the media manager. The *Oracle module* is a software plug-in for the Oracle RDBMS that connects RMAN to the client media management software, which can then make the pass to the MM server. This plug-in for Oracle is referred to as the Media Management Library (MML). Figure 4-1 shows a generalized overview of the backup topology when a media manager is used to back up to tape.

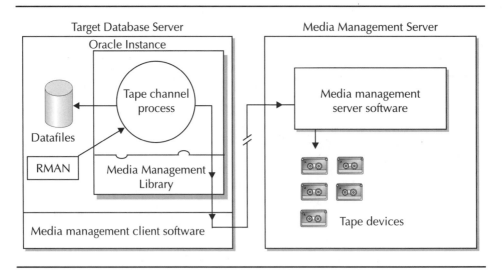

FIGURE 4-1. *Network topology when backing up to tape*

The Media Manager Catalog

The media manager is a separate subsystem in the overall backup system you will use. As previously described, it has three essential components: the Media Management Library that integrates with Oracle, the media management client, and the media management server. The MM server has multiple components, and the specifics are dependent upon the vendor. But all MM servers must have a few similar components, the most important of which (from the perspective of this chapter) is the media manager catalog.

The media manager catalog is the database of information at the MM server that holds information about the physical tapes, who has access to those tapes, and what is being stored on those tapes. It is this catalog that records the RMAN file handle when a backup is complete. The *handle* refers to the name of the backup piece that gets created when we perform a backup with RMAN. When you back up to disk, the handle is the physical filename. When backing up to tape, the handle is used in the media manager catalog to refer to a location on tape where the backups can be located.

RMAN completes a backup to tape by providing the handle name to the media manager, which records that handle in the catalog. When a restore is required, RMAN requests a specific handle (based on its own catalog) from the media manager. The media manager looks for that handle, associates it with a specific tape, and determines if that tape is available. If the tape is available, the media manager engages the tape and begins to stream the data back to RMAN so that we can rebuild the datafiles.

The Media Manager:
Other Software Components

In addition to the catalog, the MM server is comprised of two essential pieces: the device agent and the robotic interface. The *device agent* is the component that is responsible for engaging the actual tape device and passing data to and from it. The *robotic interface* refers to the software that controls any robotics that are responsible for changing tapes when they are full, or when a request is made for a tape that has been filled in the past.

From the Oracle perspective, RMAN is blind to these components. RMAN simply sends a command request to its MML, and the MM software handles the coordination of all events after that. However, it is important to be familiar with these software components because your backup and recovery success depends on them. Many problems that come from using RMAN are related to the device agent, or the robotic interface, but from the RMAN interface, these problems are nearly impossible to discern.

The Media Management Library

The MML is simply a library file that interprets generic requests from RMAN for a particular backup or restore operation, and interprets that request into the specific system call necessary at the media management server to turn that request into a reality. The MML is provided by the same vendor that supplies the MM client software and the MM server software, but you purchase and license it separately from the client and server software.

The MML is loaded into the Oracle memory space as an integrated library file when a tape channel is first allocated, and it is logically part of the Oracle RDBMS software, so that RMAN can make the correct calls to the MM client software. The integration is simple, really: When a channel to tape is allocated, Oracle looks to load a file called libobk.so. This file, located in the ORACLE_HOME/bin directory, is just a symbolic link to whichever MML file you will be using. On the Windows platform, Oracle looks for a file called orasbt.dll in the searchable path. No matter who your media management provider is, its media management DLL will be named orasbt.dll, and, usually MM providers write it to the WINDOWS\system32 directory. Those that do not will append the System Path Environment Variable with a searchable path that leads to orasbt.dll.

In the next four chapters, we discuss the linking process by which you can establish your vendor's MML file as the one RMAN initiates when a channel is allocated. For testing purposes, Oracle provides a test MML file. This library file allows you to allocate a channel to tape, but then write the backup to disk. Here, we'll show you how to use this test MML.

RMAN Workshop: *Test Tape Channels with the Oracle Default SBT Interface*

Workshop Notes

You will need access to a sufficient amount of disk space, and a directory created to place the backup piece in. In our example, we use the mount point u04, on which we created a directory called backup. Make sure you have sufficient memory available for the backup, as outlined in Chapter 2, and be aware of the disk I/O that goes to the backup location. Try to allocate space on a different controller than those that house your actual database.

Step 1. Build your backup directory:

```
$>cd /u04
mkdir backup
```

Step 2. Make sure permissions are established so that the oracle database, which operates as the user that installed the software, can write to this location:

```
ls -l backup
```

Step 3. Initiate RMAN, and connect to the target. In the following example, we are connecting locally to the target PROD. This means that an **env** command shows us that ORACLE_SID=PROD.

```
$>Rman
Rman> connect target
```

Step 4. Run your backup, using the PARMS parameter during channel allocation to specify the oracle test library file. You also need to specify a BACKUP_DIR, which is the location that RMAN will write the backup to. Here, we specify this as /u04/backup:

```
<RMAN> run {
2> allocate channel x1 type 'sbt_tape'
3> PARMS="SBT_LIBRARY=oracle.disksbt,
4> ENV=(BACKUP_DIR=/u04/backup)";
5> backup datafile 1 format='%U';}
```

Here's the output from the preceding command:

```
using target database controlfile instead of recovery catalog
allocated channel: x1
```

```
channel x1: sid=16 devtype=SBT_TAPE
channel x1: WARNING: Oracle Test Disk API
Starting backup at 04-JUN-02
channel x1: starting full datafile backupset
channel x1: specifying datafile(s) in backupset
input datafile fno=00001 name=/u02/oracle/oradata/SYSTEM01.DBF
channel x1: starting piece 1 at 04-JUN-02
channel x1: finished piece 1 at 04-JUN-02
piece handle=05dq5o7v_1_1 comment=API Version 2.0,MMS Version 8.1.3.0
channel x1: backup set complete, elapsed time: 00:01:35
Finished backup at 04-JUN-02

Starting Control File and SPFILE Autobackup at 04-JUN-02
piece handle=c-4169479667-20020604-00 comment=API Version 2.0,MMS
Version 8.1.3.0
Finished Control File and SPFILE Autobackup at 04-JUN-02
released channel: x1
```

This is a great test if you are trying to troubleshoot possible problems with your media manager backup solution and cannot get the backups to work. By allocating a "fake" tape channel, you can rest assured that RMAN is configured correctly.

CAUTION
Do not use the test MML file for production backups. If you will be backing up to disk in a production environment, allocate a disk channel. The performance of the fake MML is terrible because RMAN is allocating memory buffers for tape, not disk, and therefore is not taking advantage of the speed of disk writes versus tape writes.

If you have not successfully loaded your vendor's MML file, and you do not specify in the PARMS section of the channel allocation that you want to use Oracle's disk SBT interface, then you will receive an error when you try to allocate a channel to tape:

```
RMAN-00571: ===========================================================
RMAN-00569: =============== ERROR MESSAGE STACK FOLLOWS ===============
RMAN-00571: ===========================================================
RMAN-03009: failure of allocate command on x channel at 06/04/2002 10:32:31
ORA-19554: error allocating device, device type: SBT_TAPE, device name:
ORA-27211: Failed to load Media Management Library
```

Interfacing with the MML

When you are linking Oracle and the MML, you are establishing the means by which RMAN can pass a command that engages the MML and therefore the MM client software installed on the database server. But how do we know which MM server to engage?

To specify the MM server, you must pass an environment parameter within the RMAN session to specify the server name. Specifically, we specify the server name as an environment variable when we allocate our tape channel. As you saw in the previous RMAN Workshop example, you pass the environment variable using the PARMS option of the **allocate channel** command. Different MM products have different environment variables that they accept. Veritas NetBackup, for example, requires the parameter NB_ORA_SERV:

```
Allocate channel t1 type 'sbt_tape'
PARMS="ENV=(NB_ORA_SERV=storage1)";
```

In the preceding example, the name of the MM server is storage1, and our database server has already been registered in this server and has permissions to write to its tape devices.

In addition to the name of the server, there are numerous other parameters that we can pass at the time of the channel allocation to take advantage of management functions at the server. For instance, NetBackup offers the ability to specify the class or the schedule to use for this backup, whereas Legato allows you to specify the resource pool. More information on these parameters is provided in Chapters 5 and 6.

The SBT API

RMAN can engage different media managers with impunity because it sends the same marching orders no matter what MML has been loaded. Oracle developed RMAN with a generic API called the SBT API, which is provided to third-party vendors that wish to code integration products for Oracle database backups. This API is the means by which RMAN sends commands to the media manager.

The SBT API is responsible for sending the commands to the MM server to initiate the creation of backup files on tape. It also sends commands to search for previous backups based on the file handle in the media manager catalog. It can send commands to remove these backups, as well as write new backups and, of course, read from the backup location. There are two versions of the Oracle RMAN SBT API: 1.1 and 2.0. Version 1.1 was published and used with Oracle 8.0.x, and that's it. Since then, RMAN has made calls to the media manager using the specifications of version 2.0. You can see this version in RMAN's output when you run a backup:

```
channel x: finished piece 1 at 04-JUN-02
piece handle=1cdq5q2d_1_1 comment=API Version 2.0,MMS Version 8.1.3.0
channel x: backup set complete, elapsed time: 00:03:55
Finished backup at 04-JUN-02
```

RMAN will also return the version of the MML that it initializes at channel allocation time. This is seen during channel allocation, in the RMAN output:

```
allocated channel: x
channel x: sid=12 devtype=SBT_TAPE
channel x: VERITAS NetBackup for Oracle8 - Release 3.4GA (030800)
```

Not only is this a good way to determine your MML version, but it also means that you have successfully linked your MML in with RMAN—otherwise, it would not be able to extract the version information.

Back Up to Tape: From Start to Finish

In this section, we will do a walk-through of a backup to tape, and show the different calls made to the SBT API and how they are handled by the media manager. Again, please note that we are doing a very generic overview, and the specifics are handled by the vendor that writes the integration MML.

When you allocate a tape channel, RMAN spawns a server process at your target database. This server process then makes a call to the SBT API of sbtinit(). This call initializes the MML file and loads it into memory. It also returns to RMAN the version of SBT API supported by that MML. After calling sbtinit(), RMAN calls sbtinit2(), which supplies further configuration details to the media manager software.

After RMAN has parsed your backup command, it executes the RPC that makes the call to sys.dbms_backup_restore.backuppiececreate. At this time, the channel process calls sbtbackup(), which handles the creation of the backup piece at the specified tape location. This call informs the media manager that Oracle will begin pushing the flow of data blocks to it, so it should prepare the tape device for the onslaught.

The RMAN input buffers fill up and make the memory-to-memory write to the output buffer. When the output buffer fills, the channel process calls sbtwrite2(), which performs the write of filled output buffers to the tape location (for more details on input buffers, refer to Chapter 2). Typically, this means engaging the device agent at the MM server to access the tape itself.

When all the output buffers for a particular backup set have been cleared out, and there is no more work for sbtwrite2(), the channel session calls sbtclose2(). This flushes out any media manager buffers and commits the backup piece to tape.

After we complete the backup piece, the channel process invokes sbtinfo2(), to make sure the media manager catalog has documented the backup piece. It requests the tape, the tape location, and the expiration time of the backup from the catalog. Then, it writes the backup piece handle to the catalog.

After confirming the backup piece location, the channel process calls sbtend(), which cleans up any remaining resources and releases them for other database use. The final action performed is the deallocation of the channel process, which is terminated at the target database.

Restore from Tape: From Start to Finish

Of course, sooner or later, all that backing up you've been doing will get put to the test, and you will need to perform a restore. As with a backup, the SBT API has a specific series of steps that it goes through during a restore operation in order to get the backups on tape back into place for your database. In this section, we take a brief run-through of the SBT API during a restore operation.

When you allocate the tape channel for restore, RMAN creates a server process at the target database. This channel then calls sbtinit() to initialize the media manager software. This is identical to the initialization that would take place for a backup: the MML file is loaded into memory.

Based on the parameters of our **restore** command in RMAN, RMAN will have checked its catalog to determine the handle name of the backup required for the restore. It then takes this requested backup piece handle and passes it to the media manager using sbtrestore(). The sbtrestore() function instructs the media manager to prepare the appropriate tape for a restore operation. This means engaging the media manager catalog and finding the appropriate tape, and then (if necessary) passing the command to the robotic instruction set to get the tape. After the tape is loaded, it will need to be rewound to the backup piece starting point.

After preparing the tape for the restore, the channel process calls the sbtread2() function to read the data from the tape device and stream it to the Oracle process. This data is loaded into the input buffers, written to the output buffers, and finally written to the datafile locations as specified by the control file.

When the end of a backup piece is detected on tape, the tape channel process calls the sbtclose() function to disengage the particular tape that had that piece on it. This signals that Oracle is done with the tape. If there are more backup pieces that need to be read for the restore operation, then the channel process returns to the second step and calls sbtrestore() for a different backup piece.

After the restore is complete and RMAN requests no more backup pieces, the channel process calls the sbtend() function, which cleans up the channel resources and releases them for other use. Then the channel process is terminated, after which the media manager is free to unload any tapes that had been requested.

Using sbttest and loadsbt.exe

As mentioned previously, there are always indications as to whether you have successfully linked your MML with Oracle. The information from the channel allocation shows the MML version, for instance. However, these sorts of indicators do not guarantee success, as a failure may occur farther down the topology: at the MM client level or at the MM server. Oracle provides a utility called sbttest that can test to make sure that RMAN will be able to perform backups to tape using your MM configuration. This utility is called from the command line, and it performs a complete test. It writes a block to tape, and then requests a read of that block. In this way, it runs through the entire gamut of SBT API functions that would occur during backup and makes sure they will all be successful.

Usage of sbttest is simple, and works from the command prompt. Be sure that you have completed the full configuration of your MM configuration, and then go to the command prompt within the environment from which you will run RMAN and type **sbttest** and a test filename. The following code walks through each of the sbt() calls previously listed in the "Restore from Tape: From Start to Finish" section, and provides output on whether or not each call succeeded:

```
/u02/home/usupport> sbttest oratest_061902
The sbt function pointers are loaded from libobk.so library.
NetWorker: Cannot contact nsrexecd service on cervantes.windba.com,
Service not available.-- sbtinit succeeded
NetWorker: Cannot contact nsrexecd service on cervantes.windba.com,
Service not available.-- sbtinit (2nd time) succeeded
sbtinit: Media manager supports SBT API version 2.0
sbtinit: vendor description string=NMO v3.5.0.1
sbtinit: allocated sbt context area of 536 bytes
sbtinit: Media manager is version 3.5.0.1
sbtinit: proxy copy is supported
sbtinit: maximum concurrent proxy copy files is 0
-- sbtinit2 succeeded
-- regular_backup_restore starts .............................
MMAPI error from sbtbackup: 7501, nwora_index_ssinfo:
index connect to cervantes.windba.com failed for client
cervantes.windba.com: Program not registered
-- sbtbackup failed
```

The sbttest utility has matured impressively since its inception as a simple binary indicator of success or failure. Now, a number of parameters can be passed to tweak the exact test you would like to take your MM system through. This includes naming the database you want to test, changing the number of blocks that are written by sbttest, and specifying how to further handle the file that sbttest writes to tape. Simply typing **sbttest** from the command prompt will give you all the switches you can use, along with simple text descriptions.

The sbttest utility is only available for Unix platforms; on Windows, you can request the utility loadsbt.exe from Oracle Support. Unfortunately, this utility does not have the same capabilities as sbttest, and instead simply checks the searchable path for a file called orasbt.dll. If it finds this file, it will try to load it the same way that Oracle will during a tape backup. It will tell you if it can be loaded, but it will not attempt to write a block to tape, and so it does not "swim downstream" very far to see if the entire configuration works. As such, it is not as useful as sbttest.

Media Management Errors

Error reporting in RMAN looks much the same when reporting MM problems as it does any other problem, and this can lead to some confusion. It is critical when troubleshooting RMAN errors to be able to determine where exactly the error is coming from: is it RMAN, the target database, the catalog database, or the media manager?

The error stack in RMAN has been cleaned up significantly in Oracle9*i*; if you have ever had to figure out a problem in Oracle8*i*, you can fully appreciate just how much cleaner the stack is now. With that in mind, there are specific ways to determine if an error that is being returned in RMAN is related to the media manager. Some of them are obvious, particularly if you have not linked the MML correctly. We've shown examples of these errors already. However, if you have properly linked the MML with your Oracle installation, how can you tell if an error is related to the MML?

There are a number of different errors, but the most common error you will see related to the media manager is ORA-19511. This error is actually a blank error, meaning that Oracle supplies no text; instead, Oracle provides this as an error trap for MM errors. So if you see this error, there is no doubt that you have linked your MML correctly, and that the problem you are having is irrefutably a problem with the media manager:

```
ORA-19511: sbtbackup: Failed to process backup file
```

Other indicators of MM problems are not so clear, but are just as telling. For instance, if you ever see in the error stack RMAN referring to a "sequential file," then you are dealing with a tape backup, and the problem is due to a failed read or write to the sequential file on tape. Another common error is ORA-27206:

```
RMAN-10035: exception raised in RPC: ORA-27206: requested file
not found in media management catalog
```

Again, the wording indicates a problem communicating with the MM catalog, which is where you would need to look to resolve the problem.

In addition to actual errors, any hang you might encounter in RMAN is *usually* related to MM problems. Usually. The reason for this is that when RMAN makes an sbtwrite() call to the media manager, for instance, RMAN cannot possibly know how long this will take to complete. Therefore, RMAN does not provide any sort of time out for the operation—it will wait indefinitely for the media manager to return with either a successful write or an error. If the media manager is waiting on a particular event that has no time out, such as a tape switch or a tape load, the media manager waits, and so RMAN waits. And so you wait. And wait. Like we said, RMAN will not time out, so if you notice that RMAN is taking a particularly long time to complete, and you see no progress in V$session_longops (refer to Chapter 2), then your first instinct should be to check the media manager for an untrapped error or for an event such as a tape load or tape switch.

Legato Single Server Version

Every copy of Oracle9i Release 2 comes with an MM product that you can use, free of charge. This product, Legato Single Server Version (LSSV), is provided by Legato and is a lite version of its NetWorker product. It comes with a media management server, media management client, and the NetWorker Module for Oracle (NMO). The catch? It's only good for Oracle backups (not all your system files), and you cannot use this product to stream backups to or from a network storage device. In other words, you cannot centralize your backups to a single tape location. In addition, your target database server must have a local tape device for this to work.

The following RMAN Workshop shows LSSV set up on Windows 2000. There is a free version of LSSV for AIX, HP-UX, Linux, Solaris, and Tru64, as well as Windows. However, the most common platform that has stand-alone tapes is Windows 2000, so we chose this example first. For complete information on platform support and patches, refer to Legato's web site at www.legato.com/lssv.

RMAN Workshop: *Setup LSSV on Windows 2000*

Workshop Notes
You will need your Oracle9i version 2 (9.2.0) media for this workshop. You will also need a tape device already recognized by your operating system. (It is outside the scope of this modest little book to assist you with hardware troubleshooting. If you can see the tape in the device manager, then you are set.) Make sure you already have a tape loaded into your tape device.

You'll need about 40MB of free disk space, and, when running, LSSV will require approximately 20MB of memory. In addition, you will be modifying the system environment variables, the completion of which requires a reboot. So, schedule this installation during an acceptable downtime.

Step 1. Navigate to the root level of the first 9.2.0 CD. On this CD is a directory called lgto. Inside is a self-extracting executable file, lgto_62.exe. Extract this to a temporary directory of your choice, and then navigate to this directory and double-click the setup.exe file.

The setup is rather painless. The wizard first gives you the opportunity to choose the type of install.

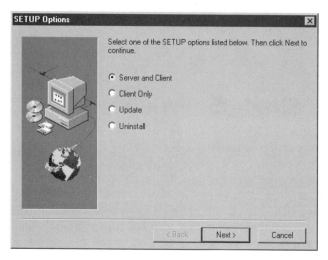

Step 2. Select Server And Client, and then click Next. The wizard displays the default directory for installation. Click Next. The Authorize NetWorker Servers screen appears: only the server on which you will be installing is allowable here. Remember, this is based on the NetWorker framework, so it carries the image of a fully functional media manager, but it is not. Type in your system name, and click Next. The installation will run through completely and finish.

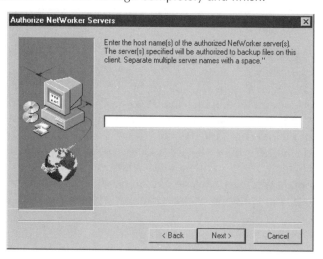

The install creates three services on your system: NetWorker Backup and Recover Server, NetWorker Power Monitor, and NetWorker Remote Exec Service. It also creates a program group with the NetWorker product and its uninstaller.

Step 3. Before you can use LSSV, you have to place its version of the orasbt.dll file in the searchable path. On your desktop, right-click My Computer and choose Properties. Then, click the Advanced tab and click the Environment Variables button to open the Environment Variables dialog box. In the System Variables list, highlight Path and click Edit. Then, at the beginning of the string, enter the following:

```
C:\Program Files\nsr\bin;
```

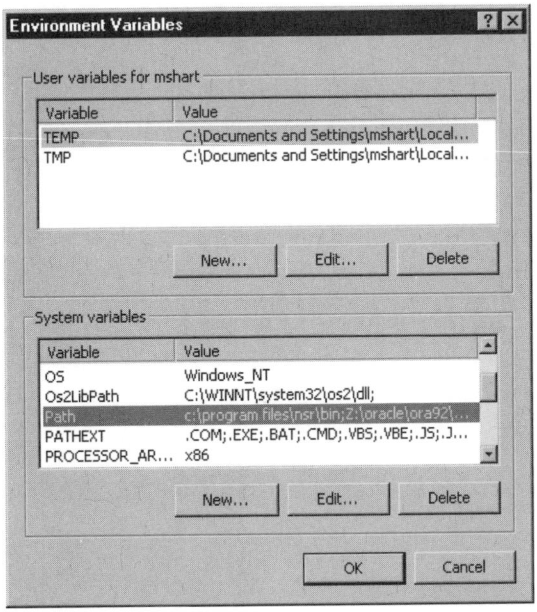

Then click OK and click OK again on the System Properties page. Unfortunately, for this change to take effect, you have to reboot the computer. Go ahead and do that now. You can now go to the NetWorker GUI to set up LSSV for tape backups from RMAN.

Step 4. Select Start | Programs | NetWorker Group | NetWorker Administrator. This opens the GUI utility that you will use to set up LSSV. When this utility opens, you see the NetWorker Servers and NetWorker Clients. Only your stand-alone system will appear here, under Servers. To set up your tape device, right-click your server name and choose Connect To This Server. There are a number of buttons here, but we will go directly to the Devices button, which has the subheading Set Up, Mount, Unmount, And Label, and click it. A small window appears that shows your server-> Devices, and underneath the devices your tape should appear automatically. If it does not, you can right-click and choose Create.

After the tape device has been established, right-click the tape device and choose Operations. This opens the Device Operations dialog box, with a graphic that represents your tape device. It will show the tape as ejected (even though your tape should be physically loaded prior to this step).

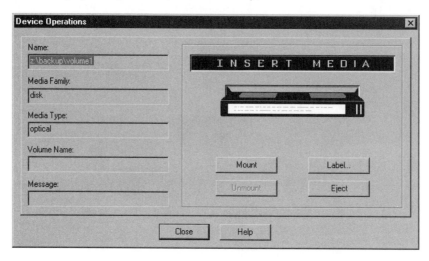

Step 5.   Click Label, which opens a new window. For the Volume Label, you can choose the default, or name it something more appropriate. Note that the Mount After Labeling check box has been selected by default, meaning Legato NetWorker will label the tape and then mount it.

Step 6.   After clicking OK, a graphic shows that the tape is being "loaded," and the big green status bar shows READY. Which is the case: you are now completely

prepared to back up to your local tape device using RMAN. Click Close, and then you can exit the NetWorker Administrator.

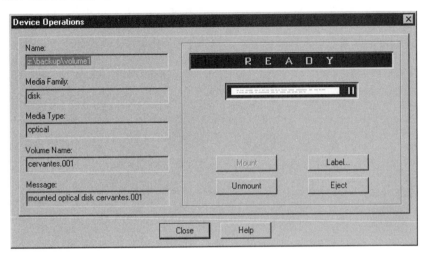

Step 7. To test your configuration, go to the command prompt, enter **rman**, and run a backup using a tape channel:

```
C:>rman
RMAN> connect target
connected to target database: PROD (DBID=4169479667)
 RMAN> run {
2> allocate channel x type 'sbt_tape';
3> backup current controlfile;}
```

After testing your configuration, you can expect an RMAN output that looks something like this:

```
allocated channel: x
channel x: sid=16 devtype=SBT_TAPE
channel x: NMO v3.5.0.1

Starting backup at 05-JUN-02
channel x: starting full datafile backupset
channel x: specifying datafile(s) in backupset
including current controlfile in backupset
channel x: starting piece 1 at 05-JUN-02
channel x: finished piece 1 at 05-JUN-02
piece handle=09dq9rn5_1_1 comment=API Version 2.0,MMS Version 3.5.0.1
channel x: backup set complete, elapsed time: 00:00:08
Finished backup at 05-JUN-02
```

Summary

In this chapter, we discussed the concepts behind how RMAN utilizes the media management software of a third-party vendor to make backups to tape. We walked through the specific steps that RMAN takes using the SBT API. We briefly discussed media management errors in RMAN. Finally, we gave a quick installation and configuration guide for using Legato Single Server Version, the free media management software provided with Oracle9*i* Release 2.

CHAPTER
5

Configuring
VERITAS NetBackup™

n the previous chapter, we discussed the underlying architecture employed by Oracle to stream backups directly to tape: Oracle leaves it up to somebody else. To provide an "out of the box" experience, another media management software product is bundled with Oracle9*i* Release 2, free of charge. But the stripped-down version has pretty severe limitations, the most obvious one being its reliance on a local tape device for backup storage. In most enterprises, tape devices are never local to production servers, but instead exist at a centralized location utilized by multiple systems throughout the network. Backups are moved across the network to these devices. To employ a networked backup and recovery system, you need to invest in a media management (MM) product. The free stuff is, well, free, and as we all know, there's no such thing as a free lunch.

In this chapter, we introduce you to one of the most widely used MM software packages on the market: VERITAS NetBackup™. VERITAS software has been in the backup business for some time. First, we talk briefly about the three VERITAS components required for successful integration with Oracle: NetBackup Server, NetBackup Client, and NetBackup for Oracle Agent. Then, we get down to the information that you need to know to get NetBackup™ configured and running for Oracle database backups. This includes setting up the NetBackup server and client, and configuring the NetBackup for Oracle integration with Oracle. We then discuss day-to-day usage, and how to configure specific elements of NetBackup that will be critical for smooth sailing through the rest of this book. This means you will learn how to ensure that your backups are being preserved, how to look at your backups from within the NetBackup Administrator interface, and how to enable client-to-client installations.

VERITAS NetBackup™ Introduction

VERITAS NetBackup provides a complete solution for protecting Oracle data. NetBackup is designed for enterprise environments and high-end databases and applications. As the industry's leading enterprise data protection solution, NetBackup provides centralized control from a single management interface. The multi-tier architecture of NetBackup provides customers with a fast, reliable, data-center-strength backup and recovery solution that can protect large Oracle environments that span terabytes to petabytes in size. The NetBackup "master" server uses other NetBackup "media" or backup servers to centrally accomplish backup and recovery tasks.

NetBackup uses storage devices that can be disk, tape, or optical. The Media Manager component of NetBackup manages the tape and optical storage and is designed so that other VERITAS storage products, such as VERITAS NetBackup

Storage Migrator™, can also share secondary storage devices. NetBackup provides extensive and automated support for most tape libraries, which means human intervention is rarely required.

Administrators can set up periodic or calendar-based schedules for automatic, unattended backup operations for clients across the storage network. These backup operations may be full or incremental backups. By carefully scheduling automatic backups, an administrator can achieve systematic and complete backups over a period of time and optimize network traffic during off-peak hours.

In addition to scheduled backups, administrators can perform manual backups of client data using the same criteria as specified for automatic backups. Manual backup operations are useful in special circumstances, such as backing up a client that missed a previously scheduled backup or preserving a system configuration prior to installing new software.

The NetBackup master server maintains a database (called the catalog) that records information about all backup and restore operations. A separate backup procedure is provided to protect the NetBackup catalog, to facilitate recovery in case of a disk failure.

VERITAS NetBackup™ includes both client and server software. Server software resides only on the platforms that manage the physical devices used for secondary storage. Client software resides on the individual client systems containing the data to be backed up. In this architecture, client software is responsible for generating the data stream to be backed up, and server software directs this data stream to a secondary storage device.

VERITAS NetBackup accommodates multiple servers working together under the administrative control of one of the servers. In this relationship, the NetBackup administrative control server is designated to be the "master" server, with the other servers designated as "media" servers, operating under control of the master server. Note, however, that a master server can also function as a media server. All NetBackup administrative functions are performed centrally from the master server, which controls all backup scheduling for each media server. Each of the media servers performs the actual backup operations under direction from the master server, and backup data stays local to the media servers and their respective storage devices. A master server and its associated media servers are referred to collectively as a NetBackup *storage domain,* and large networks may have more than one domain. Client systems back up data to NetBackup master/media servers. Figure 5-1 shows a simple master/media server configuration.

The master server in a storage domain serves a single point of administration for all backup operations in the storage domain. Administrators configure backup policies, manage all media and media pools, and configure all local and remote devices in the storage domain from the master server without having to log on to or directly access any of the media servers. In addition to retaining backup schedules

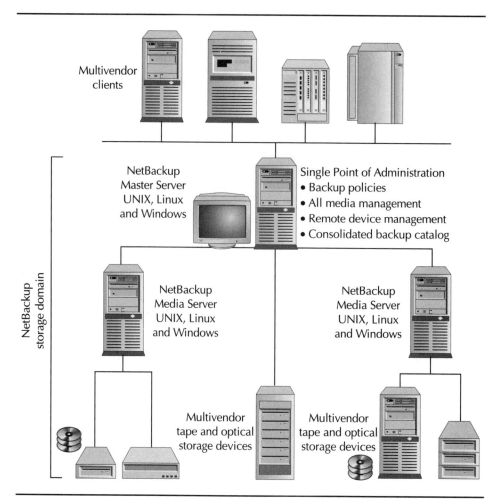

FIGURE 5-1. *A NetBackup master server/media server storage domain*

and other configuration information, the master server contains the backup catalog
for the entire storage domain. Users can browse this catalog to locate and restore files.

The actual location of the backup images in a NetBackup domain is transparent
to NetBackup administrators and users. The Media Manager component of VERITAS
NetBackup™ resides on each NetBackup server and manages secondary storage
media and the peripheral devices on those servers.

VERITAS Components for Oracle Integration

To back up Oracle databases with VERITAS NetBackup™, three software components need to be installed: NetBackup Server, NetBackup Client, and VERITAS NetBackup for Oracle.

The NetBackup Server software needs to be installed on a NetBackup master server and/or a NetBackup Media Server, while the NetBackup Client software and NetBackup for Oracle software needs to be installed on machines that are running Oracle databases. The NetBackup Client software must be installed before the NetBackup for Oracle software can be installed.

VERITAS NetBackup: The Server Software

The server software is installed on the computer that managers the storage devices, and the client software is installed on the computer that hosts the data that you want to back up. A NetBackup server also has client software installed and can be backed up like other clients. The Master Server software is responsible for the following functions:

- Contains the backup configurations and policies

- Runs the Scheduler that initiates the automated backups

- Maintains databases/catalogs that track the location and contents of all backups

- Communicates with Media Servers to initiate backup and restore processes

- Provides both a command-line interface (CLI) and a graphical user interface (GUI), which allows you to do the following:

  - Configure the backup operations.

  - Schedule automatic, unattended backups (regular backups); for example, to prevent interference with normal daytime operations, you can schedule your automatic backups to occur only at night.

  - Perform manual backups of any client.

  - Allow client users to perform their own backups and restores.

  - Control where backups are stored.

  - Control how long backup data is retained.

- Restore data to any client.

- Run reports to verify, manage, and troubleshoot backups and restores; these reports show the status or highlight problems with NetBackup servers and clients.

- Monitor the status of backup and restore jobs.

- Configure and manage your tapes and storage devices.

- Communicates with the NetBackup Media Manager (on the same system) to select media for backup and restore operations

- Communicates with NetBackup Client during a backup or restore operation

- Monitors the status of storage devices

NetBackup™ Administrator: GUI Administration

NetBackup and its Media Manager provide a comprehensive and logically designed set of interfaces that make it easy to perform all required administration, backup, and restore tasks. NetBackup gives the user a choice between using a GUI or a CLI to perform, create, and schedule RMAN backups and recoveries.

The GUIs provide the greatest ease of use with icons, pull-down menus, and full mouse support. Graphical wizards assist in the installation and configuration of devices, media, and policies.

Administrator Interfaces   The administrator interfaces provide access to all information necessary to configure and manage NetBackup and Media Manager. You can perform this administration from a single point, regardless of the number of servers or clients in the NetBackup configuration. Figure 5-2 shows a screen from the VERITAS NetBackup Administration Console, a consolidated application that offers both graphical tools and wizards for configuration. From this screen, administrators can create backup policies or define storage units. The console presents a consistent, easy-to-use window for administering data protection activities for NetBackup domains. To change domain (master server), simply select File | Change Server, or directly click the Change Server icon on the console toolbar.

The NetBackup Media Manager also has GUIs for managing its devices and media. Figure 5-3 shows the screen for managing devices. The administrator uses this screen to check and alter the status of devices. The menu version shows similar information.

Other screens allow the administrator to configure media for use under Media Manager or to perform other tasks related to Media Manager configuration and administration.

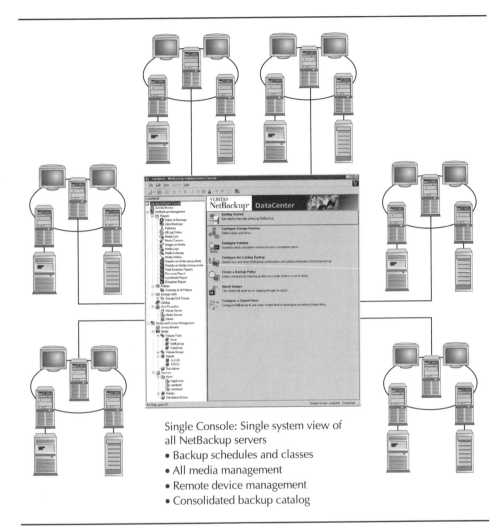

Single Console: Single system view of
all NetBackup servers
- Backup schedules and classes
- All media management
- Remote device management
- Consolidated backup catalog

FIGURE 5-2. *Single console view of all NetBackup servers*

A site administrator can even define custom menus and menu commands for the administrator GUIs. These menus will appear on the main window of the interface and contain whatever commands the administrator has added to them.

Several wizards have been designed to step novice users through common setup and configuration tasks. These wizards simplify and accelerate the process of adding

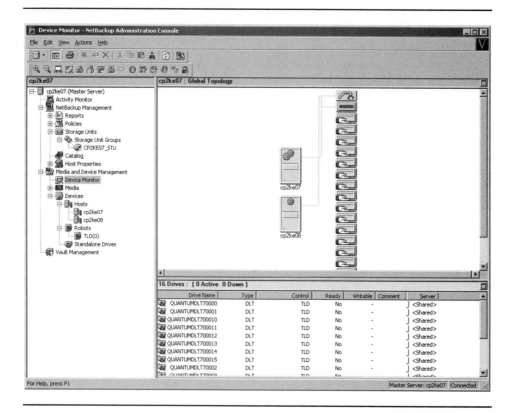

FIGURE 5-3. *Using NetBackup to manage storage devices and media*

devices, media, or backup policies, and reduce the likelihood of error. These wizards are discussed and demonstrated in more detail later in this chapter in the section "Using NetBackup for Oracle to Configure and Run Oracle Backups."

Device and Media Management   One of the most impressive features of VERITAS NetBackup™ is Media Manager, which manages the wide array of tape and optical storage devices and media supported by NetBackup. Media Manager is easy to configure and administer, thanks to a GUI that allows the administrator to centrally manage and control device and media information for all NetBackup master and media servers on the network.

The Media Manager also allows users and other VERITAS storage management applications, such as VERITAS NetBackup Storage Migrator™, to share its secondary storage devices. This eliminates the need for dedicated devices and helps administrators make the best use of their storage equipment investments.

VERITAS NetBackup™: The Client Software

The client software is a part of the VERITAS NetBackup software package and is installed on the individual client systems containing the data to be backed up. The client software, in the case of an Oracle backup, is responsible for communicating resource request (tapes) and job status to the server software.

Installation

It is possible to install and configure NetBackup on stand-alone systems or on heterogeneous client/server networks supporting hundreds or thousands of clients. The administrator first installs NetBackup software on the machine that will be the master server, and then on machines that will be media servers (if necessary), and finally on the client machines.

The entire NetBackup installation process is automated by Windows InstallShield wizards, or installation scripts on Unix machines (for example, pkgadd on Sun Solaris). When the software is installed, the administrator configures NetBackup by using the administrator interfaces.

For Unix clients, software is initially read into the server and subsequently pushed to the clients across the network. This significantly speeds up the installation process because there is no need to install client software from a CD-ROM on the individual client machines. The administrator would install software upgrades in the same manner, quickly and easily across the network. Windows clients are installed from a Windows 2000/NT domain or Active Directory (AD) server or from a CD-ROM. PC and Macintosh client software is quickly and easily installed on each client via CD-ROM.

VERITAS NetBackup: The NetBackup for Oracle Software

As an Oracle Corporation backup solutions partner, VERITAS has created database-specific support for Oracle databases using Oracle-supplied interfaces. NetBackup™ for Oracle is tightly integrated with Oracle's Recovery Manager (RMAN), which is a key component of the Oracle8, Oracle8i, and Oracle9i databases. These interfaces manage basic backup and recovery operations, automating much of the work that previously the DBA would need to perform manually.

The NetBackup server manages backup schedules for Oracle backups and communicates with the storage media. A single NetBackup server can manage multiple Oracle database backups, providing centralized storage management and leveraging high-speed and high-capacity storage devices. An example of the architecture and procedures of a typical NetBackup for Oracle environment is shown in Figure 5-4.

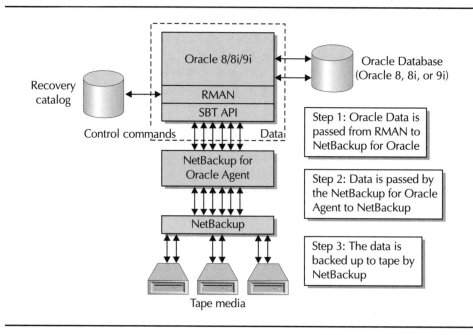

FIGURE 5-4. *Architecture for RMAN-based NetBackup for Oracle backup*

Hot Backup Support

VERITAS NetBackup for Oracle supports both cold and hot backups, so Oracle database administrators (DBAs) can create backup schedules that best suit their needs and adjust those schedules as their databases grow.

Through its integration with Oracle RMAN, NetBackup for Oracle simplifies creating and maintaining hot backups. NetBackup for Oracle manages the processes of altering the database state for backups, backing up all the appropriate files and archived redo logs, and tracking all the backup information needed for a fast and reliable recovery.

NetBackup for Oracle supports the parallel backup and restore capabilities of Oracle RMAN. This permits the user to run more than one tape device at a time for a single Oracle backup or restore, thereby reducing the time necessary to complete the operation.

Restore Support

VERITAS NetBackup™ makes restoring the data simple in large storage environments. For example, if the user needs to restore data from multiple backup tapes, NetBackup makes this process as simple as making a restore from one backup tape. NetBackup keeps track of the location of the data on the tapes required for restoring the database. NetBackup also allows recoveries to be multiplexed, significantly reducing the recovery time required.

Using NetBackup for Oracle to Configure and Run Oracle Backups

Before configuring and running an Oracle backup, be sure you have completed the following procedures:

1. Install the NetBackup Server software on the server.

2. Install the NetBackup Client software on the client or clients where you will be backing up the databases.

3. Install the NetBackup for Oracle Agent software on the machines in the NetBackup domain that have an Oracle database that you want to back up.

Once the NetBackup installation is complete, there are a number of configuration steps that are required to configure NetBackup to perform an Oracle backup. The NetBackup for Oracle configuration procedure is as follows:

1. Configure storage devices and media for NetBackup.

    a. Configure storage devices.

    b. Configure media.

2. Configure the catalog backup.

3. Set the Maximum Jobs Per Client global attribute.

4. Configure a NetBackup policy.

5. Configure the Oracle database with NetBackup.

6. Create templates and shell scripts.

7. Test NetBackup for Oracle configuration settings.

Configuring Media and Storage Devices for NetBackup

Using NetBackup to configure storage devices and media requires only a basic understanding of the NetBackup Media Manager software, which consists of three main elements:

■ **Robot Management**   Supports robotic secondary storage devices

■ **Device Management**   Lets you share secondary storage devices among different users and applications

■ **Media Management**   Tracks the location of all removable media and secondary storage devices with your system and gathers media usage statistics

An overview of the VERITAS NetBackup device management is shown in Figure 5-5.

The term *volume,* as used in regard to NetBackup, refers to the physical storage media on which NetBackup stores its backups, such as a tape or optical disk. The NetBackup Device Manager controls the actual mounting of volumes on the tape or optical storage devices in response to requests from NetBackup. These requests specify both the volume name and device density.

The NetBackup Device Manager always uses the volume database to get information about the volume. If the request involves a robot, this information includes the specific robot that has the volume and the slot location of the volume

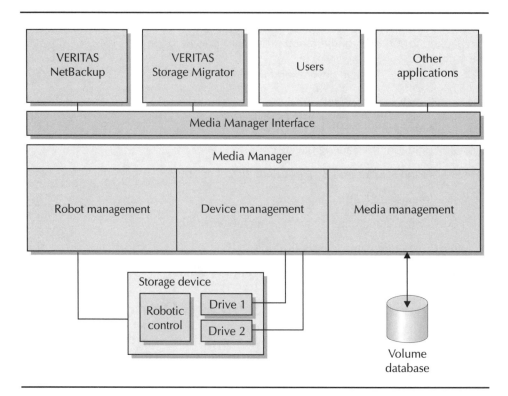

FIGURE 5-5.   *Overview of NetBackup device management*

in the robot. The device then issues a mount command to the robotic daemon controlling that robot, which automatically mounts the specified volume and returns control to NetBackup. No operator intervention is required, provided the required volume is physically in the robot.

If the volume is not in the tape library, the NetBackup Device Manager alerts the operator by sending a mount request to the console. The operator then finds the volume and inserts it into the library so the operation can proceed.

With a stand-alone drive, NetBackup attempts to use the media that is in the drive. If the drive does not contain media, the NetBackup Device Manager alerts the operator by sending a mount request to the console. The operator then finds the volume, mounts it manually, and assigns it to the correct mount request.

The NetBackup Media Manager allocates a previously unassigned volume to NetBackup whenever a new volume is required for either a stand-alone or robotic drive. Volumes allocated to NetBackup come from the volume pool designated for the specific backup files, which by default is the NetBackup volume pool. The term *volume pool* refers to a distinct set of volumes that are assigned for a specific use.

Volume pools make it possible to keep only one type of backup on a volume. For example, you could create separate pools for file backups or Oracle backups.

Configure Storage Devices

Once the NetBackup server software has been installed, a backup storage device needs to be configured. NetBackup has a Getting Started Wizard to make this process easy. The Media and Device Management node on the NetBackup Administration Console also allows a NetBackup user to configure a storage device (see Figure 5-6). However, before configuring NetBackup, you must have the storage devices attached to the server and perform all configuration steps specified by the device and operating system vendor, including installation of any required device drivers.

Configuring Volumes

The NetBackup Media Management window provides the tools required to add and manage the removable media that Media Manager controls. These media are referred to as volumes, and are assigned media IDs and other attributes that are required to track and manage the volumes. Volume setup can be accomplished either by using the wizard from the NetBackup Administration Console or through the tree view on the left side of the Administration Console, as shown in Figure 5-7.

When adding volumes to NetBackup, one of the attributes that is required is a volume pool name. A volume pool is used to identify a logical set of volumes by usage. Associating volumes with a volume pool protects them from access by unauthorized users, groups, or applications. You can create volume pools for user groups or other reasons and, as you add volumes, associate them with the appropriate pool.

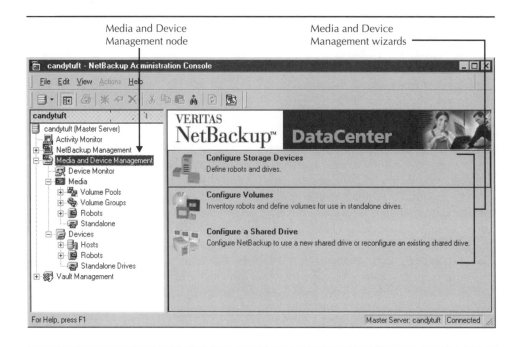

FIGURE 5-6. *Using VERITAS NetBackup to manage storage devices and media*

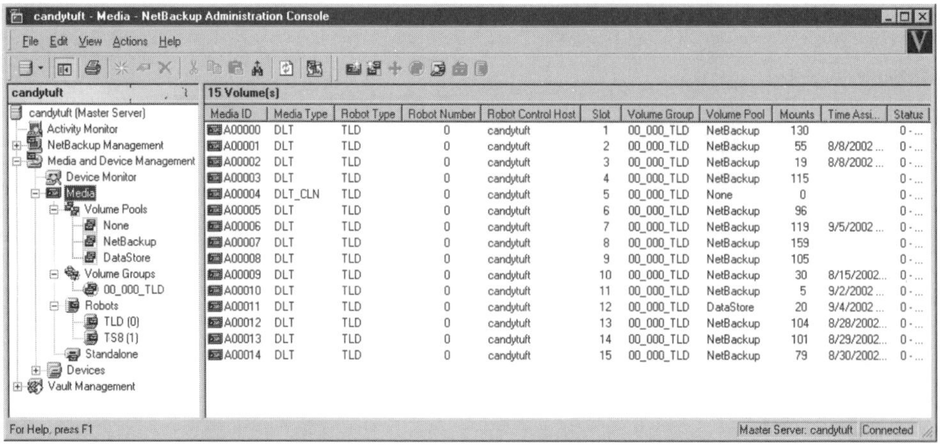

FIGURE 5-7. *Using the NetBackup Administration Console to manage media*

Scratch Pools   One option to consider when setting up volumes for NetBackup is the creation of a scratch pool. Media Manager enables administrators to configure and enable scratch pools. When applications such as VERITAS NetBackup need additional (new) media, they can obtain new media from the scratch pool. Scratch pools can be local to a single storage unit (library), or can be configured across multiple storage units. This lets the administrator add the necessary new tape volumes to the scratch pool, rather than statically assigning new media for use by specific applications.

When configured in a NetBackup domain, the media pool capability can significantly reduce operator effort. For example, assume that one of the libraries in a NetBackup storage domain has run out of available media to use. Utilizing the scratch pool feature, NetBackup can automatically and transparently acquire a scratch tape in any library in the NetBackup domain that has free media available, and use it as the media for the Oracle backup.

Setting the Maximum Jobs Per Client Global Attribute

For Oracle backups and restores, the number of jobs is hard to determine, as Oracle internally determines when and how many streams to run in parallel to optimize performance. To avoid any problems, we recommend that you enter a value of **99** for the Maximum Jobs Per Client global attribute.

To set the Maximum Jobs Per Client global attribute on a NetBackup server, first select double click on Host Properties from the NetBackup Administration Console. Then click Master Server. A hostname will appear in the right-hand panel. Right click the host icon and select Properties. From the Master Server Properties screen, select the Global NetBackup Attributes tab (see Figure 5-8). Finally, set the Maximum Jobs Per Client field to the correct value.

VERITAS NetBackup Policies

Backup policies define the rules that NetBackup follows when backing up clients. To back up an Oracle database, a policy needs to be created that is of an Oracle policy type. An Oracle policy defines the backup criteria for a specific group of one or more clients. These criteria include

- Storage unit and media to use
- Backup schedules
- Backup templates or script files to be executed on the clients
- Clients to be backed up

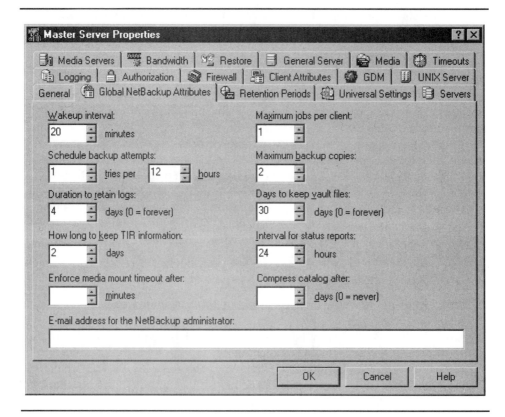

FIGURE 5-8. *NetBackup master server Properties dialog box*

To use NetBackup for Oracle, at least one Oracle policy with the appropriate schedules needs to be defined. A configuration can have a single policy that includes all clients, or there can be many policies, some of which may include only one client.

From the Administration Console, the NetBackup administrator can easily configure a NetBackup for Oracle policy either by using the NetBackup Policy Configuration Wizard or manually by using the Action menu (see Figure 5-9).

The attributes that the administrator will need to configure for their NetBackup for Oracle policies are discussed in the following section.

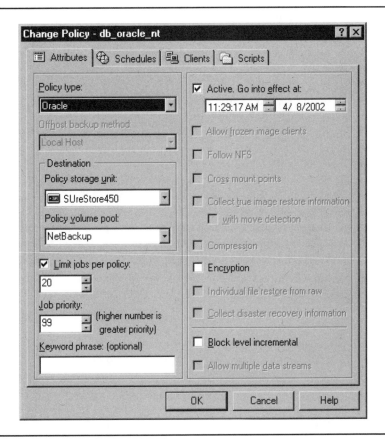

FIGURE 5-9.   *The NetBackup Change Policy screen allows the user to manually configure their Oracle backup policies.*

Attributes

The Policy Type must be set to Oracle. The destination for the Policy Storage Unit and Policy Volume Pool should be set to be consistent with the values created for the Device and Media Management values:

- **Policy Storage Unit**   Specifies the type of storage device to receive the Oracle backups. This is optional. If unspecified, the Oracle backups can go to any available storage unit. Priorities may be set, however, so that the Oracle backups may be directed first to available storage units with higher priority.

- **Policy Volume Pool**   Specifies the set of volumes (media) to use for storing the Oracle backups. If unspecified, the Oracle backups use the default NetBackup volume pool.

Scripts

This field allows you to schedule an RMAN backup through NetBackup. A user-defined template or script files can be specified in this field. A script is a KSH, CSH, or SH file on Unix and a DOS file on Windows. A script is usually created by a DBA and contains RMAN commands to perform an Oracle backup. A template on the other hand is a NetBackup internal file that contains RMAN and NetBackup information and is also used to perform an Oracle backup through RMAN (template and scripts are described in a later section of this chapter). All templates or scripts listed in the script list will be executed for the Automatic Full Backup, Automatic Differential Incremental Backup, or Automatic Cumulative Incremental Backup schedules, as specified on the Schedules tab.

All templates or scripts specified in the Scripts list are executed during manual or automatic backups. NetBackup will start backups by running the templates or scripts in the order that they appear in the Scripts list.

Clients

The client list shows the list of NetBackup clients that are a member of the policy. Your NetBackup for Oracle template or shell scripts will then be executed during a scheduled automatic backup. A NetBackup client must be in at least one policy but can be in more than one if necessary to meet the backup windows of your Oracle environment.

All policy definitions are stored in the configuration database on the NetBackup master server. In networks with more than one storage domain of NetBackup servers, clients can belong to policies on more than one master server. Although clients normally use only one master server, the ability to use an alternative master server can be an essential feature if a client's regular master server goes down and there is critical Oracle data that needs to be backed up.

Scheduling

Each policy has its own set of schedules. These schedules control the initiation of automatic backups and also specify when user operations can be initiated.

An Oracle backup requires at least two specific schedule types: an Application Backup schedule and an Automatic Backup schedule. You can also create additional schedules. All Oracle database operations are performed through NetBackup for Oracle using an Application Backup schedule. This includes Oracle backups that are started automatically. You must configure an Application Backup schedule for each NetBackup for Oracle policy that you create. This is required before you will be able to perform an Oracle backup. To help satisfy this requirement, an Application Backup schedule named Default-Application-Backup is automatically created when you configure a new Oracle policy. The backup window for an Application Backup schedule must encompass the time period during which all NetBackup jobs, scheduled and unscheduled, will occur. This is necessary because the Application Backup schedule starts processes that are required for all NetBackup for Oracle backups, including those started automatically.

For example, assume that you

■ Expect users to perform NetBackup operations during business hours, 08:00 to 13:00.

■ Configure automatic backups to start between 18:00 and 22:00.

The Application Backup schedule must have a start time of 08:00 and duration of 14 hours.

Remember, an Application Backup schedule must be created in order for RMAN to back up data to NetBackup. Without an Application Backup schedule, NetBackup cannot back up Oracle data. To schedule an RMAN backup using NetBackup, an Automatic Backup schedule needs to be created. Automatic Backup schedules can be of three types: Automatic Full Backup, Automatic Differential Incremental Backup, and Automatic Cumulative Incremental Backup. Besides creating an Automatic Backup schedule, an RMAN script or template needs to be specified in the **script** attribute of the Policy (scripts and templates are described in a later section of this chapter, "Creating Oracle RMAN Scripts Using the NetBackup for Oracle RMAN Template Generation Wizard").

Schedules can range from very basic schedules to the very complex schedules that are sophisticated enough to meet the most demanding backup requirements. From the Change Schedule – Policy dialog box, the NetBackup user has the choice of what type of backup to schedule. Choices include full, differential, cumulative, and application. The user also determines the frequency, media destination, retention period, and media multiplexing that will be used. In the example described above, the user has decided to schedule a full backup with a one-week frequency and a retention period of two weeks.

Figure 5-10 is an example of calendar-based scheduling, which allows for the user to select a specific day (or days) when a backup will occur. By simply clicking a date on the calendar, a backup will take place according to this schedule. In the example, this schedule will start backups on each Sunday.

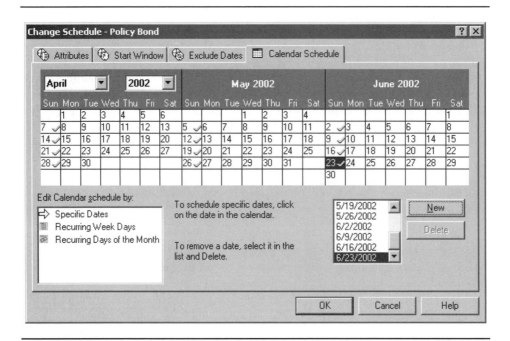

FIGURE 5-10. *VERITAS NetBackup for Oracle backups may be scheduled to initiate on specific days.*

Configuring VERITAS NetBackup™ for Oracle with Oracle RMAN

Linking Oracle RMAN with the library provided by VERITAS NetBackup for Oracle is the only Oracle requirement. Before writing to sequential devices such as tape, you must link the Oracle9i, Oracle8i, or Oracle8 Server software with the media management API library installed by NetBackup for Oracle. Oracle uses this library when it needs to write to, or read from, devices supported by Media Manager. The NetBackup for Oracle library's name depends on the specific platform. The library's name can be any one of the following:

- libobk.a64 on AIX (64 bit)

- libobk.a on AIX (32 bit)

- libobk.so.1 on Solaris, Tru64, and Digital Unix (32 bit)

- libobk.so64.1 on Solaris (64 bit)

- libobk.sl on HP-UX (32 bit)

- libobk.sl64 on HP-UX (64 bit)

- orasbt.dll on Windows NT/2000

- libobk.so on NCR, SGI, Sequent, Linux, and Data General

- libobk.so64 on SGI (64 bit)

Linking Oracle with VERITAS NetBackup for Oracle on Unix

This section documents the preferred way to link Oracle with the NetBackup for Oracle API library. The linking process is not consistent across all hardware platforms, operating system levels, and Oracle Server release levels. Operating system levels are specified when known differences occur.

Here are the steps to link Oracle9i, Oracle8i, and Oracle8 with NetBackup for Oracle on Solaris:

1. Become the Oracle user.

```
su—oracle
```

2. Shut down all the Oracle instances (SIDs). The following example is for Oracle8i:

```
Svrmgrl
onnect internal
shutdown
exit
```

Change the ORACLE_SID environment variable to any other SID that uses this Oracle installation and repeat the preceding commands.

3. Set up automatic or manual linking, described next.

To set up automatic linking, run the *oracle_link* script located in *install_path/ netbackup/bin/*. This script determines the Oracle version level and then links Oracle to NetBackup accordingly. All output from this script will be captured in a */tmp/make_trace.pid* file. To change the trace file location, change the MAKE_TRACE variable in the *oracle_link* script.

To set up manual linking, make a copy of the existing Oracle executable:

```
cd ${ORACLE_HOME}/bin
cp oracle oracle.orig
```

Starting with Oracle version 8.0.4, Oracle is shipped with default MM software. To disable this MM software, you must remove or rename the libobk file from

${ORACLE_HOME}/lib. It may be a file or a symbolic link. To satisfy this and other linking requirements, use the instructions that follow if you are using Solaris. Different linking instructions are required depending on the platform, operating system, and version of Oracle that you are running in your environment.

Step 1. Use the following instructions if your setup is Solaris (32-bit or 64-bit) using Oracle (32-bit) software. Note that for Oracle9*i* Releases 9.0.1 and 9.2 and Oracle8*i* Releases 8.1.5 and 8.1.7, Step 1 is the only step required, because for these versions, the user no longer has to make a new Oracle executable to use the NetBackup for Oracle API library. The Oracle executable always looks for the shared library:

```
cd ${ORACLE_HOME}/lib
ls -l libobk.so
```

If libobk.so exists, create

```
mv libobk.so libobk.so.orig
ln -s /install_path/netbackup/bin/libobk.so.1 libobk.so
```

Step 2. Make a new Oracle executable.

```
cd ${ORACLE_HOME}/rdbms/lib
```

For Oracle8 Releases 8.0.3, 8.0.4, 8.0.5, 8.0.5.1, and 8.0.6, make it

```
make -f ins_rdbms.mk ioracle
```

For Oracle8*i* Release 8.1.6, use Oracle-provided re-linking script—the preferred method.

```
cd $ORACLE_HOME/bin
relink oracle
```

or **make** command line

```
cd $ORACLE_HOME/rdbms/lib
make -f ins_rdbms.mk ioracle LLIBOBK=-lobk
```

Here is the procedure to verify that the library is linked. If you have carried out the preceding steps correctly, the VERITAS path should be the first one.

```
$ ldd $ORACLE_HOME/bin/oracle
libobk.so => /install_path/netbackup/bin/libobk.so
```

```
libnsl.so.1 => /usr/lib/libnsl.so.1
libsocket.so.1 => /usr/lib/libsocket.so.1
libdl.so.1 => /usr/lib/libdl.so.1
libc.so.1 => /usr/lib/libc.so.1
libaio.so.1 => /usr/lib/libaio.so.1
libm.so.1 => /usr/lib/libm.so.1
libmp.so.2 => /usr/lib/libmp.so.2
```

Linking Oracle with NetBackup for Oracle on Windows NT/2000

For the Windows NT/2000 platform, linking is not required. The installation process automatically moves orasbt.dll into the right location where Oracle can find it without human intervention.

Creating Oracle RMAN Scripts Using the VERITAS NetBackup for Oracle RMAN Template Generation Wizard

VERITAS NetBackup for Oracle simplifies the complexity of Oracle backup and recovery by providing a policy configuration wizard to make Oracle RMAN script creation easy. The wizard eliminates the complexity involved in creating Oracle RMAN backup and recovery scripts. The wizard walks the user through Oracle RMAN script creation, making script creation quick and efficient.

RMAN templates and RMAN shell scripts contain commands that are used to execute NetBackup for Oracle backup and recovery jobs. Templates or scripts must be created before NetBackup for Oracle can perform scheduled backups. These are the template files or shell scripts that are specified in policy configuration on the NetBackup server.

RMAN Templates and Shell Scripts

The NetBackup for Oracle user has two options available to create RMAN scripts to perform Oracle backups. The user can create an RMAN Template, which would be accomplished using a GUI approach via the NetBackup for Oracle RMAN Template Generation Wizard. The user also has the option of creating shell scripts via the command line. Both of these methods are described next.

Templates The NetBackup Wizard is used to create backup templates. This wizard is initiated from the NetBackup Backup, Archive, and Restore interface. The wizard does not support all the RMAN commands and options provided by Oracle. A shell script should be written for situations where a template does not provide all the required functionality.

**Creating Oracle RMAN Templates Using the NetBackup for Oracle Backup
Wizard**   The wizard solicits information interactively from the user about the
desired RMAN functions required to successfully complete Oracle backup operations.
The wizard uses the information to create a template that can be run immediately or
saved for later use in a NetBackup-specific location on the current master server. The
wizard can be launched from the NetBackup Backup, Archive, and Restore interface.
This interface can be launched from any machine where NetBackup is installed.

If NetBackup for Oracle is installed, the Backup, Archive, and Restore interface
displays an Oracle node on the backup tree. The Oracle node will display all the
SIDs that have been created on the current client. If the Backup, Archive, and
Restore interface was not launched from an Oracle SYSDBA user account, a login
dialog box will appear. The login request is required in order to populate the SID
tree. After selecting an Oracle SID, Tablespaces, Datafiles, or Archive Logs, an
Oracle RMAN backup can be started (see Figure 5-11).

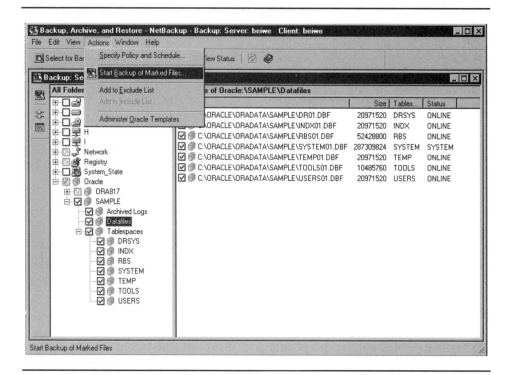

FIGURE 5-11.   *The Backup, Archive, and Restore interface browser. The user has
selected an Oracle SID and is about to start a backup.*

Selecting Actions | Start Backup Of Marked Files starts the wizard, which will capture all the necessary information required to perform an RMAN backup. Backup creation with the wizard is straightforward, as described next.

The VERITAS NetBackup for Oracle Archived Redo Logs page (see Figure 5-12) allows the user to include and select the appropriate date and time range desired to back up their Oracle Archived Redo Logs.

The VERITAS NetBackup for Oracle Backup Limits page (see Figure 5-13) provides the user with the option of specifying the I/O and backup set limits that will be used by RMAN. If the user would like to set the I/O limits for RMAN, this page can override the default values that have been predetermined by RMAN.

The VERITAS NetBackup for Oracle Template Summary page, shown in Figure 5-14, shows the options the user has to run a backup immediately and/or to save the template for later use in performing a scheduled backup. If the user would like to use the template in another schedule, the template name must be specified in the Template Name field and included in the appropriate schedule.

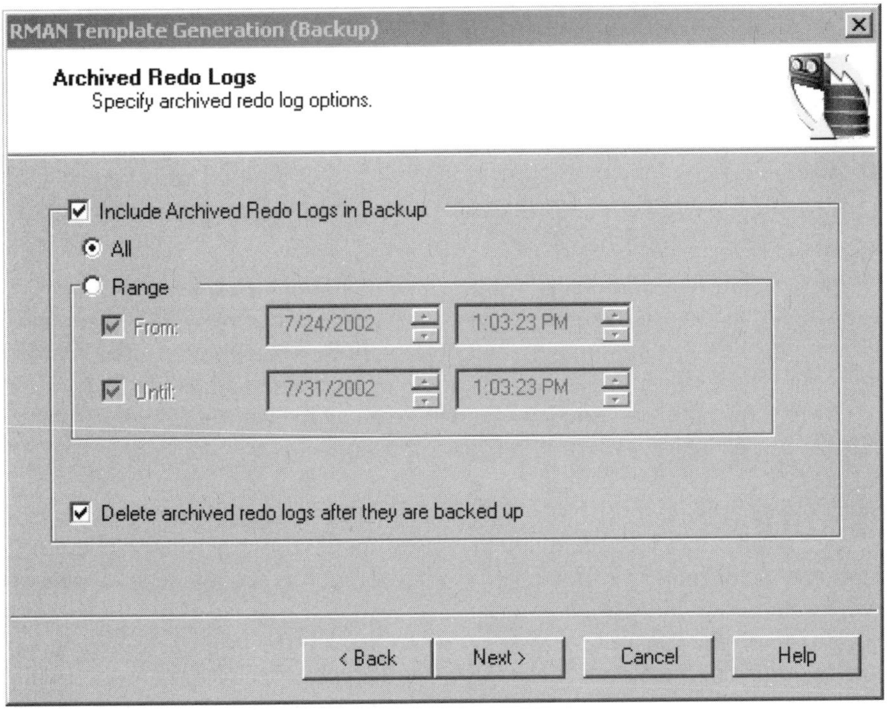

FIGURE 5-12. *The VERITAS NetBackup for Oracle Archived Redo Logs page*

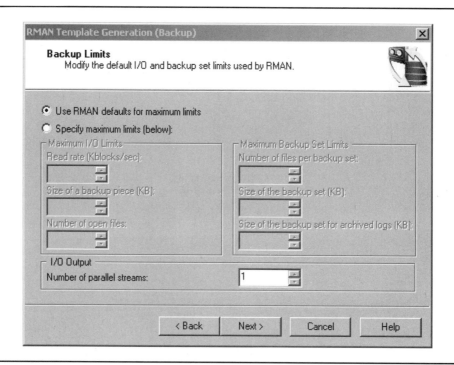

FIGURE 5-13. *The VERITAS NetBackup for Oracle Backup Limits page gives the user the ability to modify the default I/O and backup set limits used by RMAN.*

The Template Summary page displays a summary of the configuration information that the user created using the wizard. You can review the template entries in the Template Summary window, and use the Back button to find and change incorrect wizard entries. If the template information appears to be correct, you can run the template immediately after finishing the wizard or save it to a NetBackup-specific location on the current master server.

Shell Scripts   Shell scripts are written by the user and must conform to RMAN and shell syntax. Sample backup and recovery shell scripts are installed on the client with NetBackup for Oracle Agent. You can modify these scripts to meet your environment's individual requirements.

VERITAS NetBackup for Oracle also provides a utility, **bpdbsbora**, that can generate a shell script from the NetBackup for Oracle Backup Wizard template. This allows the user to create a template with the Backup Wizard and generate a shell script from the new template. The user can then run the shell script or modify the shell script further for different uses.

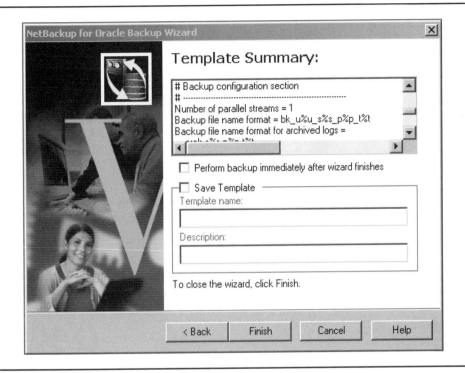

FIGURE 5-14. *VERITAS NetBackup for Oracle Template Summary page*

RMAN Workshop: *Creating an RMAN Script Using the NetBackup™ for Oracle Wizard*

Workshop Notes

For this workshop, you need an installation of Oracle database software, NetBackup server and client software, and NetBackup for Oracle Agent.

VERITAS NetBackup for Oracle includes a Backup Wizard that solicits information about desired RMAN backup operations. The wizard uses the information entered by the user to create a template that can be run immediately or saved in a NetBackup-specific location on the current master server for later use. A user-created template can be used to create a script that can be modified for each individual NetBackup user's needs.

Step 1. To start the NetBackup Backup, Archive, and Restore interface, execute the following command:

```
install_path/netbackup/bin/jbpSA &
```

If NetBackup for Oracle is installed, the Backup, Archive, and Restore interface for your Oracle client will display an Oracle node in the left pane (see Figure 5-15). Click the Backup Files tab, and expand the Oracle node to view an Oracle instance hierarchy. Select an Oracle instance to view its contents, which are then displayed in the right pane. In the right pane, select the Oracle objects that you would like to back up. Click Backup.

Step 2. The NetBackup for Oracle Wizard's Template Summary page gives the user the opportunity to save information that was collected by the wizard panel

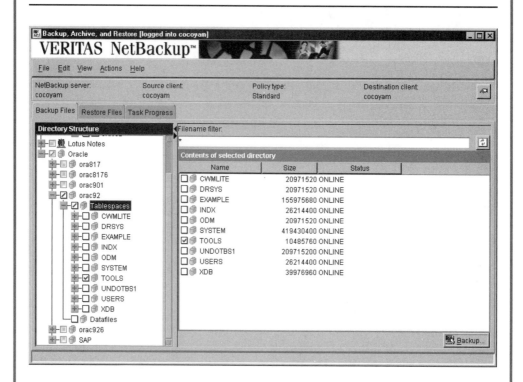

FIGURE 5-15. *The NetBackup Backup, Archive, and Restore interface*

into a new template. From the saved template, the user can generate a script by executing the NetBackup **bpdbsbora** command:

```
bpdbsbora -backup -g /tmp/abcz -t test_template.tpl
vi  /tmp/abc
```

The script /tmp/abc can then be used to run an Oracle backup from the command line, or the user can create a NetBackup schedule that will have NetBackup automatically execute the script to create an automatic Oracle backup.

Environment Variables Set Up by User   If scripts are used for Oracle backups, then the following environment variables need to be considered when creating a script:

- **NB_ORA_SERV**   Specifies the name of the NetBackup master server.

- **NB_ORA_CLIENT**   Specifies the name of the Oracle client. It is especially useful for redirecting a restore to a different client.

- **NB_ORA_POLICY**   Specifies the name of the policy to use for the Oracle backup.

- **NB_ORA_SCHED**   Specifies the name of the Application Backup schedule to use for the Oracle backup.

Oracle RMAN Environment   The way to set up environment variables depends upon the version of Oracle you are using. When connecting to a database using a TNS alias, you must use a **send** command or a **parms** operand to specify environment variables. In other words, when accessing a database through a listener, the environment variables set at the system level are not visible when RMAN is running. Two ways exist to perform setting up environment variables.

- *The first method is to use a template created by the NetBackup for Oracle Wizard.* With templates, the NetBackup for Oracle environment variables are specified on the NetBackup for Oracle Configuration Variables Wizard page. One of the benefits of using a stored template is that it gives the user the ability to use the template with the NetBackup scheduler so that automatic Oracle database backups can be performed.

- *The second method is to use shell scripts.* Use the **send** command or the **parms** operand to specify NetBackup for Oracle environment variables for use during a backup or restore. The **send** command was introduced with

Oracle8i and is also available with later versions of Oracle databases. If you are using an Oracle8.0.*x* version of RMAN, you must use the **parms** operand. The **send** command sends a vendor-specific quoted string to NetBackup for Oracle. For the following example, the code specifies what policy and server to use for an Oracle database backup (for Oracle8i or later database versions):

```
run {
allocate channel t1 type 'sbt_tape';
allocate channel t2 type 'sbt_tape';
send 'NB_ORA_POLICY=your_policy, NB_ORA_SERV=your_server';
backup
(database format 'bk_%U_%t');
}
```

The user must specify the variables in the string in the RMAN script after all channels have been allocated and before the **backup** command. The **parms** operand can also be used to set environment variables at runtime. The following example uses the **parms** operand to specify what policy and server to use for a database backup. The **parms** operand is set with each **allocate channel** command in the shell script.

```
run {
allocate channel t1 type 'sbt_tape'
parms="ENV=(NB_ORA_POLICY=your_policy, NB_ORA_SERV=your_server)";
allocate channel t2 type 'sbt_tape'
parms="ENV=(NB_ORA_POLICY=your_policy, NB_ORA_SERV=your_server)";
backup
(database format 'bk_%s_%p_%t');
}
```

Storing Oracle RMAN Templates and Shell Scripts   Once you have created your Oracle RMAN templates and shell scripts, you will want to save them so that they can be easily reused or applied to other situations. By reusing your RMAN templates and shell scripts, you will save time when creating your NetBackup for Oracle data protection strategy. The methods to save your work for later use are described next.

Storing Oracle RMAN Templates   The NetBackup Wizard saves the created backup template to a NetBackup-specific location on the current NetBackup master server. A backup template is retrieved from the master server as part of a backup (for example, server-directed, scheduled, or user-directed) and is executed on the client machine. Backup templates are associated with a policy by specifying the template's name in the policy script list. Because backup templates are stored on the server in a known location, server-directed and scheduled backups will use the same copy of the template for each client included on the policy client list.

The NetBackup for Oracle Recovery Wizard saves a restore template to a user-specified location on the client. The location specified should include a fully qualified path to a directory where the user has write access. Templates also are able to store encrypted passwords that are decrypted at runtime.

Storing RMAN Shell Scripts RMAN shell scripts must reside on the NetBackup client. Backup shell scripts are associated with a policy by specifying the filename (including path) in the policy script list. This means that for server-directed or scheduled backups, each client in the policy's client list must have a copy of the script with the same name in the same location.

The backup and recovery processes sometimes require passwords for Oracle database access and/or system user accounts. RMAN shell scripts, because a shell interprets them, store the passwords in clear text.

Use of the Command Line with NetBackup for Oracle NetBackup for Oracle allows the user to execute RMAN commands from the RMAN prompt, which allows you to automatically take advantage of all NetBackup MM functionality. Once you install and configure NetBackup for Oracle, you can run RMAN from the command line to back up an Oracle database to NetBackup. The NetBackup for Oracle user does not have to learn new commands to use the MM functionality that NetBackup provides.

Day-to-Day Usage: VERITAS NetBackup™ Maintenance Tasks

VERITAS NetBackup will require periodic maintenance to continue to operate at peak performance. Described next are some basic NetBackup maintenance tasks that will ensure that your Oracle data is being backed up properly.

Performing a Backup

NetBackup provides users with several different methods to back up their Oracle data depending on personal preference. Backups can be scheduled to perform automatically. Backups can also be executed manually if needed. The several different methods available to users are described here.

Automatic Backup of an Oracle Policy

The most convenient way to back up your Oracle database is to set up NetBackup schedules for automatic backups. When the NetBackup scheduler invokes a schedule for an automatic backup, the NetBackup for Oracle template or shell scripts will run as follows:

- In the same order as they appear in the script list

- On all clients in the client list

The NetBackup for Oracle template or shell scripts start the database backup by executing **rman**.

When the backup is started through NetBackup, NetBackup for Oracle leaves the error checking to RMAN. The **rman** command generates an error if it considers a command invalid, but allows any of the commands it normally considers valid to proceed. This means that by specifying the wrong script filename, you could start an unintended operation.

User-Directed Backup from the Client

This section describes the following procedures for performing user-directed backups.

- Executing NetBackup for Oracle templates

- Executing the NetBackup for Oracle shell script

- Executing the **rman** command

Executing NetBackup for Oracle Templates on the Client   To execute NetBackup for Oracle templates on the client, you can use either the RMAN Template Administration dialog box or the NetBackup **bpdbsbora** command. Each of these methods is described in this section.

The RMAN Template Administration dialog box is accessed from the NetBackup Backup, Archive, and Restore interface. The user can use the following commands from this dialog box to manage existing backup templates that have been created through the wizard:

- **run**   Used to execute the selected template.

- **edit**   Used to change the contents of an existing template. The selected template is loaded into the NetBackup for Oracle RMAN Template Generation Wizard.

- **delete**   Used to delete the selected template. You must be the root user (Unix), the Administrator (Windows NT/2000), or the template creator to delete a template.

■ **rename**   Used to change the name of the selected template. You must be the root user (Unix), the Administrator (Windows NT/2000), or the template creator to rename a template.

■ **view**   Used to see a summary of the selected template.

The NetBackup **bpdbsbora** command allows you to run a backup template created by the wizard. At the command prompt, type the following:

```
bpdbsbora -backup -r -t <template name>
```

In the preceding example, **-r** runs a template and **-t** identifies the template. Here is another example:

```
bpdbsbora -backup -r -t ORCL_Mon_full.tpl
```

This command will retrieve backup templates from a predetermined location on the master server. Therefore, the user only needs to specify the filename.

Executing the NetBackup for Oracle Shell Script on the Client   If you know the pathname of the NetBackup for Oracle shell script that initiates the backup, you can execute the shell script from the command prompt. For example, to perform a database backup, at the command prompt, you might enter the following:

```
/oracle8/scripts/cold_database_backup.sh
```

The Unix shell starts the database backup by executing the Oracle shell script. The Oracle shell script contains commands to execute **rman**.

The NetBackup for Oracle installation script installs sample scripts in the following location:

```
install_path/netbackup/ext/db_ext/oracle/samples/rman/
```

Executing the rman Command   As an Oracle user, you can also execute the **rman** command at the command prompt, with the RMAN command file as a parameter. For example, to perform a database backup, at the command prompt, you might enter the following:

```
rman target system/manager
RUN {
ALLOCATE CHANNEL ch00
   TYPE 'SBT_TAPE';
SEND 'NB_ORA_CLIENT=beiwe';
```

```
BACKUP
    INCREMENTAL LEVEL=0
    FORMAT 'bk_u%u_s%s_p%p_t%t'
    DATABASE
    INCLUDE CURRENT CONTROLFILE;
RELEASE CHANNEL ch00;
```

NetBackup Server Maintenance Tasks

From the NetBackup server side, there are a number of tasks that ensure that NetBackup is maintaining your Oracle backups correctly. These maintenance tasks should be performed to ensure that your data is adequately protected. Media Management is a key area where maintenance is especially important. Media Mangement maintenance tasks are discussed in more detail next.

Tracking Media Age and Number of Mounts

Because the possibility of media failure increases with age and use, the NetBackup Media Manager keeps statistics on how old the media is and how often it has been mounted. The administrator can choose to expire the physical media based on a specific date or a specified number of mounts.

If NetBackup suspects a media failure (usually due to repeated write failures), it suspends use of that volume. Similarly, it will shut down a storage device if a drive fails. In either case, NetBackup logs the reason for the action in the error database and notifies an operator to correct the problem.

Verifying Media

The verification option allows the administrator to read NetBackup media and compare its contents to the online catalog of information in NetBackup.

To verify Media,

1. In the NetBackup Administration Console, expand Master Server > NetBackup Management > Catalog.

2. Set up the search criteria for the image you wish to verify as explained in the "Search Criteria for Backup Images" table. Click Search Now.

3. Select the image you wish to verify and select Actions > Verify. The Confirm Verify dialog appears. To display information on each file that NetBackup verifies, select Log All Files Found In Image(s) Verified.

4. Click the Results tab, and then select the verification job just created to view the job results.

Duplicating NetBackup Media

By using the duplicate option, an administrator can create a second copy of media containing NetBackup images, which is convenient for making copies for offsite storage (vaulting). For advanced duplication and vaulting capabilities, VERITAS NetBackup Vault should be considered. It facilitates the managing of offsite media for disaster recovery solutions.

Administrators have the option of duplicating a multiplexed primary image into nonmultiplexed (**tar**-compatible) images on secondary media or retaining the multiplexed format of the primary image on the secondary media. The secondary media can be an exact copy of the primary media, or it may contain any subset of the (multiplexed) backup images contained on the primary multiplexed media. For example, if the primary media was created with seven multiplexed images, the secondary media may contain from one to seven multiplexed images. The duplicates are created with a single pass of the primary tape regardless of the number of multiplexes being copied, which often dramatically speeds up the duplication of multiplexed primary images. In addition, both the primary and secondary copies of a backup image may have their own unique expiration (retention) period.

Duplicate media can be done by going to the NetBackup Administration Console and expanding Master Server > NetBackup Management > Catalog. Set up the search criteria for the backup image you wish to duplicate and then select the image you wish to duplicate.

Using the NetBackup bplist Command to Browse Backups

In addition to the information from the **list** command in RMAN, you can use NetBackup's **bplist** command to list the Oracle backup pieces. The result is the list of backup filenames (Oracle backup piece names). The following example uses **bplist** to search all Oracle backups for a client named jupiter:

```
/install_path/netbackup/bin/bplist -C jupiter -t 4 -R /

/exb_n2bm5bco_1_1392342936
/exb_mabm02ko_1_1392170136
/exb_lqbltds6_1_1392083334
```

The **-t 4** in this command specifies the Oracle backups. The **-R** specifies the default number of directory levels to search, 999.

Summary

In this chapter, we discussed NetBackup for Oracle and how VERITAS utilizes Oracle's RMAN to manage the backup and recovery of Oracle data, whether for a startup with a small Oracle database or for a large Fortune 100 corporation with multiple Oracle databases and many terabytes or petabytes of data.

The following is a list of VERITAS NetBackup software solutions available to protect your mission-critical Oracle databases:

- VERITAS NetBackup™ for Oracle Agent

- VERITAS NetBackup™ for Oracle Advanced BLI Agent

- VERITAS NetBackup™ Array Integration Option (for Oracle databases)

- VERITAS NetBackup™ for Oracle ServerFree Agent

- VERITAS NetBackup™ Shared Storage Option for use with Oracle databases

- VERITAS NetBackup™ Database Archiver

CHAPTER
6

Configuring Legato
Networker Module
for Oracle

egato Networker Module for Oracle (NMO) and Legato Networker Server combine to provide efficient and reliable backup and recovery solutions for the Oracle database and its components. NMO acts as an intermediary between the primary Networker Server and RMAN. All backups and restores of the Oracle database are kicked off by RMAN. In fact, once NMO is set up, little interaction is required. The primary mode of operations will be to use RMAN.

This chapter begins with a discussion of the architecture of the Oracle backup and recovery system integrated with NMO. It then describes the basic configuration of NMO for use with Oracle and how to install NMO. You then will learn how to run and schedule RMAN backups in NMO. Finally, you will learn how to set up and run restore operations with NMO.

Architecture of the Oracle and Legato Backup and Recovery System

There are six components (one optional) in a backup and recovery system if Oracle and Networker have been configured correctly. The Oracle backup and recovery system is comprised of the following:

- The Oracle Server

- RMAN

- A recovery catalog (this is optional because the control file can be used)

The Networker system consists of the following:

- A Networker Server

- Networker Client

- Networker Module for Oracle

The Legato Networker Server is the main component of the Networker architecture. This is where all the information is stored for all backups scheduled and/or performed. The Networker Server manages all backups and restores and maintains the client indexes and storage medium.

The Legato Networker Client software is how the Networker Server communicates with the target backup node.

Legato NMO is an add-on module that allows the Networker Server and Networker Client combination to communicate with the Oracle backup and recovery system. The client software and the module work hand in hand together. The module allows the Networker system to interact with RMAN—in other words, it is the intermediary that passes information from RMAN through to the Networker system. The application programming interface (API) that is used between the two systems is Oracle System Backup to Tape (SBT). NMO also links the Oracle Server software with a media management layer (MML). This allows RMAN to back up and restore data directly to the storage media controlled by the Networker system. Figure 6-1 shows the architecture of the Oracle backup and recovery system and the Networker system.

Backup and Restore Operations

Issuing RMAN commands to the target database starts a backup of the database. Once the backup is started, the Oracle Server reads the appropriate database file, creates a backup data set, and passes it via the SBT API to NMO. NMO translates the object names of the data set into a format that can be recognized by the Networker Server, and then passes the information to the Networker Server using the network remote procedure call (RPC) protocol.

Once Networker receives the information, it creates an entry in its *client index* file, which contains information about each Oracle object being backed up. The Networker Server then stores the backup data to the storage media and writes an

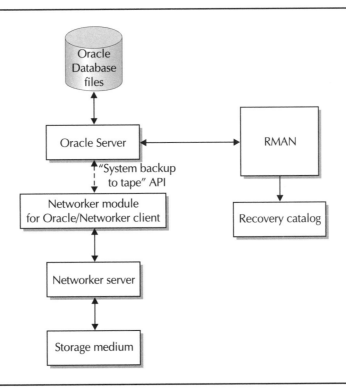

FIGURE 6-1.   *The architecture of the Networker and Oracle systems*

entry in its *media index* file, which contains information corresponding to the location and content of all storage media.

A restore initiated by RMAN works in a similar way.

Installing NMO

The Oracle Server, Networker Client, and NMO must be installed on the *same* system. The Oracle recovery catalog and the Networker Server software can reside on different systems. This chapter does not cover the installation procedures for the Networker Server or the Networker Client. For information on the installation procedures, please refer to the appropriate Legato Networker documentation.

Before proceeding with the installation of NMO, ensure that the Legato Storage Manager bundled with the Oracle Enterprise version software is removed. In Solaris, it includes the following software packages:

- ORCLclnt
- ORCLdrvr
- ORCLnode

The Networker Client software must be installed *before* you install NMO. Module Also, you do not need to install NMO for each installation of RMAN—it needs to be installed only once.

RMAN Workshop: *NMO Installation*

Workshop Notes
The following steps refer to a Sun Solaris (SPARC) installation.

Step 1. Log in as **root** on the machine on which your Oracle Server resides.

Step 2. Insert and mount the NMO CD-ROM. Then, change to the directory on the CD-ROM appropriate to your operating system:

```
#  mount /dev/<cdrom_disk_drive_name> /CD_ROM
#  cd /CD_ROM/oracle/solaris_64
```

Step 3. The NMO installation should reside on the *same* directory as the Networker Client installation. AIX, Linux, and Solaris appear to provide a choice for installing it in a different directory, but the installation will fail if you choose a different directory from the one in which the Networker Client is installed. In Solaris, modify the /var/sadm/install/admin/default file to specify the parameter

basedir=default. This ensures that the software is automatically installed in the correct directory. (Please refer to the Legato Networker Module for Oracle Installation Guide for other platforms not mentioned here.)

Step 4. Install the NMO software using the **pkgadd** command (or **swinstall** for HP-UX). Note: The Oracle database does *not* have to be shut down for this.

```
#  pkgadd -d /CD_ROM/oracle/solaris_64 LGTOnmo
```

Step 5. Link the Oracle Server with the NMO libraries. Each platform and each version of Oracle requires a different set of commands to link the libraries. Table 6-1 provides a list of commands for various operating systems and the corresponding Oracle versions.

Step 6. Log in as the owner of the oracle binaries (in other words, the ORACLE_HOME). For example, if the owner of the ORACLE_HOME is "oracle," issue the following command:

```
#  su - oracle
```

Step 7. Make sure that all the oracle instances associated with the ORACLE_HOME are shut down. In Oracle9i, the instances do *not* have to be shut down.

Step 8. Using the appropriate command from Table 6-1, link the Oracle Server file with the NMO library file.

OS	Oracle Version	Command

SUN (SPARC)	8.1.5 and 8.1.7 (64 bit)	`# cd $ORACLE_HOME/lib64`
		`# rm libobk.so`
		`# ln -s /usr/lib/libnwora.so libobk.so`

	8.1.6 (64 bit)	`# cd $ORACLE_HOME/lib64`
		`# rm libobk.so`
		`# ln -s /usr/lib/libnwora.so libobk.so`
		`# ln -s /usr/lib/libnwora.so libnwora.so`
		`# cd $ORACLE_HOME/rdbms/lib`
		`# make -f ins_rdbms.mk ioracle`

TABLE 6-1. *Library Linking Commands for NMO and Oracle Server*

OS	Oracle Version	Command
	9.0.1 (32 and 64 bit)	`# cd $ORACLE_HOME` `# ln -s /usr/lib/libnwora.so libobk.so`

	8.1.5 (32 bit)
	8.1.7 (32 bit)
		`# cd $ORACLE_HOME/lib`
		`# rm libobk.so`
		`# ln -s /usr/lib/libnwora.so libobk.so`

	8.1.6 (32 bit)	`# cd $ORACLE_HOME/lib`
		`# rm libobk.so`
		`# ln -s /usr/lib/libnwora.so libobk.so`
		`# cd $ORACLE_HOME/rdbms/lib`
		`# make -f ins_rdbms.mk ioracle`

Solaris (Intel)	8.1.5, 8.1.6, 8.1.7	`# cd $ORACLE_HOME/lib`
		`# rm libobk.so`
		`# ln -s /usr/lib/libnwora.so libobk.so`

HP-UX 11 & 11.11	8.1.5, 8.1.6, 8.1.7 (32 bit)	`# cd $ORACLE_HOME/lib`
		`# rm libobk.sl`
		`# ln -s /usr/lib/libnwora.sl libobk.sl`

	8.1.5, 8.1.6, 8.1.7 (64 bit)	`# cd $ORACLE_HOME/lib64`
		`# rm libobk.sl`
		`# ln -s /usr/lib/libnwora.sl libobk.sl`

	9.0.1 (64 bit)	`# cd $ORACLE_HOME/lib` `# ln -s /usr/lib/libnwora.sl libobk.sl`

AIX	8.1.5, 8.1.6, 8.1.7 (32 bit)	`# cd $ORACLE_HOME/lib`
		`# rm libobk.a`
		`# ln -s /usr/lib/libnwora.a libobk.a`

	8.1.5, 8.1.6, 8.1.7 (64 bit)	`# cd $ORACLE_HOME/lib64`
		`# rm libobk.a`
		`# ln -s /usr/lib/libnwora.a libobk.a`

	9.0.1 (64 bit)	`# cd $ORACLE_HOME/lib64` `# ln -s /usr/lib/libnwora.a libobk.a`

Linux	8.1.6.1	`# cd $ORACLE_HOME/rdbms/lib`
		`# make -f ins_rdbms.mk ioracle`
		`LLIBOBK=/usr/lib/libnwora.so`

TABLE 6-1. *Library Linking Commands for NMO and Oracle Server* (continued)

OS	Oracle Version	Command

	8.1.7	```# cd $ORACLE_HOME/lib```
		```# rm libobk.so```
		```# ln -s /usr/lib/libnwora.so libobk.so```

	9.0.1	```# cd $ORACLE_HOME/lib``` ```# ln -s /usr/lib/libnwora.so libobk.so```

Tru64 UNIX	8.1.5, 8.1.6	```# cd $ORACLE_HOME/lib```
		```# rm libobk.a```
		```# ln -s /usr/lib/libnwora.so libobk.so```
		```# cd $ORACLE_HOME/rdbms/lib```
		```# make -f ins_rdbms.mk ioracle```

	8.1.7	```# cd $ORACLE_HOME/lib```
		```# rm libobk.so```
		```# ln -s /usr/lib/libnwora.so libobk.so```

	9.0.1	```# cd $ORACLE_HOME/lib``` ```# ln -s /usr/lib/libnwora.so libobk.so```

TABLE 6-1. *Library Linking Commands for NMO and Oracle Server* (continued)

Configuring Networker for Client Operating System Backups

This section does not go into too much detail on configuring Networker for a client operating system backup. Refer to the appropriate Legato documentation for more detailed information.

RMAN Workshop: *Configure Networker for OS-Level Backups*

Workshop Notes

What follows is a high-level instruction guide for ensuring that your Oracle Server machine is configured in the Networker system as a client for an OS backup. This is a necessary step before NMO can be configured for use with RMAN. If your Oracle Server machine has already been configured as a client in the Networker Server, you can skip this section.

Step 1. Configure the Networker Server by identifying the Networker Server in the Server Resource section shown in Figure 6-2. The three most important fields in this dialog box are the following:

- **Name** Gives hostname of the Networker Server.
- **Parallelism** Gives the maximum number of backup data streams between the Networker Server and the storage device that can exist at the same time.
- **Administrator** Specifies which users should be granted the administrator privilege to modify and update the Networker configurations (for example, update client and media indexes, change resource configuration settings, and so on). The owner of the ORACLE_HOME (the Oracle user) should generally be given administrator privileges because when RMAN issues a **change...delete** or **delete expired backup** command, entries will be updated/removed from the client index.

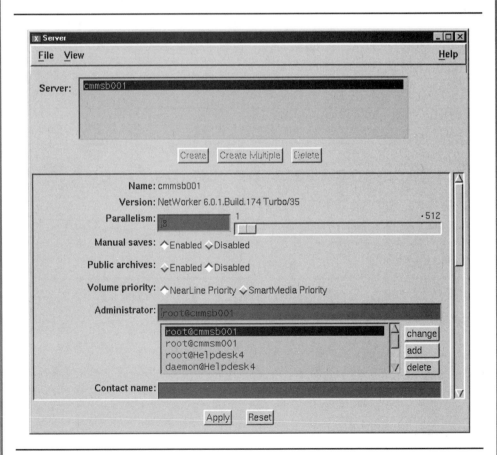

FIGURE 6-2. *Identifying the Networker Server in the Server dialog box*

Step 2. Configure appropriate resources and attributes for the Oracle Server, which is registered as a client within the Networker Server database (as per Step 1). Before NMO can be used, you must configure the Oracle Server client (the Networker Client—*not* the Oracle client). To do this, select Clients | Client Setup in the main Networker Administrator GUI to open the Clients dialog box, shown in Figures 6-3 (top) and 6-4 (bottom). General attributes of concern in this dialog box are the following:

- **Name** Specify the hostname of the Oracle Server.

- **Schedule** Use to automate scheduled backups (see "Configuring NMO for Oracle Backups," later in this chapter).

- **Browse Policy** Specify the length of time the Networker Server maintains entries for data in the online index file. This is primarily for recovery processes (the default is one month).

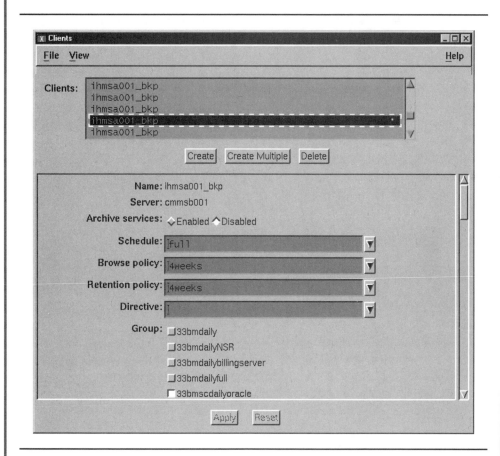

FIGURE 6-3. *Setting up a client in Networker Server—Part I*

- **Retention Policy** Specify the period of time the Networker Server keeps the information about backed up data in the online media index file (the default is one year).

- **Group** A set of Networker Client resources with preconfigured attributes (for example, start time, retries, and so forth).

- **Save Set** Specify scripts to be run in conjunction with Networker (see "Configuring NMO for Oracle Backups").

Step 3. Configure a storage device for use with Oracle backups and restores. The device can be a stand-alone tape drive or a file, or in an autochanger. Each device has to be configured in a separate way. The device configuration can be reviewed by selecting Media | Devices.

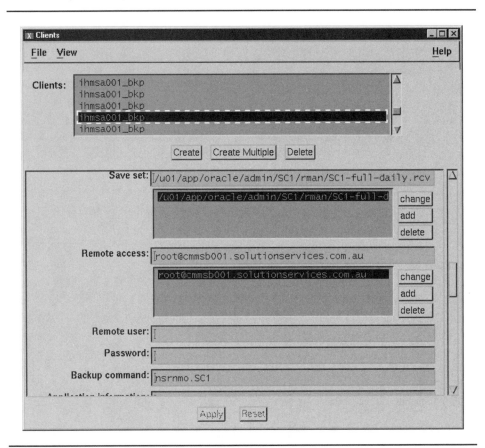

FIGURE 6-4. *Setting up a client in Networker Server—Part II*

Step 4.   Configure volume pool and label template resources. A *pool* is a collection of backup volumes that Networker uses to sort and store data. You can give each pool a meaningful and consistent name by assigning a label template to it. Doing so enables you to organize and track the backing up and labeling of data more easily. In terms of Oracle and RMAN, a volume pool can be useful if you want to back up tablespaces, archived logs, etc., onto different media sets or devices. This can be achieved by using the NSR_DATA_VOLUME_POOL environment variable within the RMAN script.

     You need to label and mount each Oracle storage device that has been configured before backup and restore operations take place.

Running and Scheduling RMAN Backups

Now you are ready to run and schedule an RMAN backup with Legato. There are a few extra configuration options that are required before this can happen. The configuration scripts have to be created and modified, and the Networker Server client setup needs additional configuration steps to allow it to interact with NMO and the Oracle Server.

RMAN Workshop: *Configuration of the nsrnmo.SID Script*

Workshop Notes
The nsrnmo.SID script is the main configuration file that contains connection information for the Networker and Oracle backup systems.

Step 1.   Connect to the Oracle Server (the Networker client server) as the owner of the ORACLE_HOME (the owner is usually "oracle"). The /usr/sbin directory contains a file called nsrnmo.SID. Keeping a copy of the original, rename this file to reflect the name of your SID (such as nsrnmo.TEST). For example:

```
# cd /usr/sbin
# cp nsrnmo.SID nsrnmo.TEST
```

Step 2.   After copying the file, edit the variables in Table 6-2 to reflect the environment settings of your site, as well as for your Oracle backup.

Variable	Description
PATH	The directory containing the Networker binaries. This field is mandatory, for example, `PATH=/usr/sbin`
ORACLE_HOME	The home directory of the Oracle Server installation. This field is mandatory, for example, `ORACLE_HOME=/app/oracle/product/8.1.7`
LD_LIBRARY_PATH	The directory containing the Oracle libraries. This field is mandatory on Tru64 only, for example, `LD_LIBRARY_PATH=/app/oracle/product/8.1.7/lib`
NSR_RMAN_ARGUMENTS	Use if parameters are required for the RMAN executable (enclose in a double-quoted string), for example, To output RMAN to a log file, you would use `NSR_RMAN_ARGUMENTS="msglog '/tmp/msglog.log' append"`
NSR_SB_DEBUG_FILE	Path and filename for detailed RMAN-specific debugging information, for example, `NSR_SB_DEBUG_FILE=/tmp/nsrdebug.log`
PRECMD	Specifies whether any pre-processing script needs to be run before the backup commences.
POSTCMD	Specifies whether any post-processing script needs to be run after the backup finishes.
TNS_ADMIN	The directory containing the Net8 configuration files (if it is other than $ORACLE_HOME/network/admin).

TABLE 6-2. *Variables To Be Set in the nsrnmo.SID File*

Configuring NMO for Oracle Backups

The Networker Server has to be configured to allow it to interact with the NMO module on the Oracle Server. Previously, we configured the Networker Server to accept the Oracle Server as a client for OS backups. This section extends this by linking RMAN with the NMO module and the Networker Client to the Networker Server (refer to Figure 6-1 for the architecture diagram of data flow).

In Step 2 of the RMAN Workshop "Configure Networker for OS-Level Backups," earlier in the chapter, the concept of a *group* was briefly introduced. A Networker backup group refers to a particular set of configuration options that can be assigned to Networker clients. These configuration options can refer to the start time, cloning, or retries. Networker comes with a "Default" backup group.

For ease of administration, create a new group for the Oracle backups with an appropriate name. For example, if the backups are for a customer XYZ, the backup group could be called XYZOracleFull. A new group can be created by selecting Customize | Groups.

Typically, the start time of the Oracle backup should be after or before the time of the OS backup. For network traffic considerations, do not run the Oracle backup at the same time.

Create a backup schedule to automate the scheduled backups for the Networker group in question. Preconfigured backup schedules are available that can be modified accordingly.

NOTE
The Networker scheduler does not determine the backup level used in an Oracle backup—it is controlled at the RMAN script level. Set the backup as Full whenever the RMAN script should be run (in other words, when a full or incremental Oracle database backup is required) and specify a level of Skip whenever no Oracle database backup is needed. If any level between 1 to 9 is specified, Networker treats it as a level of Full.

The final configuration step is to create a new client for the Oracle backups (similar to Step 2 of the RMAN Workshop "Configure Networker for OS-Level Backups").

1. Assign the client the correct Group previously created (for example, XYZOracleFull).

2. In the Save Set field, enter the path and name of the RMAN script that should be used for the scheduled backup. If required, several RMAN scripts can be specified at this point. However, the order of execution is arbitrary. If an action is required in a particular order, it may be better to use the PRECMD and POSTCMD variables of the nsrnmo.SID file. For details and examples of RMAN scripts, see the following section.

3. Set the appropriate Schedule that you previously created.

4. In the Backup Command field, enter the name of the nsrnmo.SID file that you created and modified earlier in the RMAN Workshop "Configuration of the nsrnmo.SID Script."

Creating RMAN Backup Scripts

An appropriate RMAN script must be created to perform the required type of backup. As mentioned previously, the level and type of backup is determined by the RMAN script and not by the Networker settings.

For example, the following script will perform a backup of the entire database to the group XYZOracleFull on the Networker Server of mycompany.legato.com:

```
connect target rman-user/password@SQLNetInstance1;
connect rcvcat rcat-user/password@SQLNetInstance2;
run {
    set command id to 'CMD_ID';
    allocate channel t1 type 'SBT_TAPE'
    allocate channel t2 type 'SBT_TAPE';
    send 'NSR_ENV=(NSR_SERVER=mycompany.legato.com,
    NSR_GROUP=XYZOracleFull)';
    backup full filesperset 4
    format 'FULL_%d_%u'
    (database);
    release channel t1;
    release channel t2;
    }
```

In each RMAN script, the command **connect target rman-user/password@ SQLNetInstance1** is mandatory, as it establishes the connection to the target database. The second **connect** command is required if a recovery catalog is used. An RMAN script must be created for each Oracle instance being backed up, so it is important to use some sort of file-naming convention (for example, SID_full.rcv or SID_inc.rcv). Obviously, since the usernames and passwords are stored in the RMAN script files, a minimal security setting should be granted to the file.

The **send** command in the preceding script is what sets the NSR_ environment variables. This command is supported in Oracle8i and 9i (for Oracle8, the NSR_ variables are passed through via the **parms** option; see the Legato documentation for syntax). The **parms** option is still available in Oracle8i and 9i, but setting the NSR_ variables in this way is not recommended. The following are some things to note about the **send** command:

- All NSR_ environment variables must be written in uppercase.

- When specifying the NSR_ environment variable, no spaces are allowed around the equals sign.

- The commas separating the variables are mandatory.

- The parentheses around the variables are mandatory.

- Comments are not permitted within the variable specification parentheses.

- The command can be run with three options:

  - **No option**   Sets the environment variables for all channels allocated

  - **send device_type 'SBT_TAPE'**   Sets the environment variables for all channels of that backup tape

  - **send channel <channel_name>**   Sets the environment variables for the specified channel

- The command must be put after the **allocate channel** commands and before the **backup** or **restore** commands of the RMAN script.

RMAN and NMO allow you to duplex Oracle backups—in other words, generate copies of the Oracle backup and store them on different media. In Oracle9i, this is done through the **configure...backup for device type sbt_tape to...** commands. When using this, individual NSR_ variables of NSR_DATA_VOLUME_POOL must be specified for each duplex stream (up to four copies can be made). For example, if duplex copies of datafiles and archived log files are required, the following script extract can be used:

```
...
run {
...
send 'NSR_ENV=(NSR_SERVER=mycompany.legato.com,
    NSR_DATA_VOLUME_POOL1=XYZOracleDatafile,
    NSR_DATA_VOLUME_POOL2=XYZOracleArchlogs)';
...
configure datafile backup copies for device type 'sbt_tape' to 2
configure archivelog backup copies for device type 'sbt_tape' to 2;
...
```

Oracle9i allows for *backup optimization,* in which RMAN decides whether a file should be skipped based on several criteria. As a result of this optimization, the recovery catalog and the Networker indexes can become out of sync. Therefore, it is recommended that you run the **crosscheck** command on a regular basis to synchronize the two.

Restore Commands

NMO works in conjunction with Oracle and RMAN to restore and recover a database. The restore works in basically the same way as a normal RMAN restore, as all the Networker configuration has already been done. Obviously, you can only restore data that has been backed up by NMO.

The first step is to create your restore script. The following is an example. The only difference between a "normal" RMAN restore script and one used by NMO is the environment variables (refer to "Creating RMAN Backup Scripts," earlier in the chapter, for some explanation on how to set the variables, and see Table 6-3 for a full list).

```
run {
    set command id to 'CMD_ID';
    allocate channel t1 type 'SBT_TAPE'
    allocate channel t2 type 'SBT_TAPE';
    send 'NSR_ENV=(NSR_SERVER=mycompany.legato.com,
    NSR_GROUP=XYZOracleFull)';
        restore   (database);
        recover database;
        release channel t1;
        release channel d1;
    }
```

Environment Variable	Valid Values	Description
NSR_CHECKSUM	TRUE FALSE	Specifies whether Networker should perform check summing on data.
NSR_CLIENT	Default is the hostname from which the session is initiated; it should be a valid Networker client name.	Specifies the client to be used for the backup or restore session. Recommended for all restores.
NSR_COMPRESSION	TRUE FALSE (default)	Specifies whether Networker should compress the backup data.
NSR_DATA_VOLUME_POOL	Should be a valid Networker pool name; the pool Default is used as the default.	Specifies the name of the volume pool that is to be used for the Oracle backups. It's a mandatory field if duplexing backups. This parameter will override the settings of the Networker Client if they are different.
NSR_DATA_VOLUME_POOLx (where x is 1, 2, 3 or 4)	The name of the volume pool for duplexed Oracle backups; mandatory if duplexing is used.	Each setting of this variable must be different from the other when duplexing is used.
NSR_DEBUG_FILE	Default is undefined (no debugging information is created); should be a valid pathname for the debug file.	Used for specifying a file for dumping debugging information of NMO for the SBT API.
NSR_ENCRYPTION	TRUE FALSE (default)	Specifies whether Networker performs encryption on the backup data.
NSR_GROUP	Specify a valid group name.	Specifies a valid backup group name identified in the Networker Client Resource.

TABLE 6-3. *NSR Environment Variables*

Environment Variable	Valid Values	Description
.NSR_NO_BUSY	TRUE FALSE (default)	Specifies whether the scheduled backup waits for the Networker Server if it is busy. A setting of TRUE means it will fail immediately if the server is busy.
NSR_NWPATH	Valid pathname for the directory of the Networker binaries.	Is mandatory if the Networker installation directory is different from the default installation path.
NSR_SAVESET_ EXPIRATION	Default is the Retention Policy setting in the client configuration; otherwise, specify a valid date.	Specifies the date when the save set becomes recyclable. Primarily used for Networker 6 and above.
NSR_SERVER	Specify a valid Networker Server name; default is the local host.	The hostname of the Networker Server that will perform the Oracle backup; a recommended but *not* mandatory setting.

TABLE 6-4. *NSR Environment Variables*

The restore script should be run via the command line, such as in the following example:

```
# rman target rman-user/password@SQLNetInstance1 rcvcat
rcat-user/password@SQLNetInstance2 cmdfile
'/app/oracle/admin/TEST/scripts/restore.rcv'
```

NSR Environment Variables

This section describes various NSR_ variables that can be set in an RMAN session for an Oracle backup or restore. See "Creating RMAN Backup Scripts," earlier in the chapter, for rules that should be followed when specifying NSR_ environment variables.

Summary

The Networker suite of products combine with the Oracle Server and RMAN to provide an efficient and relatively simple interface for database backup and recovery. This chapter has given an overview of how the Networker and Oracle systems fit together in terms of data and information flow. We have covered the various components of the two systems and how they should be installed and configured. Using this information, you should now be able to configure RMAN to interact with NMO and create RMAN scripts for your backup and recovery needs.

CHAPTER
7

RMAN and Tivoli
Storage Manager

his chapter introduces you to Tivoli Storage Manager and Tivoli Data Protection and describes how you can use the data protection software to interface RMAN to Tivoli Storage Manager.

Tivoli Storage Manager

Tivoli Storage Manager (TSM) is a popular backup/recovery software tool that allows you to back up files and raw logical volumes on virtually any platform to a wide array of tape library systems. It is set up as a client/server system in which the client backs up files to the server and the server keeps track of the backup objects, their versions, and other relevant information.

Introducing TSM to the DBA

If your installation uses TSM, then you need to understand how a basic TSM-based backup/recovery system works. Then, you can add TDP to that scenario and make RMAN backups to TSM. See Figure 7-1. What follows is a basic introduction to TSM, in which we deal with only those aspects of TSM that are necessary for the DBA to understand. The discussion assumes that the TSM server and client are on a Unix operating system. The end of this chapter includes a section, "TDP on Windows," that details the differences between Unix and Windows installations.

TSM Server

The TSM server controls the storage libraries and the actual storage of backup objects. When installed, it creates a database that stores the details of all the backups. This database can be queried using SQL through an administrator tool.

Backup objects are stored in storage pools. Storage pools are made up of disk partitions or tapes and tape libraries.

TSM Client

The TSM client has three pieces to it: a backup/archive client, an administrator interface program, and an API library.

TSM makes two kinds of copies of a file: backup and archive. A backup copy can have multiple versions and is what is normally thought of when discussing backups. An archive is a copy that does not allow versioning and can exist on the server for a long period of time. It is typically used when you want to keep a backup of a file for a long time after the file has been removed from the original system. All RMAN backups are backup copies, so we will not discuss archive copies any more in this introduction.

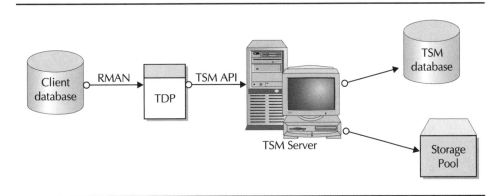

FIGURE 7-1. *RMAN Backup to TSM using TDP*

The backup/archive client installs by default in the /opt/tivoli/tsm/client/ba/bin directory. The **dsmc** program allows you to do a backup or restore files. The administrative interface, **dsmadmc**, allows you to log in to the server database and query the database using SQL. This is installed in the /opt/tivoli/tsm/client/admin/bin directory.

The client API is installed in /opt/Tivoli/tsm/client/api/bin and is used by programs to interface to the TSM server. TDP uses this client API to talk to TSM.

States of a Backup Object

When a file is copied from the client to the server, a backup copy of the file is created on the server and can be in one of three states: active, inactive, or expired. The latest copy is the active one, previous copies are inactive, and the copies ready for immediate removal are marked expired.

The states are set and managed by the TSM server. Files can expire in many ways. If we are keeping three versions of a file, then when the fourth copy arrives, the oldest one is marked expired. When a file is removed from the client, one or more of the backup copies may be expired. The DBA needs to understand the following parameters that control the number of versions, retention period of copies, and so forth. These parameters are stored on the TSM server. Later in this chapter, you will see how to define these parameters when you create a structure called a copy group.

- **VEREXISTS**   Specifies the number of copies of a file to be kept on the server. This includes the active copy also.

- **RETEXTRA** Specifies the time to keep the inactive copies. Suppose it is set to seven days. After seven days, the inactive copies will be marked expired and deleted from the server. This means that if you did not do a backup in the seven days, then you will end up with only the active copy. Once a file is deleted from the client, all backup copies are marked inactive, and how many of the backup copies remain on the server and for how long are controlled by the three parameters listed next.

- **VERDELETED** Specifies how many inactive copies to keep. Others are marked expired and are ready for immediate removal.

- **RETEXTRA** Specifies how long to keep the inactive copies. This applies to all copies but the last one.

- **RETONLY** Specifies how long to keep the last inactive copy.

Data Storage Policy

As the DBA, you devise a backup policy based on the requirements of the application. The requirements that you need to identify are directly tied to the parameters just discussed: the number of backup versions to keep, the retention period for inactive copies, the number of deleted versions to keep, and so forth.

Many applications may have similar requirements, and the TSM administrator creates policy domains that can cater to these. Every policy domain has a number of policy sets, but only one of them is active. Every policy set has one or more management classes associated with it. One of these management classes is designated as the default management class for a policy set. Every management class has a backup copy group and/or an archive copy group. The copy group is where you specify the actual details of the backup. The policy set and the policy domain are for administering clients with similar requirements under one umbrella. So, the DBA needs to understand the copy group parameters. See Figure 7-2.

Copy Group

There can be only one copy group for a management class and it is always called Standard. When you create a copy group, you supply critical information that directly corresponds to your backup requirements. Later in this chapter, you will see how to create a copy group. The parameters supplied to create a copy group are explained here:

- **TYPE** Backup or Archive. In our case, this is always Backup.

- **DESTINATION** The storage pool that will hold the backup objects.

- **VEREXISTS, VERDELETED, RETEXTRA, and RETONLY** Refer to the earlier section "States of a Backup Object" for an explanation of these parameters.

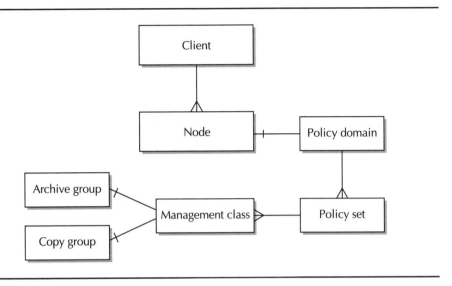

FIGURE 7-2. *Backup Client and TSM system objects*

Registering a Node on the Server

A TSM client needs to identify itself to a TSM server before the client can use the services of the server. This authentication is tied to the concept of a node. When a node is defined by the TSM administrator, it defines a name for the node, the password associated with the node, the maximum number of tape mounts, whether deleting a backup from the client will delete the corresponding backup from TSM, and so on. The client uses this node to back up its files to the server.

Suppose a copy group has been created to match your requirements. It is associated with a management class, which belongs to a policy set that belongs to a policy domain. The TSM administrator can then create a new node by the process of registration. When registering, the node gets associated with a policy domain, node name, password, tape mount, and delete options. TSM requires administrators and clients to identify themselves using the password for the node.

The following command registers a node called kitefin.

```
Register node kitefin domain=ora_kitefin password=set4now maxnummp=5
backdelete=YES archdelete=YES
```

This node can then be used from the client to back up data to the TSM server. A client can use any number of nodes to back up data. For instance, one node can be used to back up Oracle data and a different node can be used to back up non-Oracle data.

Client Options Files

Once a node has been registered by the TSM server, the client can target that node for backups. This is done using two files on the Unix client, dsm.sys and dsm.opt. If the client is on a Windows platform, it uses only one option file, dsm.opt. The end of this chapter includes a section, "TDP on Windows," that deals with the differences in TSM in the two environments, Unix and Windows.

The dsm.sys File

This file specifies one or more server names, sort of like TNS service names, that give the details of the TSM server and other configuration information necessary to do a backup. A server name entry, like a TNS entry, is made up of many parameters that specify the client address, TSM server address, node name that was registered for this client, and other information. Of these parameters, the DBA has to give special attention to three:

- **inclexcl**   Specifies what directories and files should be excluded from the backup. If you want to back up to a nondefault management class, you specify that as an include.

- **passwordaccess**   Can be set to one of two values. If set to **prompt**, every time a backup command is issued, the TSM server will authenticate your connection by asking for the password. If set to **generate**, then no password is asked for.

- **users**   If this keyword is present, then the users allowed to use TSM to back up files are listed. If this keyword is not present, then any user on the client can back up to the server using this server name.

Here is an example of a dsm.sys options file:

```
**********************************************************************
* dsm.sys
**********************************************************************
Servername              general
*    QUERYSCHEDPERIOD   12   (DFLT)
     COMMmethod         TCPip
     TCPClientaddress   xxx.xxx.xxx.xxx
     TCPPort            1500
     TCPServeraddress   xxx.xxx.xxx.xxx
     nodename           general
     Inclexcl           /usr/tivoli/tsm/client/ba/bin/inclexcl.aix
     SCHEDLogRetention  5
     SCHEDLogName       /usr/tivoli/tsm/client/ba/bin/dsmcsched.log
```

```
        SCHEDMODE                       PROMPTED
        CHAngingretries                 0
        ERRORLOGRetention               5
        COMPRESSION                     YES
        TCPNODELAY                      YES
        PasswordAccess                  Generate
*-*-*-*-*
Servername                              oracle
        COMMmethod                      TCPip
        TCPClientaddress                xxx.xxx.xxx.xxx
        TCPPort                         1500
        TCPServeraddress                xxx.xxx.xxx.xxx
        nodename                        node-oracle
*       inclexcl                        /usr/tivoli/tsm/client/ba/bin/inclexcl.ora
        SCHEDLogRetention               5
        SCHEDLogName                    /usr/tivoli/tsm/client/ba/bin/dsmcsched-o.log
        SCHEDMODE                       PROMPTED
        CHAngingretries                 0
        ErrorLogRetention               5
        COMPRESSION                     YES
        TCPNODELAY                      YES
        PasswordAccess                  Prompt
```

This example shows a system that has two nodes defined. The first server definition, **general**, is for backing up all the files on the system other than the Oracle database-related files. The second server definition is to be used with TDP to back up Oracle files.

The dsm.opt File

Normally, the only line in this file specifies the server name to use if one is not given in the backup/restore commands. Here is an example of a dsm.opt file:

```
****************************************************************
* Tivoli Storage Manager
*
*
*
* Sample Client User Options file for UNIX (dsm.opt.smp)
*
****************************************************************
*  This file contains an option you can use to specify the TSM
*  server to contact if more than one is defined in your client
*  system options file (dsm.sys).  Copy dsm.opt.smp to dsm.opt.
```

```
 *   If you enter a server name for the option below, remove the
 *   leading asterisk (*).
 ******************************************************************
Servername      oracle
```

How a Backup Object Is Stored on the Server

Suppose we back up a file /oradata/exp/epprd/exp1.dmp by issuing the following command:

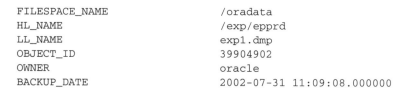

```
dsmc selective /oradata/exp/epprd/exp1.dmp.
```

This is stored on the server like this (HL stands for high level and LL stands for low level):

```
        FILESPACE_NAME              /oradata
        HL_NAME                     /exp/epprd
        LL_NAME                     exp1.dmp
        OBJECT_ID                   39904902
        OWNER                       oracle
        BACKUP_DATE                 2002-07-31 11:09:08.000000
```

Once you understand all of this, you are ready to install and configure TDP. As far as a TSM server is concerned, TDP is just another client that would like to use its services.

Tivoli Data Protection

RMAN, as it is installed from the Oracle CD-ROM, is capable of backing up files to disk only. While this is a viable solution for some small installations, most DBAs will find this of limited use. So, Oracle has published a media management API that allows vendors like Tivoli to develop software that can interface to RMAN on one side and the storage manager on the other side. This interface software then allows RMAN to back up to the storage manager directly. One such intermediate product is Tivoli Data Protection (TDP) from Tivoli. TDP allows RMAN to back up and restore files to and from TSM directly. This software requires its own license for every client.

Installing TDP

As you saw earlier, the Tivoli backup/archive client installs, by default, at /opt/tivoli/tsm/client/ba/bin. By default, TDP installs at /opt/tivoli/tsm/client/oracle/bin. You should be root to install the software. The TDP software is supplied as packages that need to be installed using the operating system utilities that are specific to the OS.

For instance, on AIX, use **smitty** to install TDP; on HP, use **swinstall**; and on Solaris, use the **pkgadd** command.

On all of these platforms, TDP is made up of three packages: the actual TDP software, the license, and the TDP utilities. Every version of TDP requires a minimum version of TSM API and the server software. The configuration and examples here refer to the latest version of the TDP software as of this writing, which is 2.2.1. This requires TSM server version 4.1.0 or above and TSM API version 4.2.1 or above on the client. TDP for Oracle 2.2.1 implements Oracle-defined media management API 2.0. Backups done using older versions of TDP can be restored using this version.

The biggest change from TDP version 2.1 is that all the options that use to be environment variables are now specified in the tdpo.opt file. So, the RMAN scripts written for use with TDP 2.1 need to be changed. (Please don't forget to check your installation guide for the latest details.) For example, on the Solaris OS, the TDP CD-ROM contains the file TDPOracle32.pkg. This file contains the three packages that need to be installed. We can install all three packages together by issuing the following command:

```
Pkgadd -d TDPOracle32.pkg
```

The license package creates a file called agent.lic in the opt/tivoli/tsm/client/ oracle/bin directory. Every TDP client requires a license. The first time you install TDP, you need to order the software CD-ROM with the license package in it. Subsequently, the later versions of TDP can be downloaded from Tivoli's web site, and the same agent.lic license file can be used with the new versions. Also, if you have a license for multiple clients, the agent.lic file can be copied from one client to another, as long as they are on the same platform.

Relinking RMAN and TDP

After installing the TDP packages, you need to relink RMAN. To do this, follow these steps:

1. Shut down all oracle instances that use the Oracle software.

2. Go to ORACLE_HOME/lib.

3. On AIX, remove libobk.a; on HP, remove libobk.sl; and on Solaris, remove libobk.so. If you are running Oracle9i, this file will not be present, so you don't have to delete it.

4. Create a soft link **ln –s /usr/lib/libobk.<a,so,sl> libobk.<a,so,sl>**.

5. Start the oracle instances.

Creating a Copy Group for TDP Backups

It is a good practice to create a separate management class, policy set, and policy domain for the TDP backups. The copy group created for the TDP backups should have the following parameters defined as specified:

VEREXISTS	1
VERDELETED	0
RETEXTRA	0
RETONLY	0

Essentially, this says that there will be no versioning, and that as soon as a file is deleted from the client, it should be marked expired in TSM and should be removed.

Registering the TDP Node with the TSM Server

As you saw earlier, any client needs to be registered with the server under a node name before the client can use the services of the server. So, come up with a node name for this TDP client and then register it under the policy domain that was created specially for TDP backups. The TSM administrator, when creating a new node by registering the node, should set the following parameters carefully according to the needs of the DBA:

- **BACKDELETE** Should be set to YES so that when an object is deleted in the RMAN catalog, that object can be deleted on the TSM server immediately. If this is set to NO, then objects that are removed from the RMAN catalog will not be removed from TSM.

- **MAXNUMMP** Specifies the maximum number of tape mounts and should not exceed the maximum number of physical drives that TSM uses. Talk to your TSM administrator for the maximum allowed. Set this to match the maximum number of channels allocated in your RMAN **allocate channel** command in your backup scripts, if that number does not exceed the maximum number of physical drives.

Once a node is registered, go to the client and create a server entry in the dsm.sys file that refers to this node and the TSM server.

Configuring dsm.sys for TDP

For TDP to work, set the **passwordaccess** parameter to the value **prompt**. This means TSM will ask for a password for every backup command. This is not the preferred way of doing a backup and will certainly not work in an automation script. TDP provides a utility called TDPCONF that can be used to overcome this problem.

Configuring dsm.opt for TDP

TDP for Oracle uses its own dsm.opt file. In this file, you specify the server name from dsm.sys that you wish to use. The location of this dsm.opt file is specified in another options file, tdpo.opt. The location of tdpo.opt is directly supplied to the RMAN **allocate channel** command. Next, we discuss the tdpo.opt file in detail.

Configuring the tdpo.opt File

You configure all the options for TDP in a file called tdpo.opt. This file can be located anywhere and is specified in the RMAN **allocate channel** command:

```
Allocate channel tdp1 type 'sbt_tape' parms
...ENV=(TDPO_OPTFILE=/u01/app/oracle/admin/tdp/bin/tdpo.opt)'
```

The default location for the tdpo.opt file is the default TDP installation directory, /opt/tivoli/tsm/client/oracle/bin.

Here is an example of the tdpo.opt file from a production system. The key parameters are explained in Table 7-1.

```
********************************************************************
* Tivoli Storage Manager - Tivoli Data Protection for Oracle
*
********************************************************************
DSMI_ORC_CONFIG      /u01/app/oracle/admin/tdp/bin
DSMI_LOG             /u01/app/oracle/admin/tdp/log
TDPO_FS              tdp_filesystem
TDPO_NODE            tdp_node
TDPO_OWNER           oracle
TDPO_PSWDPATH        /u01/app/oracle/admin/tdp/bin
TDPO_DATE_FMT        1
TDPO_NUM_FMT         1
TDPO_TIME_FMT        1

*TDPO_MGMT_CLASS2     mgmtclass2
*TDPO_MGMT_CLASS3     mgmtclass3
*TDPO_MGMT_CLASS4     mgmtclass4

*tdpo_trace_flags         orclevel0 orclevel1 orclevel2
*tdpo_trace_file          /u01/app/oracle/admin/tdp/log/tdpo.trace
*tdpo_trace_max           10000
```

Parameter	Explanation
DSMI_ORC_CONFIG	Says where to find the dsm.opt file for backups using TDP. TDP for Oracle uses its own dsm.opt file and, as described earlier, this chooses the server name for the backups.
DSMI_LOG	Designates the location for the error log (tdpoerror.log).
TDPO_FS	The filespace name for the backup. Earlier, you saw how a file is stored on the TSM server and how the filespace name corresponds to the mount point. For TDP backups, the value specified here would be the filespace name.
TDPO_NODE	Name of the node that you wish to use for your backup.
TDPO_OWNER	This value is used as the owner of the backup in the storage specification.
TDPO_PSWDPATH	Where the password file generated by the TDPOCONF utility is stored. TDPOCONF is explained in the following section.

TABLE 7-1. *TDP Backup Parameters*

How to Avoid Entering Passwords in Backup Scripts

TDP supplies a utility called TDPOCONF. When you run this utility, it asks you for a password, encrypts it, and stores it in the location specified in the TDPO_PSWDPATH parameter in the tdpo.opt file. TDP then uses this password and supplies it to the TSM server automatically, whenever required. To create the password file, go to /opt/Tivoli/tsm/client/oracle/bin and execute the following command:

```
tdpoconf  password  -tdpo_optfile=<complete path name of the
   tdpo.opt file>
```

You will be asked for the old password and then a new password, and then a file called TDP.<*node name*> will be created in the directory specified by the parameter TDPO_PSWDPATH. The original password for the node is required to run this command. The original password is the one with which the TSM administrator registered the node.

Testing TDP Setup

After configuring TDP, you should test the setup using the **sbttest** program provided by Oracle. This is found in ORACLE_HOME/bin. To run this, first set the TDPO_OPTFILE variable as shown next.

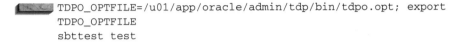
```
TDPO_OPTFILE=/u01/app/oracle/admin/tdp/bin/tdpo.opt; export
TDPO_OPTFILE
sbttest test
```

The test should successfully execute and return a message similar to this:

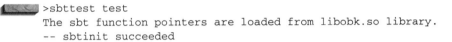
```
>sbttest test
The sbt function pointers are loaded from libobk.so library.
-- sbtinit succeeded
```

TDP on Windows

On the Windows platform, TDP installs under the regular TSM directory, c:\program files\tivoli\tsm. On Windows, the TSM client uses only one options file, dsm.opt. So, all the details you saw in dsm.sys on the Unix platform are specified in dsm.opt. If you want to use different nodes for backup, define multiple dsm.opt files and specify the correct one at the time of backup. You can specify it in the TDPO_ORC_CONFIG parameter in the tdpo.opt file. As usual, the fully qualified name of the tdpo.opt file is specified in the RMAN **allocate channel** command.

Using RMAN and TDP to Back Up the Database

At this point, you are ready to use RMAN and TDP together. As you are aware, the RMAN **allocate channel** command takes a parameter called **type** that can be disk or sbt_tape. For TDP backups, this should be set to sbt_tape:

```
Allocate channel tdp1 type 'sbt_tape'
```

Database objects stored on the TSM server by TDP for Oracle are stored as backup objects. For each backup:

- The FILESPACE_NAME is taken from the tdpo.opt file parameter TDPO_FS.

- The LL_NAME is uniquely generated using the format statement specified in the **backup** command.

■ The OBJECT_ID is uniquely generated.

■ The OWNER value is taken from the TDPO_OWNER parameter in the tdpo.opt file.

For example, suppose you have a tablespace called WHSEDATA in your database and you want to back up this tablespace. You issue a command similar to the following:

```
Run
{ allocate channel tdp1 type 'sbt_tape' parms
      'ENV=(TDPO_OPTFILE=/u01/app/oracle/admin/tdp/bin/tdpo.opt)';
   backup
      format 'df_%t_%s_%p'
      (tablespace whsedata);
   release channel tdp1;
}
```

This may create a backup object that looks like this on the TSM server:

FILESPACE_NAME	What You Designated in TDPO_FS
HL_NAME	//
LL_NAME	df_2_468686952_1 based on your format
OBJECT_ID	39905726
OWNER	What you designated in TDPO_OWNER

Duplex Copy

In Oracle 8.1.7 and Oracle9*i*, you can create duplicate copies of your backups to different locations. A maximum of four copies are allowed. TDP for Oracle version 2.2.1 supports this feature. In Oracle 8.1.7, you specify this option with the **set duplex** command, and in Oracle9*i*, you can use the **set backup copies** command. When you want to use this option, you need to configure the following additional parameters in the tdpo.opt file:

```
TDPO_MGMT_CLASS_2
TDPO_MGMT_CLASS_3
TDPO_MGMT_CLASS_4
```

These parameters specify different management classes for backing up the files. As you saw earlier, the management class has the copy group associated with it, and the copy group specifies the destination storage pool for the data. So, if we want to get four copies of the backup, we would create four different copy groups that target four different storage pools. Then, we would associate these copy groups with four different management classes, and associate these four management classes with the same policy set. Of these, the first management class may be the default.

Duplex copying affects the MAXNUMMP parameter also. If you are using two duplex copies, for example, then you should set the value of MAXNUMMP to the product of two times the maximum channel allocation in your RMAN backup scripts. Make sure that this doesn't exceed the maximum physical drives allocated to TSM.

TDP Utilities

TDP for Oracle provides two utilities for special operations. One is tdpoconf, which you already used for password generation. The other is tdposync.

TDPOCONF

This utility can be used to generate a password file or to show the details of the existing environment. These two options for the command are shown here:

```
tdpoconf      password  -TDPO_OPTFILE=<>
tdpoconf      showenvironment   -TDPO_OPTFILE=<>
```

Here is an example of the output from the **showenvironment** option of the **tdpoconf** command.

```
#tdpoconf showenvironment
-TDPO_OPTFILE=/u01/app/oracle/admin/tdp/bin/tdpo.opt
TDP FOR ORACLE INFORMATION
 Version:             2
 Release:             2
 Level:               1
 Sublevel:            0
 Platform:            32bit TDP Oracle SUN
TSM SERVER INFORMATION
 Server Name:         ORACLE
 Server Address:      xxx.xxx.xxx.xxx
 Server Type:         AIX-RS/6000
 Server Port:         1500

 Communication Method: TCP/IP
SESSION INFORMATION
 Owner Name:          oracle
 Node Name:           TDP_NODE
```

```
Node Type:               TDP Oracle SUN
DSMI_DIR:                /opt/tivoli/tsm/client/api/bin
DSMI_ORC_CONFIG:         /u01/app/oracle/admin/tdp/bin
TDPO_OPTFILE:            /u01/app/oracle/admin/tdp/bin/tdpo.opt
Password Directory:      /u01/app/oracle/admin/tdp/bin
Compression:             FALSE
```

TDPOSYNC

When the policy domain parameter **backdelete** is not set to yes or the copy group parameters are not set correctly, then the RMAN catalog and the TSM server can go out of synchronization. That is, you may have deleted the old backups that you don't care about anymore from the RMAN catalog, but those backups may not have been removed from the TSM server. This situation can be rectified by taking two steps:

1. Ask the TSM administrator to update the node registration and set BACKDELETE=yes. Check the copy group parameters to make sure that they are what the TDP wants—that is, **VEREXISTS** is set to 1, **VERDELETED** to 0, and so forth.

2. Run the **tdposync** command to identify and remove the unwanted backups from the server.

The **tdposync** command checks for objects on the TSM server that are not in the RMAN catalog. Then, it presents the information to you and allows you to delete or exit without deleting. Here is how you run the **tdposync** command. Specify the full name for the tdpo.opt file in the TDPO_OPTFILE option.

```
tdposync syncdb -TDPO_OPTFILE=<>
```

This prompts you for the username, password, and the connect string to the RMAN catalog. Then, it checks the backup information in the catalog against the TSM server database and gives you a pick window that displays a list of backups that may be out of sync. You can then pick the ones you want to delete. Please note that this process cannot be rolled back.

Troubleshooting

Look at the sample tdpo.opt file in the erlier section "Configuring the tdpo.opt File." You will see three parameters at the end that deal with tracing. These parameters help the DBA trace the TDP process while it is running, and the output file is useful to the Tivoli support personnel when debugging your problem.

Summary

It should be clear from this chapter that the DBA plays a middleman in setting up and making things work with TDP and TSM. In particular, the DBA should do the following:

- Help the Unix/Windows administrator install TDP.

- Specify the backup requirements to the TSM administrator so that the TSM administrator can create the copy group, management classes, and so forth correctly.

- Configure the tdpo.opt file.

- Help the Unix/Windows administrator run the tdpoconf utility to generate the encrypted password.

- Make sure the DBA username is added to the client options file (dsm.sys or dsm.opt) so that the DBA user can run **tsm** commands

CHAPTER
8

Configuring
HP OmniBack II v4.0

his brief chapter is not intended to replace Hewlett-Packard's OpenView *OmniBack II UNIX Integration Guide Release A.04.00* (HP OBII UIG), but rather to enhance and supplement it, especially in regard to the relinking and configuration areas. This chapter also covers the requirements for shutting down, mounting, and reopening a NOARCHIVELOG database via OmniBack PREEXEC and POSTEXEC scripts. Additionally, it also describes how to use a different tape drive for restoring than what you use for backing up.

Linking OmniBack Libraries for RMAN Usage

The first thing that you need to do is install OmniBack II. This installation is outside the scope of this chapter and can be found in Hewlett-Packard's OmniBack II v4.0 Installation documentation. From an Oracle point of view, the latest OmniBack patches (including the OmniBack Oracle8 patch) must be installed and pushed out to every OmniBack client machine. Note that OmniBack II v4.0 references "Oracle8" everywhere in the HP documentation, but the Oracle8 module is valid for both Oracle8.x and 9.x databases. (OmniBack has two separate Oracle modules: Oracle7 for Enterprise Backup Utility, and Oracle8 for RMAN.)

There are slightly different linking configuration requirements between Oracle8.x and 9.x systems, which are not covered in the HP documentation. After you install the most current OmniBack Oracle8 patch, you must link each individual HP-UX ORACLE_HOME directory to the OmniBack libraries prior to usage. You must do this with all Oracle processes running out of that ORACLE_HOME directory down. Oracle8.x is slightly more complicated than Oracle9.x, because the 8.x oracle executable must be relinked to include the OmniBack libraries. The linking directions published in HP's OBII UIG are somewhat incorrect for Oracle8.x environments, and are unsuitable for Oracle9.x environments.

Because this book is written primarily for Oracle9i users, the following workshop demonstrates relinking Oracle9i for OmniBack II usage. The methodology for Oracle8.x can be found at the end of the chapter in the section "OmniBack and Oracle8i: Workshops."

RMAN Workshop: *Relinking Oracle9.x OmniBack II on HP-UX 11.00*

Workshop Notes
This workshop handles relinking for Oracle9i releases only.

Step 1. Sign on as the **oracle** user. Shut down all Oracle databases and all other Oracle-related processes (listener and so forth) tied to the ORACLE_HOME being configured.

Step 2. Change to the 64-bit lib directory by typing **cd ${ORACLE_HOME}/lib**. Back up what the libobk.sl symbolic link is initially pointing to (i.e., **ll libobk.sl > libobk.sl.ORIG**), as this information will be required in the future when applying Oracle patches to this ORACLE_HOME. (If this file does not exist, skip to Step 4.)

Step 3. Delete the existing 64-bit libobk.sl symbolic link file (type **rm libobk.sl**).

Step 4. Symbolically link in the 64-bit OmniBack library by typing **ln -s /opt/omni/lib/libob2oracle8_64bit.sl libobk.sl**.

Step 5. Check to see if the link is valid by typing **strings libobk.sl**. You should see quite a bit of text information—if nothing is returned, the link is invalid and should be dropped and re-created.

Step 6. Change to the 32-bit lib directory by typing **cd ${ORACLE_HOME}/lib32**. Back up what the libobk.sl symbolic link is initially pointing to (i.e., **ll libobk.sl > libobk.sl.ORIG**), as this information will be required in the future when applying Oracle patches to this ORACLE_HOME. (If this file does not exist, skip to Step 8.)

Step 7. Delete the existing 32-bit libobk.sl symbolic link file (type **rm libobk.sl**).

Step 8. Symbolically link in the 32-bit OmniBack library by typing **ln -s /opt/ omni/lib/libob2oracle8.sl libobk.sl**.

Step 9. Check to see if the link is valid by typing **strings libobk.sl**. You should see quite a bit of text information—if nothing is returned, the link is invalid and should be dropped and re-created.

OmniBack Linking and Oracle Patchset Installations

Another relinking issue appears when you are installing an Oracle patch into an HP-UX ORACLE_HOME. Oracle patch installations will error out when compiling certain sets of executables if the OmniBack libraries are still linked into the ORACLE_HOME. The Oracle Universal Installer may or may not recognize these errors. The OmniBack information should be removed from the ORACLE_HOME prior to a patch installation. Instructions are provided in the following RMAN Workshop to back out the OmniBack-related changes of an ORACLE_HOME directory so that an Oracle patch can be cleanly applied. Then the OmniBack libraries can be relinked into the patched ORACLE_HOME.

The following RMAN Workshop describes backing out OmniBack links for Oracle9i. For instructions on Oracle8.x, see the section at the end of this chapter "OmniBack and Oracle8i: Workshops."

RMAN Workshop: *Backing Out OmniBack Links to Cleanly Apply Oracle9.x Patches*

Workshop Notes
With the OmniBack II libraries linked into the ${ORACLE_HOME}, relinking errors will occur when applying Oracle patches if the OmniBack II changes are not first backed out of the ORACLE_HOME being patched.

Step 1.   Sign on as the **oracle** user. Shut down all Oracle databases and all other Oracle-related processes (listener and so forth) tied to the ORACLE_HOME being patched.

Step 2.   Change to the 64-bit lib directory by typing **cd ${ORACLE_HOME}/lib**.

Step 3.   Delete the existing 64-bit libobk.sl symbolic link file (type **rm libobk.sl**).

Step 4.   Display the backup file to see how to relink this library (type **cat libobk.sl.ORIG**). Symbolically relink the library back to the original Oracle value (for example, type **ln –s liblsm.sl libobk.sl** if your libobk.sl.ORIG file shows that liblsm.sl was originally linked to libobk.sl).

Step 5.   Check to see if the link is valid by typing **strings libobk.sl**. You should see quite a bit of text information—if nothing is returned, the link is invalid and should be dropped and re-created.

Step 6.   Change to the 32-bit lib directory by typing **cd ${ORACLE_HOME}/lib34**. Delete the existing 32-bit libobk.sl symbolic link file (type **rm libobk.sl**). Display the backup file to see how to relink this library (type **cat libobk.ORIG**). Symbolically relink the library back to the original Oracle value (for example, type **ln –s liblsm.sl libobk.sl**).

Step 7. Check to see if the link is valid by typing **strings libobk.sl**. You should see quite a bit of text information—if nothing is returned, the link is invalid and should be dropped and re-created.

Step 8. Apply the Oracle patch as normal. When completed, follow the steps listed earlier in the "Relinking Oracle9.x OmniBack II on HP-UX 11.00" RMAN Workshop.

OmniBack Configuration for Oracle

Once the ORACLE_HOME has been linked to the OmniBack libraries, each individual database must be configured within OmniBack. Configuration includes telling OmniBack where the ORACLE_HOME directory is, the name of the SID, and the user IDs and passwords for the Target database (and optionally for the Catalog database). OmniBack stores this information internally. OmniBack does not use RMAN stored scripts—every OmniBack Oracle8 backup script is kept within the confines of OmniBack, not within an Oracle database.

OmniBack provides two different methods to provide this configuration information—one is a command-line program, and the other is through the standard OmniBack GUI program. Certain inconsistencies have been noticed with the way that each of the programs store OmniBack client names (especially on the Windows platforms), so using *both* methods is highly recommended—especially if backup jobs are submitted both via the command line and via the GUI program.

Once a database is configured in OmniBack, the GUI program can be used to set up an OmniBack Oracle8 backup job. The GUI program to create an Oracle8 backup job is fairly easy to use and thus will not be covered here.

Configuring an Oracle Database Within OmniBack II

OmniBack requires a minimum of three pieces of information to configure an Oracle database—four if an RMAN catalog is being used—in the following order:

1. ORACLE_SID name

2. ORACLE_HOME directory

3. User ID and password for the Target database

4. User ID and password for the Catalog database (optional)

There are two different ways to provide this information to OmniBack. One way is to configure a database via the command line. The configuration program is named /opt/omni/lbin/util_oracle8.exe under HP-UX, and C:\Program Files\

OmniBack\bin\util_oracle8.exe under Windows. Both require the same parameters in the aforementioned order. For example,

```
/opt/omni/lbin/util_oracle8.exe  -CONFIG DB01\
/u01/app/oracle/product/9.2.0 targetid/password@DB01\
catalogid/password@CAT1
```

Note that this command must be run as root under HP-UX, and that valid TNS connect strings must exist (whether HP-UX or Windows). To validate the configuration, run the following:

```
/opt/omni/lbin/util_oracle8.exe  -CHKCONF DB01
```

If it comes back with a return value of 0, then everything is configured correctly. If it does not come back with a value of 0, then reissue the **util_oracle8.exe -CONFIG** command with the correct information.

The other way to configure a database for OmniBack is through the OmniBack II Manager GUI program. When you create a new "Oracle8 Server" backup job (which is the correct option regardless of whether Oracle8.x or Oracle9.x is being run) by clicking Add Backup and then Blank Oracle Backup, OmniBack goes out and searches every HP-UX and Windows OmniBack Oracle8 client to build a drop-down list of SIDs. If the chosen database has never been configured before, a GUI box will pop up requesting the required information.

OmniBack stores this information behind the scenes according to client hostname. Sometimes, the command-line version of the command and the GUI version of the command will come up with different hostnames, especially on the Windows servers. For example, one version of the command will store information behind the scenes under the client name SERVER1, while the other may store it under SERVER1.COMPANY.COM. Therefore, it is always a good idea to configure an Oracle database using both the command-line and GUI versions.

Note that Oracle passwords are stored internally (and encrypted) by OmniBack. If the target or catalog password is changed (or any other information provided to OmniBack), OmniBack needs to be updated to reflect the changes by rerunning the **util_oracle8.exe -CONFIG** configuration command.

The OmniBack GUI can be used to configure the rest of the backup. RMAN backup scripts stored in an RMAN catalog are not used in OmniBack. OmniBack stores all backup scripts on the OmniBack Cell Server host. An example of an OmniBack II Oracle8 Barlist backup script, for backing up a NOARCHIVELOG mode database, is shown here:

```
BARLIST "rman_Cold_DB01"
OWNER oracle dba server1.company.com
DYNAMIC 1 1
PREEXEC "ob_pre_DB01.sh" -on_host server1.company.com
```

```
POSTEXEC "ob_post_DB01.sh" -on_host server1.company.com
DEVICE "DLT_01"
{
    -sync
    -pool "rman_TEST_Daily"
}
DEVICE "DLT_02"
{
    -sync
    -pool "rman_TEST_Daily"
}
DEVICE "DLT_03"
{
    -sync
    -pool "rman_TEST_Daily"
}
DEVICE "DLT_04"
{
    -sync
    -pool "rman_TEST_Daily"
}
DEVICE "DLT_05"
{
    -sync
    -pool "rman_TEST_Daily"
}
DEVICE "DLT_06"
{
    -sync
    -pool "rman_TEST_Daily"
}
DEVICE "DLT_07"
{
    -sync
    -pool "rman_TEST_Daily"
}
DEVICE "DLT_08"
{
    -sync
    -pool "rman_TEST_Daily"
}
DEVICE "DLT_09"
{
    -sync
    -pool "rman_TEST_Daily"
}
DEVICE "DLT_10"
{
    -sync
```

```
    -pool "rman_TEST_Daily"
}
CLIENT "DB01" server1.company.com
{
    EXEC ob2rman.exe
    -args {
       "-backup"
    }
    -input {
       "run {"
       "allocate channel 'dev_0' type 'sbt_tape'"
       "parms'ENV=(OB2BARTYPE=Oracle8,OB2APPNAME=DB01,
          OB2BARLIST=rman_Cold_DB01)';"
       "allocate channel 'dev_1' type 'sbt_tape'"
       "parms'ENV=(OB2BARTYPE=Oracle8,OB2APPNAME=DB01,
          OB2BARLIST=rman_Cold_DB01)';"
       "allocate channel 'dev_2' type 'sbt_tape'"
       "parms'ENV=(OB2BARTYPE=Oracle8,OB2APPNAME=DB01,
          OB2BARLIST=rman_Cold_DB01)';"
       "backup incremental level <incr_level> filesperset 1"
       "format 'rman_Cold_DB01<DB01_%s:%t:%p>.dbf'"
       "tablespace users"
       ";"
       "}"
    }
    -public
    -profile
}  -protect days 92
```

OmniBack and Cold Backups

Another issue not covered in the HP OBII UIG is having OmniBack do everything to back up a NOARCHIVELOG mode database—in other words, shut it down, mount it, back it up, and then open it. OmniBack has PREEXEC and POSTEXEC jobs that can be configured to run immediately before and after the actual RMAN backup. These jobs execute as root (even though the backup job is configured under the oracle user ID), but normally the oracle ID is used to perform all Oracle-related shutdowns and startups. The **su** command can be used to change to the **oracle ID**, but there is a limitation that OmniBack cannot do a **su** command directly inside of the PREEXEC or POSTEXEC job; however, it can call an **at** program, which then calls the **su** command. There is a problem with the **at** command and datafiles over 2GB in size that needs to be resolved on each HP-UX system. The whole thing seems unnecessarily complicated, but it does work well once everything is appropriately configured.

File Size Limitations and Starting the Database with the at Command

There's a bug in HP-UX that manifests itself as an HP-UX 27 error ("File too large") if a datafile is over 2GB in size *and* the database is started via the **at** command. To fix this problem, prior to running any **at** command, the system file /var/adm/cron/.proto needs to be modified by changing the **ulimit $l** line to **ulimit unlimited**. If this line is not changed, an HP-UX 27 error will show up the first time Oracle attempts to read or write more than 2GB of the way into a datafile that is larger than 2GB—which may be several hours (or days!) after the database is opened after the backup.

These are surmountable problems, but overcoming them requires setting up several shell scripts to accomplish the goal, which are shown in the following code samples. The PREEXEC script is ob_pre_DB01.sh, and the POSTEXEC script is ob_post_DB01.sh. The other scripts are called by these scripts, and are all required to perform a cold RMAN backup.

Script 1: ob_pre_DB01.sh

```
#!/bin/sh
# Set Up Name of Wait File; Export to Environment
export ORA_WAIT_FILE=/tmp/ora_ob_pre_DB01.$$.wait

# Delete Wait File, if it exists
if [ -f ${ORA_WAIT_FILE} ]
then
/usr/bin/rm ${ORA_WAIT_FILE}
fi

# Kick off Database-Specific Job
/usr/bin/at -f /scripts/ora_su_pre_DB01.sh now
```

```
/usr/bin/echo "Waiting for "${ORA_WAIT_FILE}"..."

# Wait for Oracle Database to be Shutdown and Mounted ...
until ( [ -f ${ORA_WAIT_FILE} ] )
do
    /usr/bin/sleep 15
done

# Remove Wait File
/usr/bin/rm ${ORA_WAIT_FILE}
exit 0
```

Script 2: ora_su_pre_DB01.sh

```
#!/bin/sh

/usr/bin/su - oracle -c /scripts/ob_shutdown_mount_DB01.sh >>\
/scripts/log/ora_su_pre_DB01.log 2>&1

/usr/bin/touch ${ORA_WAIT_FILE} >> /scripts/log/ora_su_pre_DB01.log 2>&1

exit 0
```

Script 3: ob_shutdown_mount_DB01.sh

```
#!/bin/sh
export PATH=${PATH}:/usr/local/bin
export ORAENV_ASK=NO
export ORACLE_SID=DB01
. oraenv
sqlplus /nolog <<EOF
connect / as sysdba
shutdown immediate;
startup mount;
exit;
EOF
```

Script 4: ob_post_DB01.sh

```
#!/bin/sh
# Set Up Name of Wait File; Export to Environment
export ORA_WAIT_FILE=/tmp/ora_ob_post_DB01.$$.wait

# Delete Wait File, if it exists
if [ -f ${ORA_WAIT_FILE} ]
then
```

```
    /usr/bin/rm ${ORA_WAIT_FILE}
fi

# Kick off Database-Specific Job
/usr/bin/at -f /scripts/ora_su_post_DB01.sh now

/usr/bin/echo "Waiting for "${ORA_WAIT_FILE}"..."

# Wait for Oracle Database to be Opened ...........
until ( [ -f ${ORA_WAIT_FILE} ] )
do
    /usr/bin/sleep 15
done

# Remove Wait File
/usr/bin/rm ${ORA_WAIT_FILE}

exit 0
```

Script 5: ob_su_post_DB01.sh

```
#!/bin/sh
/usr/bin/su - oracle -c /scripts/ob_alter_open_DB01.sh >> /scripts/log/ora_su_post_DB01.log 2>&1
/usr/bin/touch ${ORA_WAIT_FILE} >> /scripts/log/ora_su_post_DB01.log 2>&1
exit 0
```

Script 6: ob_alter_open_DB01.sql

```
#!/bin/sh
export PATH=${PATH}:/usr/local/bin
export ORAENV_ASK=NO
export ORACLE_SID=DB01
. oraenv
sqlplus /nolog <<EOF
connect / as sysdba
alter database open;
exit;
EOF
```

Changing the Tape Drive for Restores

RMAN backups from OmniBack are initiated from OmniBack (either via the command line or through the GUI), whereas RMAN restores are initiated from RMAN. Standard OmniBack file system restores easily allow for changing tape devices; but for Oracle8 restores, there are no specific OmniBack-related RMAN commands to be run from the RMAN> command prompt. Unless told differently, OmniBack will use the same tape device for restoration as it used to back up. Using the same tape device for restoration may present a problem if the tape device is malfunctioning or is unavailable for usage by the restoring machine (for example, it's on a different network, to which the restoring machine does not have access, or it's in need of repair). OmniBack provides a command that can be run prior to initiating the RMAN restoration that can direct OmniBack to use a different tape device.

The following command must be run as root:

```
omnidbutil -changebdev <FromDev> <ToDev> [-session <SessionID>]
```

For example, the command **omnidbutil -changebdev DLT_10 DLT_04 -session 2002/08/05-34** will now directOmniBack to use the new tape drive (DLT_04) instead of the original tape drive (DLT_10) for any files that are restored from the 2002/08/05-34 backup session.

OmniBack and Oracle8i: Workshops

While this book concentrates on Oracle9i, the methodology for relinking tasks is different enough in Oracle8.x that we have included this section of RMAN Workshops. The first workshop walks you through relinking Oracle8.x OmniBack on the HP-UX 11.00 operating system, and corresponds to the similarly named workshop for Oracle9.x that appeared earlier in the chapter.

RMAN Workshop: *Relinking Oracle8.x OmniBack II on HP-UX 11.00*

Workshop Notes
This workshop covers only Oracle8.x.

Step 1.   Sign on as the **oracle** user. Shut down all Oracle databases and all other Oracle-related processes (listener and so forth) tied to the ORACLE_HOME being relinked. Back up the current ${ORACLE_HOME}/bin/oracle file by coping it before starting (type **cd ${ORACLE_HOME}/bin**, and then type **cp -p oracle oracle.ORIG**).

Step 2.   Change to the 32-bit lib directory by typing **cd ${ORACLE_HOME}/lib**. Back up what the libobk.sl symbolic link is initially pointing to (i.e., **ll libobk.sl > libobk.sl.ORIG**), as this information will be required in the future when applying Oracle patches to this ORACLE_HOME.

Step 3.   Delete the existing 32-bit libobk.sl symbolic link file (type **rm libobk.sl**).

Step 4.   Symbolically link in the 32-bit OmniBack library by typing
ln -s /opt/ omni/lib/libob2oracle8.sl libobk.sl.

Step 5.   Check to see if the link is valid by typing **strings libobk.sl**. You should see quite a bit of text information—if nothing is returned, the link is invalid and should be dropped and re-created.

Step 6.   If this is a 64-bit ORACLE_HOME, the same steps need to be performed for the 64-bit library. (If this is a 32-bit ORACLE_HOME, skip to Step 10.) Change to the 64-bit lib directory by typing **cd ${ORACLE_HOME}/lib64**. Back up what the libobk.sl symbolic link is initially pointing to (i.e., **ll libobk.sl > libobk.sl.ORIG**), because this information will be required in the future when applying new Oracle patches to this ORACLE_HOME.

Step 7.   Delete the existing 64-bit libobk.sl symbolic link file (type **rm libobk.sl**).

Step 8.   Symbolically link in the 64-bit OmniBack library by typing
ln -s /opt/ omni/lib/libob2oracle8_64bit.sl libobk.sl.

Step 9.   Check to see if the link is valid by typing **strings libobk.sl**. You should see quite a bit of text information—if nothing is returned, the link is invalid and should be dropped and re-created.

Step 10.   Change to the ${ORACLE_HOME}/rdbms/lib directory by typing
cd ${ORACLE_HOME}/rdbms/lib.

Step 11.   Back up the current env_rdbms.mk file by typing
cp -p env_rdbms.mk env_rdbms.mk.ORIG.

Step 12.   Edit the env_rdbms.mk file, changing the LIBMM and LLIBMM statements as follows (the commented out LIBMM and LLIBMM statements were the original values):

```
## 08-OCT-2001: START CHANGE:
##Change for new OmniBack II v4.0 Linking Instructions
##Replace LIBMM and LLIBMM Entries
##LIBMM=$(LIBHOME)$(LIB_PREFIX)$(LIBMMNAME).$(LIB_EXT)
##LLIBMM=$(LDLIBFLAG)$(LIBMMNAME)
LIBMM=
LLIBMM=
## 08-OCT-2001: END CHANGE
```

Step 13. Recompile the oracle executable by typing one of the following statements, depending on whether this is a 32-bit or 64-bit ORACLE_HOME:

```
For a 32-bit ORACLE_HOME:
make -f ins_rdbms.mk ioracle "LLIBOBK=/opt/omni/lib/libob2oracle8.sl"
For a 64-bit ORACLE_HOME:
make -f ins_rdbms.mk ioracle "LLIBOBK=/opt/omni/lib/libob2oracle8_64bit.sl"
```

This final workshop describes backing out OmniBack links so that an Oracle8.x software installation can be safely patched up. This corresponds to the similarly named workshop for Oracle9.x that appears earlier in the chapter.

RMAN Workshop: *Backing Out OmniBack Links to Cleanly Apply Oracle8.x Patches*

Workshop Notes
With the OmniBack II libraries linked into the ${ORACLE_HOME}, relinking errors will occur when applying Oracle patches if the OmniBack II changes are not first backed out of the ORACLE_HOME.

Step 1. Sign on as the **oracle** user. Shut down all Oracle databases and all other Oracle-related processes (listener and so forth) tied to the ORACLE_HOME being patched.

Step 2. Change to the 32-bit lib directory by typing **cd ${ORACLE_HOME}/lib**.

Step 3. Delete the existing 32-bit libobk.sl symbolic link file (type **rm libobk.sl**).

Step 4. Display the backup file to see how to relink this library (type **cat libobk.sl.ORIG**). Symbolically relink the library back to the original Oracle value (normally, **ln -s libdsbtsh8.sl libobk.sl** or **ln -s liblsm.sl libobk.sl** is used).

Step 5. Check to see if the link is valid by typing **strings libobk.sl**. You should see quite a bit of text information—if nothing is returned, the link is invalid and should be dropped and re-created.

Step 6. If this is a 64-bit ORACLE_HOME, the same steps need to be performed for the 64-bit library. (If this is a 32-bit ORACLE_HOME, skip to Step 8.) Change to the 64-bit lib directory by typing **cd ${ORACLE_HOME}/lib64**. Delete the existing 64-bit libobk.sl symbolic link file (type **rm libobk.sl**). Display the backup file to see how to relink this library (type **cat libobk.ORIG**). Symbolically relink the library back to the original Oracle value (type **ln -s libdsbtsh8.sl libobk.sl** or **ln -s liblsm.sl libobk.sl**).

Step 7.   Check to see if the link is valid by typing **strings libobk.sl**. You should see quite a bit of text information—if nothing is returned, the link is invalid and should be dropped and re-created.

Step 8.   Change to the ${ORACLE_HOME}/rdbms/lib directory by typing **cd ${ORACLE_HOME}/rdbms/lib**.

Step 9.   Back up the current env_rdbms.mk file by typing **cp -p env_rdbms.mk env_rdbms.mk.OB2**.

Step 10.   Replace the original env_rdbms.mk file by typing **cp -p env_rdbms.mk.ORIG env_rdbms.mk**.

Step 11.   Recompile the oracle executable by typing **make -f ins_rdbms.mk ioracle**.

Step 12.   Apply the Oracle patch as normal. When completed, follow the steps listed under the "Relinking Oracle8.x OmniBack II on HP-UX 11.00" RMAN Workshop (instead of starting from scratch for editing the env_rdbms.mk file, you can use the OB2 backup copy of the env_rdbms.mk file that you made in Step 9).

Summary

Using RMAN with HP's OmniBack is straightforward once Oracle and OmniBack are correctly configured. This chapter covered linking the OmniBack libraries into an ORACLE_HOME directory, and providing the specific Oracle information (SID name, ORACLE_HOME, and user IDs) to OmniBack so that database-specific backup jobs can be created in OmniBack. An example of an OmniBack backup script (a Barlist) for an Oracle database was included. HP-UX shell scripts were also provided to run a cold RMAN backup. Standard Oracle RMAN restore commands are used for restoration and recovery, but since these do not allow for specifying a different tape device, the OmniBack command for this function was also covered.

PART
III

Using RMAN
Effectively

CHAPTER
9

RMAN Backups

ow that we have covered all the startup essentials, we are actually ready to use RMAN to back up something. In this chapter, we are going to talk all about doing backups with RMAN. From offline backups to online backups, backups of archived redo logs to incremental backups, we will cover it all. We will look at how to back up entire databases and individual database datafiles. So, with that in mind, let's move on!

Benefits of RMAN Backups vs. Scripted Backups

So, why use RMAN to back up your databases? You may already be doing online backups with some wonderfully crafted, home-grown scripts, and you may be asking yourself, "Why should I start using RMAN when my scripts work so reliably?" In this section, we hope to answer that question.

I'm sure your scripts never fail. Trust me, though, there are scripts out there that others have crafted that do break. This raises two problems. First, when the script breaks, the database backup fails. Second, when the script fails, someone has to fix it. You might be a wizzo Unix scripter. Unfortunately, after you take that DBA job on the international space station (NASA, I volunteer!), there is no guarantee that the person following behind you will be an equally gifted Unix scripter. That poor person is going to be sitting there looking at your marvelous code and cussing you up one side and down the other. His or her boss isn't going to be happy, and, most important, the database will be at risk. Of course, the other possibility is that you will be the one having to debug the "code from hell" since it was your predecessor, the shell scripter from nether regions, who went to work on the space station. Therein lies one big plus for RMAN—it is supported by Oracle. So, you can go to Oracle with your RMAN woes.

Of course, there are a number of other positives to using RMAN, including these:

- RMAN will detect corrupted blocks and report them to you.

- RMAN can back up your database online without having to put the tablespaces in hot backup mode. Thus, the additional (sometimes quite significant) redo generated during a hot backup is reduced.

- RMAN will automatically track new datafiles and tablespaces for you, which means you no longer have to add new tablespaces or datafiles to scripts.

- RMAN will only back up used data blocks (up to the high water mark (HWM)). Thus, RMAN backup images typically are smaller than those of online backup scripts.

- RMAN provides easy, automated backup, restore, and recovery operations. RMAN tracks all the backups needed to recover the database that you will require in the event that a restore will be required, and will restore only those objects that are needed.

- RMAN can work fairly seamlessly with third-party media management products.

- RMAN supports incremental backup strategies.

- With RMAN, you can actually test your backups without restoring them. Try that with your backup scripts!

- If you use the repository, then RMAN provides a nice, centralized reporting facility.

RMAN Compatibility Issues

Before you haul off and start doing backups, you need to consider some compatibility issues. Your enterprise probably has differing versions of Oracle running, and you need to consider RMAN compatibility issues as you plan your backup strategy. Not all databases are compatible with all RMAN versions, and when you add in the recovery catalog to the mix, things get even dicier. The following are some general rules to keep in mind:

- Any version of the Oracle database that is version 8 or later can be the host for a recovery catalog. As a result, an Oracle 8.0 database can host a recovery catalog for Oracle 8.0.x, 8.1.x (8i), 9.0.x (9i), or 9.2.x (9iR2).

- If you are using a recovery catalog, it must have been created with a version of the RMAN executable at the same or higher version number.

- If you are running RMAN version 8i, 9i, or 9iR2, then you cannot create a recovery catalog in an Oracle 8.0 database.

- Do not use an RMAN 8.0 executable with a recovery catalog schema created by an RMAN version that is version 8i or later.

- In general, you should try to use the RMAN executable that is at the same version as your database. There are some cases where a given database version can use a different RMAN executable version.

Table 9-1 lists the versions that allow exceptions to the preceding rules.
Note that there is a case with 8.1.6 and 8.1.7 in which use of RMAN version 8.0.6.1 is supported. In this event, if the recovery catalog you are using was created

Database Version	Allowed RMAN Executable Versions	Database Version and Catalog Schema Version
8.1.6	8.0.6.1	Oracle 8.x database (or later) and a catalog schema created by RMAN version 8.0.6
8.1.6	8.0.6.1	Oracle 8.1.x (or later) database, with a catalog schema created by RMAN version 8.1.6 (or later)
8.1.6	8.1.5	Oracle 8.1.x (or later) database, with a catalog schema created by an RMAN version that is equivalent to or greater than the RMAN version being used to back up the database
8.1.6	8.1.6	Oracle 8.1.x (or later) database, with a catalog schema created by an RMAN version that is equivalent to or greater than the RMAN version being used to back up the database
8.1.7	8.0.6.1	Oracle 8.x (or later) database, with a catalog schema created by RMAN version 8.0.6
8.1.7	8.0.6.1	Oracle 8.1.x (or later) database, with a catalog schema created by an RMAN version that is equivalent to or greater than the RMAN version being used to back up the database
8.1.7	8.1.x	Oracle 8.1.x (or later) catalog database, with a catalog schema created by an RMAN version that is equivalent to or greater than the RMAN version being used to back up the database
9.0.1	9.0.1	Oracle 8.1.x (or later) catalog database, with a catalog schema created by an RMAN version that is equivalent to or greater than the RMAN version being used to back up the database
9.2	9.0.3	Oracle 8.1.x (or later) catalog database, with a catalog schema created by an RMAN version that is equivalent to or greater than the RMAN version being used to back up the database

TABLE 9-1. *RMAN Compatibility Matrix*

by an 8i or later version of RMAN, you need to make one update to the recovery catalog before you can use it with RMAN version 8.0.6.1. You need to issue the following SQL statement, logged in as your catalog schema owner:

```
UPDATE CONFIG SET VALUE='080004' WHERE NAME='COMPATIBLE';
```

Finally, if you are faced with having to create more than one recovery catalog, there is no reason that all recovery catalogs cannot be maintained in the same database, as long as the database is version 8i or later. This still makes for a single recovery catalog database, which facilitates easy enterprise-wide reporting from that database.

Offline RMAN Database Backups

Okay, so you think this RMAN thing sounds good, and the first few chapters were sure interesting. Time to really put the beast to work! The first backup topic we will discuss is performing offline (or cold) backups of the Oracle database. An offline RMAN backup is taken with the database mounted, but not open (obviously). If you have set up your default configuration settings for RMAN (as we discussed in Chapter 3), then an offline RMAN backup is fairly straightforward.

Offline Backups Using Default Settings

To do an offline backup, first you sign in to RMAN (in the example we provide for this backup, we are not using a recovery catalog). Next, you use the RMAN commands **shutdown** and **startup mount** to mount the database, which is the condition that the database must be in to perform an offline backup. Once the database has been mounted, simply issue a **backup database** command and the backup will occur. Here is an example of the commands you would issue to perform an offline backup via RMAN :

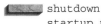

```
shutdown
startup mount
backup database;
startup
```

RMAN Workshop: *Do an Offline Backup*

Workshop Notes

This workshop assumes that your database has been configured with automatic channels as shown in Chapter 3. It also assumes that you have configured a database account called backup_admin for backups (as described in Chapter 3). It also assumes if you are using the MML layer, that it has been configured.

Step 1.   Start up RMAN

```
C:\>rman target=backup_admin/robert
```

Step 2.   Shut down the database with the **shutdown immediate** command.

```
RMAN> shutdown immediate
```

Step 3.   Mount the database with the **startup mount** command.

```
RMAN> startup mount
```

Step 4.   Now, back up the database with the **backup database** command.

```
RMAN> backup database;
```

Step 4.   Use the **alter database open** command to open the database.

```
RMAN> alter database open;
```

Here is an example of a complete offline RMAN backup following these steps:

```
C:\>rman target=acct_back/robert
Recovery Manager: Release 9.2.0.1.0 - Production
Copyright (c) 1995, 2002, Oracle Corporation.  All rights reserved.
connected to target database: ROBT (DBID=3395799962)
RMAN> shutdown immediate
using target database controlfile instead of recovery catalog
database closed
database dismounted
Oracle instance shut down
RMAN> startup mount
connected to target database (not started)
Oracle instance started
database mounted
<some database startup output was removed here to save space>
RMAN> backup database;
Starting backup at 13-JUN-02
using target database controlfile instead of recovery catalog
allocated channel: ORA_DISK_1
channel ORA_DISK_1: sid=10 devtype=DISK
allocated channel: ORA_DISK_2
channel ORA_DISK_2: sid=13 devtype=DISK
channel ORA_DISK_1: starting full datafile backupset
channel ORA_DISK_1: specifying datafile(s) in backupset
input datafile fno=00001 name=D:\ORACLE\ORADATA\ROBT\SYSTEM01.DBF
input datafile fno=00005 name=D:\ORACLE\ORADATA\ROBT\USERS01.DBF
input datafile fno=00004 name=D:\ORACLE\ORADATA\ROBT\TOOLS01.DBF
input datafile fno=00003 name=D:\ORACLE\ORADATA\ROBT\INDX01.DBF
input datafile fno=00002
name=D:\ORACLE\ORADATA\ROBT\ROBT_TEST_RECOVER_02.DBF
channel ORA_DISK_1: starting piece 1 at 13-JUN-02
channel ORA_DISK_2: starting full datafile backupset
channel ORA_DISK_2: specifying datafile(s) in backupset
input datafile fno=00010 name=D:\ORACLE\ORADATA\ROBT\ROBT_RBS_01.DBF
input datafile fno=00011
name=D:\ORACLE\ORADATA\ROBT\ROBT_TEST_TBS_01.DBF
input datafile fno=00007
name=D:\ORACLE\ORADATA\ROBT\ROBT_TEST_RECOVER_01.DBF
```

```
input datafile fno=00006
name=D:\ORACLE\ORADATA\ROBT\ROBT_TEST_RECOVER_03.DBF
channel ORA_DISK_2: starting piece 1 at 13-JUN-02
channel ORA_DISK_1: finished piece 1 at 13-JUN-02
piece handle=D:\BACKUP\ROBT\BACKUP_0RDQU150_1_1 comment=NONE
channel ORA_DISK_1: backup set complete, elapsed time: 00:07:13
channel ORA_DISK_2: finished piece 1 at 13-JUN-02
piece handle=D:\BACKUP\ROBT\BACKUP_0SDQU153_1_1 comment=NONE
channel ORA_DISK_2: backup set complete, elapsed time: 00:07:11
Finished backup at 13-JUN-02
Starting Control File Autobackup at 13-JUN-02
piece handle=D:\BACKUP\ROBT_C-3395799962-20020613-00 comment=NONE
Finished Control File Autobackup at 13-JUN-02
RMAN> alter database open;
```

Note that in the preceding example and the RMAN Workshop, that there are really very few commands. Since we have already defined default configuration settings (refer to Chapter 3), RMAN automatically uses the default settings. We really didn't have to do anything but issue the **shutdown** and **startup mount** commands to the database, issue the **backup database** command, and then sit back and watch. Pretty easy, huh? RMAN has backed up our database datafiles, our control file, and our server parameter file (assuming we have configured it to do so). Once it's done, all we need to do is issue the **alter database open** command, and our backup is complete.

In this example, Oracle created two backup sets, each of which contains a single backup piece. As you can see from the output, these backup pieces will be created in the D:\BACKUP\ROBT directory:

```
piece handle=D:\BACKUP\ROBT\BACKUP_0RDQU150_1_1 comment=NONE
```

NOTE
If you are not using an Oracle Server Parameter File (spfile), then you cannot back up your database text-based init.ora parameter file with RMAN.

Finally, we might have opted to connect to the recovery catalog when we did this backup (and this applies to all backups that we will do in this chapter). To connect to the recovery catalog, all you need to do is start RMAN slightly differently at the command line:

```
C:\>set oracle_sid=recover
C:\>rman target=sys/robert catalog=rcat_owner/password@robt
```

One interesting thing to note here is that when we connected to our recovery catalog owner, we did so using Oracle NET because we had our ORACLE_SID set to the SID of our database rather than the recovery catalog. When you do a backup with a recovery catalog, you need to use a service name and Oracle Net to connect either to the database you are backing up or to the catalog. We generally recommend using the networking connection to connect to the catalog.

One other thing to note quickly is that if we had not configured automated backups of our control file, RMAN would still back up the control file as long as we were backing up datafile 1. The control file would be backed up into the backup set that contains datafile 1. You would also want to do a separate control file backup after your database backup was complete, so you would have the most current control file backed up (as the control file backed up with the backup set will not have the complete information on the current backup in it). Note that this control file, if it must be recovered, is a bit more complicated to recover than if you have configured control file autobackups. Because of this we strongly suggest that you configure control file autobackups on your system.

Offline Backups Without Using Configured Defaults

What if we had not configured default settings (see Chapter 3)? Or what if the defaults were not what we wanted to use (maybe we want to back up to disk this time instead of using a configured default tape device)? In this case, we have a few more things that we need to do. Let's look at an example of such a backup and determine what it is doing:

```
shutdown
startup mount
run
{
allocate channel c1 device type disk format 'd:\backup\robt\robt_%U';
allocate channel c2 device type disk format 'd:\backup\robt\robt_%U';
backup database;
backup current controlfile;
}
```

In the Beginning, Shut Down and Mount the Database
This example looks a bit more complicated than the earlier example. First, we have the **shutdown** and **startup mount** commands that we had in the previous example. Then, we have a **run** block, which is a set of one or more statements contained within the confines of braces that are executed together as a block. Oracle will not run any of the statements until the entire block of statements has been entered. Once all the statements have been entered, the **run** block is completed with the closing brace. Once the closing brace has been put in place (followed, of course, by the ENTER key), the **run** block is compiled and executed.

NOTE
*This book was written using Oracle9i Release 2. In this release of RMAN (9i, in general), many commands that previously had to run within the confines of a **run** block no longer need to. We deliberately do not use **run** blocks unless required by this release. Many of the backup and restore/ recover commands you will see in this and the next chapter will work in previous versions but will need to be run in the confines of a **run** block.*

Allocate Channels

In the preceding code example, we have several different RMAN commands within the confines of the **run** block. First, the **allocate channel** commands allocate a channel each to RMAN for the database backup. We have discussed channels already (Chapter 3, for example), but let's look into their use a bit more for a moment.

First, a word on backup sets and backup set pieces. Each time we create a channel, this implies that we are going to create one or more backups sets. There are some exceptions to this statement, but generally this is true, so for the sake of this discussion, assume this is a true statement. Let's quickly define some terms:

- **Backup sets**   Logical entities, one or more of which will be created for each channel you define (generally, it's one backup set per channel).

- **Backup pieces**   The actual physical files that the backed up data resides in. One or more backup pieces may be associated with each backup set.

You can control the overall backup set size with the **backup** command (or, alternatively, you can configure a default value for it), or you can control the overall backup piece size with the **allocate channel** command (again, this can be configured when you configure default channels). We will discuss limiting backup set sizes a bit more later in this chapter.

The **allocate channel** command defines to which device a given channel (and thus, an individual backup set) is to be allocated. This device might be a disk (type disk) or a tape drive (type sbt). If we were allocating a channel to a tape system, we might also include certain parameter settings required by the MML vendor that we are using. An example of an **allocate channel** command to tape using an MML vendor, VERITAS Netbackup (Chapter 5), might look like this:

```
allocate channel t1 type sbt parms='ENV=(NB_ORA_CLASS=RMAN_db01)';
```

This particular channel is being allocated to a tape device (refer to Chapters 4 through 8 for more on allocating RMAN channels to MML devices). Having allocated two channels to the backup, RMAN will automatically try to parallelize the backup stream among those channels. Thus, since we have allocated two channels, two different backup sets will be created and each backup set will have one backup piece. The size is defined in bytes, but you can use the *k*, *m*, or *g* place holders to indicate kilobytes, megabytes, or gigabytes, respectively, as required. Here is another example of the **allocate channel** command:

```
allocate channel t1 type disk maxpiecesize=100m;
```

In this example, we have limited the maximum size of each individual piece of a backup set (remember that each channel will create a single backup set) created through that channel to 100MB. This is a great way to ensure that you do not create an individual backup piece that is larger than your tape or file system will handle. Here is another example that we want to look at quickly:

```
allocate channel t1 type disk maxpiecesize=100m format='d:\backup\robt\robt_%U.bak'
```

In this example, we have used the **format** parameter to define where the backup pieces will be put on the disk and what the naming convention will be for the backup pieces. Note the %U format placeholder. In this case, %U (which is the default value used by RMAN) will be replaced by a set of characters that will make the backup piece name unique. The resulting name will include the database name (robt) followed by an underscore and then an eight-character mnemonic that consists of the following:

- The backup set identifier. Each backup set is assigned a unique identifying number by RMAN when it is created.

- The time the backup set piece was created.

Following the eight-character mnemonic will be an underscore, followed by the backup set piece number. The backup set piece number uniquely identifies each piece of the backup set, therefore this number is unique to that backup set. Finally, another underscore will be followed by the copy number of the backup set piece. Each multiplexed backup set piece copy has it's own unique number assigned to it. If you are not multiplexing, the copy number will be the number 1.

An example of the resulting backup set piece names might look like this:

```
recover_16E112V9_1_1
```

Note in this filename that the time component of the 8-character mnemonic is not readily discernable, but that's not really a problem. The important thing about the use of the %U placeholder is that it guarantees that the name of each backup set piece is unique. Of course, several different mnemonics are available for use with the **format** command, but generally %U will suffice. We added the instance name to the name and the extension just out of habit and good practice. Finally, there are a number of other options with the **allocate channel** command. Check out Appendix A for the entire syntax of the **allocate channel** command.

NOTE
You might have noticed we are using SBT instead of SBT_TAPE. Oracle9i has changed SBT_TAPE to just SBT, but SBT_TAPE is still usable for backward compatibility.

Backup Is the Name of the Game

Moving on now with our example code, after we have allocated the channels, it's time to back up the database with the **backup** command (using the **database** option). The sum result of the **backup database** command is that RMAN will proceed to use the two channels we created and back up the database. The command is a bit different than the **backup database** command we issued earlier, as this **backup database** command is issued within the confines of a **run** command block. We had to perform this backup using a **run** block because we manually allocated the channels with the **allocate channel** command.

The **backup** command also takes care of the control file and server parameter file (spfile) for us if datafile 1 is getting backed up (which it always will during an offline backup or any full backup, which is the default). Where this control file backup is stored depends on the setting of the **controlfile autobackup** parameter. If the **controlfile autobackup** parameter is set to off, then the control file is included in the database backup set along with the server parameter file (if an spfile is being used). If the **controlfile autobackup** parameter is set to on, then the control file and spfile backup will be made to a separate control file backup piece. You can force RMAN to put the control file in the database backup set by including the **include current controlfile** clause in the **backup database** command (assuming you are not backing up datafile 1). Better yet, as we have done in our example, a separate backup of the control file is a good idea to ensure that you have a control file backup that is current, including the most recent database backup.

NOTE
RMAN will only back up a server parameter file (spfile). It will not back up text-based init.ora files.

The **backup database** command comes with a number of different options (and is in fact a subset of the larger **backup** command). Let's look at the use of some of the options of the **backup** command.

Backup Command Options

Now that we have introduced you to the **backup** command, let's look at the number of different options you can use with it. These **backup** command options can be used with many of the various **backup** command flavors, such as **backup database** (which we have just covered), **backup tablespace**, **backup datafile**, and other backup options, which we will cover later in this chapter. There are a number of different options available for use with the **backup** command that allow you to do such things as provide a naming format for individual backup pieces, or limit the size of those backup pieces. The **backup** command even allows you to manually decide which channels will be used to back up what, should you wish to override the choices that RMAN makes otherwise. So, let's look at some of the options that you can use with the **backup** command.

Tags

Each backup in Oracle can be assigned a tag. This applies to full backups, tablespace backups, datafile backups, incremental backups, and even backup copies (all of which will be discussed in this chapter). Here is an example of assigning a tag to a full backup:

```
backup database tag='test backup';
```

In this example, note we used the **tag** parameter to identify this backup. Each tag should be unique, and RMAN will allocate a tag to each backup set using a default naming convention if one is not assigned. The same tag can be applied to multiple backups, and the latest backup will be restored by default.

Limiting the Size of a Backup Set

The following example builds on our previous example by adding a new parameter, **maxsetsize**:

```
backup database maxsetsize=50m tag='test backup';
```

Using this parameter we have limited the maximum size of the backup set to 50MB. This is handy if your tape has a size limit or if your disks can only handle datafiles that are a certain size. Oracle will split the backup into multiple backup sets, each no larger than the **maxsetsize** parameter that you defined.

The **maxsetsize** parameter can also lead to a problem in that it limits the overall size of an individual backup set. Thus, if you have a datafile in your backup set that is larger than the defined limit, the backup will fail, as shown in the next example (some output has been removed for brevity).

```
RMAN> set maxcorrupt for datafile 1 to 10;
RMAN> run
2> {
3> allocate channel c1 device type disk format 'd:\backup\robt\robt_%U';
4> allocate channel c2 device type disk format 'd:\backup\robt\robt_%U';
5> backup maxsetsize=50m tag='test backup' database;
6> }
allocated channel: c1
allocated channel: c2
Starting backup at 13-JUN-02
RMAN-00571: ===========================================================
RMAN-00569: =============== ERROR MESSAGE STACK FOLLOWS ===============
RMAN-00571: ===========================================================
RMAN-03002: failure of backup command at 06/13/2002 22:07:47
RMAN-06183: datafile or datafilecopy larger than SETSIZE: file# 1
D:\ORACLE\ORADATA\ROBT\SYSTEM01.DBF
```

So, be careful using this restriction and see whether you instead can use the **maxpiecesize** parameter of the **allocate channel** command.

Also, you can use the **configure** command to create default limits on the size of backup sets and limits on the backup piece size, if that is your preference. Refer to Chapter 3 for more information on this command.

Modifying the Retention Policy for a Backup Set

In the next example, two backup statements are using the **keep** parameter to override the default retention policy (refer to Chapter 3 for more on using the **configure** command to set a default retention policy):

```
backup database keep forever;
backup database keep until time='sysdate+180';
```

In the first example, we will keep the backup set forever. In the second example, we will keep the backup for only 180 days after the day it was taken. As we mentioned in Chapter 3, beware of retention because it is no guarantee that the physical files of your backup will actually be protected. Also, if you back up to disk, somebody can easily go out and physically remove the backup pieces.

Overriding the configure exclude Command

You can configure RMAN to exclude in your backups datafiles that have not changed since the last backup, by issuing the **configure exclude** command (which is discussed in Chapter 3). If you want to ensure that RMAN backs up these datafiles, you can include the **noexclude** parameter in the **backup** command as follows:

```
backup database noexclude keep forever tag='test backup';
```

Checking the Database for Errors with the backup Command

Another handy RMAN feature is the ability to use RMAN to actually scan the database for physical and logical errors without actually doing a backup. This is facilitated through the use of the **validate** parameter of the **backup** command. Here is an example of the use of this option:

```
backup validate database;
```

NOTE
*Even though some of the text generated during an RMAN **validate** run will make it look like a backup set is being created, this is not the case. No RMAN backup file pieces will be generated during the **validate** run.*

Skipping Offline, Inaccessible, or Read-Only Datafiles

Sometimes, you will have a datafile in your database that has a status other than ONLINE. In the case of read-only datafiles, you may not want to back them up every time you do a backup of the database. In the case of offline or inaccessible datafiles, RMAN backups will fail if you don't do something to indicate to RMAN to just skip the missing datafiles. This is what the **skip** parameter is used for. You can skip offline, read-only, or inaccessible datafiles (or all three) as required. Here are some examples of how to do this:

```
backup database skip readonly;
backup database skip offline;
backup database skip inaccessible;
backup database skip readonly skip offline skip inaccessible;
```

The **inaccessible** parameter causes Oracle to skip files that cannot be read at all. These files are not physically on the disk (for example, if the datafiles have been deleted from the disk or moved to another location). Data files that are offline but physically still in place are skipped using the **offline** parameter. Finally, the **skip readonly** parameter is used to cause Oracle to skip backing up a read-only datafile. Of course, you can use the **configure** command to indicate that Oracle should not back up read-only tablespaces at all, which leads us to our next section.

Forcing a Backup of Read-Only Datafiles

In the preceding section, we showed you how to cause a backup to skip read-only datafiles, but this can be a bit tedious. Oracle offers backup optimization to make life a bit easier. We talked about backup optimization in Chapter 3 in association with the **configure** command. Backup optimization will cause RMAN to not back up unchanged tablespaces (for example, read-only tablespaces) by default. If you want a specific backup to be forced to ignore that configuration setting, you can use the **force** parameter to ensure that all datafiles are backed up. Here is an example:

```
backup database force;
```

Backing Up Datafiles
Based on Their Last Backup Time

Oracle allows you to indicate in your backup process, if you prefer, to only back up database datafiles that have not been backed up since a given time. This is handy if you have added new datafiles (as we discuss first in this section) or if you only want to back up datafiles that have changed in a given number of days. Let's look at each of these choices in a bit more detail.

Backing Up Only Newly Added Datafiles

Here is a neat option you can use. Suppose you have just added four or five new datafiles to the database and you want to back them up without having to back up the entire database. Well, you could just back up the individual datafiles (as we will show you later in this chapter), but there is an easier way. You can use the **not backed up** option of the **backup** command, and RMAN will only back up datafiles that have not been backed up. Here is an example:

```
backup database not backed up;
```

Backing Up Files Not Backed Up in a Specific Time Period

So, perhaps you have a backup strategy in which you back up only specific datafiles on specific nights. The **since time** option is also really handy if you need to restart a failed backup. If the backup fails, you can use this option, after you have corrected the cause of the failure, to restart the backup. For example, let's assume that your tape system died two days ago in the middle of a backup. You finally got the tape system fixed, so how would you restart the backup? Simply issue this command:

```
backup database not backed up since time='sysdate - 2';
```

In this case, RMAN will only back up those datafiles that have not been backed up within the last two days. Note that you can express the time in the format of the databases NLS_DATE format, or you can use a SQL date expression such as the one in our example. An additional parameter to the **since time** option applies to archive log backups to ensure that each archive log is backed up a certain number of times before it is removed. We will cover that option later in this chapter.

Checking for Logical Corruption During a Backup

By default, RMAN checks for physical corruption of database blocks. If any corruption is discovered, the backup will fail, by default. If you want even more error checking, you can configure a backup to check for logical corruption using the **check logical** option of the **backup** command. Here are a couple of examples of the use of this option:

```
backup check logical database;
backup validate check logical database;
```

The first example will physically back up the database as it is checking for logical corruption. The second example just validates the database blocks performing a logical database verification without performing an actual physical backup of the database. Note that if you wish the backup to continue through a given number of errors, you need to set the **maxcorrupt** parameter first. This requires using a **run** block, as shown in this example:

```
run {
set maxcorrupt for datafile 1,2,3,4,5,6,7 to 10;
backup validate check logical database;
}
```

Making Copies of Backups on Our RMAN Copier

Perhaps you wish to create multiple copies of the backup pieces of a backup set. While this can be configured by default, you can also use the **copies** parameter to configure a specific backup to create multiple copies of the backup pieces. (You could also use the **set backup copies** parameter.) Here is an example of this option in use:

```
backup database copies=2;
```

Perhaps you have configured different default channels, one to disk and one to tape. You can use the **device type** parameter to define which automatic channel device you wish to use when the backup begins. Here is an example:

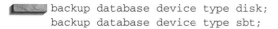
```
backup database device type disk;
backup database device type sbt;
```

Capturing the Elusive Control File

The **include current controlfile** option creates a snapshot of the current control file and places it into each backup set produced by the **backup** command. Here is an example of the use of this command:

```
backup database device type disk include current controlfile;
```

By default, if you do a backup of datafile 1, the control file will get backed up anyway. So this parameter comes in much more handy if you are doing tablespace or datafile backups. Also, if automated backups of control files is configured, then this command can cause the current control file to be stored in the backup set also (so you have two copies of the control file, though they might be slightly different if you are running in ARCHIVELOG mode).

Introducing the set Command

Well, we are done with offline backups. We have covered a great deal of material. Before we move on to discuss online backups—and now that you have some idea of how RMAN commands work when backing up—we should take a quick detour and look at the RMAN **set** command.

The **set** command is used to define settings that only apply to the current RMAN session. In other words, the **set** command is a lot like the **configure** command (refer to Chapter 3), but the settings are not persistent. You can use the **set** command one of two ways, depending on the **set** command you need to use. You can use it outside a **run** block for these operations:

- To display RMAN commands in the message log, use the **set echo** command.

- To specify a database's database identifier (DBID), use the **set DBID** command.

Certain **set** commands can only be used within the confines of a **run** block. The most common are

- The **set newname** command is useful if you are performing TSPITR or database duplication. The **set newname** command **allows you to specify new database datafile names. This is useful if you are moving the database to a new system and the file system names are different. You need to use the switch** command in combination with the **set newname** command. You will see examples of this in later chapters.

- Using the **set maxcorrupt for datafile** command enables you to define a maximum number of data block corruptions allowed before the RMAN operation will fail.

- Using the **set archivelog destination** command allows you to modify the archive_log_dest_1 destination for archived redo logs.

- Using **set** with the **until** clause of the **set** command enables you to define a specific point in time, an SCN, or a log sequence number, to be used during database point-in-time recovery.

- Using the **set backup copies** command enables you to define how many copies of the backup files should be created for each backup piece in the backup set.

- Using the **set command id** setting enables you to associate a given server session to a given channel.

- Using the **set controlfile autobackup format for device type** command enables you to modify the default format for control file autobackups.

When doing backups, you may well need to use some of these commands. For example, if you wish to do a backup that creates two copies of each backup piece that is created, and you want to allow for ten corruptions in datafile 3, you would craft a backup script that looks like this:

```
run
{
set maxcorrupt for datafile 3 to 10;
set backup copies = 2;
backup database;
}
```

Online RMAN Database Backups

We have spent the first half of this chapter on offline backups and the **set** command. If you are interested in online backups, then this section (and the following one) is for you. Still, don't skip the previous sections, because they present a great deal of foundational information that won't be repeated here. If you are jumping into the chapter at this point, first go back and read the previous sections. If you have read the first half of the chapter already and you find that you are a bit punchy, then take a short break before you forge on.

In this section, we first discuss several different kinds of online backups: backups of the entire database, tablespace backups, and datafile backups. We then look at archive log file backups and, finally, backups of the control file and parameter files.

Online Database Backups

As described in Chapters 1 and 3 in detail, to perform online backups with RMAN, our database must be in ARCHIVELOG mode. If your database is not in ARCHIVELOG mode, RMAN will generate an error if you try to perform an online backup. So, having ensured that we are in ARCHIVELOG mode, we are ready to do our first RMAN online backup.

NOTE
*From this point on in this chapter, we assume that you have configured default channels (refer to Chapter 3), unless we need to point out something specifically. This saves you typing and allows us to leave out commands such as **allocate channel**, giving us more space to give you important information.*

You will find that online backups are not all that different from offline backups. In fact, they are a bit simpler because you don't have to mess with shutting down and then mounting the database. When you have your defaults configured (refer to Chapter 3), then an online backup is as simple as this:

```
backup database plus archivelog;
```

This command does it all. First, the process does a log switch (using the **alter system archivelog current** command). Next, it backs up any existing archived redo logs. Then, the actual database backup occurs. At this point, another log switch occurs (using the **alter system archivelog current** command), and RMAN backs up the remaining archived redo logs (using the **backup archivelog all** command). Finally, the autobackup of the control file and spfile occurs. Because a full database backup will always include datafile 1, which belongs to the SYSTEM tablespace, there will always be a backup of the control file and spfile.

RMAN Workshop: *Do an Online Backup*

Workshop Notes
This workshop assumes that your database has been configured with automatic channels as shown in Chapter 3. It also assumes that you have configured a database account called backup_admin for backups (as described in Chapter 3).

It also assumes that if you are using the MML layer, it has been configured. Finally, your database must be configured for and operating in ARCHIVELOG mode.

Step 1. Start up RMAN.

```
C:\>rman target=backup_admin/robert
```

Step 2. Start the backup.

```
RMAN> backup database plus archivelog;
```

Here is an example of a complete offline RMAN backup following these steps:

```
C:\>rman target=backup_admin/robert
RMAN> backup database plus archivelog;
Starting backup at 15-JUN-02
current log archived
using target database controlfile instead of recovery catalog
configuration for DISK channel 3 is ignored
allocated channel: ORA_DISK_1
channel ORA_DISK_1: sid=13 devtype=DISK
channel ORA_DISK_1: starting archive log backupset
channel ORA_DISK_1: specifying archive log(s) in backup set
input archive log thread=1 sequence=351 recid=13 stamp=464457020
channel ORA_DISK_1: starting piece 1 at 15-JUN-02
input archive log thread=1 sequence=352 recid=14 stamp=464609012
input archive log thread=1 sequence=353 recid=15 stamp=464609115
channel ORA_DISK_1: finished piece 1 at 15-JUN-02
piece handle=D:\BACKUP\ROBT\BACKUP_20DR2QJ8_1_1 comment=NONE
channel ORA_DISK_1: backup set complete, elapsed time: 00:00:11
channel ORA_DISK_1: starting archive log backupset
channel ORA_DISK_1: specifying archive log(s) in backup set
input archive log thread=1 sequence=357 recid=19 stamp=464610450
input archive log thread=1 sequence=358 recid=20 stamp=464611007
input archive log thread=1 sequence=359 recid=21 stamp=464611921
channel ORA_DISK_1: starting piece 1 at 15-JUN-02
channel ORA_DISK_1: finished piece 1 at 15-JUN-02
piece handle=D:\BACKUP\ROBT\BACKUP_22DR2QJK_1_1 comment=NONE
channel ORA_DISK_1: backup set complete, elapsed time: 00:00:03
Finished backup at 15-JUN-02
Starting backup at 15-JUN-02
using channel ORA_DISK_1
channel ORA_DISK_1: starting full datafile backupset
input datafile fno=00001 name=D:\ORACLE\ORADATA\ROBT\SYSTEM01.DBF
input datafile fno=00005 name=D:\ORACLE\ORADATA\ROBT\USERS01.DBF
input datafile fno=00004 name=D:\ORACLE\ORADATA\ROBT\TOOLS01.DBF
```

```
input datafile fno=00003 name=D:\ORACLE\ORADATA\ROBT\INDX01.DBF
input datafile fno=00002
name=D:\ORACLE\ORADATA\ROBT\ROBT_TEST_RECOVER_02.DBF
input datafile fno=00010 name=D:\ORACLE\ORADATA\ROBT\ROBT_RBS_01.DBF
input datafile fno=00011 name=D:\ORACLE\ORADATA\ROBT\ROBT_TEST_TBS_01.DBF
input datafile fno=00007
name=D:\ORACLE\ORADATA\ROBT\ROBT_TEST_RECOVER_01.DBF
input datafile fno=00006
name=D:\ORACLE\ORADATA\ROBT\ROBT_TEST_RECOVER_03.DBF
channel ORA_DISK_1: starting piece 1 at 15-JUN-02
channel ORA_DISK_1: finished piece 1 at 15-JUN-02
piece handle=D:\BACKUP\ROBT\BACKUP_23DR2QJU_1_1 comment=NONE
channel ORA_DISK_1: backup set complete, elapsed time: 00:04:56
Finished backup at 15-JUN-02
Starting backup at 15-JUN-02
current log archived
using channel ORA_DISK_1
channel ORA_DISK_1: starting archive log backupset
channel ORA_DISK_1: specifying archive log(s) in backup set
input archive log thread=1 sequence=360 recid=22 stamp=464612416
channel ORA_DISK_1: starting piece 1 at 15-JUN-02
channel ORA_DISK_1: finished piece 1 at 15-JUN-02
piece handle=D:\BACKUP\ROBT\BACKUP_25DR2R2K_1_1 comment=NONE
channel ORA_DISK_1: backup set complete, elapsed time: 00:00:04
Finished backup at 15-JUN-02
Starting Control File and spfile Autobackup at 15-JUN-02
piece handle=D:\BACKUP\ROBT_C-3395799962-20020615-02 comment=NONE
Finished Control File and spfile Autobackup at 15-JUN-02
```

We have now completed an entire online database backup! Next, we will look at tablespace backups.

NOTE
A full database backup should be contrasted against an incremental backup (as we will discuss later in this chapter) in that a full database backup cannot be used as a base for application of incremental backups.

Tablespace Backups

Occasionally, you will wish to do tablespace-level backups instead of backups of the entire database. This might be before you drop a partition that is specific to that tablespace, or perhaps just after you have made the tablespace read-only. To do a

Important!

When you first try a hot backup with RMAN, you might run into a problem with RMAN reporting that it is missing archived redo logs that are required for recovery. This often occurs if your database has been switched in and out of ARCHIVELOG mode and you removed old archived redo logs that belonged to the database when it was previously in ARCHIVELOG mode. In this event, you might get an RMAN error message like the following when trying to do an online backup of the database:

```
RMAN> backup database plus archivelog;
Starting backup at 15-JUN-02
RMAN-00571: ===========================================================
RMAN-00569: =============== ERROR MESSAGE STACK FOLLOWS ===============
RMAN-00571: ===========================================================
RMAN-03002: failure of backup command at 06/15/2002 10:05:46
RMAN-06059: expected archived log not found, lost of archived log compromises
recoverability
ORA-19625: error identifying file D:\ORACLE\ADMIN\ROBT\ARCH\ROBT_201.ARC
O/S-Error: (OS 2) The system cannot find the file specified.
```

This error indicates that RMAN is looking for some archived redo logs that no longer exist. These archived redo logs likely were generated when the database was previously in ARCHIVELOG mode. Oracle gets confused in this event and thinks that the archived redo logs need to be backed up, when they really don't. To correct this problem, so we can do a backup, we need to issue the command **crosscheck archivelog all**. The result of this command is that Oracle will check for the existence of the archived redo logs stored in the control file, against those actually stored on disk. During the crosscheck operation, Oracle will assume that any archived redo log that is missing is lost and will not try to back it up.

tablespace-level backup, we simply use the **backup** command with the **tablespace** parameter:

```
backup tablespace users;
```

If we want to back up any archived redo logs at the same time, we would issue the command like this:

```
backup tablespace users plus archivelog;
```

Or perhaps we want to also make sure our current control file is backed up:

```
backup tablespace users include current controlfile plus archivelog;
```

Of course, you are not really backing up a tablespace, but rather the datafiles associated with that tablespace. Oracle just converts the tablespace name into a list of datafiles that are associated with that tablespace. Normally, a control file backup will not occur during these backups unless you have configured automatic control file backups (refer to Chapter 3) to occur (and you are not backing up datafile 1). Of course, if you use the **include current controlfile** parameter, then the control file will be backed up.

NOTE
RMAN will not prevent you from doing a tablespace or datafile backup in NOARCHIVELOG mode (as long as the database is not open). However, these backups are not really all that usable when the database is in NOARCHIVELOG mode (unless you back up all the tablespaces and datafiles at the same time).

Datafile Backups

You might want to back up specific database datafiles of the database. Perhaps you are getting ready to move them to a new device and you wish to back them up before you move them. RMAN allows you to back up a datafile using the **backup** command with the **datafile** parameter followed by the filename or number of the datafiles you wish to back up. The following are examples of some datafile **backup** commands:

```
backup datafile 2;
backup datafile 'd:\oracle\oradata\robt\users01.dbf';
backup datafile 'd:\oracle\oradata\robt\users01.dbf' plus archivelog;
```

Again, the control file and the spfile will get backed up if datafile 1 is backed up or if automated control file backups are configured. In the last example, the archived redo logs will get backed up as well.

Archived Redo Log Backups

For a number of reasons, you might well want to back up your archived redo logs, but not back up the database. In this event, you use the **backup archivelog** command. To back up all of the archived redo logs, simply issue the command **backup archivelog all**. Optionally, you might want to back up a specific range of archived redo logs, for which you have several options available, including time, SCN, or redo log sequence number (or a selected range of those values). Here are some examples of backing up the archived redo logs:

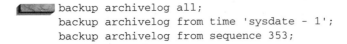

```
backup archivelog all;
backup archivelog from time 'sysdate - 1';
backup archivelog from sequence 353;
```

Once you have backed up archived redo logs, you may want to have RMAN remove them for you. The **delete input** option allows you to perform this operation. The **delete input** option can also be used with datafile copies (which we will discuss later in this chapter) or backup set copies. Here are a couple of examples of using the **delete input** parameter on an archived redo log backup:

```
backup archivelog all delete input;
backup archivelog from sequence 353 delete input;
```

You can also instruct RMAN to make redundant copies of your archived redo logs. In the following example, we use the **not backed up *n* times** parameter of the **backup** command to make sure that we have backed up our archived redo logs at least three times. Any archived redo logs that have already been backed up three times will not be backed up again.

```
backup archivelog not backed up 3 times;
```

Also, you can use the **until time** parameter with the **backup** command to ensure that a certain number of days' worth of archived redo logs remain on disk:

```
backup archivelog all delete input until time 'sysdate - 2';
```

NOTE
*Use of the **not backed up** parameter and use of the **delete input** parameter are somewhat mutually exclusive. The **delete input** parameter will remove the archived redo log regardless of how many times it has been backed up.*

Control File and Parameter File Backups

Just as with archived redo logs, sometimes you may just want to back up the control file or the server parameter files. RMAN provides specific commands for these functions as well. Use the **backup spfile** command to back up the server parameter file. This is handy if you have made a configuration change to the database, for example. To back up the control file, you can use the **current controlfile** parameter of the **backup** command to generate a copy of the current control file. The **current controlfile** parameter also comes with a **for standby** clause that will create a backup control file for use with a standby database.

You can use the **controlfilecopy** parameter of the **backup** command to create a backup set that contains an externally created backup of the control file. This control file backup might be the result of the **alter database backup controlfile to 'filename'** SQL command or the use of the RMAN **copy** command (covered later in this chapter) to create a control file backup. Also, you can back up a standby database control file that was created with the **alter database create standby controlfile** command. The benefit of this feature is that you can take external control file backup files and register them with RMAN and create a backup set that contains the control file backup in it. Here are some examples of the use of this parameter:

```
backup current controlfile;
sql "alter database backup controlfile to ''d:\backup\robt\contf_back.ctl''";
backup controlfilecopy 'd:\backup\robt\contf_back.ctl';
```

Backup Set Backups

Perhaps you like to back up to disk first, and then back up your backup sets to tape. RMAN supports this operation in Oracle9i through the use of the **backup** command. Here is an example. Suppose we issued a **backup database** command, and the entire backup set went to disk because that is our configured default device. Now we wish to move that backup set to tape. We could issue the **backup** command with the **backupset** parameter, and Oracle would back up all of our backup sets to the channel that is allocated for the backup.

You can choose to back up all backup sets with the **backup backupset** command, or you can choose to back up specific backup sets. Further, you can only back up from disk to disk, or disk to tape. There is no support for tape-to-tape or tape-to-disk backups. The **delete input** option, which we previously discussed in regard to archive log backups, is also available with backup set backups. When used, the **delete input** option will cause the files of the source backup set to get deleted after a successful backup. Here are some examples of this command:

```
backup backupset all;
backup backupset all
format='d:\backup\newbackups\backup_%U.bak'
tag='Backup of backupsets on 6/15'  channel 'ORA_DISK_1';
backup backupset completed before 'sysdate - 2';
backup backupset completed before 'sysdate - 2' delete input;
backup backupset completed after 'sysdate - 2' delete input;
```

An example of a backup strategy here might be to perform RMAN backups to disk, and then to back up the backup sets to tape with the **backup backupset** command. Perhaps you want to keep two days' worth of your backup sets on disk. You could then issue two commands. First, issue the **backup backupset completed before 'sysdate -2'** command to back up the last two days of backups. Then, to back up and then remove any backup sets older than two days, issue the **backup backupset completed after 'sysdate - 2' delete input** command, which would cause one final backup of the old backup sets and then remove them.

NOTE
Backup set backups are very handy if you want to back up your control file automated backups elsewhere, and still have the catalog track the location of the backup set.

Copies

Okay, all this new-fangled talk of backup sets and pieces is just blowing your mind. You ask, "Can't I just make a copy of these database datafiles?" Well, I'm here to make you feel better. With RMAN, you can just make copies of your different database structures, and that's what we are going to talk about in this chapter. First, we will review the upside, and downside, to creating copies instead of backup sets. Then, we will look at how we create datafile copies, control file copies, and archived redo log file copies.

Introducing Copies

RMAN can create an exact duplicate of your database datafiles, archived redo logs, or your control file. An RMAN copy is just that—it is simply a copy of the file with the name and/or location changed. No backup pieces or anything else to worry about. Copies can only be made to disk, and you cannot make incremental copies. The database must be either mounted or open to make copies. A history of the copies made is kept in the database control file, so you can track when copies have been made and where they reside.

The RMAN copy process provides some of the same protections as normal RMAN backup sets, such as checking for corrupted blocks and, optionally, logical corruption. One of the unfortunate shortcomings of the **copy** command is that you have to define specific objects that it will operate on. In other words, if I want to make copies of archived redo logs, I have to specify a different filename for each **copy** command. I cannot simply define a range of archived redo logs that I want to copy. As a result, the **copy** command can get a bit tedious if you need to copy a number of files. So, let's move on and look at how to use the **copy** command.

Datafile Copies

RMAN can be instructed to make datafile copies via the **copy** command. Note that this can be done with the database online or offline, as RMAN will ensure that the datafile copy is consistent. With the **copy** command, you can create copies of datafiles, or even copies of other datafile copies. The **copy** command with the **datafile** parameter is used to create the datafile copy. Here are some examples:

```
copy datafile 3 to 'd:\backup\datafilecopy\users01.dbf.bak';
copy datafile 'd:\oracle\oradata\users01.dbf' to 'd:\backup\datafilecopy\users01.dbf.bak';
```

You can also use the **copy** command with the **datafile copy** parameter to copy datafile copies elsewhere:

```
copy datafilecopy 'd:\backup\datafilecopy\users01.dbf.bak'
to 'd:\backup\robt\users01.dbf.bak';
```

You can also back up a datafile copy with the **backup** command using the **datafile copy** parameter. As with archived redo logs, you can also use the **delete input** parameter to remove the datafile copy if you wish. Here is an example of this operation:

```
Backup datafilecopy 'd:\backup\robt\users01.dbf.bak' delete input;
```

NOTE
A datafile copy can be made with the database mounted or, if the database is in ARCHIVELOG mode, with the database open.

Control File Copies

Control file copies can also be made with the **copy** command through the use of either the **copy current controlfile** or **copy controlfilecopy** commands. The **copy current controlfile** command is used to create a copy of the current control file to d:\backup\controlfile.backup, as seen in the following code example:

```
copy current controlfile to 'd:\backup\controlfile.backup';
```

If you wished to create a control file for use with a standby database that you are creating, then you would use the **for standby** clause as shown here:

```
copy current controlfile for standby to 'd:\backup\controlfile.backup';
```

Further, you can create copies of control file copies by using the **controlfilecopy** parameter of the **copy** command:

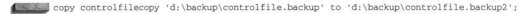
```
copy controlfilecopy 'd:\backup\controlfile.backup' to 'd:\backup\controlfile.backup2';
```

As with datafile copies, you can back up control file copies into backup sets, as shown in this example (note that the **delete input** option is not available for control file copy backups):

```
backup controlfilecopy 'd:\backup\controlfile.backup2';
```

ARCHIVELOG File Copies

Having copies of archived redo logs can be helpful. It's certainly easier to mine a copy of an archived redo log with Oracle's LogMiner product than to have to first extract that archived redo log out of a backup set. The **copy** command allows you to create copies of archived redo logs using the **archivelog** parameter of the **copy** command. Unfortunately, as we mentioned earlier, the use of **copy archivelog** requires us to list each archived redo log by name, rather than specify some temporal range with which to make copies of the archived redo logs by. Here is an example of making an ARCHIVELOG file copy:

```
copy archivelog 'd:\oracle\admin\robt\arch\robt_351.arc' to 'd:\backup\robt\robt_351.arc';
```

Incremental RMAN Backups

I hope you have made it this far through the book without much difficulty, and have been able to get at least one good backup of your database done. Now we are going to move on to the topic of incremental backups in RMAN. Through incremental backups, RMAN allows you to back up just the data blocks that have changed since the last incremental backup. The following are the benefits of incremental backups:

- Less overall tape or disk usage
- Less network bandwidth required
- Quicker backup times

You can do incremental backups either online or offline, and in either ARCHIVELOG mode or NOARCHIVELOG mode, which is pretty handy. Keep in mind that if you choose an incremental backup strategy, a give and take exists in terms of the benefits. While you are deriving a benefit in the reduction of overall backup times (and this may be significant), the cost comes on the recovery side.

Because Oracle will need to use several backup sets to recover the database if an incremental strategy is used, the time required to recover your database can significantly increase.

NOTE
If you choose to do incremental backups on a NOARCHIVELOG mode database, make sure you shut down the database in a consistent manner each time you back up the database.

The Base Backup

When doing an incremental backup, the first thing you will need is an *incremental base backup*. This backup is the backup that all future incremental backups will be based on. Each time you perform a backup of the database, you assign that backup an incremental level identifier through the use of the **incremental** parameter of the **backup** command. A base backup will always have an incremental value of 0, and you must have a base backup to be able to perform any type of incremental backup. If you do not have a base backup and you try to perform an incremental backup (using a backup level other than 0), then RMAN will perform a base backup for you automatically. Here is an example of performing a base incremental backup:

```
backup incremental level = 0 database;
```

Differential vs. Incremental Backups

Now, we need to decide how we want to perform our incremental backups. We can use one of two methods:

- Differential
- Cumulative

Each of these is a different method of performing an incremental backup. Let's look at these two different types of incremental backup types in a bit more detail.

Differential Backups

This is the default type of incremental backup that RMAN will generate. With a differential backup, RMAN backs up all blocks that have changed since the last backup at the same differential level or lower. Understanding how this all works can get a bit confusing. Figure 9-1 should help you better understand the impacts of using different levels.

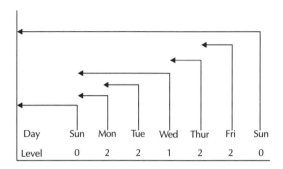

Day	Sun	Mon	Tue	Wed	Thur	Fri	Sun
Level	0	2	2	1	2	2	0

FIGURE 9-1.   *Differential backups*

In this example, we have a level 0 differential backup being taken on Sunday. This backup will back up the entire database. Following that, on Monday and Tuesday we perform level 2 differential backups. Mondays backup will only back up the blocks changed since Sunday's differential backup. Tuesday's backup will only back up the blocks changed since Monday's differential backup since its backup level (two) is the same as the backup level on Monday's backup. Thus, Tuesday's backup will not include the blocks contained in Monday's backup. Thus, for recovery purposes, we will need both Monday's and Tuesday's backups, along with Sunday's backup.

On Wednesday, we take a level 1 differential backup. This backup, since this is a level 1 backup, will back up all the blocks contained in Monday's and Tuesday's level 2 backups. Following Wednesday's backup, Thursday and Friday backups are level 2 (much like Monday and Tuesday backups). Finally, on the following Sunday, we do another base-level backup.

Here is an example of a differential level 2 backup being executed:

```
backup incremental level = 2 database;
```

Cumulative Backups

RMAN provides another incremental backup option, the cumulative backup. When used, this option will cause backup sets to back up changed blocks for all backup levels including the backup level that you have selected to back up. This is an optional backup method and requires the use of the **cumulative** keyword in the **backup** command. Again, this can all be somewhat confusing, so let's look at an example:

See Figure 9-2 for another example of the impacts of cumulative backups using different levels.

In Figure 9-2, just as in Figure 9-1, we have a level 0 differential backup being taken on Sunday. This backup will back up the entire database. Following that, on

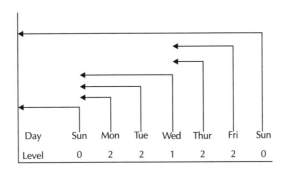

FIGURE 9-2.   *Incremental backups*

Monday we perform a level 2 backup. Now things change a little bit. On Tuesday, we perform another level 2 differential backup. Note that this time, the backup will not only contain changed blocks since Monday's backup, but will also include the blocks that were contained in Monday's backup as well. Thus, a cumulative backup accumulates all changed blocks for any backup level equal to or less than the level of the backup. As a result for recovery purposes, we will need only Tuesday's backup, along with Sunday's base backup.

On Wednesday, we take a level 1 differential backup. This backup, since this is a level 1 backup, will back up all the blocks contained in Monday's and Tuesday's level 2 backups. Following Wednesday's backup, Thursday and Friday backups are level 2 (much like Monday and Tuesday backups). Finally, on the following Sunday, we do another base-level backup.

Here is an example of the creation of a level 2 cumulative backup:

```
backup incremental level = 2 cumulative database;
```

Incremental Backups Options

Oracle allows you to perform incremental backups of not only the database, but also tablespaces, datafiles, and datafile copies. Control files, archived redo logs, and backup sets cannot be made as incremental backups. Additionally, you can choose to back up the archived redo logs at the same time. Here are some examples:

```
backup incremental level=0 tablespace users;
backup incremental level=2 tablespace users;
backup incremental level=0 datafile 4;
backup incremental level=3 datafile 4;
backup incremental level=1 database plus archivelog;
```

RMAN Workshop: *Do an Incremental Backup*

Workshop Notes
This workshop assumes that your database has been configured with automatic channels as shown in Chapter 3. It also assumes that you have configured a database account called backup_admin for backups (as described in Chapter 3). It also assumes that if you are using the MML layer, it has been configured. Finally, your database must be configured for and operating in ARCHIVELOG mode.

Step 1.   Start up RMAN.

```
C:\>rman target=backup_admin/robert
```

Step 2.   Perform a level 0 incremental backup. Include the archived redo logs in the backup set, and then remove them after the backup.

```
backup incremental level = 0 database plus archivelog delete input;
```

Step 3.   The next day, perform a level 2 incremental backup. Again, include the archived redo logs in the backup and remove them after they are backed up.

```
backup incremental level = 2 database plus archivelog delete input;
```

That about covers RMAN backups. The next chapter will be even more fun, because in it we discuss how to restore these backups and recover our databases.

Getting Started

We have covered a number of different backup options, and you may be left wondering where you should start. Let us make a suggestion or two. We recommend that you start with a test database, one that is very unimportant (better yet, one you have created for just this process). Here is an RMAN Workshop to get you started!

RMAN Workshop: *Get Your Database Backed Up!*

Workshop Notes
This workshop is more of an overall list of things that you will need to accomplish to get your database backed up. We have covered a great deal of ground in the last few chapters and we felt it would be a good idea to summarize everything important up to this point.

Step 1.   Set up a special account in your test database that will be responsible for backup operations. Configure the account as described in Chapter 3. Note that you can opt to use the SYS account, but we prefer to use a separate account. Here is an example:

Step 2.   Set up your MML layer and be clear on what it requires you to do when performing backup and recovery commands.

Step 3.   As we describe in Chapter 3, use the **configure** command to configure a separate default channel for each device that you are backing up to, unless your specific device supports multiple channels (as some do). Set the default degree of parallelism, as shown in Chapter 3, such that each of the channels will be used during the backup. If you need to configure maximum set sizes, do so; otherwise, don't bother with that now.

Step 4.   Use the **configure** command to configure automated backups of your control file and spfile (if you are using one). For now, let them be created in the default location. You will want to change this later, but for now, just leave it there.

Step 5.   Make sure your operating system backup backs up your Oracle RDBMS software (this also makes sure your control file backups will be backed up!).

Step 6.   At first, we suggest that you don't use a recovery catalog. Once you have the RMAN basics down pat and you are ready to deploy RMAN to the enterprise, then you can consider a recovery catalog.

Step 7.   For the first few trials, run your database in NOARCHIVELOG mode if you can. Shut down and mount your database and execute a few **backup database** commands. Make sure the backup sets are getting created where you expect them to.

Step 8.   Go to Chapter 10 and recover the database. We suggest you make cold backups of the entire database, control file, and online redo logs (using the **cp** or **copy** command) first, just in case you run into some learning curves.

Step 9.   Once you are good at recovering databases in NOARCHIVELOG mode, put the database in ARCHIVELOG mode and do the same thing again. Back up the database using the **backup database plus archivelog** commands.

Step 10.   Go to Chapter 10 and do some recoveries. Become an RMAN recovery expert before you go any further.

Step 11.   Play around with the **crosscheck** command, the **list** command, and the **report** commands (see Chapter 14 for more details on these commands). Become really comfortable with these commands and their purpose.

Step 12. If you have a large enterprise environment (say, over ten databases), then go ahead and add a recovery catalog to the mix, and connect to it and back up your database with it. Beyond the requirements of mixed recovery catalog schemas depending on the version of RMAN you will be using, we strongly encourage you to use a separate recovery catalog for development/test and production databases. Again, we suggest that you run through the gambit of backup and restore situations while using a recovery catalog before you move on.

Step 13. Once you are very comfortable with RMAN, create scripts to automate and schedule the process. For example, if you are running on Unix, a script such as the following could be scheduled through **cron** (we include an offline and online script here):

```
# For offline backups, use this script
#!/bin/ksh
# for offline backups, avoid shutdown aborts at all costs!
rman target rman_backup/password<<EOF
shutdown immediate
startup mount
backup database;
alter database open;
quit
EOF
```

If you are doing online backups, use this script!

```
#!/bin/ksh
rman target rman_backup/password<<EOF
backup database plus archivelog;
quit
EOF
```

These are korn shell scripts, which is one of the more commonly used shell scripting languages in Unix. Of course, RMAN works on a number of different platforms, so you can use the scripting language you are most comfortable with. In this script, we use what is known as a *here* document. That's what the EOF is in the fourth line of the first script and the third line of the second script. A here document acts like the user is "here" and typing the input that you see listed from the EOF on the top line, until the closing EOF several lines later. Optionally, you could just use a command script created by a text editor and call it from the RMAN command line like this:

```
rman target rman_backup/password @backup.cmd
```

in which case your backup.cmd script would look like this for an offline backup:

```
shutdown immediate
startup mount
backup database;
alter database open;
quit
```

For a hot backup, it would look like this:

```
backup database plus archivelog;
quit
```

You can also store scripts in RMAN using the RMAN **create script** command. We will discuss stored RMAN scripts in Chapter 13, since storing scripts in RMAN requires a recovery catalog.

Step 14.   Before you move your backups into production, test restores of the backups you have set up in your test environments. Make sure you are comfortable that everything works as it should. We suggest that you use your old backup strategy in dual until you have successfully tested several restores.

Step 15.   Move your RMAN backup strategy into production carefully. Do it one system at a time. Choose your least "visible" systems to convert first. We suggest that you do several test recoveries as you move out into production and continue (if possible) to do dual backups on each database until you have recovered that production database on a test box with an RMAN backup successfully. Also, you might want to consider separate archived redo log backups, if that is required.

Step 16.   Perform disaster recovery and test backups often. We also suggest that, at least once a week, you execute a **restore database validate check logical** command on each database to make sure that the database is recoverable.

You will note that with each of these steps, we err on the side of caution. We leave it up to you to decide when you feel you are comfortable with your RMAN setup. There is just nothing more disheartening than trying to restore your database and getting the following error message from RMAN:

```
RMAN-00571: ===========================================================
RMAN-00569: =============== ERROR MESSAGE STACK FOLLOWS ===============
RMAN-00571: ===========================================================
RMAN-03002: failure of restore command at 07/07/2002 17:14:55
RMAN-06026: some targets not found - aborting restore
```

Summary

In this chapter we have covered RMAN backups galore. We looked at how to do offline backups and online backups using RMAN. We also looked at RMAN incremental backups. We also looked at the impact of configured defaults on backups, and how much easier they make the backup process. We also looked at the number of options you can use with backups, such as using tags, overriding the default retention policy and forcing backups of read-only datafiles. We looked at methods of detecting database corruption with RMAN. All in all it's been a full chapter, but we hope you have found it to be a worthwhile one. You are now a step closer to being a RMAN expert, but the real fun is yet to come, and that's recovery. Hang on, because that's coming up next.

CHAPTER
10

RMAN Restore
& Recovery

ll of your planning and backing up is about to pay off. This chapter is about restoring your backups and then recovering your database. We will first address some basic issues regarding the overall recovery process. Then, we will look at the different methods that you might need to use to restore your RMAN backups to disk and recover your Oracle database in the event of an outage. We strongly suggest that you test these different types of recoveries on a test database somewhere, as you never quite know when you will need to recover your database, and what the conditions of that recovery will be.

You will find that this chapter is an introduction to foundational restores in RMAN. The number of situational recovery permutations that might exist for a given database is pretty large, so it's important that you understand not only the mechanics of recovery (as we will discuss here) but also how it works in concert with Oracle's architecture. In this chapter, you will find some rather straightforward recovery situations. In Chapter 12, we will address some of the more advanced recovery techniques. In Chapter 19, we will plow through a number of different recovery case studies. We suggest you read this chapter, and test each of the recoveries documented here. Then, look at the more advanced situations in Chapter 12. Once you are really good at recoveries, look at Chapter 19 and try out some of those restores.

RMAN Restore and Recovery Basics

In this chapter, we will be discussing the concepts of restores and recoveries. In RMAN parlance, "restore" and "recover" have different meanings. A *restore* implies that we are accessing a previously made backup set to get one or more objects from it and restore them to some location on disk. A restore is separate from a recovery, then, in that a *recovery* is the actual process of making a database consistent to a given point in time so that it can be opened, generally through the application of redo (contained in online redo logs or archived redo logs).

If the Oracle RDBMS is anything, it is particular. The database is particular about the state of the data within the database and demands that it be consistent to a given state in time when the database is started. If the database is consistent, then it will open; if it isn't consistent, then it will not open. Through the use of rollback segments, this consistency is maintained while the database is up and running. When the database is shut down normally, the datafiles are made consistent again. As you've likely noticed, the ongoing theme here is consistency.

Unfortunately, inconsistency can creep into the database through myriad causes. An abnormal shutdown of the database (as happens with a shutdown abort, or due to power loss on the server) will leave it in an inconsistent state. Oracle hates inconsistency, and it refuses to just start the database in the face of this demon.

Of course, other problems can plague your database. You can lose database datafiles through the loss of a disk, or perhaps lose the entire database. It is because these kinds of losses occur that you back up your database datafiles with RMAN. The problem is that when you restore those datafiles, they are likely to be inconsistent. Worse yet, those restored datafiles are likely to be anywhere from a few hours old to several days old—which safely qualifies as really inconsistent.

As we said, Oracle is a stickler about consistency. When you try to restart the database after recovering datafiles, Oracle is going to detect that those datafiles are in an inconsistent state. How does it do this? Recall from Chapter 1 our discussion of the SCN. Oracle tracks the current SCN in the datafile headers of each database datafile and in the database control file. Oracle goes through three stages when opening the database: nomount, mount, and open. When the database startup enters the open stage, Oracle begins to attempt to open the database. As it opens the database, it checks the SCN in the control file against the SCNs in each of the database datafiles. If the SCNs don't match, Oracle knows that something is amiss with the database and that it is inconsistent.

Other checks occur during startup, as well, and some of these are not consistency checks. For example, Oracle checks each datafile for a bit that indicates the datafile is in hot backup mode. If this bit is set, Oracle will not open the database. In this event, a simple **alter database datafile end backup** command will suffice to restart the database. Oracle might also determine, while trying to open the database, that a given datafile is missing. The solution to this problem might be as easy as mounting the file system the datafile is on, or perhaps a restore of the datafile will be required.

If Oracle discovers that the database is inconsistent, it needs to determine whether it can recover the database based on the online redo logs, or whether it's going to require archived redo logs to do the trick. If it can perform the recovery with the online redo logs, then Oracle will perform crash recovery (or instance recovery in the case of OPS). If Oracle cannot make the database consistent with the online redo logs, then it will stop the startup process and report that media recovery is required.

Media recovery is a condition where Oracle will require archived redo logs to recover the database and make it consistent if the database is in ARCHIVELOG mode. If the database is in NOARCHIVELOG mode, then a restore/recovery of a consistent backup of the database will likely be required. This chapter is all about recovery of your database. There are all kinds of recoveries that you can do. Sometimes you will need to recover the entire database, and sometimes you will just need to recover a few datafiles. We will discuss all of these different possibilities in this chapter.

Well, we have highlighted the issues that revolve around restore and recovery of your database. Now it's time to hit the road and see how this all works in practice.

Before You Can Restore the Database

In this chapter, we are going to approach the restore and recovery process from the beginning, assuming you have nothing left of your database except a backup somewhere. So, first we are going to look at restoring the spfile, if you are using one, and then we will look at restoring the control file. Once we have those preliminaries out of the way, we will move on to the bigger topic of restoring and recovering the database. Of course, your specific recovery situation may not require recovery to this depth. You might have just lost a few datafiles, or perhaps you want to perform a point-in-time recovery. Some restores will need to use these preliminary steps and others will not. We think that between the layout of this chapter and the case studies later in this book, you will be quite confident as to what you will need to restore and when.

Finally, you will note that in most of the examples we use, we will not be connecting to a recovery catalog unless the operation is different when using the recovery catalog. This lends to some consistency in our examples and saves a few pages with duplicate results. So, keep an eye out for any notes that we might include about recovery catalog issues.

Before RMAN Can Get Going

Before RMAN can do its thing, you need to do a few things first. Preparation is the mother of success, someone once said, and this is so true when it comes to restoring your database. You need to work with your system administrator to make sure the following are done before you attempt your restore/recovery:

- The OS parameters are configured for Oracle.

- Your disks are configured correctly and are the correct sizes.

- The tape drives are installed, and the tape software is installed and configured.

- Your network is operational.

- The Oracle RDBMS software is installed.

- The MML is configured.

- Ancillary items are recovered from backups that RMAN does not back up, which include

  - The database networking files (for example, sqlnet.ora and listener.ora)

  - The oratab file, if one is used

■ The database parameter files, if they are not spfiles and are not backed up by RMAN

■ Any RMAN control file backups that were made to disk if you have enabled autobackup of control files

Once these items have been restored, then you are ready to begin restoring your Oracle database. If you are using a recovery catalog, you will want to recover it first, of course. Then, you can recover the remaining databases.

When you start recovering databases, you need to start by recovering the spfile (if you are using one and it was backed up), followed by the control file. The next two sections cover those topics for you.

Restoring the spfile

If you are not using Oracle9i Release 2 and if you are not using an spfile, then this section really does not apply to you. As a result, you will need to restore your spfile (or your database parameter file) from an operating system backup. On the other hand, if you have started using spfiles and you have backed them up using RMAN's control file autobackup abilities, then you are in good shape!

Recall from Chapter 9 that we suggested that if you are performing RMAN database backups without a recovery catalog, you might want to note the DBID of your database for restore and recovery purposes. This is one of those times that this comes in handy, though it is not 100 percent critical.

Let's look at how we recover the spfile in a bit more detail.

Recovering the spfile from an Autobackup Using RMAN

If you have lost your spfile, you will want to recover it from the control file autobackup set if you are using this feature. As we have already described, Oracle will by default back up the spfile (along with the control file) to the $ORACLE_HOME/dbs or $ORACLE_HOME/dbs directory (depending on the operating system). If you choose to use the default location (or if you back up to an alternate disk location), you will probably want to back up these backup sets themselves to another backup media such as tape (which RMAN can do for you).

The general procedure to restore the spfile is to first set your ORACLE_SID and then log into RMAN. Then you need to set the DBID, so that RMAN will know which database spfile it is looking for. We have to start the database instance at this point in the operation. Generally, Oracle can start a database instance in this case without any parameter file or spfile being present. Oracle will use the default values assigned to the various parameters when starting the database instance. If there is some reason that you cannot allow Oracle to use these defaults, then you need to create a temporary parameter file to start the Oracle instance.

Having started the instance, if you are using the default location to back up your control file autobackup to, you can simply issue the **restore spfile from autobackup** command, and RMAN will look for the control file backup set that contains the most current spfile backup. Once the spfile is recovered, you need to shut down the instance and restart it to allow your new spfile parameters to take effect. If you are using a nondefault location, then you will need to allocate a channel pointing to that location, and then you can restore the spfile using the same method.

When you issue the **restore spfile from autobackup** command, Oracle will look in the default location for automated control file backup sets (or in the location you defined with the **allocate channel** command). Since you used the **set dbid** command, RMAN knows your database's DBID. It uses the DBID to search through the defined directory to look specifically for the most current control file backup sets for your database. When RMAN creates the control file autobackup pieces, it uses a default naming convention. The following graphic shows an example of an automated control file backup set piece and how the naming convention is used.

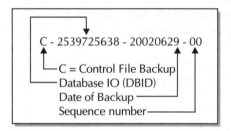

Keep in mind that if we are not using a recovery catalog (and if we are not using a control file, which is likely), Oracle doesn't know for sure what the name of the most current control file backup piece is. Thus, Oracle constructs the name of the control file backup piece based on the default naming standard that is used for those backup sets (which we will document later in this chapter). Oracle will traverse the directory, looking backward in time for a control file backup set for your database. By default, Oracle will look for one created within the last ten days. If it cannot find a backup set created within that time period, it will generate an error. If Oracle finds a valid backup set, it will proceed to restore the spfile for you.

You can modify how far back RMAN will look for a control file autobackup by using the **maxseq** and **maxdays** parameters of the **restore** command. Here are a couple of examples of recovering control files. First, we use the default settings of the **restore** command:

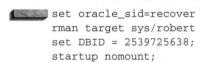

```
set oracle_sid=recover
rman target sys/robert
set DBID = 2539725638;
startup nomount;
```

```
restore spfile from autobackup;
shutdown immediate;
```

Next, we use the **maxseq** and **maxdays** parameters to look back beyond the default ten days:

```
set oracle_sid=recover
rman target sys/robert
set DBID = 2539725638;
startup nomount;
restore spfile from autobackup maxseq 200 maxdays 100;
shutdown immediate;
```

Here is an example of recovering the spfile in the case that you have configured control file autobackups to be made to another directory location:

```
set oracle_sid=recover
rman target sys/robert
set DBID = 2539725638;
startup nomount;
run
{
set controlfile autobackup format for device type disk to
'd:\backup\recover\controlf\%F';
restore spfile from autobackup;
}
shutdown immediate;
```

Recover the spfile with dbms_backup_restore   In some very rare situations you might need to use the **dbms_backup_restore** package to restore a backed up spfile. Before we talk about the **dbms_backup_restore** package in detail, let's talk about the naming convention of the automated control file/spfile backup sets for a second. Each automated control file backup piece name follows a naming convention that starts with C- followed by the database DBID. Following the database DBID is the date of the backup and then a sequence number that uniquely identifies the sequence of the backup in the day (so, this morning's backup will have 01 in the sequence number, and this afternoon's backup will have 02 in the sequence number position).

Now that you have the database instance started and the automated control file backup set piece identified, it's a snap to recover the spfile. Start SQL*Plus using the privileged "sys as sysdba" login. Next, you will use several different procedures and functions in the RMAN package **dbms_backup_restore** to complete the restore. This package is available to you any time the Oracle instance has been started. You are going to need to create a little PL/SQL script. Let's look at an example of such a script:

```
declare
devtype varchar2(256);
done boolean;
begin
devtype:=dbms_backup_restore.deviceallocate(NULL);
dbms_backup_restore.restoresetdatafile;
dbms_backup_restore.restorespfileto('d:\backup\recctl01.ctl');
dbms_backup_restore.restorebackuppiece('d:\backup\recover\C-2539725638-
20020629-00', DONE=>done);
END;
/
```

First, we declare a few variables. Next, we define the device we want to allocate for the operation with the **deviceallocate** function. If we define it as NULL, then Oracle will use the disk device by default. Of course, if you are using a tape device, then you would allocate it slightly differently, as shown in this example:

```
devtype:=dbms_backup_restore.deviceallocate(type=>'sbt',
params=>'ENV=(NB_ORA_CLASS=RMAN_db01));
```

In this example, we allocated a device to tape instead of disk and defined the tape class that the MML will use. (We will discuss the **dbms_backup_restore** procedure, and a number of its options, in more detail in Chapter 12.)

Continuing with our example, having defined the device, we indicate to Oracle that we will be restoring from a database backup set by using the **restoresetdatafile** procedure. We then instruct Oracle to recover the control file from the backup set, and we provide the name and location that we want to restore the control file to with the **restorespfileto** procedure. Finally, we use the **restorebackuppiece** command to indicate the backup set piece that the restore should come from. You complete the PL/SQL script with the **end** command, followed by the /. Oracle will then fire off the restore of the control file and restore the control file to the location that you indicated that Oracle should restore it to.

Recovering an spfile When Using a Recovery Catalog
If you are using a recovery catalog, restoring the most current spfile is as simple as issuing the **restore spfile** command after starting (nomount) the Oracle instance. RMAN will use the recovery catalog to locate the most current control file backup and extract that backup for your use. Here is an example:

```
set oracle_sid=recover
rman target sys/robert catalog rcat_manager/password@robt
```

```
startup nomount;
restore spfile from autobackup;
shutdown immediate;
```

Note that we shut down the database after the restore. Again, this is to make sure that the database will be restarted using the correct parameter value settings.

Recovering the spfile When Not Using a Recovery Catalog or Autobackup

This operation is not unlike previous operations. There is an additional complication this time, as there is no easily identifiable backup set to restore the spfile from since we are not using control file autobackups. You will use the same procedure used in that section to restore the spfile in this situation. What makes it a bit more complicated is that you will not know for sure which backup sets will contain a control file backup (which will also contain an spfile), and the naming conventions are not the same.

If possible, you might want to keep track of the output of the **list backup** command from RMAN after a backup. This will make it somewhat easier to locate the backup set pieces you are looking for because this command lists each backup set and its associated pieces, what each backup set piece contains, and its name. Here is an example of the output of this command:

```
RMAN> list backup;
using target database controlfile instead of recovery catalog
List of Backup Sets
===================
BS Key  Size        Device Type Elapsed Time Completion Time
------- ----------  ----------- ------------ ---------------
68      176K        DISK            00:00:06     29-JUN-02
        BP Key: 68   Status: AVAILABLE   Tag: TAG20020629T140829
        Piece Name: D:\BACKUP\RECOVER\BACKUP_2FDS83B1_1_1
  List of Archived Logs in backup set 68
  Thrd Seq    Low SCN    Low Time    Next SCN    Next Time
  ---- ------ ---------- ---------   ----------  ---------
   1    7      393235    27-JUN-02  395155       27-JUN-02
   1    8      395155    27-JUN-02  395208       27-JUN-02
   1    9      395208    27-JUN-02  395266       27-JUN-02
   1    10     395266    27-JUN-02  395797       27-JUN-02
   1    11     395797    27-JUN-02  395900       27-JUN-02
   1    12     395900    27-JUN-02  396065       27-JUN-02
   1    13     396065    27-JUN-02  396143       27-JUN-02
   1    14     396143    27-JUN-02  416201       27-JUN-02
   1    15     416201    27-JUN-02  416531       27-JUN-02
BS Key  Size        Device Type Elapsed Time Completion Time
------- ----------  ----------- ------------ ---------------
69      619K        DISK            00:00:11     29-JUN-02
```

```
        BP Key: 69   Status: AVAILABLE   Tag: TAG20020629T140829
        Piece Name: D:\BACKUP\RECOVER\BACKUP_2GDS83B1_1_1
  List of Archived Logs in backup set 69
  Thrd Seq     Low SCN    Low Time  Next SCN    Next Time
  ---- ------- ---------- --------- ---------- ---------
   1    16     416531     27-JUN-02 436816     27-JUN-02
   1    17     436816     27-JUN-02 437324     27-JUN-02
   1    18     437324     27-JUN-02 437444     28-JUN-02
   1    19     437444     28-JUN-02 437963     28-JUN-02
   1    20     437963     28-JUN-02 458182     28-JUN-02
   1    21     458182     28-JUN-02 458257     28-JUN-02
   1    22     458257     28-JUN-02 458280     28-JUN-02
   1    23     458280     28-JUN-02 458407     28-JUN-02
   1    24     458407     28-JUN-02 502309     29-JUN-02
BS Key   Type LV Size       Device Type Elapsed Time Completion Time
-------  ---- -- ---------- ----------- ------------ ---------------
70       Full    128K       DISK         00:00:12    29-JUN-02
        BP Key: 70   Status: AVAILABLE   Tag: TAG20020629T140852
        Piece Name: D:\BACKUP\RECOVER\BACKUP_2HDS83BM_1_1
  List of Datafiles in backup set 70
  File LV Type Ckp SCN    Ckp Time  Name
  ---- -- ---- ---------- --------- ----
   4      Full 502325     29-JUN-02 D:\ORACLE\ORADATA\RECOVER\TOOLS0
1.DBF
   5      Full 502325     29-JUN-02 D:\ORACLE\ORADATA\RECOVER\USERS0
1.DBF
BS Key   Type LV Size       Device Type Elapsed Time Completion Time
-------  ---- -- ---------- ----------- ------------ ---------------
71       Full    111M       DISK         00:02:56    29-JUN-02
        BP Key: 71   Status: AVAILABLE   Tag: TAG20020629T140852
        Piece Name: D:\BACKUP\RECOVER\BACKUP_2IDS83BN_1_1
  List of Datafiles in backup set 71
  File LV Type Ckp SCN    Ckp Time  Name
  ---- -- ---- ---------- --------- ----
   1      Full 502329     29-JUN-02 D:\ORACLE\ORADATA\RECOVER\SYSTEM
01.DBF
   3      Full 502329     29-JUN-02 D:\ORACLE\ORADATA\RECOVER\INDX01
.DBF
BS Key   Size       Device Type Elapsed Time Completion Time
-------  ---------- ----------- ------------ ---------------
72       2K          DISK         00:00:06    29-JUN-02
        BP Key: 72   Status: AVAILABLE   Tag: TAG20020629T141231
        Piece Name: D:\BACKUP\RECOVER\BACKUP_2JDS83IK_1_1
  List of Archived Logs in backup set 72
  Thrd Seq     Low SCN    Low Time  Next SCN    Next Time
  ---- ------- ---------- --------- ---------- ---------
   1    25     502309     29-JUN-02 502392     29-JUN-02
```

```
BS Key  Type LV Size       Device Type Elapsed Time Completion Time
-------  ---- -- ---------- ----------- ------------ ---------------
73      Full 1M         DISK        00:00:15     29-JUN-02
        BP Key: 73   Status: AVAILABLE   Tag:
        Piece Name: D:\BACKUP\RECOVER\C-2539725638-20020629-00
    spfile Included: Modification time: 26-JUN-02
```

We will cover the output generated by this command in detail in Chapter 13, but for now, only the last six lines of the report are important.

Note the spfile Included notation in the last line. This indicates that this backup set (which has a unique backup set key number of 73) has an spfile backup in it. It also gives us the specific piece name (note that in this case, this was an automated backup of a backup set, so the piece name takes that naming convention) that we can use to restore. You can use the **dbms_backup_restore** package to restore the spfile, as we demonstrated in the previous section.

If you don't have the piece association, you are just going to have to play some hit and miss. You can get the available piece names off your recovery media and then attempt to restore the spfile using the **dbms_backup_restore** package from each of these until you find it.

Restoring the Backed Up spfile with an Operational Database Online

Extracting a copy of your spfile from a database backup with the database up is really easy regardless of whether you are using a control file or a recovery catalog. You should note that this operation will result in a text parameter file, and not an spfile, so you will need to convert it if you wish it to be an spfile.

If you are not using a recovery catalog and you have enabled automatic backups of control files, just issue the following command:

```
RMAN> restore spfile to pfile 'd:\backup\test.ora' from autobackup;
```

This command will restore the spfile to a file called test.ora in a directory called d:\backup. Again, with any autobackup restore, RMAN will only look for the past seven days to find a control file automatic backup piece unless you supply **maxseq** and **maxdays** parameter values.

If you are not using a recovery catalog and are not using control file autobackups, or if you are using a recovery catalog, then this is the command you would use:

```
RMAN> restore spfile to pfile 'd:\backup\test.ora';
```

In this case, Oracle will use the control file of the database to locate the most current backup set to restore the spfile from. So, now that you have your spfile back, you are ready to go out and recover your control file.

Restoring the Control File

Restoring a control file is similar to restoring your spfile. There are several different types of control file recovery situations you might encounter, but each is very similar.

Restoring the control file is not much different from restoring your spfile. First, the database needs to be mounted, so to restore the control file, you should have already restored your spfile, or have created one, and mounted your database. Once that occurs, you are ready to proceed to recover the control file for your database. Now, let's look at that process in more detail.

Recovering the Control File from an Autobackup Using RMAN

If you have lost your control file, you will want to recover it from the control file autobackup set if you are using this feature. As we have already described, Oracle will, by default, back up the control file to the $ORACLE_HOME/dbs or $ORACLE_HOME/dbs directory (depending on the operating system). If you choose to use the default location, you will probably want to back up these backup sets themselves to another backup media such as tape (which RMAN can do for you).

The general procedure to restore the control file is to first set your ORACLE_SID and then log into RMAN. Then, you need to set the DBID, so that RMAN will know which database control file it is looking for (you will usually have already performed these steps to recover the spfile of the database).

If you are not using the default location for your control file autobackups, then you will need to allocate a channel before you can restore the control file. Once the channel is allocated, to restore your control file use the **restore controlfile from autobackup** much like the **restore spfile** command you used earlier. Once the command is issued, RMAN will look for the control file backup set that contains the most current control file backup. Once the control file is recovered, you will need to mount the database and perform an incomplete recovery.

As with spfile recoveries, when you issue the **restore controlfile** command, Oracle will look in the default location for automated control file backup sets (or in the location you defined with the **allocate channel** command). Since you used the **set dbid** command, RMAN knows your database's DBID. It will use the DBID to search through the directory with the control file backups to look for the most current control file backup sets for your database.

Keep in mind that if we are not using a recovery catalog, Oracle doesn't know for sure what the name of the most current control file backup piece is. Thus, Oracle constructs the name of the control file backup piece based on the default naming standard used for those backup sets (which we will document later in this chapter). Oracle will traverse the directory, looking backward in time for a control file backup set for your database. By default, Oracle will look for one created within the last ten days. If it cannot find a backup set created within that time period, it will generate an error. If Oracle finds a valid backup set, it will proceed to restore the control file for you.

As with spfile restores, you can modify the default by using the **maxseq** and **maxdays** parameters of the **restore** command. Here are a couple of examples of recovering control files. First, we use the default settings of the **restore** command:

```
set oracle_sid=recover
rman target sys/robert
set DBID = 2539725638;
startup nomount;
restore controlfile from autobackup;
```

Next, we use the **maxseq** and **maxdays** parameters to look back beyond the default ten days:

```
set oracle_sid=recover
rman target sys/robert
set DBID = 2539725638;
startup nomount;
restore coontrolfile from autobackup maxseq 200 maxdays 100;
```

Here is an example of recovering the spfile in the case that you have configured control file autobackups to be made to another directory location:

```
set oracle_sid=recover
rman target sys/robert
set DBID = 2539725638;
startup nomount;
run
{
set controlfile autobackup format for device type disk to
'd:\backup\recover\controlf\%F';
restore controlfile from autobackup;
}
```

Recover the Control File with dbms_backup_restore   In some very rare situations, you might need to use the **dbms_backup_restore** package to restore a backed up control file. In particular, if you have not enabled automated backups of your control file and you are not using a recovery catalog, this may be the only method you will have to restore your control file in the event of a complete loss of all of your control files.

Recall that each automated control file backup piece name follows a naming convention that starts with C- followed by the database DBID. Following the database

DBID is the date of the backup and then a sequence number that uniquely identifies the sequence of the backup in the day.

Once you have the database instance started and the automated control file backup set piece identified, it's a snap to recover the control file. Start SQL*Plus using the privileged "sys as sysdba" login. Next, you will use several different procedures and functions in the RMAN package **dbms_backup_restore** to complete the restore. This package is available to you any time the Oracle instance has been started. You are going to need to create a little PL/SQL script. Let's look at an example of such a script:

```
declare
devtype varchar2(256);
done boolean;
begin
devtype:=dbms_backup_restore.deviceallocate(NULL);
dbms_backup_restore.restoresetdatafile;
dbms_backup_restore.restorecontrolfileto ('d:\backup\recctl01.ctl');
dbms_backup_restore.restorebackuppiece('d:\backup\recover\C-2539725638-
20020629-00', DONE=>done);
END;
/
```

First, we declare a few variables. Next, we define the device we want to allocate for the operation with the **deviceallocate** function. If we define it as NULL, then Oracle will use the disk device by default. Of course, if you are using a tape device, then you would allocate it slightly differently, as shown in this example:

```
devtype:=dbms_backup_restore.deviceallocate(type=>'sbt',
params=>'ENV=(NB_ORA_CLASS=RMAN_db01));
```

In this example, we allocated a device to tape instead of disk and defined the tape class the MML will use.

Continuing with our example, having defined the device, we indicate to Oracle that we will be restoring from a database backup set by using the **restoresetdatafile** procedure. We then instruct Oracle to recover the control file from the backup set, and we provide the name and location that we want to restore the control file to with the **restorecontrolfile** procedure. Finally, we use the **restorebackuppiece** command to indicate the backup set piece that the restore should come from. You complete the PL/SQL script with the **end** command, followed by the /. Oracle will then fire off the restore of the control file and restore the control file to the location that you defined via the **restorecontrolfileto** procedure.

Recovering a Control File Using a Recovery Catalog

If you are using a recovery catalog, restoring the most current control file backup is as simple as issuing the **restore controlfile** command. RMAN will use the recovery catalog to locate the most current control file backup and extract that backup for your use. Here is an example:

```
set oracle_sid=recover
rman target sys/robert catalog rcat_manager/password@robt
# Note - We would issue a startup nomount
# and restore control file from autobackup here if we needed to.
# shutdown immediate here if we recovered the control file.
startup nomount;
restore controlfile;
# mount the database in preparation for a restore.
alter database mount;
```

Recovering a Lost Control File

In the event that only your control file was lost, then recovery of the control file and your database is fairly simple. The commands to recover the control file are the same; you just need to simulate incomplete recovery in order to open the database. If you are running in NOARCHIVELOG mode, this would be the method you would use:

```
set oracle_sid=recover
rman target sys/robert
set DBID = 2539725638;
startup nomount;
restore controlfile from autobackup;
alter database mount;
recover database noredo;
alter database open resetlogs;
```

If you are running in ARCHIVELOG mode, recovery is only slightly different:

```
set oracle_sid=recover
rman target sys/robert
set DBID = 2539725638;
startup nomount;
restore controlfile from autobackup;
alter database mount;
recover database;
alter database open resetlogs;
```

Recovering a Control File Online

Extracting a copy of your control file from a database backup while the database is up is really easy regardless of whether you are using a control file or a recovery catalog.

If you are not using a recovery catalog and you have enabled automatic backups of control files, just issue the following command:

```
RMAN> restore controlfile to 'd:\backup' from autobackup;
```

This command will restore the spfile to a file called test.ora in a directory called d:\backup. Again, with any autobackup restore, RMAN will only look for the past seven days by default to find a control file automatic backup piece. Use **maxseq** and **maxdays** to modify this default.

If you not using a recovery catalog and are not using control file autobackups, or if you are using a recovery catalog, then this is the command you would use:

```
RMAN> restore controlfile to 'd:\backup';
```

In this case, Oracle will use the control file of the database to locate the most current backup set to restore the control file from. Of course, you could use the manual restore process, using the **dbms_backup_restore** procedure, which we discussed earlier in this section.

RMAN Workshop: *Recover Your Control File*

Workshop Notes

For this workshop, you will need an installation of the Oracle software and an operational test Oracle database. Also, determine your database DBID by looking at the DBID column of the V$DATABASE view of your database.

> **NOTE**
> *For this workshop, the database is in ARCHIVELOG mode.*

Step 1. Ensure that you have configured automated backups of your control files.

```
configure controlfile autobackup on;
```

Note that in this case we are accepting that the control file backup set pieces will be created in the default location.

Step 2.   Complete a cold backup of your system. In this workshop, we will assume that the backup is to a configured default device:

```
set oracle_sid=recover
rman target rman_backup/password
backup database;
```

Step 3.   Shut down your database:

```
shutdown immediate;
```

Step 4.   Rename all copies of your database control file. Do not remove them just in case your backups cannot be recovered.

Step 5.   Now, start your database. It should complain that the control file cannot be found.

```
startup;
```

Step 6.   Recover your control file with RMAN using your autobackup of the control file:

```
set DBID = <enter the DBID of the database here>;
restore controlfile from autobackup;
```

Step 7.   You will need to restart your database by simulating incomplete recovery:

```
recover database;
alter database open resetlogs;
```

Restore and Recover the Database in NOARCHIVELOG Mode

If your database is in NOARCHIVELOG mode, you will be recovering from a full, offline backup, and point-in-time recovery won't be possible. If your database is in ARCHIVELOG mode, read the "Database Recoveries in ARCHIVELOG Mode" section later in this chapter. If you are doing incremental backups of your NOARCHIVELOG database, then you will also want to read "What If I Use Incremental Backups," later in this chapter.

Introducing the restore and recover Commands

If you are running in NOARCHIVELOG mode, and assuming you actually have a backup of your database, performing a full recovery of your database is very easy. First, clean everything out. Clean out any datafiles that might be left over, and clean out the old redo logs and the old control files. You don't want any of those files lying around. Since you are in NOARCHIVELOG mode, you will need to start afresh.

Having cleaned out your datafiles, control files, and redo logs, you are ready to start the recovery process. First, recover the control file from your last backup, as we demonstrated earlier in this chapter. Alternatively, you can use a backup control file that you created at some point after the backup you wish to restore from. Do not use the **create control file** command, or you will not be able to restore your backup.

For this example, we assume that you are not using a recovery catalog. We also assume you want to recover from the most current backup, which is the default setting for RMAN. If you want to recover from an older backup, you need to use the **set time** command, which we will discuss later in this section.

The differences in recovery with and without a recovery catalog are pretty much negligible once you are past the recovery of the spfile and the control file. So, we will only demonstrate recoveries without a recovery catalog. First, let's look at the RMAN commands you will use to perform this recovery:

```
startup mount;
restore database;
recover database noredo;
alter database open resetlogs;
```

Looks pretty simple. Of course, these steps assume that you have recovered your spfile and your database control files. The first command, **startup mount**, mounts the database. So, Oracle reads the control file in preparation for the database restore. The **restore database** command is next, which causes RMAN to actually start the database datafile restores. Following this command is the **recover database noredo** command, which instructs RMAN to perform final recovery operations in preparation for opening the database. Since the database is in NOARCHIVELOG mode, and there are no archived redo logs to apply and the online redo logs are missing, the **noredo** parameter is required. If the online redo logs were intact, the **noredo** parameter would not be needed.

Finally, we open the database with the **alter database open resetlogs** command. Since we have restored the control file and we need the online redo logs rebuilt, we will need to use the **resetlogs** command. In fact, you will probably use **resetlogs** with about every NOARCHIVELOG recovery you do. So, let's look at this recovery in action:

```
d:>set oracle_sid=recover
d:>rman target sys/robert
RMAN> startup mount;
database mounted
 RMAN> restore database;
Starting restore at 17-JUN-02
allocated channel: ORA_DISK_1
channel ORA_DISK_1: sid=11 devtype=DISK
channel ORA_DISK_1: starting datafile backupset restore
channel ORA_DISK_1: specifying datafile(s) to restore from backup set
restoring datafile 00001 to D:\ORACLE\ORADATA\RECOVER\SYSTEM01.DBF
restoring datafile 00003 to D:\ORACLE\ORADATA\RECOVER\INDX01.DBF
restoring datafile 00004 to D:\ORACLE\ORADATA\RECOVER\TOOLS01.DBF
restoring datafile 00005 to D:\ORACLE\ORADATA\RECOVER\USERS01.DBF
channel ORA_DISK_1: restored backup piece 1
piece handle=D:\ORACLE\ORA912\DATABASE\06DR6T5C_1_1 tag=TAG20020617T000042
   params=NULL
channel ORA_DISK_1: restore complete
Finished restore at 17-JUN-02
RMAN> recover database noredo;
Starting recover at 17-JUN-02
using channel ORA_DISK_1
starting media recovery
media recovery complete
Finished recover at 17-JUN-02
RMAN> alter database open resetlogs;
```

Well, we now have a happy bouncing baby database back again! Woo hoo!

NOTE
*Use the **restore database noredo** command
when your online redo logs are not available.
Use the **restore database** command without
the **redo** parameter when your online redo logs
are available during the recovery.*

Recovery and Using Your Existing Control File

If your control file (or files) is intact, and you are recovering your NOARCHIVELOG
mode database, then you can use the old control file without restoring a control file
from a backup. However, the procedure is just a bit different than if you are doing
a recovery with a backup control file. First, we start our RMAN recovery as we
normally would:

```
startup mount;
restore database;
```

Now, to finish the recovery, we need to use SQL*Plus and trick Oracle into thinking we are performing incomplete recovery, as shown here:

```
D:\ >sqlplus "sys as sysdba"
SQL*Plus: Release 9.2.0.1.0 - Production on Mon Jul 1 12:30:04 2002
Copyright (c) 1982, 2002, Oracle Corporation.  All rights reserved.
Enter password:
Connected to:
Oracle9i Enterprise Edition Release 9.2.0.1.0 - Production
With the Partitioning, Oracle Label Security, OLAP and Oracle Data Mining options
JServer Release 9.2.0.1.0 - Production
SQL> recover database until cancel;
ORA-00279: change 527968 generated at 06/30/2002 11:51:21 needed for thread 1
ORA-00289: suggestion : D:\ORACLE\ADMIN\RECOVER\ARCH\ARC00028.001
ORA-00280: change 527968 for thread 1 is in sequence #28
Specify log: {<RET>=suggested | filename | AUTO | CANCEL}
Cancel
Media recovery cancelled.
SQL> alter database open resetlogs;
Database altered.
```

Restoring from an Older Backup

You probably have more than one backup that you have taken of your database, and you may well want to recover from some backup other than the most current one. In this case, you need to use the **set** command in conjunction with the rest of the restore process. We will talk about the **set time** command in detail later in this chapter, but here is an example of using it to restore a backup that is a few days older than our default backup:

```
-- We assume that we have already recovered the control file
-- If not, you will need to manually use the recover until cancel
-- command as described earlier in the section "A Word About
-- Your Control File".
startup mount;
run
{
SET UNTIL TIME "TO_DATE('06/30/02 13:00:00','MM/DD/YY HH24:MI:SS')";
restore database;
recover database noredo;
alter database open resetlogs;
}
```

Note that, in this case, the **set until time** command is in the confines of a **run** block. This is a requirement if you want to use the **set until time** command. Also note that we have established the set time as June 30, 2002, at 13:00:00. This will cause Oracle to find the backup taken closest to this time, but not beyond it. Thus, if you took three backups on 6/30/02, one at 8 A.M., the second at 12:50 P.M., and the last at 8 P.M., then RMAN would restore the 12:50 P.M. backup.

If you don't want to have to use a **run** block, you can alternatively set the time restriction in the **restore** command itself, as shown here:

```
-- We assume that we have already recovered the control file
-- If not, you will need to manually use the recover until cancel
-- command as described earlier in the section "A Word About
-- Your Control File".
startup mount;
restore database UNTIL TIME "TO_DATE('06/28/02 13:00:00','MM/DD/YY HH24:MI:SS')";
recover database noredo;
alter database open resetlogs;
```

Restoring to a Different Location

Of course, we don't always have the luxury of restoring back to the original file system names that the Oracle files resided on. For example, during a disaster recovery drill, you might have one big file system to recover to, rather than six smaller-sized file systems. That can be a bit of a problem, because by default RMAN is going to try to restore your datafiles to the same location that they came from when they were backed up. So, how do we fix this problem?

Enter the **set newname for datafile** and **switch** commands. These commands, when used in concert with **restore** and **recover** commands, allow you to tell RMAN where the datafiles need to be placed. For example, if our datafiles were originally backed up to d:\oracle\data\recover and we wanted to recover them instead to e:\oracle\data\recover, we would first issue the **set newname for datafile** command for each datafile, indicating its old location and its new location. Here is an example of this command's use:

```
set newname for datafile 'd:\oracle\data\recover\system01.dbf'
to 'e:\oracle\data\recover\system01.dbf';
```

Note that we define both the original location of the file and the new location that RMAN should copy the file to. Once we have issued **set newname for datafile** commands for all of the datafiles we want to restore to a different location, we proceed as before with the **restore database** and **recover database** commands. Finally, before we actually open the database, we need to indicate to Oracle that we do, once and for all, really want to have it use the relocated datafiles that we have restored. We do this by using the **switch** command.

The **switch** command will cause the datafile locations in the database control file to be changed so that they reflect the new location of the Oracle database datafiles. Typically, you will use the **switch datafile all** command to indicate to Oracle that you wish to switch all datafile locations in the control file. Alternatively, you can use the **switch datafile** command to switch only specific datafiles.

If you use the **set newname for datafile** command and do not switch all restored datafiles, then any nonswitched datafile will be considered a datafile copy by

RMAN, and RMAN will not try to use these nonswitched datafiles when recovering
the database. Here is an example of the commands that you might use for a restore
using the **set newname for datafile** command:

```
startup nomount
set DBID=2539725638
restore controlfile from autobackup;
alter database mount;
run
{
set newname for datafile 'd:\oracle\oradata\recover\system01.dbf' to
'e:\oracle\oradata\recover\system01.dbf';
set newname for datafile
'd:\oracle\oradata\recover\recover_undotbs_01.dbf' to
'e:\oracle\oradata\recover\recover_undotbs_01.dbf';
set newname for datafile 'd:\oracle\oradata\recover\users01.dbf' to
'e:\oracle\oradata\recover\users01.dbf';
set newname for datafile 'd:\oracle\oradata\recover\tools01.dbf' to
'e:\oracle\oradata\recover\tools01.dbf';
set newname for datafile 'd:\oracle\oradata\recover\indx01.dbf' to
'e:\oracle\oradata\recover\indx01.dbf';
restore database;
recover database noredo;
alter database open resetlogs;
switch datafile all;
}
```

Note that if the recovery is not successful but the files were restored successfully,
the datafiles restored will become datafile copies and will not be removed.

RMAN Workshop: *Recover Your NOARCHIVELOG Mode Database*

Workshop Notes
For this workshop, you will need an installation of the Oracle software and an
operational test Oracle database.

> **NOTE**
> *For this workshop, the database is in
> NOARCHIVELOG mode.*

Step 1.   Set the ORACLE_SID, and then log into RMAN. Ensure that you have configured automated backups of your control files. Because this is an offline backup, we will need to shut down and mount the database:

```
set oracle_sid=recover
rman target rman_backup/password
configure controlfile autobackup on;
shutdown immediate;
startup mount;
```

Note that in this case, we are accepting that the control file backup set pieces will be created in the default location.

Step 2.   Complete a cold backup of your system. In the workshop, we will assume that the backup is to a configured default device:

```
backup database;
```

Step 3.   Shut down your database:

```
shutdown immediate;
```

Step 4.   Rename all database datafiles. Also rename the online redo logs and control files. (Optionally, you can remove these files if you don't have the space to rename them and if you can afford to really lose your database, should something go wrong.)

Step 5.   Startup mount your database and restore your control file:

```
startup nomount;
set DBID = <enter the DBID of the database here>;
restore controlfile from autobackup;
alter database mount;
```

Step 6.   Recover your database with RMAN using the backup you took in Step 2:

```
restore database;
recover database noredo;
alter database open resetlogs;
```

Step 7.   Complete the recovery by backing up the database again:

```
shutdown immediate;
startup mount;
backup database;
```

> **NOTE**
> *If your online redo logs had not been removed, you would have used the **recover database** command instead of **recover database noredo**.*

Database Recoveries in ARCHIVELOG Mode

Typically, you will find production databases in ARCHIVELOG mode because of one of more requirements, such as the following:

- Point-in-time recovery

- Minimal recovery time service-level agreements with customers

- The ability to do online database backups

- The ability to recover specific datafiles while the database is available to users

When the database is in ARCHIVELOG mode, you have a number of recovery options that you can choose from:

- Full database recovery

- Tablespace recoveries

- Datafile recoveries

- Incomplete database recovery

We will cover the first three items in this section. Later in this chapter, we will look at incomplete database recoveries. With each of these types of recoveries, you will find that the biggest difference from NOARCHIVELOG mode recovery is the application of the archived redo logs, as well as some issues with regard to defining when you wish to recover to if you are doing incomplete recovery. For now, let's start with looking at a full database recovery in ARCHIVELOG mode.

NOTE
Recoveries of spfiles and control files are the same regardless of whether or not you are running in ARCHIVELOG mode.

Point-of-Failure Database Recoveries

With a point-of-failure database recovery (also known as a full database recovery), you hope that you have your online redo logs intact; in fact, any unarchived online redo log must be intact. If you lose your online redo logs, you are looking at an incomplete recovery of your database; you should reference Chapter 11 for more information on incomplete recoveries. Finally, we are going to assume that at least one control file is intact. If it is not, then you will need to recover a control file backup, and again you are looking at an incomplete recovery (unless your online redo logs are intact).

So, in this first example, we have lost all of our database datafiles. Our online redo logs and control files are safe, and we just want our database back. In this case, we opt for a full recovery of our database to the point of the failure. Here is the command set we will use to perform this restore operation:

```
shutdown;
startup mount;
restore database;
recover database;
alter database open;
```

And here is an actual restore operation:

```
RMAN> restore database;
Starting restore at 27-JUN-02
allocated channel: ORA_DISK_1
channel ORA_DISK_1: sid=11 devtype=DISK
allocated channel: ORA_DISK_2
channel ORA_DISK_2: sid=12 devtype=DISK
channel ORA_DISK_1: starting datafile backupset restore
channel ORA_DISK_1: specifying datafile(s) to restore from backup set
restoring datafile 00002 to D:\ORACLE\ORADATA\RECOVER\RECOVER_UNDOTBS_01.DBF
restoring datafile 00004 to D:\ORACLE\ORADATA\RECOVER\TOOLS01.DBF
restoring datafile 00005 to D:\ORACLE\ORADATA\RECOVER\USERS01.DBF
channel ORA_DISK_2: starting datafile backupset restore
channel ORA_DISK_2: specifying datafile(s) to restore from backup set
restoring datafile 00001 to D:\ORACLE\ORADATA\RECOVER\SYSTEM01.DBF
restoring datafile 00003 to D:\ORACLE\ORADATA\RECOVER\INDX01.DBF
channel ORA_DISK_1: restored backup piece 1
piece handle=D:\BACKUP\RECOVER\BACKUP_12DS0PJM_1_1 tag=TAG20020626T193932 params=NULL
channel ORA_DISK_1: restore complete
channel ORA_DISK_2: restored backup piece 1
piece handle=D:\BACKUP\RECOVER\BACKUP_13DS0PJO_1_1 tag=TAG20020626T193932 params=NULL
```

```
channel ORA_DISK_2: restore complete
Finished restore at 27-JUN-02
RMAN> restore database;
Starting restore at 27-JUN-02
using channel ORA_DISK_1
using channel ORA_DISK_2
skipping datafile 1; already restored to file D:\ORACLE\ORADATA\RECOVER\SYSTEM01.DBF
skipping datafile 3; already restored to file D:\ORACLE\ORADATA\RECOVER\INDX01.DBF
skipping datafile 2; already restored to file
D:\ORACLE\ORADATA\RECOVER\RECOVER_UNDOTBS_01.DBF
skipping datafile 5; already restored to file D:\ORACLE\ORADATA\RECOVER\USERS01.DBF
channel ORA_DISK_1: starting datafile backupset restore
channel ORA_DISK_1: specifying datafile(s) to restore from backup setrestoring
datafile 00004 to D:\ORACLE\ORADATA\RECOVER\TOOLS01.DBF
channel ORA_DISK_1: restored backup piece 1
piece handle=D:\BACKUP\RECOVER\BACKUP_12DS0PJM_1_1 tag=TAG20020626T193932 params=NULL
channel ORA_DISK_1: restore complete
Finished restore at 27-JUN-02
RMAN> recover database;
Starting recover at 27-JUN-02
using channel ORA_DISK_1
using channel ORA_DISK_2
starting media recovery
media recovery complete
Finished recover at 27-JUN-02
RMAN> alter database open;
database opened
```

Looks pretty easy, and it is. However, there are a few things to realize about restore operations like this. First of all, Oracle touts that if the file is there already and it doesn't need to be recovered, it will not recover it. After reading the Oracle documentation, you might think that if you lose a single datafile, all you need to do is run the **restore database** command and Oracle will only recover the datafile you lost.

What really happens is that Oracle will determine whether the file it's going to restore already exists. If so, and the file that exists is the same as the file it's preparing to restore, then RMAN will not restore that file again. If the file on the backup image is different in any respect from the existing datafile, then RMAN will recover that file. So, if you lose a datafile or two, you will want to do a datafile or tablespace recovery instead, which we will talk about shortly.

Let's take a moment now and look at what's happening during each step of the restore/recovery process. Each of these steps is quite similar for any type of ARCHIVELOG restore. After we have recovered our spfile and control files, if that was required, we have the **restore database** command, which causes RMAN to begin restoring all database datafiles. Note that, in this case, the database has to be down because we are restoring critical tablespaces, namely the SYSTEM tablespace. While many ARCHIVELOG recoveries can be done online, a full database point-in-time restore cannot.

Once the datafiles have been restored, Oracle will move on to the next command, the **recover database** command. This command is much like the **recover database** command that you would issue from inside SQL*Plus in that it will cause the Oracle RDBMS to start recovering the database to the point of failure by applying the archived redo logs needed to perform a full point-in-time recovery. An additional benefit that you get from RMAN is that it will restore the needed archived redo logs from disk, so that they can be applied during the recovery process. Once Oracle has recovered the database, then it's as simple as an **alter database open** command and Oracle will finish the process of opening the database for use.

NOTE
If you attempt a full database restore and it fails, all recovered datafiles will be removed. This can be most frustrating if the restore has taken a very long time to complete. We suggest that you test different recovery strategies, such as recovering tablespaces (say four to five tablespaces at a time), and see which works best for you and which method best meets your recovery SLA and your disaster recovery needs.

RMAN Workshop: *Complete Recovery of Your ARCHIVELOG Mode Database*

Workshop Notes
For this workshop, you will need an installation of the Oracle software and an operational test Oracle database.

NOTE
For this workshop, the database must be configured for and running in ARCHIVELOG mode.

Step 1.   Ensure that you have configured automated backups of your control files:

```
set oracle_sid=recover
rman target rman_backup/password
configure controlfile autobackup on;
```

Note that in this case we are accepting that the control file backup set pieces will be created in the default location.

Step 2. Because this is an online backup, there is no need to shut down and then mount the database. Complete an online backup of your system. In this case, we will back up the database and the archived redo logs. Once the archived redo logs are backed up, we will remove them. In this workshop, we will assume that the backup is to a configured default device:

```
backup database plus archivelog delete input;
```

Step 3. Shut down your database.

```
shutdown immediate;
```

Step 4. Rename all database datafiles. Also rename the control files. Do not rename your online redo logs for this exercise. (Optionally, you can remove these files if you don't have the space to rename them and if you can afford to really lose your database, should something go wrong.)

Step 5. Startup mount your database and restore your control file:

```
startup nomount;
set DBID = <enter the DBID of the database here>;
restore controlfile from autobackup;
alter database mount;
```

Step 6. Recover your database with RMAN using the backup you took in Step 2.

```
restore database;
recover database;
alter database open resetlogs;
```

Step 7. Complete the recovery by backing up the database again:

```
shutdown immediate;
startup mount;
backup database;
```

Tablespace Recoveries

Perhaps you have just lost datafiles specific to a given tablespace. In this event, you can opt to just recover a tablespace, rather than the entire database. One nice thing about tablespace recoveries is that they can occur while the rest of the database is humming along. For example, suppose you lose your accounts payable tablespace, but your accounts receivable tablespace is just fine. As long as your application doesn't need to access the accounts payable tablespace, you can be recovering

that tablespace while the accounts receivable tablespace remains accessible. Here
is an example of the code required to recover a tablespace:

```
sql "alter tablespace users offline";
restore tablespace users;
recover tablespace users;
sql "alter tablespace users online";
```

As you can see, the recovery process is pretty simple. First, we need to take the
tablespace offline. We use a new command, **sql**, to perform this action. Enclosed in
quotes after the **sql** command is specific SQL that we want the database to execute;
in this case, we are taking the users tablespace offline with the command **alter
tablespace users offline**. Next, we restore the datafiles associated with the tablespace,
and then we recover the tablespace. Finally, we use the **sql** command again to issue
the **alter tablespace users online** command, and the recovery of the users tablespace
is complete.

NOTE
*You cannot recover an individual tablespace or
datafile to a point in time different from that of
the rest of the database.*

You can also recover multiple tablespaces in the same command set, as shown
in this code snippet:

```
sql "alter tablespace users offline";
sql "alter tablespace data offline";
restore tablespace users, data;
recover tablespace users, data;
sql "alter tablespace users online";
sql "alter tablespace data online";
```

Datafile Recoveries

Second cousin to a tablespace recovery is a datafile recovery, which is a very
granular approach to database recovery. Here, we can replace lost database datafiles
individually, while the rest of the tablespace remains online. Datafile recovery allows
the DBA to recover specific datafiles while allowing the rest of the tablespace to
remain online for users to access. This is particularly a nice feature if the datafile
was empty or sparsely populated, as opposed to the entire tablespace. Here is some
sample code required to recover a datafile:

```
sql "alter database datafile 3 offline ";
sql "alter database datafile 'd:\oracle\oradata\users01.dbf' offline ";
```

```
restore datafile 3;
restore datafile 'd:\oracle\oradata\users01.dbf';
recover datafile 3;
recover datafile 'd:\oracle\oradata\users01.dbf';
sql "alter database datafile 3 online";
sql "alter database datafile 'd:\oracle\oradata\users01.dbf' online ";
```

We recovered a couple of datafiles in this example, using a couple of different methods of defining which datafile we were recovering. First, we used the **sql** command again and took the offending datafiles offline with an **alter database datafile offline** command (they may be already offline in some cases, but we want to make sure).

Before we move on, let's look closer at one component of the **alter database** command: how we reference datafiles. There are two different ways to reference datafiles. The first is to reference the datafile by number, and that's what we did with datafile 3. The second is to reference a datafile by name, 'd:\oracle\oradata\ users01.dbf'. Either method is acceptable, but we often find that the use of the datafile number is easier. Generally, when a datafile is missing or corrupt, Oracle will give you both the datafile name and number in the associated error message, as shown in this example:

```
ORA-01157: cannot identify/lock data file 4 - see DBWR trace file
ORA-01110: data file 4: 'D:\ORACLE\ORADATA\RECOVER\TOOLS01.DBF'
```

Notice in this listing that datafile 4 is associated with the tools01.dbf datafile. Often, it's much easier to just indicate that you want to restore datafile 4 than to indicate you want to restore d:\oracle\oradata\recover\tools01.dbf.

Once we have taken our datafiles offline, we will restore them (again using either the file number or the filename) and then recover them. Finally, we will bring the datafiles online again, which will complete the recovery process.

What If I Use Incremental Backups?

Oracle will determine automatically if you are using an incremental backup strategy when you restore your datafiles and will automatically apply the required incremental backup sets as required. You do not need to do anything different to recover in these cases.

During a restore using an incremental backup, the **restore** command will only restore the base backup. Once that restore is complete, you will issue the **recover** command, which will cause the incremental backups to be applied to the database, and then the archived redo logs will be applied. Once that is complete, then you can open the database as usual.

Note that since the database will likely be applying multiple backup sets during the recover process, your recovery will likely take longer than you might otherwise expect. However, depending on a number of factors (data change velocity being a large factor), applying incremental backup sets can be faster than the application of a generous amount of redo, and thus the incremental backup solution can be a faster one. Therefore, the ultimate benefit of incremental backups is a quicker backup strategy (and a smaller overall space requirement for the backup set pieces) at the expense of a potentially slower recovery timeline.

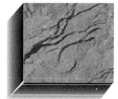

CHAPTER
11

Using Oracle9i
Enterprise Manager for
Backup Implementations

o, we've been encouraging a command-line interface usage of RMAN to this point, with the exception of the media manager configuration. It is critical to understand how to build and execute RMAN commands because sometimes you will encounter situations in which you have no other choice but to use the RMAN command-line interface. That being said, if you use a centralized utility as a DBA to administer multiple database environments, that utility can be extremely useful to schedule and monitor backup jobs.

Oracle provides an excellent management utility suite, known collectively as Enterprise Manager (EM). This set of utilities can be used for nearly every DBA task that you will ever need to perform, from space management to performance tuning to advanced setup like Data Guard and Advanced Replication. Buried in there, as well, is an interface to RMAN.

This chapter first discusses setting up Oracle9i Enterprise Manager 9.2.0.1 for enterprise usage, so that you can discover and manage remote database nodes. After that, we will forego a larger discussion of the usefulness of EM (although we encourage you to explore it extensively) and dive right into using EM for backup and recovery. We will discuss setting up jobs and event notification, as well as scheduling manual RMAN jobs. We think that after our brief introduction, you will find that EM can be an integral part of your backup and recovery strategy.

Is Enterprise Manager right for you? Well, that's a tricky question. There is a learning curve involved with EM, between getting all of its moving parts configured to familiarizing yourself with its quirks and foibles. But if you are a dedicated GUI user, EM provides an excellent way of doing advanced database administration without knowing all the views and queries and DML involved. And if you have a dozen or more databases that you are responsible for, there is no better way than to use EM to consolidate your administration and make it easier on yourself to get everything done efficiently.

Enterprise Manager Installation

In this chapter, we discuss only the most recent version of Enterprise Manager. Like many components in Oracle (and RMAN specifically), each successive version of EM includes excellent improvements, ranging from the refinement of existing functionality to entirely new options and features. Because of this, we recommend always staying up to date with your EM installation, even if your databases cannot remain quite so current. Another reason we discuss only Enterprise Manager 9.2.0.1, which ships with Oracle9i Release 2, is that it would be easy to lose focus of our real goal, backup and recovery, and immerse ourselves in discussing the differences and similarities between each particular version of EM.

If you will be calling on EM from a system that already has a 9.2 Enterprise or Standard Edition installation, then there is no installation task you need to perform because EM installs by default with any database installation. This holds true unless you chose a Custom Installation and deselected Enterprise Manager Components.

If you will be installing EM on a client system for remote administration of your databases, you will need to insert your 9iR2 media and run the setup executable. As you navigate through the installer, you come to a screen that gives you three installation options: Oracle9i Database, Oracle9i Management and Integration, and Oracle9i Client. If you install the Oracle9i Database, you get all EM components installed, no questions asked. If you are going to install EM on a system with no database locally installed (or if you need to install the latest EM on a system with an earlier database version), you will choose either of the two remaining choices, depending on which piece of EM's three-tier architecture you need to install: the Oracle Management Server (OMS) or just the client access utilities.

If you want to run the OMS locally, you need to select Oracle9i Management And Integration, and then on the next screen select Oracle Management Server. The OMS requires a repository for metadata to be contained in. If you are going to connect to an existing OMS repository, you specify this now. Otherwise, choose to install a new repository. This installation will also include all the client (first-tier) software, so you will not need a separate installation.

Enterprise Manager's Three-Tier Architecture

EM uses a distinct three-tier architecture for connecting to and managing databases in the enterprise. The three tiers are the client utilities, the Oracle Management Server (OMS), and the database nodes. The client utilities are the suite of utilities you run from your desktop to perform management duties, based out of the Enterprise Manager Console. The second tier, the OMS, stands at the core of the EM philosophy, providing the metadata and job-handling functionality necessary to scale up the client EM connections to the enterprise. It manages administrative user accounts, schedules and runs jobs and events, and manages the flow of information between the EM Console and the database nodes. The OMS gains access to the database on the database nodes via the *Intelligent Agent*. Installed by default with every database installation since Oracle 7.3, the Agent is responsible for connecting to the database and gathering requisite information, along with local execution of jobs scheduled out of the OMS.

If all you need is the client utilities, choose Oracle9i Client, and then choose the Administrator installation. This will install just those utilities needed to make a connection to a preexisting OMS, or an OMS that you will install at one of your database servers.

Configuring Enterprise Manager

From the standpoint of configuration, you must put in quite a bit of legwork initially before you can successfully use EM for backup and recovery purposes. The backup and recovery wizards that are part of EM require the usage of an OMS, as these wizards rely on the ability to run a job at the target nodes. To run these jobs, we have to have our OMS running, and we have to have our agents running at the target databases. There is no configuration necessary for the client software.

Creating and Configuring the OMS

Creating the OMS is straightforward: Oracle provides a GUI wizard, known as the Enterprise Manager Configuration Assistant (EMCA), to walk you through the steps of the OMS configuration. This wizard is installed by default with any of the three installation options mentioned previously. On Windows systems, it can be run from Start | Programs | Oracle-OraHome92 | Configuration And Migration Tools; on Solaris, you execute the file emca from the ORACLE_HOME/bin directory.

RMAN Workshop: *Build the Oracle Management Server*

Workshop Notes
For this workshop, you need an installation of the Oracle software that includes the OMS. The impact on your system can be severe, so consider yourself warned:

- The impact of an OMS varies from system to system, but a baseline, inactive memory utilization comes to roughly 280–300MB for the OMS process, and 60MB for the Agent (no, we're not kidding).

- You need 35MB of free space on disk, for the repository tablespace's datafile. This needs to be on the system that contains the database you will use for the repository.

For the sake of this section, we assume you are configuring the OMS locally to the system from which you are running EM.

Step 1. In the EMCA, select Oracle9i Management And Integration, and then select Oracle Management Server.

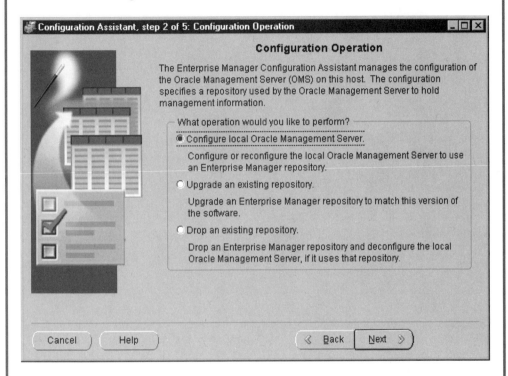

Step 2. Choose to create a new repository for OMS data. The repository is a set of database tables you create within a schema in a database of your choice. Be sure the database is a reliable one; any loss of service of that repository renders your EM setup unusable and makes your backup jobs fail. When asked by the EMCA, if you choose a Typical repository, the wizard will actually create a local database on your behalf to house the repository. If you already have a database you would like to use,

or will connect to a remote database, choose Custom instead, and then select the radio button In Another Existing Database. Then click Next.

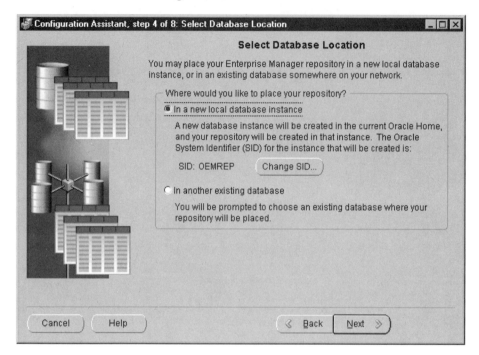

Step 3. Provide a username with DBA privileges, and a Net connect string to make the connection and create the OEM user. The next step offers a default name of the database schema that will be used. You will rarely (if ever) log in as this user, so the default works as fine as anything. Next, you select the tablespace for the OEM user. The default, again, is fine. Definitely let it create its own tablespace. If necessary, modify the default location of the datafile. After that, you simply need to review your choices and click Finish.

Step 4. The creation of the repository can take a little time. Get your coffee, read up on all the excellent features you are getting yourself into, and wait for the creation to complete. After this is done, you are ready to use EM. Open the EM Console by clicking Start | Programs | Oracle-OraHome92 | Enterprise Manager Console. Choose the option Login To The Oracle Management Server. The username and password will always be sysman/oem_temp. You will be prompted to immediately change this password. You will have to specify your OMS the first time you connect to it. Click the icon next to Management Server.

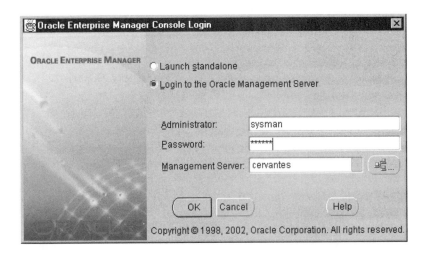

When the box appears, click Add and then type the name of the computer on which your OMS has been configured. Click OK, make sure your username and password are correct, and choose OK. Congratulations! You have EM set up and ready to roll.

The Intelligent Agent

After you have completed the configuration of your OMS, you have two out of three tiers ready to go. To prepare the third tier—your database server—you need to start the agent. The Intelligent Agent is a daemon that runs on your database server that listens for commands coming from the OMS and passes those commands down to any databases running on that system.

To start the Agent on a Windows system, you simply start the service, OracleOraHome92Agent (this name will reflect the name you gave your ORACLE_HOME, to the format Oracle<*home_name*>Agent). On Unix systems, you can navigate to your ORACLE_HOME/bin directory and type

```
Agentctl start
```

The AGENTCTL utility has four main commands: **start**, **stop**, **status**, and **restart**. You can also use it to set blackouts, but that's a conversation best left to a different book. By the way, AGENTCTL exists on the Windows platform as well, in case you are needing a command-line utility.

The Agent must be running on every database server that you want to connect to via EM. No Agent, no connection. It's that simple.

IP Addresses, DNS, and Enterprise Manager

If you haven't already noticed, the Agent will not work properly on a system that is receiving its IP address via DHCP. DHCP is a system by which a network administrator can serve out IP addresses at the time a system starts, instead of hard-coding the IP address in the system's network files. The Agent uses the utility **nslookup** to resolve information about the host, and therefore the database that runs on that host. The **nslookup** utility requires access to a DNS server that can resolve your hostname to an IP address. If you are using DHCP, you are probably not registered at a DNS server, or the name is a floating name that changes along with your IP address if you reboot.

The OMS also requires a fixed IP address to work successfully. So if you are thinking about putting the OMS on your laptop, make sure it has a fixed IP. Essentially, the way to test whether the OMS or the Agent will run successfully is to use the **nslookup** command from the command prompt to check both your IP address and your *hostname.domainname*, as follows. If both of these are successful, your Agent and OMS will be, too.

```
nslookup cervantes.windba.com
nslookup 123.123.123.123
```

There are ways around this restriction, but you should get used to the idea that Oracle Support will tell you that any hack of this basic requirement makes your system unreliable for job and event processing, and therefore will utter those most famous of phrases: "That is unsupported." Tragedy? Maybe. But then again, the truth usually is.

Node Discovery

After you have your agents up and running on your servers, it's time to head back to your EM Console, connect to the OMS, and then make the connections to your servers. The process of finding and gathering initial information about the databases running on different servers is called *node discovery*. The discovery process identifies, via the Intelligent Agent, any and all targets running on a computer (referred to here as a *node*). A target, in this sense, can refer to a database, the Oracle TNS Listener, or an Oracle HTTP server.

Node discovery takes place at the EM Console from the Navigator menu, by clicking Discover Nodes. This opens a wizard to walk you through the process. In the first step, you name the nodes you would like to discover, separated by commas, spaces, tabs, or newlines. Note, too, that you can import a longer list of nodes using the Import button in the lower-right corner.

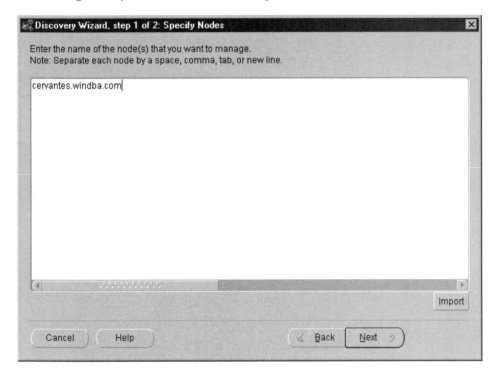

After the discovery completes, you will see your nodes listed in the left column of the EM Console. If you expand the node tree, you will see the subfolders for databases, listeners, and HTTP servers. Drilling down under Databases, you will see all databases configured on that system. If you click the database itself, you will get some rudimentary information about the database, such as the ORACLE_HOME and some listener information.

Be sure when you list the nodes for discovery that you include the server that contains your catalog database. If you will be using a recovery catalog and scheduling your backups with EM, the catalog database will need to have an agent running on its server, and it will need to be discovered.

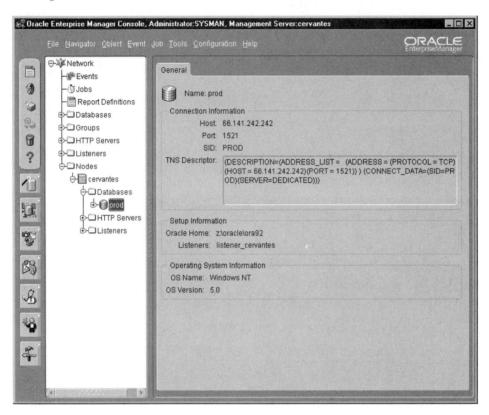

If you attempt to drill down any farther into the database by clicking the + sign next to a database name, you will be asked to provide a username and password. You can provide any username or password that can make a legitimate connection to the database, but we suggest you always use an SYSDBA connection (using the Connect As drop-down menu in the Database Connect Information dialog box). If this is a username that you will always connect to this database as, then leave the Save As Preferred Credential check box selected and click OK.

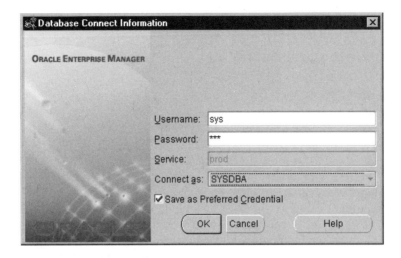

The drop-down context menu from the database gives you access to the core database administration interface of EM. From instance configuration to datafile storage information, you can use this interface to perform nearly all important administration tasks. It is outside the scope of this book to delve deeply into the usage of each tool, but we encourage you to explore at your leisure all that EM has to offer.

Preferred Credentials

We mentioned this only briefly in the previous section, but it is a feature (yeah, okay, more like a requirement) of EM worth taking note of: If you have a username and password combination that you will be using each time you connect to a database from within EM, you can store this username and password in the OMS so that you don't have to type them each time you connect to the database. This is done via Preferred Credentials.

In addition, Preferred Credentials are required if you will be doing any "lights out" administration using EM jobs. To schedule a job to run in the middle of the night requires that the job have access to password information. By using Preferred Credentials, you avoid hard-coding passwords in less secure file systems. If you will use any of the EM backup and recovery features, you will need credentials set, as these features all use jobs.

RMAN Workshop: *Setting Up Preferred Credentials for EM*

Workshop Notes

Preferred Credentials are required for backup and recovery via EM, so be sure to go through this exercise. The only information needed is the usernames and passwords you will be setting in EM.

Step 1.   To set up preferred credentials, select Configuration | Preferences to open the Preferences window. Select the Preferred Credentials tab, which lists all targets currently known to the EM user you are logged in as. Targets can be databases, listeners, HTTP servers, or nodes. For the sake of backups, we only need to worry about the database and node targets. If you select the database that you previously connected to (and left the Save As Preferred Credential check box selected), you will notice a check mark in the Credentials column, as well as the username and hidden password that you used to connect.

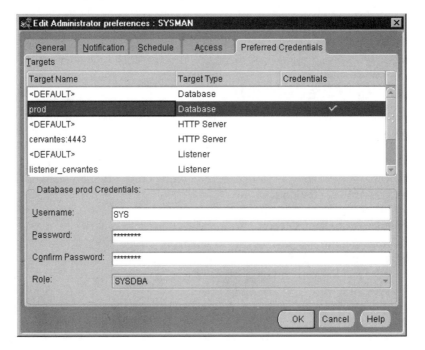

Step 2.   You can go through each of your databases and supply the username, password, and role (NORMAL, SYSOPER, or SYSDBA) for each database individually. Alternatively, if you will be logging in to every database, or even most of the

databases, as the same user, it behooves you to take advantage of the <DEFAULT> setting. For every type of target, you can specify a set of credentials that will be used by default for each of the individual targets. For instance, you can set the default username and password for the database type target to the same username/password that you use to connect to every database in the enterprise. This saves you quite a bit of hassle down the road.

Step 3. If you will be using jobs, you have to set a Preferred Credential for the node, as well as the target. The node credentials specify the user that will be used to run jobs at the OS level at your database server. Typically, you will use the oracle user that installed the Oracle software. If not, be sure to give a highly privileged username and password.

Step 4. On Windows systems, the user you specify for the node must be a member of the local Administrators group, and the user must have the Log On As A Batch Job right. To enable this right for the user, go to the Control Panel and choose Administrative Tools. Then, choose Local Security Policy. In the Local Security Settings window, expand the Local Policies tree and highlight User Rights Assignment. Then, double-click Log On As A Batch Job, click Add, and select your user. This is all it takes.

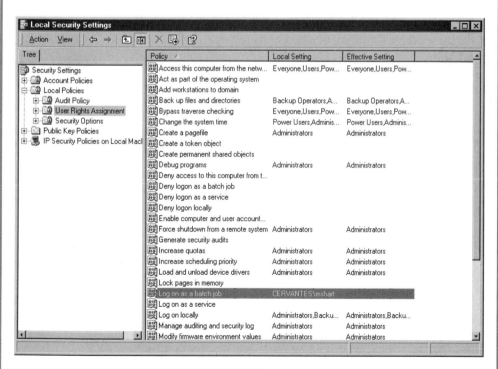

Are we glossing over quite a bit of information about credentials and authentication? You bet. But there are too many caveats and exceptions to document without completely losing our focus here. Try the Oracle Enterprise Manager documentation (you can find it all at http://technet.oracle.com) for more information.

Scheduling Jobs

Once you have your credentials squared away, you can use EM for what it's really good for: automation of jobs. In a minute, we will talk about setting up jobs for backups, but it's good to familiarize yourself with EM's job system by setting up and running a quick little job. Remember, you have to have your credentials set up for jobs to work, and if you are running on Windows 2000, you have to provide the Logon As Batch Job privilege to the preferred user.

RMAN Workshop: *Schedule an Insert Job*

Workshop Notes
You will need to create a new test user with resource privileges on a target database that has been discovered by your OMS.

Step 1. Create a dummy user and small table from sqlplus:

```
Create user dummy identified by dummy
Default tablespace users
Temporary tablespace temp;
grant connect, resource to dummy;
connect dummy/dummy
create table new_data (column1 number);
```

Step 2. Connect as **dummy** and make sure you can insert a row into the new_data table:

```
Insert into new_data values (1);
commit;
```

Step 3. In your EM Console, right-click Jobs and choose Create Job to open the Create Job dialog box, which allows you to create your job.

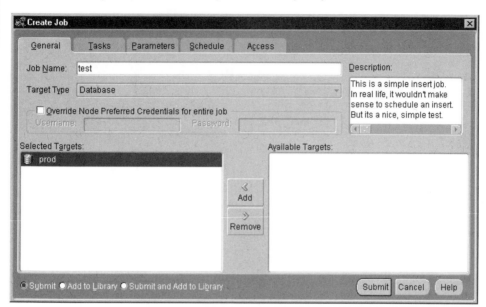

On the General tab, name the job **TEST**, and choose Database in the Target Type drop-down list. From the Available Targets box on the right, choose the target on which you created the user dummy, and move it to the Selected Targets box on the left by clicking Add.

Step 4. Move to the second tab, Tasks. From the list in the right column, choose Run SQL*Plus Script and then select Add to move it to the left column.

Step 5. On the Parameters tab in the Script Text box, type the following:

```
insert into new_data values (1);
commit;
```

Step 6. Select the Override Preferred Credentials check box and type in the username **dummy** and your dummy password.

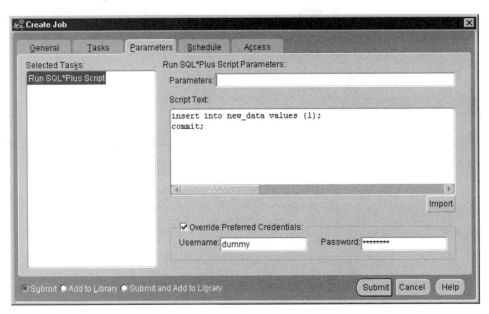

Step 7. On the Schedule tab, choose On Interval and set the interval to be every two minutes. Then click Submit.

From the EM Console, if you have Jobs highlighted, you can see the job move from a status of Submitted to Scheduled. After two minutes have passed, you can take a look at the History tab to see what has happened to your job.

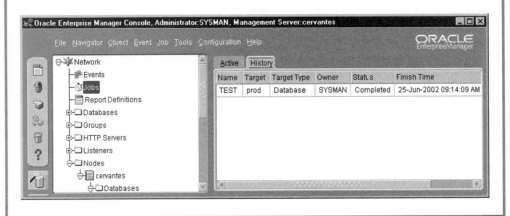

The Job Library

At any time, you can add a scheduled job to the Job Library, a stored set of jobs that can be used in the future, even if they are not currently scheduled. In this way, you can store a job that is not currently needed, but may be needed again some time in the future. Instead of deleting the job and having to build it again from scratch, you merely store it in the Job Library, and then remove it from the current job queue.

To add a job to the Job Library, select Jobs from the main EM Console. Then, on the right side of the screen, right-click the job that you want to add and choose Copy Job To Library. Then, if you want to view the Job Library, right-click Jobs from the main EM Console and choose Job Library. The Job Library window shows all stored jobs, which you can edit by changing the access and schedules, and then submit or delete the job.

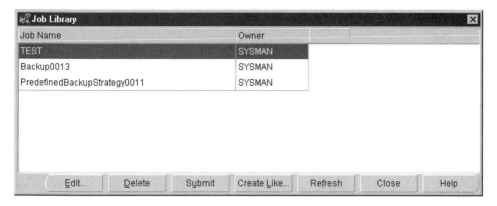

Event Notification

Enterprise Manager has the ability to monitor different types of activities on your database and node, and to respond to that activity based on parameters that you provide. EM refers to this functionality as Event Notification: when an event is encountered, you will be notified. These events can range from performance threshold levels to node outages to job failures. When a job fails, for instance, the event is noted and EM responds by sending you an e-mail message informing you of the failure. In this way, there are no surprises when your backup job fails. Instead of having to check the backups each morning when you come in, you can sit back and wait for an e-mail message to inform you of any failures.

The Event Notification subsystem can alert you to an event via e-mail or a page. In this chapter, we only provide the steps for setting up e-mail notification when a job fails.

RMAN Workshop: *Set Up E-Mail Notification for Job Failure*

Workshop Notes

To proceed with this exercise, you must have the name of your SMTP (outgoing e-mail) server and, of course, your own e-mail address. The SMTP server must be accessible from the system on which your OMS runs.

Step 1. You will be setting up your e-mail account to send an e-mail message to you when an event occurs on your system that warrants notification. In the EM Console, select Configuration | Configure Paging/Email to open the Configure Paging/Email dialog box. In the SMTP Mail Gateway list box, enter the name of the SMTP server that routes outgoing e-mail. You will not need an incoming mail server (IMAP or POP) because EM only sends mail, it does not receive it. In the Sender's SMTP Mail Address list box, provide your e-mail address (you will be sending e-mail messages to yourself). Then, click OK.

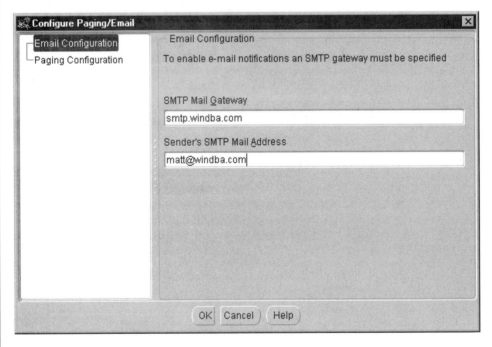

Step 2. Next, you have to set up the e-mail receiver. In the EM Console, select Configuration | Preferences to open the Preferences window (where we set Preferred Credentials), and click the Notification tab. Then, click the Email tree. In the Receiver's Email list box, specify your e-mail address. In the optional Subject Prefix list box, specify a prefix of **EM Notification**. Then, in the lower-right corner, click the Test button. This gives you a confirmation screen that the e-mail was sent or notifies you that a failure occurred. Failures here are most often a misspelling in the SMTP server name or your e-mail address, so check your spelling carefully.

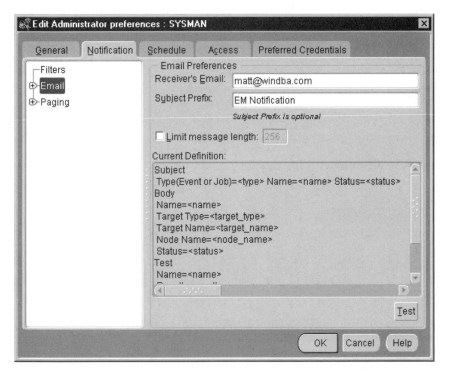

Step 3. Next, you have to configure your EM User (SYSMAN by default) for e-mail notification. In this example, we will configure the user to receive only e-mail about failed jobs. In the EM Console, select Configuration | Manage Administrators, highlight your administrator, and click Edit. This opens a Preferences dialog box for managing the administrator. Click the Notification tab. This opens the Filters options. By default, all options are selected for both e-mail and paging

notification. For the sake of this exercise, deselect every check box except Fail under Job Filters.

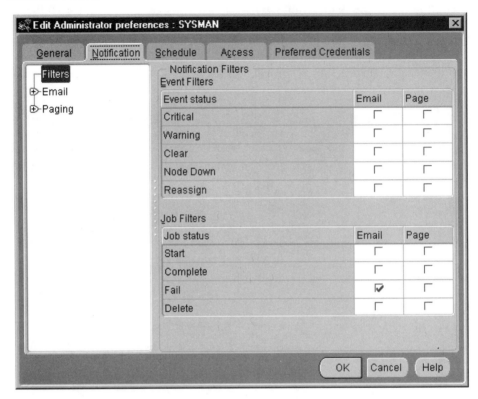

Step 4. Click the Schedule tab. By default, the schedule is completely clear, meaning that there is no time scheduled for notification. Highlight the hours during which you would like to be e-mailed, and then click the legend box at the bottom titled Email. In the following example, we highlighted the entire 24-hour day.

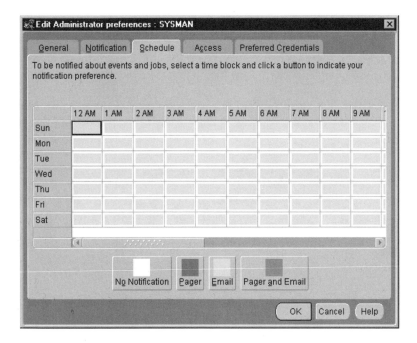

Step 5. Click the Access tab, and for your administrator account, select the check box for Notify. Then click OK. The EM administrator has been set up to receive e-mails for job failures.

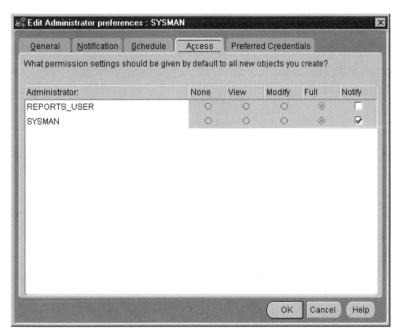

Step 6.   You're not quite done yet. While the user has been scheduled to receive e-mail notification of any job failure at any time during the day, the job itself is not configured to send e-mail when it fails. To do this, navigate to the Jobs tree in the main EM Console window. With Jobs highlighted, double-click the Test job we created earlier in this chapter. When the job appears in a new window, click the Access tab. This will look very familiar. Choose your administrator user from the list, and click the Notify check box. Now you are ready to receive e-mails should this Test job fail.

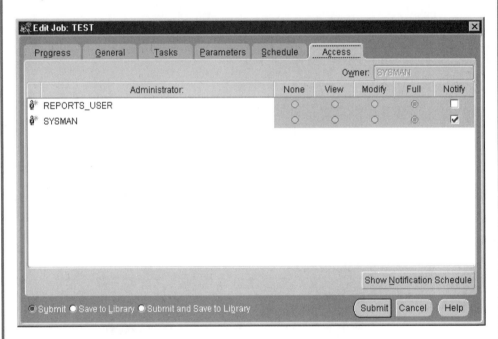

Step 7.   So let's make it fail, shall we? Log in to SQL*Plus and run the following code:

```
connect dummy/dummy;
drop table new_data;
```

Step 8.   Log in to your e-mail account and watch the e-mails pile up. The Test job was set to insert a row into new_data every two minutes, so you can expect an e-mail from EM every two minutes, notifying you of this failure.

You will get an e-mail from yourself with a subject of EM Notification JOB TEST FAILED. The body of the message will look something like this:

```
Name : TEST
Target Name : prod
Target Type : Database
Node Name : cervantes
Status : FAILED
```

STEP 9.   To stop the e-mail barrage, delete the TEST job. From the main EM Console, select Jobs, and highlight the TEST job. Right-click it and choose Remove Job. Optionally, you can also right-click the Jobs tree in the main EM Console and choose Clear Job History to remove the sordid history of our TEST job.

Congratulations! You now have EM up, running, and configured. Granted, we've raced through the configuration and skipped over a lot of excellent EM functionality, but you're at least far enough to successfully configure and monitor backup jobs using EM. So, without further ado....

The EM Backup Management Utilities

Now that you have EM set up, you can move on to the really good stuff: building RMAN jobs that back up the database. The interfaces for this are the Backup Management utilities, a set of windows that guide you through the backup and recovery process. You can access these utilities from the Tools | Database Tools | Backup Management menu. From there, you can access a screen for backup, recovery, maintenance, or to build backup configurations and then access those backup configurations. A *backup configuration* is a set of backup parameters, such as the number of channels or the media management environment setup, that the OMS stores in its repository on your behalf. The *Backup Configuration Library* is the means by which you access and edit this library of stored configurations.

Although it doesn't show it on the outside, EM is really just building RMAN commands underneath the GUI. Now that you've been introduced to the kinds of commands you would write directly to RMAN, looking at EM will seem to be asking slightly different questions, but that's because it's not framing the argument in quite the same way. When you make direct calls to RMAN, you are making literal commands to do specific actions. EM, on the other hand, is framing your backups based on the outcome you desire. So, it will ask questions about how you want your backups to act, and then construct the commands on your behalf. Again, EM is trying to make complicated actions seem a bit simpler.

In addition, it is worth noting here that EM is building jobs that are executed at the target sites themselves. This means one very important thing: the EM backup and recovery jobs will be using the RMAN executable that is found in the

ORACLE_HOME of the database you are connecting to. Thus, EM is an excellent form of version control to eliminate possible compatibility problems (refer to Chapter 2).

Let's go through the Backup Management tools one at a time to see how they can work to our benefit.

The Backup Wizard

You cannot connect to any of the backup utilities without first highlighting a database from the main EM Console. After doing so, select Tools | Database Tools | Backup Management and click Backups. This gives you access to the Backup Wizard, a step-by-step process for building an RMAN command and then submitting it at the target destination via an EM job.

The very first decision you will make is whether you want a predefined backup strategy or a customized strategy. If you choose the predefined strategy, a series of pages will ask you generic questions about your database. The first Backup Wizard page, Backup Frequency, asks you how often your database is updated. If it is updated infrequently, the wizard suggests a weekly full backup. If your database is a heavily used OLTP system, the wizard suggests a weekly full backup along with daily incremental backups. It will also give you the opportunity to set a retention policy and automatically delete backups past a certain number of copies.

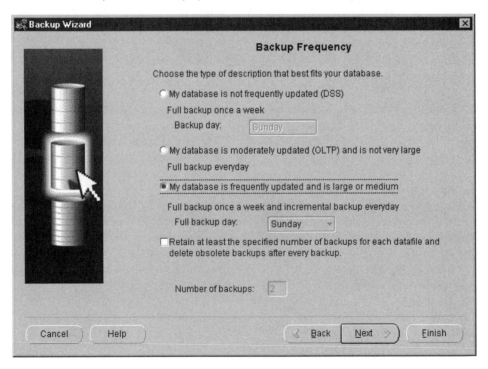

The next Backup Wizard page asks you to specify the time of day to run the backup job, suggesting that you set it to 12:00 A.M. (which is pretty good advice). Next, the Configuration page asks you to specify a backup configuration. If you have not made any new backup configurations, at least one exists by default. This one will be named the same as the database you are connected to and will back up your database using one channel, to disk, at a location derived from the name of the first datafile of the database (the system.dbf file). Obviously, this isn't an ideal backup strategy, but this allows a means by which EM can build a backup job for you with next to no information provided.

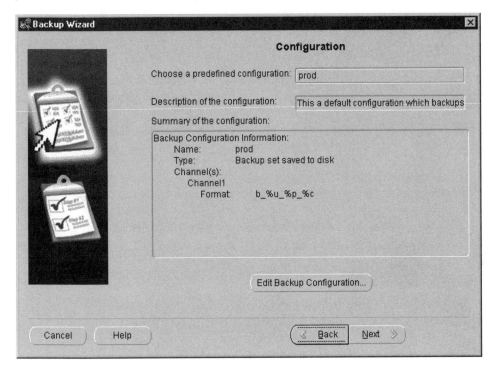

The final wizard page allows you to choose which database to submit the job to. This way, you can set up a single job to back up multiple databases in the same fashion. Then, you just click Finish, and the job is submitted into the EM job queue and can be viewed from Jobs in the main EM Console. One final screen appears from the Backup Wizard, giving you a summary of the actions that will be taken, including a look at the RMAN script it has built based on your answers. This is your last chance to cancel the backup job if it does not fit your needs.

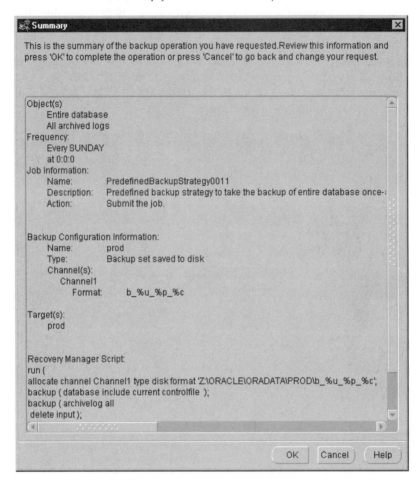

If you choose to submit a customized backup, the wizard will ask you to determine the following elements of your backup:

- The granularity of the backup: full database, tablespace, datafile, or archive log backup.

■   Whether or not you want to perform automatic backup cleanup based on the retention policy you determine in the Maintenance Wizard (see the upcoming "The Maintenance Wizard" section).

■   Whether you want your archive logs backed up along with the database and, if so, whether you want only a selected subset of the archive logs or all of them.

■   How to delete the archive logs that are backed up by RMAN.

■   Whether this will be a full or incremental backup.

■   Whether you want an online or offline backup.

■   The stored backup configuration. Again, there is a default one if you have not configured any yet (we go through the Backup Configuration Wizard next).

■   Whether you want to override the retention policy for this backup job.

■   The schedule for how frequently this backup will run. This is the same scheduling window you saw when you created a job earlier in this chapter.

■   The name and description for this backup job.

■   Whether you want to schedule this job now or simply add it to the Job Library for later use.

Next, we need to discuss the Maintenance Wizard and backup configurations. Due to dependencies of the Maintenance Wizard on the specifics of your backup configurations, we will first discuss backup configurations.

Backup Configurations

A backup configuration is the means by which we can set and store the parameters for any particular backup, so that we don't have to set them again and again. With backup configurations, we can store information about channels, back up filename formats, and the usage of a recovery catalog. We can tune our backups for optimal performance using the performance backup parameters.

Backup configurations are not really an optional part of a backup strategy that includes EM. Whenever you create any backup, recovery, or maintenance job through EM, it asks for a backup configuration. EM uses them to determine the nature of what you want done: Do you want one channel or two channels? Do you want tape channels or disk channels? Do you want to connect to a recovery catalog or use the target database control file?

Think of backup configurations as precreated shortcuts that save you from having to specify the same information over and over again. And these configurations are decoupled from specific databases, so they can be used generically against a multitude of different databases, on different nodes, that are all running agents that have been discovered by your OMS. This is similar in many ways to the new persistent configurations in Oracle9i, as you can tell, but the persistent configurations that you set manually with RMAN only apply to a single database; backup configurations in EM can be used for any database, as long as you keep the backup specifications generic enough.

Without wasting another breath, let's set up a backup configuration that allocates two disk channels, backs up to a local disk drive, and uses a recovery catalog. If you do not have a recovery catalog established, don't worry. You can skip the recovery catalog steps with absolutely no impact on the exercise—they are provided merely to assist with a maintenance exercise later in the chapter.

RMAN Workshop: *Create a Backup Configuration*

Workshop Notes
For this exercise, you need a running EM Console that has your nodes discovered and, if you desire, a recovery catalog already set up with the target databases registered.

Step 1.   Before you can create a backup configuration, you must highlight the database you expect will be backed up with this configuration. After it is highlighted, select Tools | Database Tools | Backup Management | Create Backup Configuration to open the Create Backup Configuration dialog box.

Step 2. On the General tab, give the configuration a name, which is limited to 30 characters or less. You can optionally give a description as well.

Step 3. On the Channels tab, you will see Channel 1 already set up. The only thing to change for Channel 1 is the location on disk where you want your backups to reside. We have chosen /u04/backup_data/b_%u_%p_%c. Note that you can change the backup to an image copy at this stage, if you desire.

Step 4. Below Channel 1, click the Insert button. Channel 2 will appear in the list. Highlight this channel, and change the backup location. We have chosen /u02/backup_data/b_%u_%p_%c, so that we are putting half the backup on a different physical disk.

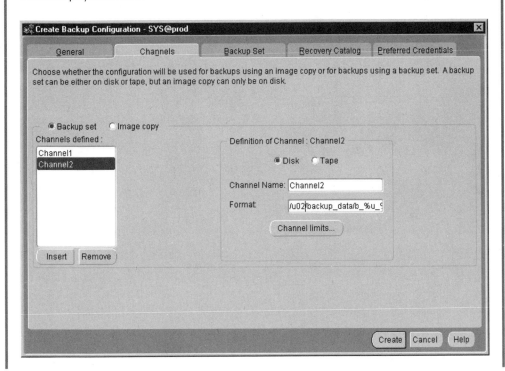

Step 5. Still on the Channels tab, click the Channel Limits button. A smaller window appears, allowing you to manage RMAN's resource usage more closely. Chapter 15 discusses these parameters in detail. Here, we take the defaults, and click OK.

Step 6. On the Backup Set tab, click the check box Override Recovery Manager Defaults. Now you can change the maximum number of files per backup set. For the sake of this exercise, we will leave this setting at the default.

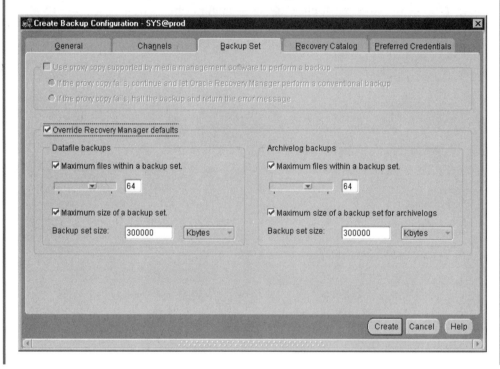

Step 7.   On the Recovery Catalog tab, select the In A Recovery Catalog radio button, and then enter the name and password of your recovery catalog owner. Specify the service name that will connect you to your catalog database.

Step 8. On the Preferred Credentials tab, there is nothing you need do if you have set up the preferred credentials for your target databases in EM as a SYSDBA user. If not, you need to override the EM preferred credentials here with a username and password that can log in to your target as SYSDBA.

Step 9. Click Create. If the target database that you highlighted at the beginning of this exercise is not registered in the catalog you specified, you get a message telling you so. It also offers to register the database on your behalf. Click Register.
   To view the configuration, select Tools | Database Tools | Backup Management | Backup Configuration Library. This will display a listing of all stored configurations. From here, you can edit the configuration if necessary.

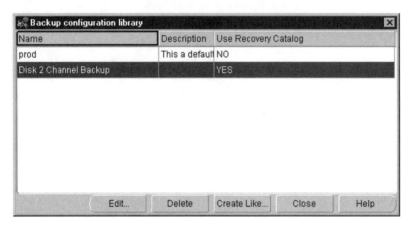

The Maintenance Wizard

The Maintenance Wizard is responsible for two things: setting the backup and retention policies, and performing recovery catalog–specific commands. If you choose the former, you will be prompted for the following information:

■ Whether or not to automatically back up the control file and server parameter file, and, if so, where exactly to back them up to.

■ Here you can turn backup optimization on, and also set any tablespaces that you want to skip on backup.

■ You can set the retention policy to a recovery window of days, or set it to a number of backups to retain.

■ Set the default backup configuration to be used by the chosen database.

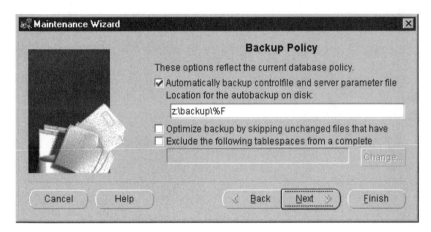

When you are finished with the configuration, EM shows you a summary page and then submits the job. This is submitted as a one-time job and does not need to be deleted from the Jobs screen.

You can also perform three recovery catalog–specific operations from the maintenance screen: register databases, resynchronize the catalog, and reset the database.

To register a database, you have to specify a backup configuration. This may seem a little counterintuitive, but the backup configuration is the means by which you specify the catalog database connection information. So, be sure to specify a backup configuration that contains your recovery catalog credentials.

The Maintenance Wizard's final page, Multiple Targets, is the most powerful: here, you get a list of all the discovered databases known to EM. Using this utility, you can choose to register multiple databases as a single job, so that you don't have to go through and do the registration for each database. The register database job that is created is a one-time job, and does not need to be deleted.

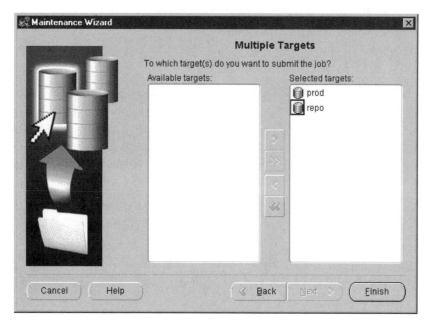

If you choose the Resynchronize Catalog option in the Maintenance Wizard, then you must specify a backup configuration again to make the recovery catalog connection. After the backup configuration, you can set the schedule for the resync job. Here again, the power of using EM shines through: you can automate the **resync** command as a job so that it executes on a regular basis. In addition, after you set the schedule, you can select multiple target databases, so that you can set one job that resynchronizes all of your databases regularly without any intervention.

The final option from the Maintenance Wizard is the **reset database** command. All you need to do for this command is specify the backup configuration that has the information to connect to the recovery catalog. The reason for resetting your database is spelled out in Chapter 3.

The Recovery Wizard

There is a time and place for every tool in your tool belt, and the Recovery Wizard is no different. It has a very straightforward interface for doing straightforward recovery operations: the whole database, datafiles, tablespaces, or block media recovery. Moreover, the Recovery Wizard is extremely effective if you have been performing your backups using EM: you have all of your credentials set up for your nodes correctly, you have your jobs and job failure established, and you have set up your EM backup configurations. Would you ever use the Recovery Wizard if you were using command-line scripts for backup? Absolutely not. The wizard only provides a benefit when EM has already been established and used to perform backups. Otherwise, trying to get it to work for you while the database is down wastes valuable time.

If you have been using EM for backups, the Recovery Wizard is an excellent, and dare I say intelligent, little utility. Just starting it will give you an indication. It will tell you the status of your database (open, mounted, and so forth), and will tell you, based on the status, what your options are. For instance, if your database is only in NOMOUNT mode and you need to restore a control file, it will indicate what your choices are (if you will use your recovery catalog or control file autobackups).

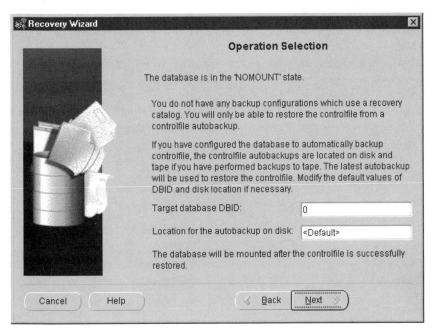

Once your database is mounted, the Recovery Wizard shows its true colors: full restore and recovery, the most basic of tasks. You can also perform a more specific task: just restore, just recover, or perform block media recovery.

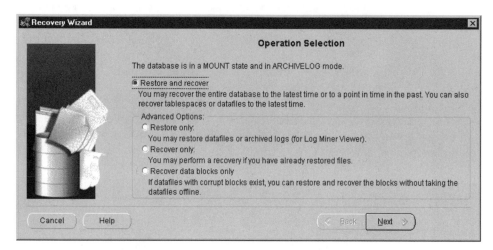

Other than block media recovery, all of these options will ask you what granularity you desire: the full database, tablespaces, or datafiles. It will then ask whether you want to perform a complete or a point-in-time recovery. It will give you the opportunity to rename any files, in case the original location has been lost. Finally, it will give you a summary screen, on which you choose your backup configuration. Obviously, you should be choosing the backup configuration that you used to create those backups now required for recovery.

The Recovery Wizard has certain criteria for the option screens that it presents to you. Based on the status of the target database you are connected to, there are three option states:

- If the database is at nomount, you can restore the control file.

- If the database is mounted but not open, restoring the control file is not an option.

- If the database is open, you can restore any tablespace except SYSTEM.

Block media recovery is pretty slick running out of the Recovery Wizard. It asks you whether you want to do the recovery from the corruption list (V$DATABASE_BLOCK_CORRUPTION) or want to specify the blocks themselves based on a datafile list or a tablespace list. Then, you give your backup configuration, and it's off and running. To use the corruption list, you have to run a job in EM called the RMAN job, which does a **backup database validate** to see which blocks are corrupt, and populate the V$DATABASE_BLOCK_CORRUPTION view.

Be sure that if you will be using the Recovery Wizard, you have configured EM to notify you for all job failures. Once completed, the Recovery Wizard packages your choices as an EM job that calls RMAN at the specified target. If for any reason it fails, you need to know immediately. Recovery is not something to take lightly or to fumble your way through. Usually, you have someone breathing down your neck, users calling constantly, and a real live revenue stream waiting for you.

So, don't leave anything up to chance. If you use EM for recovery, test the different recovery options, and make sure you are comfortable with the wizard format and that you know the outcome of each choice it presents. Often, the Recovery Wizard won't give you the flexibility or interactive ability that you need to get a restore and recovery done as quickly as possible, so be willing to walk away from your GUI and write the commands at the command prompt. But, if you understand exactly what your recovery situation requires and you are familiar with your EM configuration, then the wizard is an invaluable time saver for an enterprise DBA.

Summary

In this chapter, we discussed the installation and configuration of the different components necessary to use Oracle9i Enterprise Manager for backup and recovery of your target databases. We walked through setting up jobs and event notification. Then, we discussed how to use the wizards available for configuring and running backup and recovery jobs.

CHAPTER
12

RMAN Advanced
Recovery Topics

his chapter introduces you to some advanced recovery topics. We start with a topic that tends to cause the most trouble and confusion when it comes to recovery topics, incomplete recoveries. Then, we look at some miscellaneous recovery topics. We will then look at tablespace point in time recovery, followed by a look at how you can verify your backups. Finally, we will look at the **dbms_backup_restore** package that is associated with RMAN.

Incomplete Recoveries

An incomplete recovery is just what it sounds like—a recovery of the database that is incomplete. It is similar to a complete recovery in many respects; the basic command set is the same, but with a few added wrinkles. The possible causes of an incomplete recovery are numerous, such as the loss of online or archived redo logs or a major user error that has seriously compromised the database. Incomplete recoveries impact the entire database; in other words, you cannot perform an incomplete recovery on just one part of the database because it would result in that part of the database having a different system change number (SCN, or point in time if you prefer) than the remainder of the database.

The point about incomplete recovery impacting the entire database is an important point to make, and many junior DBAs get caught by this. Oracle demands that a database be consistent at startup, and if it is not consistent, Oracle will complain bitterly. To illustrate the point, consider an example in which a user who has his own tablespace has just mistakenly truncated a table in that tablespace, for which he has no backup. He calls you in a panic and asks you to recover just that tablespace to the point in time before he issued the truncate operation.

At first thought, the junior DBA might think that he can just restore the datafiles of the offending tablespace and recover them to a time before the truncate operation was executed. Seems somewhat logical, doesn't it? (In fact, that's what a logical backup is for.) So, the junior DBA restores the datafiles and recovers the tablespace to a point in time before the truncate operation. Now he's feeling pretty good about himself. Unfortunately, his euphoria is short lived because when he tries to open his database, RMAN slaps him with this message:

```
ERROR at line 1:
ORA-01113: file 3 needs media recovery
ORA-01110: data file 3: 'D:\ORACLE\ORADATA\RECOVER\INDX01.DBF'
```

Oracle is basically saying (in this case), "You recovered the datafile all right, but you didn't do enough recovery on it, and it's not consistent with the rest of the database!" So, as you can see, incomplete recovery is not the solution to all of your woes, but it can be the solution to some of them.

Incomplete recovery certainly has its place. If you need to take your entire database back to the same point in time, or if you lose your active, online redo logs, you will need to do some form of incomplete recovery.

Next, we look at the **resetlogs** command because it is common to just about every incomplete recovery situation there is, and then we discuss actual incomplete recovery methods, including time-, SCN-, log sequence–, and cancel-based recoveries.

Using the resetlogs Command

During incomplete recoveries, you pretty much always need to use the **resetlogs** command when opening the database because you are deviating from an already established stream of redo that exists, and you need to indicate this to Oracle. The **resetlogs** command really represents the end of one logical life of your database, and the beginning of the next logical life of your database. This logical lifespan of a database is known as an *incarnation*. Each time you use **resetlogs**, you are creating a new incarnation of the database. This can be critical with regard to recovery, as we will discuss later in this section.

With each use of the **resetlogs** command, the SCN counter is not reset. However, Oracle does reset other counters, such as the log sequence number, and the contents of the online redo logs are reset (and re-created if required). Recovering a database by using a backup that was taken before you issued the **resetlogs** command can be complicated at best, and thus a section is dedicated to this process later in the chapter.

The bottom line of this discussion is that any time you issue the **resetlogs** command when opening a database, you need to back up the database, if at all possible. As you will see later in this chapter, recovery from a previous incarnation can be frustrating (and time consuming if you don't have a recovery catalog). Recovery through **resetlogs** is a complex task that requires a number of things to go just right to work. So, don't depend on it.

Establishing a Point to Recover To

One of the things you need to do when performing incomplete recovery with RMAN is to establish a recovery target. The recovery target is the point at which you wish to terminate the recovery process and can be identified based on a point in time, a specific SCN, or a log sequence number. The recovery target can be established in a number of different ways. First, you can use the **set** command along with the **until time**, **until SCN**, or **until sequence** parameter within a **run** block, as shown in this example, which uses the **set until time** command to establish the recovery target as 3 P.M. on July 1, 2002:

```
run
{
set until time "to_date('07/01/02 15:00:00','mm/dd/yy hh24:mi:ss')";
```

```
restore database;
recover database
alter database open resetlogs;
}
```

When this command is issued, RMAN looks for the backup set closest to, but not including or after, this period of time, and restores the database from that backup set. If the database it in NOARCHIVELOG mode, then recovery will stop at that point; otherwise, during the execution of the **recover** command, Oracle will apply the archived redo logs (and any incremental backups that need to be applied) up to, but not including, the defined recovery target.

You can also opt to use the **until time**, **until SCN**, or **until sequence** commands directly in the **restore** and **recover** commands, which eliminates the need for the **run** block entirely. Here is an example of the use of the **until time** command when restoring and recovering a database:

```
-- We assume that your control file is intact
startup mount;
restore database UNTIL TIME "TO_DATE('06/28/02 13:00:00','MM/DD/YY HH24:MI:SS')";
recover database UNTIL TIME "TO_DATE('06/28/02 13:00:00','MM/DD/YY HH24:MI:SS')";
alter database open resetlogs;
```

Time-Based Recovery

In the previous section, we provided some examples of time-based recovery. This type of recovery allows you to recover the database as it looked consistently at a specific time. Of course, if you don't have backups or archived redo logs available to restore the database to the time you are requesting, then Oracle will generate an error somewhat like this one:

```
RMAN-00571: ===========================================================
RMAN-00569: =============== ERROR MESSAGE STACK FOLLOWS ===============
RMAN-00571: ===========================================================
RMAN-03002: failure of restore command at 07/02/2002 21:33:02
RMAN-20207: UNTIL TIME or RECOVERY WINDOW is before RESETLOGS time
```

The bottom line is that you need to make sure you have a backup of your database that was taken before the time you wish to recover to. You also need all of your archived redo logs. In Chapter 14, we discuss the **list** and **report** commands that allow you to determine what backups are available for RMAN to restore from.

SCN-Based Recovery

We talked about the SCN in detail in Chapter 1. Oracle allows you to recover the database to a specific SCN. In practice, this is not a frequently used recovery method, but it's nice to know it's available. We will use it later in this chapter to recover to a previous database incarnation. Here is an example of a recovery to a specific SCN:

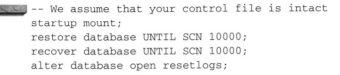

```
-- We assume that your control file is intact
startup mount;
restore database UNTIL SCN 10000;
recover database UNTIL SCN 10000;
alter database open resetlogs;
```

In this case, we restore up to, but not including, SCN 10000.

Log Sequence–Based Recovery

RMAN allows you to perform a recovery up to a specific archived redo log sequence number. This is handy if there is a gap in your archived redo logs, which generally means that you can only recover up to the point where the gap begins. Here is the command to perform this recovery in RMAN:

```
-- We assume that your control file is intact
startup mount;
restore database UNTIL SEQUENCE 100 thread 1;
recover database UNTIL SEQUENCE 100 thread 1;
alter database open resetlogs;
```

In this case, we restore up to, but not including, log sequence 100 of thread 1.

Other RMAN Recovery Topics

We have covered a number of different restore operations that you can do with RMAN, but a few more topics remain to go over. In this section, we discuss more of the restore operations that are available to you. First, we look at how to restore archived redo logs from your backup sets. Next, we look at restoring control file copies from backup. Then, we move on to discuss restoring datafile copies and backup set backups. Finally, we discuss validating your backups, an important feature in RMAN.

Read-Only Tablespace Recovery Considerations

By default, RMAN will not restore read-only datafiles when you do a full database restore, even if the read-only datafile is not there. To restore a read-only datafile during a full recovery, you need to include the **check readonly** parameter in the **restore** command:

```
restore database check readonly;
```

Note that the RMAN behavior is different if you issue a **recover tablespace** or **recover datafile** command. When you use either of these two **recover** commands, recovery occurs regardless of the read-only nature of the tablespace.

Archived Redo Log Restores

During the normal course of recovery with RMAN, there is no real need to recover the archived redo logs. However, restoring one or more archived redo logs may be required occasionally. For example, you might want to use Log Miner to mine some information from the archived redo log files stored in your backups. In this event, RMAN allows you to restore specific archived redo logs by using the **restore archivelog** command, as shown in these examples:

```
restore archivelog all;
restore archivelog from logseq=20 thread=1;
restore archivelog from logseq=20 until logseq=30 thread=1;
```

You might want to have Oracle restore the archived redo logs to a location other than the default location. To do this, use the **set** command with the **archivelog destination to** parameter:

```
run
{
set archivelog destination to "d:\oracle\newarch";
restore archivelog all;
}
```

Note that there is no alternative to the **set** command, so a **run** block is required. Finally, be aware that RMAN will not restore an archived redo log to disk if it determines that the archived redo log already exists. Even if you change the destination to a destination other than the default archivelog destination, Oracle will not recover an archived redo log to that new destination.

Datafile Copy Restores

You can restore your database datafiles from a datafile copy (as opposed to a backup set). To do this, use the **restore from datafilecopy** command and then use the **recover** command as you normally would to recover the database (or tablespace or datafile), as shown in this example:

```
restore (datafile 5) from datafilecopy;
recover datafile 5;
sql "alter database datafile 5 online;"
```

Note that when you issue a **restore** command, it will identify the most current copy of the datafiles that need to be restored and then restore those datafiles from that copy. The most current copy of a datafile might be within a datafile copy rather than a backup set. In that case, Oracle will recover the datafile copy. Also note that the use of parentheses is important; if they are not used, this command will fail.

Recovering Corrupted Data Blocks

Up to this point, most of the restore methods (full database, tablespace, and datafile) have been available in versions of RMAN prior to Oracle9i. In Oracle9i, a brand-new feature is available that is the most granular type of restore you can make with RMAN. With *block media recovery (BMR)* you can now do block-level recoveries to repair logically or physically corrupted blocks in your Oracle database, even while the associated datafile is online and churning away the whole time.

So, just how do we do a block media recovery? It's easy, as demonstrated in the following example. Suppose you receive the following error message when querying an Oracle table:

```
ORA-01578: ORACLE data block corrupted (file # 19, block # 44)
ORA-01110: data file 19: 'd:\oracle\oradata\data\mydb_maintbs_01.dbf'
```

This message is telling you that a block in the MAINTBS tablespace is corrupted. Of course, you need to do something about that. Before Oracle9i, you would have had to recover the datafile from a backup. During this recovery, all data within that datafile would be unavailable to the users.

Now, with Oracle9i, we can use BMR to recover just the corrupted blocks. This is facilitated through the **blockrecover** command. In the preceding example, the **blockrecover** command would look like this:

```
blockrecover datafile 19 block 44;
```

You can recover multiple blocks in multiple datafiles at the same time, if you like. Here are two examples of using **blockrecover** for such an operation:

```
BLOCKRECOVER DATAFILE 19 BLOCK 44,66,127;
BLOCKRECOVER DATAFILE 19 BLOCK 44 DATAFILE 22 BLOCK 203;
```

Of course, Oracle tracks block corruption that occurs during backups and copies. If a backup or copy operation has detected corruption, the operation will fail by default because Oracle will allow zero corruption in a backup. Of course, you can configure RMAN to allow a set amount of corruption, but this is not a recommended practice.

If you want to see all database corruption that might be detected by RMAN, you can use the **backup validate database** command, which populates the views V$BACKUP_CORRUPTION and V$DATABASE_BLOCK_CORRUPTION with the results of all corrupted blocks. If corruption occurs during a copy operation, the V$COPY_CORRUPTION view indicates which backup sets contain corruption. Note that V$BACKUP_CORRUPTION is a historical view of past corruption. V$DATABASE_ BLOCK_CORRUPTION is a view of current block corruption. Once you have corrected the database block corruption, rerun the **backup validate database** command, and then query V$DATABASE_BLOCK_CORRUPTION to ensure that no further corruption exists.

As we mentioned already, you can query the view V$DATABASE_BLOCK_ CORRUPTION for details on corrupted blocks. To make it easy to correct corrupted blocks in V$DATABASE_BLOCK_CORRUPTION, you can use the **blockrecover** command with the **corruption list restore** parameter:

```
BLOCKRECOVER CORRUPTION LIST RESTORE UNTIL TIME 'SYSDATE - 5';
```

In this case, we will restore all corrupted blocks on our corrupt block list that are no older than five days old. You can also use the **until time** and **until sequence** keywords with this command.

Recovering to a Previous Incarnation

Recall from our earlier discussion about the **resetlogs** command that an incarnation of a database is a representation of a specific logical lifetime for that database. As a hotshot DBA, you may find yourself in an odd restore situation in which you need to restore your database using a backup that took place from before the last time you opened the database using the **resetlogs** command. In this section, we discuss how to recover your database from a previous incarnation both with a recovery catalog (a rather easy task) and without a recovery catalog (plan for time and frustration). Finally, we will cover a rather unique recovery situation in which you need to recover through the **resetlogs** command.

Recovering to a Previous Incarnation with a Recovery Catalog

One of the three good reasons to use a recovery catalog is that doing so makes recovering from a previous incarnation easy (the other two being the ability to store scripts and easier recovery of the control file). Let's look at an example of recovering from a previous incarnation. In this example, we assume we have done backups using a recovery catalog and that we have recently done a point-in-time recovery using **resetlogs**. Now, we need to recover our database using a backup taken from a point in time before we issued our **resetlogs** command. First, we need to list the database incarnations by using the **list incarnation** command (covered in detail in the next chapter):

```
RMAN> list incarnation;
List of Database Incarnations
```

```
DB Key  Inc Key DB Name  DB ID            CUR Reset SCN  Reset Time
------- ------- -------- ---------------- --- ---------- ----------
1       2       RECOVER  2539725638       NO  763059     08-JUL-02
1       123     RECOVER  2539725638       YES 764905     09-JUL-02
```

In this list, we discover that there have been two different incarnations of our database, incarnation key 2 and incarnation key 123. The CUR column indicates that we are on incarnation key 123 right now (since it says YES). So, we need to switch back to incarnation 2 of the database.

Now that we know which incarnation we want to recover, we proceed to do the recovery (we removed some of the output here to make this example clearer):

```
RMAN> startup force nomount
Oracle instance started
RMAN> reset database to incarnation 2;
database reset to incarnation 2 in recovery catalog
RMAN> restore controlfile;
Finished restore at 10-JUL-02
RMAN> restore database until scn 764904;
 Finished restore at 10-JUL-02
RMAN> recover database until scn 764904;
starting media recovery
media recovery complete
Finished recover at 10-JUL-02
RMAN> alter database open resetlogs;
database opened
new incarnation of database registered in recovery catalog
starting full resync of recovery catalog
full resync complete
```

The following steps describe what we have done in this example:

1. Start the instance. We don't mount it, though, because we first want to get a control file that is associated with the incarnation of the database we wish to recover.

2. Use the **reset database to incarnation** command to indicate to RMAN which incarnation's backup sets we wish to be considered for the recovery.

3. Issue the **restore controlfile** command, prompting RMAN to restore the most current control file for us.

4. Mount the database.

5. Restore the database, doing an SCN-based restore (discussed earlier in this chapter). We have decided to restore the database to the SCN just before the last **resetlogs** (which was at SCN 764905), so we issue the **restore database** command, limiting the restore to SCN 764904.

6. Issue the **recover** command, again limiting the recovery of the database to SCN 764904, and wait for the recovery to complete.

7. Open the database, resetting the online redo logs.

Now, when we run the **list incarnation** command, the results are as follows:

```
RMAN> list incarnation;
List of Database Incarnations
DB Key  Inc Key DB Name  DB ID             CUR Reset SCN  Reset Time
------- ------- -------- ----------------- --- ---------- ----------
1       2       RECOVER  2539725638        NO  763059     08-JUL-02
1       123     RECOVER  2539725638        NO  764905     09-JUL-02
1       245     RECOVER  2539725638        YES 764905     10-JUL-02
```

Note the new incarnation of the database that has been created (with incarnation key 245). Also note that the reset SCN for this new incarnation is the same as that of incarnation 123 (which was the active incarnation). The reset time, however, reflects the actual time that this incarnation was created.

Recovering to a Previous Incarnation Without a Recovery Catalog

This type of recovery is a bit trickier because you do not have the luxury of the **reset database to incarnation** command. We have to manually recover the correct control file using the **dbms_backup_restore** procedure before we can do anything. First, again, we want to list our database incarnations:

```
RMAN> list incarnation;
List of Database Incarnations
DB Key  Inc Key DB Name  DB ID             CUR Reset SCN  Reset Time
------- ------- -------- ----------------- --- ---------- ----------
4       4       RECOVER  2539725638        NO  316908     25-JUN-02
5       5       RECOVER  2539725638        YES 394300     10-JUL-02
```

Here, we want to go back to incarnation 4, and in particular to SCN 394299 (or we could choose a time if we preferred). First, we need a control file that is from that incarnation. To get our control file, we list our backups with the **list backup file** command (discussed in more detail in the next chapter). Here is an example of the output from this command (again, cleaned up for brevity):

```
RMAN> list backup by file;
List of Datafile Backups
========================

File Key      TY LV S Ckp SCN    Ckp Time   #Pieces #Copies Tag
---- -------  -  -- - ---------- ---------- ------- ------- ----------------
1    33       B  F  A 394144     09-JUL-02  1       1       TAG20020709T2353
2    32       B  F  A 394128     09-JUL-02  1       1       TAG20020709T2353
```

```
3    33     B  F  A  394144      09-JUL-02 1           1          TAG20020709T2353
4    32     B  F  A  394128      09-JUL-02 1           1          TAG20020709T2353
5    32     B  F  A  394128      09-JUL-02 1           1          TAG20020709T2353


List of Archived Log Backups
============================
Thrd Seq    Low SCN    Low Time   BS Key  S #Pieces #Copies Tag
---- ------- ---------- ---------- ------- - ------- ------- --------------
1    7       393235     27-JUN-02 31       A 1        1        TAG20020709T23
1    8       394122     09-JUL-02 34       A 1        1        TAG20020709T23


List of Controlfile Backups
===========================
CF Ckp SCN Ckp Time  BS Key  S #Pieces #Copies Tag
---------- --------- ------- - ------- ------- ---
394396      10-JUL-02 36      A 1       1
394220      09-JUL-02 35      A 1       1


List of SPFILE Backups
======================
Modification Time BS Key  S #Pieces #Copies Tag
---------------- ------- - ------- ------- ---
26-JUN-02          36      A 1       1
26-JUN-02          35      A 1       1
```

Look at the section of the report titled "List of Controlfile Backups." The CF Ckp column indicates the SCN that the control file was created at. In this case, we want the SCN that is equivalent to or less than 394299. So, from this report, it appears that we want to restore the control file from the backup set with a backup set key number 35. Before we can recover the control file, though, we need to find out more about this backup set. So, let's use the **list backupset** command to generate a bit more detail about our backup set:

```
RMAN> list backupset 35;
List of Backup Sets
===================
BS Key  Type LV Size        Device Type Elapsed Time Completion Time
------- ---- -- ---------- ----------- ------------ ---------------
35       Full   1M           DISK        00:00:08     09-JUL-02
          BP Key: 35   Status: AVAILABLE   Tag:
          Piece Name: D:\ORACLE\ORA912\DATABASE\C-2539725638-20020709-00
     Controlfile Included: Ckp SCN: 394220      Ckp time: 09-JUL-02
```

Now, let's restore our control file. We use the **dbms_backup_restore** command to do this, as you learned in Chapter 10. Here is an example of restoring the control file (recall that this is done from SQL*Plus):

```
startup force nomount;
declare
devtype varchar2(256);
```

```
done boolean;
begin
devtype:=dbms_backup_restore.deviceallocate(NULL);
dbms_backup_restore.restoresetdatafile;
dbms_backup_restore.restorecontrolfileto
('d:\oracle\oradata\recover\control01.ctl');
dbms_backup_restore.restorebackuppiece('D:\ORACLE\ORA912\DATABASE\
C-2539725638-20020709-00', DONE=>done);
dbms_backup_restore.restoresetdatafile;
dbms_backup_restore.restorecontrolfileto
('d:\oracle\oradata\recover\control02.ctl');
dbms_backup_restore.restorebackuppiece
('D:\ORACLE\ORA912\DATABASE\C-2539725638-20020709-00', DONE=>done);
dbms_backup_restore.restoresetdatafile;
dbms_backup_restore.restorecontrolfileto
('d:\oracle\oradata\recover\control03.ctl');
dbms_backup_restore.restorebackuppiece
('D:\ORACLE\ORA912\DATABASE\C-2539725638-20020709-00', DONE=>done);
dbms_backup_restore.devicedeallocate(NULL);
END;
/
```

Now we are getting somewhere. We have the latest control file from the incarnation we are interested in, so we are on our way home. Next, we need to mount our database, restore and recover the database to the SCN that we are interested in, and then open it.

However, there is one little problem. Between the time we backed up our last archived redo log and the time we issued the **resetlogs** command, we might have generated a few SCNs. So that we know exactly where to recover to, we can find out what the high SCN number is in the last archived redo log we will apply. From the earlier **list backup by file** command, we find that archive log sequence number 8 appears to be the last one we want to apply. It is in backup set 34, so let's look at that backup set:

```
RMAN> list backupset 34;
List of Backup Sets
===================
BS Key  Size        Device Type Elapsed Time Completion Time
------- ----------- ----------- ------------ ---------------
34      2K          DISK           00:00:05     09-JUL-02
        BP Key: 34    Status: AVAILABLE   Tag: TAG20020709T235731
        Piece Name: D:\BACKUP\RECOVER\BACKUP_19DT65VF_1_1
  List of Archived Logs in backup set 34
  Thrd Seq     Low SCN    Low Time  Next SCN   Next Time
  ---- ------- ---------- --------- ---------- ---------
  1    8       394122     09-JUL-02 394209     09-JUL-02
```

The highest SCN in this archived redo log is 394208, which is just a bit below our target, 394301. Still, this gives us a clear target of which SCN we need to recover to. Using the 394308 SCN, then, we will recover our database. Here is that part of this exercise:

```
RMAN> alter database mount
database mounted
RMAN> restore database until scn 394301;
 Finished restore at 10-JUL-02
RMAN> recover database until scn 394301;
starting media recovery
media recovery complete
Finished recover at 10-JUL-02
RMAN> alter database open resetlogs;
database opened
new incarnation of database registered in recovery catalog
starting full resync of recovery catalog
full resync complete
```

If you want to recover based on time, then you need to get the backup times for the archived redo logs so that you know what the latest time you can restore to is for a given incarnation. Once you have recovered the control file for the incarnation, determine which is the oldest archived redo log backup for that incarnation (it will have the lowest low SCN listed on the report).

The problem with the RMAN reports, as you might have noticed, is that they only have dates, and no times, associated with them. So, we have to go to SQL*Plus to determine to what time we can restore. In our case, we know that backup piece 34 contains the oldest archived redo log we have available for this incarnation (as we demonstrated earlier). To determine the time of the last record in that archived redo log file, we can perform a simple join between **V$backupset** and **V$backup_redolog**:

```
select a.recid, to_char(b.next_time, 'mm/dd/yy hh24:mi:ss')
from v$backup_set a, v$backup_redolog b
where a.recid=34
and a.set_stamp=b.set_stamp
and a.set_count=b.set_count;
```

The following is the result:

```
     RECID TO_CHAR(B.NEXT_TI
---------- -----------------
        34 07/09/02 23:57:08
```

So, as long as we are going to restore to any time before 23:57:08, we are in good shape. If we need to restore to a point in time beyond 23:57:08, we better be looking for some additional archived redo logs (which apparently don't exist).

Tablespace Point-In-Time Recovery

Your user has dropped a table in error…in fact, the user has dropped three tables, truncated two more tables, and then called you asking for your help in getting it all back. Fortunately for you, RMAN allows you to do tablespace point-in-time recovery (TSPITR). There are a number of cases where TSPITR might come in handy. Such situations might include accidentally dropping a table, as in our opening example, or perhaps a big bulk data load program ended up logically corrupting data. A number of possibilities exist.

To learn how to perform a TSPITR, you need to be familiar with a few terms:

- **Auxiliary instance**   A temporary instance that you create. RMAN uses this instance to perform TSPITR. After you complete your TSPITR, the auxiliary instance can be removed.

- **Auxiliary set**   The set of remaining target database files that you need to perform TSPITR. This set includes a backup control file, rollback and undo segment tablespace datafiles, the SYSTEM tablespace datafiles, online redo logs of the auxiliary database, and, optionally, a temporary tablespace in the auxiliary database.

- **Recovery set**   The set of tablespaces/datafiles that you wish to perform TSPITR on.

- **Target database**   The database you are actually going to perform TSPITR on.

Performing TSPITR

The basic steps of successful TSPITR are as follows:

1. Prepare the auxiliary instance.

2. Perform the actual TSPITR.

3. Perform post-TSPITR activities on the target database.

Let's look at each of these steps in more detail next.

Prepare the Auxiliary Instance

The first thing we need to do is get an auxiliary instance up and running. As already defined, an auxiliary instance is just a temporary instance that RMAN uses to perform TSPITR. The auxiliary instance must reside on the same box as the target database, and you will never be able to execute any type of DML on the auxiliary instance.

Before we can start TSPITR, we need to get the auxiliary instance ready. This is a manual process that RMAN has no part in, but it's not unlike creating a normal database instance. To create the auxiliary instance, perform these actions:

1. Create the password file.

2. Create the database parameter file.

3. If you are running Oracle on Windows NT, add the database service with the **oradim** program.

4. Start the auxiliary instance and check to make sure that you have network connectivity.

You should be familiar in general with each of these steps, as these are typical DBA tasks. Basically, it's a lot like creating an instance in preparation for issuing the **create database** command. We need to note a few issues specific to TSPITR, however, so let's do that quickly.

The Auxiliary Instance Parameter File   The parameter file of the auxiliary database is a separate parameter file from the one used on the target database. You configure the parameter file for the auxiliary instance in much the same way you configure a normal database parameter file. You need to include a few additional parameters in this parameter file, which are listed in Table 12-1.

Parameter Name	Optional/ Required	Comment
db_name	Optional	The same name as the target database.
lock_name_space	Required	Should be a name that is unique among all other databases on the system that you are creating your auxiliary database on. In our examples, we will use aux1.
db_file_name_convert or **db_file_name_convert_n**	Optional	Can be used to define a set of file-naming conversion patterns for datafiles in the auxiliary database as they are restored by RMAN. This is an alternative to using the **configure auxname** RMAN command. Note that Oracle9i supports up to five different directories, which is handy in the event your file systems are sized differently.

TABLE 12-1.   *Auxiliary Instance Parameter File Parameters of Interest*

Parameter Name	Optional/ Required	Comment
log_file_name_convert or **log_file_name_convert_n**	Optional	Can be used to define a set of file-naming conversion patterns for redo log files in the auxiliary database as they are restored by RMAN. This is an alternative to using the **set newname** RMAN command. As with the **db_file_name_convert** command, up to five of these directories may be defined in Oracle9i.
control_files	Required	The control file parameter defines the names and locations of the auxiliary instance control files. The control files should be unique in name from any existing control file in the location(s) you intend on creating the control files in.
remote_login_passwordfile	Optional/ Required	Used to allow RMAN to connect to the auxiliary database via Oracle Networking services. Requires the presence of a current password file. If you will be connecting to the auxiliary database locally, then this doesn't need to be set.
Compatible	Required	Must be the same as the target database's setting.
db_block_size	Optional/ Required	If set on the target database, must be set in the auxiliary database to the same value.

TABLE 12-1. *Auxiliary Instance Parameter File Parameters of Interest* (continued)

Each of these parameters is further defined in the Oracle reference manual, if you need further information on how to configure them. For our example, we simply copied the target instance parameter file and made a few changes to it. Here is a copy of the resulting auxiliary database instance parameter file:

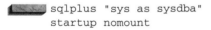
```
# These parameters already existed for the target database and
# required no changes.
db_name=recover
db_block_size=8192
db_cache_size=8388608
timed_statistics=TRUE
shared_pool_size=16777216

# Note that remote_loging_passwordfile must be set to exclusive
# if we want to connect to the aux database through RMAN via Oracle Net.
remote_login_passwordfile=EXCLUSIVE
compatible=9.2.0

# These parameters required changes to directory locations
# to reflect the new database instance.
background_dump_dest=d:\oracle\admin\auxil\bdump
core_dump_dest=d:\oracle\admin\auxil\cdump
user_dump_dest=d:\oracle\admin\auxil\udump
control_files=("d:\oracle\oradata\aux1\control01.ctl",
               "d:\oracle\oradata\aux1\control02.ctl",
               "d:\oracle\oradata\aux1\control03.ctl")

# These are new parameters that are exclusive to the aux database
lock_name_space=aux1
db_file_name_convert=
('d:\oracle\oradata\recover','d:\oracle\oradata\aux1')
log_file_name_convert=
('d:\oracle\oradata\recover','d:\oracle\oradata\aux1')
instance_name=aux1
```

Starting the Auxiliary Instance and Checking Network Connectivity   Now
that we have everything in place, we can start our auxiliary instance. To do so, we
simply use the **startup nomount** command, as shown in this example:

```
sqlplus "sys as sysdba"
startup nomount
```

Once you have started the instance, connect to it using Oracle Net to ensure
your network connectivity is correct.

Verify That the Tablespace Is Transportable

Later in this chapter, we list a number of restrictions with regard to TSPITR. RMAN uses
the transportable tablespace feature of Oracle to perform TSPITR, so the tablespace itself
must be transportable. A number of different factors can cause a tablespace to not be
transportable. Oracle provides a view, TS_PITR_CHECK, that enables you to determine

whether or not a tablespace is transportable. If the tablespace is not transportable, then RMAN will fail in attempting to do TSPITR. Here is an example of querying the TS_PITR_CHECK view:

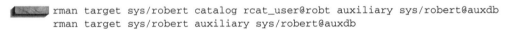

```
select obj1_owner "Object Owner" , obj1_name "Object Name", obj1_type "Ojbect Type",
 ts1_name "Tablespace Name" , reason
from ts_pitr_check
where ts1_name='USERS';

Object Owner  Object Name  Ojbect Type      Tablespace Name
------------- ------------ ---------------- ---------------
REASON
------------------------------------------------------------
SYS            BOGUS_TABLE  TABLE            USERS
Sys owned tables not allowed in Recovery Set
```

In this example, the tablespace USERS is not transportable because a table called BOGUS_TABLE in it is owned by SYS. Since a tablespace is not transportable if the SYS user owns an object in it, TSPITR recovery will not be possible for that tablespace (which is what the REASON column tells us).

Perform the Actual TSPITR

To perform the actual recovery, we need to connect to RMAN. The connection string we are going to use is a bit different because we need to connect to the target database, the auxiliary database, and the recovery catalog (if we are using one) all at the same time. To connect to the auxiliary database, we use the **auxiliary** command-line parameter, along with the **target** and **catalog** parameters, as shown in these examples:

```
rman target sys/robert catalog rcat_user@robt auxiliary sys/robert@auxdb
rman target sys/robert auxiliary sys/robert@auxdb
```

Of course, you could also choose to set the auxiliary database as your Oracle SID, and use an RMAN startup command line like this:

```
set oracle_sid=aux1
rman target sys/robert@recover auxiliary sys/robert
```

This can eliminate some of the networking hassles that you might experience, and make the entire process of creating and using the auxiliary database a bit easier.

Now that you have connected to RMAN, you can easily perform your TSPITR by issuing the **recover tablespace** command using the **until time**, **until scn**, or **until sequence** parameter, as shown here:

```
recover tablespace production until time "to_date('01/05/03 22:00:00',
'mm/dd/yy hh24:mi:ss')";
recover tablespace production until scn 44555;
recover tablespace production until sequence 22 thread 1;
```

Of course, you may need to allocate channels and the like if you do not have default channels configured. Once you have issued the **recover** command, Oracle performs several actions, including restoring the datafiles to the auxiliary instance and enabling it, recovering the tablespaces in the auxiliary instance, and then transporting the recovered tablespaces to the target database (along with the required import and export operation for a transportable tablespace).

Perform Post-TSPITR Activities on the Target Database

There are a few actions that you need to perform once your TSPITR is complete. First, you should reconnect RMAN to just the target database (and the recovery catalog if you are using one) and back up the tablespaces you just recovered. Once you have completed the backup, you will want to bring the tablespace online (RMAN leaves the tablespace offline after TSPITR). Finally, you will want to shut down the auxiliary instance.

TSPITR Restrictions

TSPITR has a number of restrictions, a quick summary of which follows:

- You can't restore tablespaces with objects owned by SYS.

- Any tablespace with replicated master tables cannot be recovered with TSPITR.

- Tablespaces with snapshot logs are not supported.

- You can't restore tablespaces that contain rollback segments.

- You can restore a tablespace that contains a partitioned object where the partitions of that object span multiple tablespaces.

- If an object within the tablespace to be recovered has one of the following types, then TSPITR is not supported:

  - VARRAY

  - Nested tables

  - External files

Additionally, TSPITR cannot be used to recover a dropped tablespace. You also will not be able to recover older object statistics.

Finally, there are some restrictions with regard to TSPITR if you are using RMAN without a recovery catalog:

- The current physical structure of the undo and rollback segments in the target database must be unchanged between the point you wish to recover to and the current point. In other words, the rollback segments can't change during the recovery.

■ Once you have completed TSPITR on a given tablespace, all previous backups of that tablespace are no longer usable for future TSPITR recoveries of that tablespace. This is why a backup of the tablespace after TSPITR is very important, in case you need to run another TSPITR.

Verifying Your Backups Are Recoverable

Of course, backups are not useful if they are not recoverable. RMAN provides a method of checking the restorability of your database without actually restoring it. RMAN offers you a couple of options. In this section, we look at some different ways to verify that your database backups, and thus your database, are recoverable. First, we will look at the **verify** and **check logical** options of the **restore** command. Then, we will look at the **validate backupset** command.

Restoring with the verify and check logical Commands

The **restore** command comes with some great options that allow you to verify that your database is recoverable and that the backup itself is valid. First, you can use the **validate** parameter of the **backup** command to cause RMAN to check the backup sets and make sure your database is recoverable. When the **validate** option is used, Oracle checks the most current backup set that will be needed to recover your database, ensuring that it is complete. This option also checks any datafile copies and archive redo log backup sets that will be required for recovery and ensures that they are all complete. Additionally, the **validate** option does a general validation of the backup sets to ensure that they are intact. Validation doesn't take very long, and is one way to ensure that your database is recoverable. Here is an example of a **validate** operation on our database:

```
RMAN> restore database validate;
Starting restore at 05-JUL-02
using channel ORA_DISK_1
using channel ORA_DISK_2
channel ORA_DISK_1: starting validation of datafile backupset
channel ORA_DISK_2: starting validation of datafile backupset
channel ORA_DISK_1: restored backup piece 1
piece handle=D:\BACKUP\RECOVER\BACKUP_4QDSM5IB_1_1 tag=TAG20020703T221224 params=NULL
channel ORA_DISK_1: validation complete
channel ORA_DISK_2: restored backup piece 1
piece handle=D:\BACKUP\RECOVER\BACKUP_4RDSM5IC_1_1 tag=TAG20020703T221224 params=NULL
channel ORA_DISK_2: validation complete
Finished restore at 05-JUL-02
```

Another, more complete check of the most current backup set is the **check logical** parameter of the **restore** command. This command causes RMAN to check the backups of the database, if they pass a physical corruption check, for logical corruption within the data and index segments backed up. If logical errors are found, Oracle will respond in one of two ways:

- If the **maxcorrupt** parameter has been set and this count is not exceeded during the restore check logical operation, RMAN will populate the Oracle V$ table V$DATABASE_BLOCK_CORRUPTION with a list of corrupted block ranges.

- If **maxcorrupt** is exceeded during the operation, then the operation will terminate.

By default, **maxcorrupt** is set to 0, so any logical corruption will cause the operation to fail. The **maxcorrupt** parameter default is modified via the **set** command and can only be established within the confines of a **run** block. Additionally, **maxcorrupt** is set for each datafile individually, not collectively. The following is an example of setting **maxcorrupt** to allow for some corruption to appear, and then logically validating backups of our database. In this example, we have set **maxcorrupt** for all the datafiles in out database (1 through 5), and we not only are checking that the latest backup sets are present and recoverable, but also are looking for logical corruption within the backup sets:

```
RMAN> run {
2> set maxcorrupt for datafile 1,2,3,4,5,6 to 5;
3> restore database check logical validate;
4> }
executing command: SET MAX CORRUPT
Starting restore at 05-JUL-02
using channel ORA_DISK_1
using channel ORA_DISK_2
channel ORA_DISK_1: starting validation of datafile backupset
channel ORA_DISK_2: starting validation of datafile backupset
channel ORA_DISK_1: restored backup piece 1
piece handle=D:\BACKUP\RECOVER\BACKUP_4QDSM5IB_1_1 tag=TAG20020703T221224 params=NULL
channel ORA_DISK_1: validation complete
channel ORA_DISK_2: restored backup piece 1
piece handle=D:\BACKUP\RECOVER\BACKUP_4RDSM5IC_1_1 tag=TAG20020703T221224 params=NULL
channel ORA_DISK_2: validation complete
Finished restore at 05-JUL-02
```

Using the validate backupset Command

Using the **restore** command with the **validate** and/or **check logical** parameters only checks the most current backup set. There may well be times that you want to check a specific backup set. To do this, you use the **validate backupset** command. To use this command, you first need to determine the backup set key that you want to back up. Each backup set, when it is made, is assigned a unique identifier called the *backup set key*. To determine the key assigned to the backup set you are interested in, you can use the **list backupset** command (covered in Chapter 13), as shown in the following example:

```
RMAN> list backupset;
List of Backup Sets
===================
BS Key  Type LV Size        Device Type Elapsed Time Completion Time
------- ---- -- ---------- ----------- ------------ ---------------
141     Full    320K         DISK        00:02:09     03-JUL-02
        BP Key: 141   Status: AVAILABLE   Tag: TAG20020703T221224
        Piece Name: D:\BACKUP\RECOVER\BACKUP_4QDSM5IB_1_1
   List of Datafiles in backup set 141
   File LV Type Ckp SCN    Ckp Time  Name
   ---- -- ---- ---------- --------- ----
   2       Full 647435     03-JUL-02
D:\ORACLE\ORADATA\RECOVER\REVDATA.DBF
   4       Full 647435     03-JUL-02
D:\ORACLE\ORADATA\RECOVER\TOOLS01.DBF
   6       Full 647435     03-JUL-02
D:\ORACLE\ORADATA\RECOVER\REVINDEX.DBF

BS Key  Type LV Size        Device Type Elapsed Time Completion Time
------- ---- -- ---------- ----------- ------------ ---------------
142     Full    113M         DISK        00:03:28     03-JUL-02
        BP Key: 142   Status: AVAILABLE   Tag: TAG20020703T221224
        Piece Name: D:\BACKUP\RECOVER\BACKUP_4RDSM5IC_1_1
   List of Datafiles in backup set 142
   File LV Type Ckp SCN    Ckp Time  Name
   ---- -- ---- ---------- --------- ----
   1       Full 647439     03-JUL-02
D:\ORACLE\ORADATA\RECOVER\SYSTEM01.DBF
   3       Full 647439     03-JUL-02
D:\ORACLE\ORADATA\RECOVER\INDX01.DBF
   5       Full 647439     03-JUL-02
D:\ORACLE\ORADATA\RECOVER\USERS01.DBF
```

Here, we are interested in the report's BS Key column, which lists the backup set key number. Notice that the files in the backup set also are listed, as are the date and time of the backup. All of this information should make it easy to identify the backup set you wish to validate. Once you have determined the set you need to check, then validating the backup set is as easy as running the **validate backupset** command, as shown in the next two examples.

```
RMAN> validate backupset 141;
using channel ORA_DISK_1
using channel ORA_DISK_2
channel ORA_DISK_1: starting validation of datafile backupset
channel ORA_DISK_1: restored backup piece 1
piece handle=D:\BACKUP\RECOVER\BACKUP_4QDSM5IB_1_1
tag=TAG20020703T221224 params=NULL
channel ORA_DISK_1: validation complete

RMAN> validate backupset 141 check logical;
using channel ORA_DISK_1
using channel ORA_DISK_2
channel ORA_DISK_1: starting validation of datafile backupset
channel ORA_DISK_1: restored backup piece 1
piece handle=D:\BACKUP\RECOVER\BACKUP_4QDSM5IB_1_1
tag=TAG20020703T221224 params=NULL
channel ORA_DISK_1: validation complete
```

The Guts of RMAN: the dbms_backup_restore Package

As we discussed in Chapter 2 and demonstrated in some of the examples in the last few chapters, the **dbms_backup_restore** package is really the heart of RMAN. It is through calls to this package that RMAN does almost all of its work. Unfortunately, much of this package is undocumented by Oracle, and it is subject to change with any version of Oracle. This section attempts to give you a quick overview of some of the major functions and procedures of this package, as they exist in Oracle9i Release 2.

The **dbms_backup_restore** package comes with about 160 various procedures and functions, many of which you will never need to use. Table 12-2 lists and describes some of the more commonly used procedures for special recovery situations.

Procedure	Description
restoreSetDataFile	Indicates the beginning of a restore operation (but does not cause the actual restore to take place)
restoreSetDataFileTo	Defines the datafile to restore and the location to restore it to

TABLE 12-2. *Common **dbms_backup_restore** Packages*

Procedure	Description
restorecontrolfileto	Defines the location to restore a control file to
restorebackuppiece	Causes the restore to actually execute
devicedeallocate	Deallocates the device allocated by the **deviceallocate** function
applysetdatafile	Indicates the beginning of an incremental restore
applydatafileto	Defines the datafile to apply the incremental restore to
applybackuppiece	Actually causes the restore to occur
restoresetarchivelog	Indicates the beginning of an archive log restore
restorearchivedlog	Defines the archived redo log sequence and thread to restore

TABLE 12-2. *Common **dbms_backup_restore** Packages* (continued)

One commonly used function is **deviceAllocate**, which allocates a device for sequential I/O.

Finally, if you are really interested in what is going on in the bowels of RMAN, you can enable the **debug** switch at the command line. When in debug mode, RMAN will output each command as it's called (including the calls to **dbms_backup_restore**).

CHAPTER
13

Maintaining RMAN

ntropy is a nasty result of the second law of thermodynamics. Basically, *entropy* describes the tendency of an ordered system to become disordered, the result of which is the requirement to maintain that system. RMAN is no different. When using RMAN, you have to maintain a number of things to keep it running smoothly.

In this chapter, we talk all about maintaining RMAN. From the **crosscheck** command to retention policies to redundancy policies, everything you need to know about keeping RMAN from falling apart is provided here. After we have talked about RMAN maintenance issues, we will discuss some issues specific to the recovery catalog, including an introduction to the recovery catalog schema itself.

RMAN Maintenance

You didn't think you could just start using RMAN and not have to do anything to maintain it, did you? The truth is that RMAN is fairly maintenance free, but there are a few maintenance-related things you need to be aware of, which we address in this section. First, we are going to talk about the **crosscheck** command, which is followed by a discussion of retention policies. Next, we discuss the **change** command, and then the **delete** command. Finally, we end this section with a discussion of cataloging your existing database backups in RMAN.

Cross-Checking RMAN Backups

You may encounter situations in which backup set pieces or copies are listed in the control file or recovery catalog but do not physically exist on the backup media (disk or tape). The physical files that comprise the backup or copy might have been deleted, either by some process (for example, a separate retention policy for the tape management system that you are using or a damaged tape) or perhaps by the loss of a physical device that had backup set pieces on it.

In cases where the RMAN catalog and the physical backup destinations are out of synchronization, the **crosscheck** command is used to validate the contents of the RMAN information in the control file or the recovery catalog against the actual physical backup set pieces that are on the backup media.

When using the **crosscheck** command, we are interested in the status of each backup set or copy. Each backup set or copy has status codes that are listed in the STATUS column of the views V$BACKUP_SET for backup set pieces and V$DATAFILE_COPY for copies if you are using a control file, and RC_BACKUP_SET for backup set pieces and RC_DATAFILE_COPY for copies if you want to look in the recovery catalog. There are several different backup status codes, but for now we are interested primarily in two:

■ **A** Available; RMAN assumes the item is available on the backup media.

■ **X** Expired; the backup set piece or the copy is stored in the RMAN catalog (meaning the control file or the recovery catalog) but is not physically on the backup media.

It is the purpose of the **crosscheck** command to set the status of the RMAN catalog to either AVAILABLE (status code A) or EXPIRED (status code X). When the **crosscheck** command is executed, RMAN checks each backup set or copy listed in the catalog and determines if it is on the backup media. If it is not, then that piece will be marked as EXPIRED and will not be a candidate for any restore operation. If the piece exists, then it will maintain its AVAILABLE status. If a backup piece or copy was previously marked EXPIRED and it becomes available again (for example, after the recovery of a failed disk drive), then the **crosscheck** command will return that piece's status to AVAILABLE.

In the following example of the execution of the **crosscheck** command, we are checking the status of all backup sets and determining whether they exist on the backup medium:

```
RMAN> crosscheck backup;
using target database controlfile instead of recovery catalog
allocated channel: ORA_DISK_1
channel ORA_DISK_1: sid=13 devtype=DISK
allocated channel: ORA_DISK_2
channel ORA_DISK_2: sid=14 devtype=DISK
crosschecked backup piece: found to be 'AVAILABLE'
backup piece handle=D:\ORACLE\ORA912\DATABASE\C-2539725638-20020710-00 recid=35
stamp=466821903
crosschecked backup piece: found to be 'AVAILABLE'
backup piece handle=D:\ORACLE\ORA912\DATABASE\C-2539725638-20020710-01 recid=36
stamp=466877683
Crosschecked 2 objects

crosschecked backup piece: found to be 'EXPIRED'
backup piece handle=D:\BACKUP\RECOVER\BACKUP_16DT65ML_1_1 recid=31 stamp=466818775
crosschecked backup piece: found to be 'EXPIRED'
backup piece handle=D:\BACKUP\RECOVER\BACKUP_17DT65MV_1_1 recid=32 stamp=466818786

Crosschecked 2 objects
```

In this example, we have cross-checked a total of four backup set pieces. Notice that the **crosscheck** command has two parts to its output. The first part lists all the backup set pieces that were found to be available. The second part provides a list of those backup set pieces that were not found on the backup media, and that were thus set to an expired status by RMAN. Note that the **crosscheck** command will not change a backup set piece with a status of DELETE to AVAILABLE. Any backup marked with a status of DELETE cannot be changed.

You can also cross-check datafile backups, tablespace backups, control file backups, and SPFILE backups. Additionally, you can be selective in the specific backup you want to cross-check by identifying the tag associated with that backup. You can even cross-check all backups taken based on the device used or based on a time period. The following are several examples of cross-checking backups:

```
crosscheck backup of datafile 1;
crosscheck backup of tablespace users;
crosscheck backup of controlfile;
crosscheck backup of spfile;
crosscheck backup tag='SAT_BACKUP';
crosscheck backup completed after 'sysdate - 2';
crosscheck backup completed between 'sysdate - 5' and 'sysdate - 2;
crosscheck backup device type sbt;
```

The first example is a cross-check of backups. As you might expect, you also can cross-check archive log backups:

```
RMAN> crosscheck archivelog all;
released channel: ORA_DISK_1
released channel: ORA_DISK_2
allocated channel: ORA_DISK_1
channel ORA_DISK_1: sid=13 devtype=DISK
allocated channel: ORA_DISK_2
channel ORA_DISK_2: sid=14 devtype=DISK
validation succeeded for archived log
archive log filename=D:\ORACLE\ADMIN\RECOVER\ARCH\ARC00013.001 recid=35 stamp=467044186
validation succeeded for archived log
archive log filename=D:\ORACLE\ADMIN\RECOVER\ARCH\ARC00014.001 recid=36 stamp=467070583
Crosschecked 2 objects

validation failed for archived log
archive log filename=D:\ORACLE\ADMIN\RECOVER\ARCH\ARC00012.001 recid=34 stamp=466961070
Crosschecked 1 objects
```

You can cross-check archived redo log backups based on a number or criteria, including time, scn (specific or high/low range), or log sequence number. You can even use the **like** parameter, along with wildcards, to cross-check specific archivelog backups. Here are some variations in the **crosscheck** command:

```
crosscheck archivelog like 'ARC001.log';
crosscheck archivelog 'D:\ORACLE\ADMIN\RECOVER\ARCH\ARC00012.001';
crosscheck archivelog like '% ARC00012.001';
crosscheck archivelog from time "to_date('07-10-2002', 'mm-dd-yyyy')";
crosscheck archivelog until time "to_date('07-10-2002', 'mm-dd-yyyy')";
crosscheck archivelog from sequence 12;
crosscheck archivelog until sequence 522;
```

To cross-check copies, use the **crosscheck copy** command. You can cross-check datafile copies, control file copies, archive redo log copies, and archived redo logs (on disk). Here are two examples of cross-checking these kinds of objects:

```
crosscheck copy of datafile 5;
crosscheck datafilecopy 'd:\oracle\oradata\recover\recover_users_01.dbf';
```

RMAN Workshop: *Using the crosscheck Command*

Workshop Notes

This workshop assumes that you have a functional Oracle database running in ARCHIVELOG mode. Additionally this workshop assumes that you are backing up your database to disk.

This workshop assumes that you have a tablespace called USERS in your database, and that one datafile is associated with the USERS tablespace.

Step 1. Using RMAN, back up the USERS tablespace.

```
RMAN> backup tablespace users;
Starting backup at 08-SEP-02
using channel ORA_DISK_1
using channel ORA_DISK_2
channel ORA_DISK_1: starting full datafile backupset
channel ORA_DISK_1: specifying datafile(s) in backupset
input datafile fno=00005 name=D:\ORACLE\ORADATA\RECOVER\USERS01.DBF
channel ORA_DISK_1: starting piece 1 at 08-SEP-02
channel ORA_DISK_1: finished piece 1 at 08-SEP-02
piece handle=D:\BACKUP\RECOVER\BACKUP_1VE25VC0_1_1 comment=NONE
channel ORA_DISK_1: backup set complete, elapsed time: 00:00:09
Finished backup at 08-SEP-02
```

Step 2. Look at the output of the backup and determine the backup set piece that has just been created. The backup set piece is highlighted in the output in Step 1.

Step 3. Remove the backup piece from the disk.

Step 4. Issue the **crosscheck** command to determine the status of the backup set piece. RMAN will detect that the backup set piece has been removed and mark it expired.

```
RMAN> crosscheck backup;
using channel ORA_DISK_1
using channel ORA_DISK_2
crosschecked backup piece: found to be 'AVAILABLE'
backup piece handle=D:\ORACLE\ORA912\DATABASE\C-2539725638-20020908-01 recid=54
stamp=472055188
Crosschecked 1 objects
crosschecked backup piece: found to be 'EXPIRED'
backup piece handle=D:\BACKUP\RECOVER\BACKUP_1VE25VC0_1_1 recid=53 stamp=472055171
Crosschecked 1 objects
```

Validation of RMAN Backups

RMAN provides the **validate** command that allows you to examine a given backup set and verify that it can be restored. With this command, you can choose which backup sets to verify, whereas the **validate** parameter of the **restore** command allows RMAN to determine which backup set to validate.

Here is an example of the use of the **validate** command. Note that you must pass the primary key ID of the backup set that you wish to validate. This primary key can be determined by running the **list backupset summary** command. Here is an example of getting the primary key of the backup set and validating that backup set:

```
RMAN> list backupset summary;
List of Backups
===============
Key     TY LV S Device Type Completion Time #Pieces #Copies Tag
------- -- -- - ----------- --------------- ------- ------- --------------
37      B  F  A DISK        28-AUG-02       1       1
38      B  F  A DISK        29-AUG-02       1       1
39      B  A  X DISK        01-SEP-02       1       1       TAG20020901T110901
40      B  A  X DISK        01-SEP-02       1       1       TAG20020901T110901
41      B  F  A DISK        01-SEP-02       1       1
42      B  A  X DISK        01-SEP-02       1       1       TAG20020901T110959
43      B  A  X DISK        01-SEP-02       1       1       TAG20020901T110959
44      B  F  A DISK        01-SEP-02       1       1
45      B  F  A DISK        01-SEP-02       1       1       TAG20020901T123047
46      B  F  A DISK        01-SEP-02       1       1       TAG20020901T123047
47      B  F  A DISK        01-SEP-02       1       1

RMAN> validate backupset 40;
```

Backup Retention Policies

In Chapter 3, we mentioned configuration of a retention policy for RMAN backups and copies. A *retention policy* is a method of managing backups and copies and specifying how long you want to keep them on your backup media. You can define two basic types of retention policies: the *recovery window backup retention policy* and the *backup redundancy backup retention policy*. We will talk more about those shortly.

Each redundancy policy is persistent until changed or removed (or the control file is rebuilt using the **create controlfile** command). Additionally, the two redundancy policies are mutually exclusive. Finally, even with a redundancy policy, physical backup pieces are not removed until you use the **delete** command with the **obsolete** parameter to remove them.

Now, let's look at each of these retention policies in some more detail. After that, we will look at how we manage RMAN backups and copies that are made obsolete as a result of the retention policies.

Recovery Window Backup Retention Policy

The use of this type of retention policy is based on the latest possible date that you want to be able to recover your database to. With a recovery window backup retention policy, you can direct Oracle to make sure that if you want to be able to recover your database to a point in time two weeks ago, you will be able to do so.

For example, assume that today is Monday, and you have three backups. The first backup was taken the day before, on Sunday, the second backup was taken on the previous Thursday, and the last backup was taken ten days ago last Saturday. If the recovery window is set to 7 days, then the first two backups (Sunday's and Thursday's) would be considered current. However, the backup taken ten days ago, on the previous Saturday, would be considered obsolete. If we wanted to establish this 7-day redundancy policy for RMAN, we would use the **configure** command with the **retention policy to recovery window** parameter, as seen here:

```
configure retention policy to recovery window of 7 days;
```

Backup Redundancy Backup Retention Policy

When the backup redundancy backup retention policy is used, RMAN will maintain *x* number of database backups, starting with the most current backup. For example, suppose you have configured a backup redundancy of 3, and you did backups on Monday, Tuesday, Wednesday, and Thursday. Because the retention policy is set to 3, Oracle will obsolete the Monday backup as soon as the Thursday backup is successfully completed.

The backup window backup retention policy is enabled using the **configure** command with the **retention policy to redundancy** parameter. If we wanted to set the backup window backup retention policy to 3, you would use the following command:

```
configure retention policy to redundancy 3;
```

Retention Policy Maintenance

When a given backup or copy meets the criteria of a backup retention policy and becomes obsolete, RMAN does not automatically remove that backup or copy. RMAN marks the backup or copy as obsolete. You can determine which backups RMAN has marked as obsolete with the **report obsolete** command (we will look at the **report** command in the next chapter):

```
report obsolete;
```

Of course, when you view the backups that have been made obsolete, you might find that there are some that you want to retain. In this event, you would use the RMAN **change** command with the **keep** parameter to change the status of the backups you want to retain. When you use this command, the backups or copies impacted are considered to be *long-term backups* and are not subject to the chosen retention policy.

With the **change** command, you can modify a backup so that it will be retained forever, or you can define a new date for that backup or copy to be made obsolete by RMAN. Furthermore, you can define that any logs associated with that backup should be retained as well, ensuring the backup will always be recoverable to the current point in time (consider the impact that this might have on storage, however). Finally, you can obsolete a backup manually with the **change nokeep** command. Here are several examples of the **change** command in use to override an established retention policy:

```
-- Run the list backup command to get the backup key we need
-- This is just a partial listing of the list backup output
-- We bolded the backup set key values that we will be using.
RMAN> list backup;

List of Backup Sets
===================
BS Key  Size        Device Type Elapsed Time Completion Time
------- ----------  ----------- ------------ ---------------
31      56K         DISK          00:00:04     09-JUL-02

BS Key  Type LV Size        Device Type Elapsed Time Completion Time
------- ---- -- ----------  ----------- ------------ ---------------
32      Full    368K        DISK          00:00:28     09-JUL-02

BS Key  Type LV Size        Device Type Elapsed Time Completion Time
------- ---- -- ----------  ----------- ------------ ---------------
33      Full    111M        DISK          00:03:43     09-JUL-02

-- change a backup so it will be retained forever. 220 is the backup key
-- that we get from the list backup RMAN command
-- Change backup 31 from an obsolete status to a keep status.
change backupset 31 keep forever logs;
```

```
-- change a backup so it will be kept for 7  more days
change backupset 32 keep until time 'sysdate + 7' logs;

-- Obsolete a backup
change backupset 33 nokeep;
```

When you change a backup or copy, you have to reference the key that is associated with that backup. As you can see from the example, you find this key by using the **list backup** or **list copy** command, which are described in the next chapter.

Once you have reviewed the report, you can then direct RMAN to actually remove the backups with the RMAN **delete** command with the **obsolete** parameter:

```
delete obsolete;
```

If you have a backup that you don't want to make subject to the chosen redundancy policy, you can use the **keep** parameter of the **backup** command to indicate an alternate retention criteria for that backup. For example, here are some **backup** commands that define an alternate retention criteria for the backups being performed:

```
backup database keep forever;
backup database keep until time "to_date('01/01/05','mm/dd/yy')";
backup database keep 5 days;
```

The change Command

We introduced the **change** command earlier in this chapter and explained how it can be used to modify the retention window assigned to a specific backup. The **change** command allows you to change the status of a backup. You might have a case where one of your backup media devices becomes unavailable for a period of time (perhaps someone spilled a drink down the power supply). In this event, you can use the **change** command to indicate that the backups on that device are unavailable.

Once you have properly scolded the employee for fiddling around in your hardware area with a drink and have fixed the device, you can change the status of that backup set with the **change** command again, so that it will take on an available status. You can also change a backup status to unavailable, indicating that the backup is not currently available. This effectively disqualifies the backup from consideration during restore and recovery operations, but protects the backup record from being removed during the execution of the **delete expired** command. Here are some examples of the use of the **change** command:

```
change backup of database tag = 'GOLD'  unavailable;
change backup of database like '%GOLD%' unavailable;
change backupset 33 unavailable;
change backupset 33 available;
change archivelog 'd:\oracle\mydb\arch\arch_001.arc' unavailable;
```

Using the **change** command, you can modify the status of archived redo log backups. For example, you can modify the status to unavailable for all archived redo logs that have been backed up at least a given number of times. You can also change the status of all backups that occurred using a given device. Examples of these operations are shown next:

```
change archivelog all backed up 5 times to device type disk unavailable;
change backup of database device type disk unavailable;
```

You can also use the **change** command to delete backup sets (physically on the backup media and from the control file and recovery catalog). The **delete** parameter is used for this operation. First, you need to identify the RMAN backup IDs of the backups that you wish to remove. Use either the **list backup** or **list copy** command (which are covered in detail in the next chapter) to perform this operation. Here is an example of how to get the backup ID using the **list backup** command (we have modified the output somewhat to save space):

```
RMAN> list backup of database;
List of Backup Sets
===================
BS Key  Type LV Size       Device Type Elapsed Time Completion Time
------- ---- -- ---------- ----------- ------------ ---------------
117     Full    111M        DISK        00:03:35     14-JUL-02
        BP Key: 119   Status: AVAILABLE   Tag: TAG20020714T194153
        Piece Name: D:\BACKUP\RECOVER\BACKUP_17DTISSH_1_1
  List of Datafiles in backup set 117
  File LV Type Ckp SCN    Ckp Time  Name
  ---- -- ---- ---------- --------- ----
   1      Full 402784     14-JUL-02 D:\ORACLE\ORADATA\RECOVER\SYSTEM01.DBF
   3      Full 402784     14-JUL-02 D:\ORACLE\ORADATA\RECOVER\INDX01.DBF

BS Key  Type LV Size       Device Type Elapsed Time Completion Time
------- ---- -- ---------- ----------- ------------ ---------------
118     Full    368K        DISK        00:04:27     14-JUL-02
        BP Key: 120   Status: AVAILABLE   Tag: TAG20020714T194153
        Piece Name: D:\BACKUP\RECOVER\BACKUP_16DTISSD_1_1
  List of Datafiles in backup set 118
  File LV Type Ckp SCN    Ckp Time  Name
  ---- -- ---- ---------- --------- -----------------------------------------
   2      Full 402781     14-JUL-02
D:\ORACLE\ORADATA\RECOVER\RECOVER_UNDOTBS_01.DBF
   4      Full 402781     14-JUL-02 D:\ORACLE\ORADATA\RECOVER\TOOLS01.DBF
   5      Full 402781     14-JUL-02 D:\ORACLE\ORADATA\RECOVER\USERS01.DBF
```

The results of this report provide us with a detailed list of all database backups and the backup piece identifiers. We can then remove either the entire backup set, by using the BS Key identifier, or individual backup pieces, by using the BP Key identifier. Let's assume we want to remove both backup sets. The BP Key IDs for these sets are 117 and 118. Once we have this information, we simply need to use the **change** command with the **delete** parameter, and our backup will be gone. Here is what we would do to remove these backup sets:

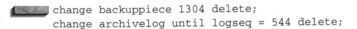

```
RMAN> change backupset 117, 118 delete;
using channel ORA_DISK_1
using channel ORA_DISK_2
List of Backup Pieces
BP Key  BS Key  Pc# Cp# Status      Device Type Piece Name
------- ------- --- --- ----------- ----------- -------------------------
119     117     1   1   AVAILABLE   DISK
D:\BACKUP\RECOVER\BACKUP_17DTISSH_1_1
120     118     1   1   AVAILABLE   DISK
D:\BACKUP\RECOVER\BACKUP_16DTISSD_1_1
Do you really want to delete the above objects (enter YES or NO)? yes
deleted backup piece
backup piece handle=D:\BACKUP\RECOVER\BACKUP_17DTISSH_1_1 recid=31
stamp=467235756
deleted backup piece
backup piece handle=D:\BACKUP\RECOVER\BACKUP_16DTISSD_1_1 recid=32
stamp=467235731
Deleted 2 objects
```

In this example, backup sets 117 and 118, as well as all the associated backup pieces, will be removed. Here are some additional examples of other options for the **change** command that will result in the removal of backup set pieces:

```
change backuppiece 1304 delete;
change archivelog until logseq = 544 delete;
```

RMAN Workshop: *Using the change Command*

Workshop Notes

This workshop assumes that you have a functional Oracle database running in ARCHIVELOG mode. Additionally, this workshop assumes that you are backing up your database to disk.

This workshop assumes that you have a tablespace called USERS in your database and that one datafile is associated with the USERS tablespace.

Step 1.   Using RMAN, back up the USERS tablespace.

```
RMAN> backup tablespace users;
Starting backup at 08-SEP-02
using channel ORA_DISK_1
```

```
using channel ORA_DISK_2
channel ORA_DISK_1: starting full datafile backupset
channel ORA_DISK_1: specifying datafile(s) in backupset
input datafile fno=00005 name=D:\ORACLE\ORADATA\RECOVER\USERS01.DBF
channel ORA_DISK_1: starting piece 1 at 08-SEP-02
channel ORA_DISK_1: finished piece 1 at 08-SEP-02
```
piece handle=D:\BACKUP\RECOVER\BACKUP_21E2608U_1_1 comment=NONE
```
channel ORA_DISK_1: backup set complete, elapsed time: 00:00:17
Finished backup at 08-SEP-02
```

Step 2.   Look at the output of the backup and determine the backup set piece that has just been created. The backup set piece is highlighted in the output in Step 1.

Step 3.   Use the list **backup of tablespace users** command to determine the backup key of the backup set piece that you need to mark as deleted in the control file or recovery catalog. Note in the following output that we have highlighted the backup set key and the related backup set piece.

```
RMAN> list backup of tablespace users;
List of Backup Sets
===================
BS Key  Type LV Size        Device Type Elapsed Time Completion Time
------- ---- -- ---------- ----------- ------------ ---------------
55      Full    64K          DISK         00:00:12    08-SEP-02
        BP Key: 55    Status: AVAILABLE    Tag: TAG20020908T144127
          Piece Name: D:\BACKUP\RECOVER\BACKUP_21E2608U_1_1
  List of Datafiles in backup set 55
  File LV Type Ckp SCN    Ckp Time  Name
  ---- -- ---- ---------- --------- ----
  5       Full 655126     08-SEP-02 D:\ORACLE\ORADATA\RECOVER\USERS01.DBF
```

Step 4.   Simulating an unrecoverable media failure, remove the backup set piece.

Step 5.   Use the **change backuppiece** command to change the status flag of this backup set piece from available to deleted.

```
RMAN> change backuppiece 55 delete;
using channel ORA_DISK_1
using channel ORA_DISK_2
List of Backup Pieces
BP Key  BS Key  Pc# Cp# Status      Device Type Piece Name
------- ------- --- --- ----------- ----------- -------------------------
55      55      1   1   AVAILABLE   DISK
D:\BACKUP\RECOVER\BACKUP_21E2608U_1_1
Do you really want to delete the above objects (enter YES or NO)? yes
```

```
deleted backup piece
backup piece handle=D:\BACKUP\RECOVER\BACKUP_21E2608U_1_1 recid=55
stamp=472056097
Deleted 1 objects
```

Step 6.   Now, use the **list backup of tablespace users** command to determine that the backup set piece is no longer available for use during a recovery.

```
RMAN> list backup of tablespace users;
```

The delete Command

All good things must come to an end, and the same is true about the life of a given backup set. With a retention policy, we can mark backups whose usefulness and lifetime are at an end. As we mentioned already, enforcement of a redundancy policy does not remove the backups from the catalog, but rather just marks the backups with a status of obsolete. The same is true with the **crosscheck** command, which we discussed earlier in this chapter. The **crosscheck** command marks obsolete backups and copies as expired, but does not remove them.

Enter the **delete** command, the grim reaper of RMAN. It is the dark raven that swoops down and puts the kibosh on your backups and copies. With the **delete** command, you can remove any backups that have been made obsolete based on a retention criteria, and you can change the status of any expired backups in the recovery catalog or control file to a status of DELETED. Here are a couple of examples of the **delete** command in use:

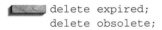

```
delete expired;
delete obsolete;
```

When you issue a **delete** command, RMAN will request that you confirm your instructions. Once you have confirmed your instructions, RMAN will complete the **delete** operation.

NOTE
Once a backup has been marked with a delete status, you cannot get it back. You can still recover the backup, if it's physically available, using the dbms_backup_restore procedure.

RMAN Workshop: *Using the delete Command*

Workshop Notes
This workshop builds on the previous workshop, "Using the **change** Command," which deals with using the **crosscheck** command.

Step 1. Having determined that the backup set piece is missing, we want to mark is as permanently missing. From the RMAN prompt, issue the **delete expired backup** command.

```
RMAN> delete expired backup;
using channel ORA_DISK_1
using channel ORA_DISK_2
List of Backup Pieces
BP Key  BS Key  Pc# Cp# Status       Device Type Piece Name
-------  -------  --- --- -----------  ----------- ----------
53       53      1   1   EXPIRED      DISK
D:\BACKUP\RECOVER\BACKUP_1VE25VC0_1_1
Do you really want to delete the above objects (enter YES or NO)?
```

Step 2. Review the objects listed to be marked with a deleted status. If they can all be marked as deleted, reply to the prompt with a YES and press ENTER. Review the output for a successful operation.

```
deleted backup piece
backup piece handle=D:\BACKUP\RECOVER\BACKUP_1VE25VC0_1_1 recid=53
stamp=472055171
Deleted 1 EXPIRED objects
```

Cataloging Other Backups in RMAN

Before you used RMAN, you might have been doing manual backups of your database datafiles. Wouldn't it be nice to be able to record those backups in RMAN? Well, the **catalog** command enables you to record datafile backups, archivelog backups, and control file backups in RMAN, and these backups can later be used to restore and recover the database. Here are some examples of the use of this command to catalog old datafile backups:

```
-- first, backup the users tablespace
sqlplus sys/robert as sysdba
alter tablespace users begin backup;
host copy d:\oracle\oradata\recover\users01.dbf d:\backup\recover\users01.dbf.backup
alter tablespace users end backup;
alter system archive log current;
host copy d:\oracle\admin\recover\arch\*.* d:\backup\recover
-- get a list of archivelog files that were created
host dir d:\backup\recover
alter database backup control file to 'd:\backup\recover.ctl'
quit

-- Now, catalog the backup in rman
rman target sys/robert
catalog datafilecopy 'd:\backup\recover\users01.dbf.backup';
-- Replace arc001.log with the list of archive logs you generated earlier
```

```
catalog archivelog 'd:\backup\recover\arc001.log';
-- Now catalog the control file.
catalog controlfilecopy 'd:\backup\recover.ctl';
```

Recovery Catalog Maintenance

Use of the recovery catalog involves some additional maintenance activities, which include upgrading the catalog during a database upgrade or migration, manually resetting the database incarnation, and resynchronizing the recovery catalog after certain database operations. This section describes those activities, as well as other maintenance considerations, including removing a database from the recovery catalog and use of the Oracle EXP/IMP utilities to back up the recovery catalog. Finally, this section reviews the different recovery catalog views and what they are used for.

Database Migration/Upgrade Issues

As you upgrade your Oracle databases, you need to upgrade your recovery catalog as well. As you saw in Chapter 9, there are some strict rules with regard to the version of the database you are using, the version of RMAN, and the version of the recovery catalog.

You can determine what version your recovery catalog is by querying the VERSION column of the RCVER view in the recovery catalog–owning schema:

```
SQL> select version from rcver;

VERSION
------------
09.02.00
```

As long as the version of the recovery catalog is at the same level or higher than your database, you will be in good shape. Thus, if you are storing multiple databases in the same recovery catalog, it's okay to upgrade the catalog to a higher version, even if only one of the databases stored in the recovery catalog is being upgraded.

To upgrade your recovery catalog, simply issue the command **upgrade catalog** from RMAN. RMAN will prompt you to enter the **upgrade catalog** command again. RMAN will then upgrade the recovery catalog for you.

Manually Resetting the Database Incarnation (reset catalog)

As we have already covered in earlier chapters, each time the **resetlogs** parameter is used when you open an Oracle database, a new incarnation of the database is created. If this is done during an RMAN operation, then the recovery catalog will be correctly updated. However, if you manually issue a **resetlogs** command (through SQL*Plus, for example), you need to reset the database incarnation in the recovery catalog. This is done with the **reset database** command:

```
reset database;
```

Manually Resynchronizing the Recovery Catalog (resync catalog)

When RMAN uses a recovery catalog, it uses a resynchronization process to ensure that the recovery catalog is consistent with the target database control file. Generally, Oracle performs database resynchronization itself after RMAN operations such as backups and recoveries, so you really don't need to resync the recovery catalog often. One example of the need to resync the recovery catalog is if you are running backups sometimes with and sometimes without a recovery catalog. To manually get Oracle to resync the recovery catalog, use the **resync catalog** command:

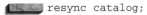
```
resync catalog;
```

When Oracle synchronizes the recovery catalog, it first creates a snapshot control file and compares it to the recovery catalog. Once that comparison is complete, Oracle will update the recovery catalog so it is in synch with the database control file.

Purging Recovery Catalog Records

You might have noticed that very few records get removed from the recovery catalog. Unmaintained, old backups will sit forever in the recovery catalog with a deleted status flag associated with them. So, how do you fix this problem? Oracle provides the solution with the $ORACLE_HOME/rdbms/admin/prgrmanc.sql script, which will remove all records in your recovery catalog with a deleted status. We recommend that you run this script periodically to control the size of your recovery catalog.

If you want to remove old incarnation records from the recovery catalog, then you will want to remove these incarnations from the DBINC table. Use the RC_DATABASE_INCARNATION view to determine which incarnations you wish to remove. Record the DBINC_KEY value for each incarnation you wish to remove. Then, to remove the incarnation, use SQL*Plus and issue a **delete** command to remove the incarnation from the DBINC table using the DBINC_KEY values you previously recorded. Here is an example of the **delete** SQL command that you would use:

```
DELETE FROM dbinc WHERE dbinc_key=2;
```

Unregistering Your Database with the Recovery Catalog

Removal of a database from the recovery catalog is done through SQL*Plus. First, you need to determine the DBID of the database you wish to remove from the recovery catalog. Then, you log in to the recovery catalog schema and query the DB table to determine the recovery catalog database key for the database you wish to unregister. The following is an example of this operation:

1. Go to the database you wish to unregister and get its DBID:

```
SQL> select dbid from v$database;
      DBID
----------
2539725638
```

2. Connect to the recovery catalog–owning schema and determine the DB_KEY of the database in the recovery catalog:

```
SQL> select db_key from db where db_id=2539725638;
    DB_KEY
----------
         1
```

3. Use the **dbms_rcvcat.unregisterdatabase** procedure to unregister the database from the recovery catalog (this procedure takes the DB_KEY and the DB_ID that we just found as parameters):

```
-- The syntax for this procedure is:
-- dbms_rcvcat.unregisterdatabase(db_key, db_id)
exec dbms_rcvcat.unregisterdatabase(1, 2539725638);
```

Recovery Catalog Schema Objects

There are a number of different objects in the recovery catalog that you can query. Many of these objects have related V$ views that provide the same information from the control file. Appendix B contains a list of the V$ views and their related recovery catalog objects that are related to RMAN.

Backing Up the Recovery Catalog

The procedure for using RMAN to back up a database can be found in Chapter 9, and it just so happens that it is perfectly okay to use RMAN to back up your recovery catalog database. Just make sure you have a sound recovery strategy, so you can restore your recovery catalog as quickly as possible. Also, remember that losing the recovery catalog is not the end of the world. Even if you are using a recovery catalog, you can still recover your databases later without it. All you really need is a backup of the database control file (or, in a really bad situation, some fancy work with **dbms_backup_restore**!). The really important thing to note is that you need to test your entire recovery strategy. Only then can you know, and be comfortable with, your ability to recover your databases.

RMAN Stored Scripts

If you find that you are often doing the same RMAN operations over and over, then you would probably like to be able to store those operations somewhere and execute them when needed. Of course, you could create a command file, which is just a text file physically located on disk somewhere, with the RMAN commands and then execute the command file from the RMAN command-line interface using the **cmdfile** parameter, as shown in this example:

```
rman target robert/password cmdfile=run_backup.cmd
```

Or, you can run a command file from within RMAN itself, using the @ command:

```
@run_backup.cmd
```

RMAN offers another option, which is to store scripts in the recovery catalog. As you might guess, this requires that you use a recovery catalog, so if you are not using one, you will not be able to store RMAN scripts. This section shows you how to store scripts in the recovery catalog and how to manage those scripts.

Creating Stored Scripts

To store a script in the recovery catalog, you use the **create script** RMAN command. Each stored script is assigned a name when you create it. You can create scripts that do backups, recoveries, and maintenance of your databases. To create a script, you must be connected to the recovery catalog. Here is an example of using the **create script** command to create a backup script:

```
create script my_backup_script
{ backup database plus archivelog;}
```

Changing Stored Scripts

To change a stored script, you need to delete it first using the **delete script** (described next), and then re-create it using the **create script** command.

Deleting Stored Scripts

To drop a script, you use the **delete script** command. You must be connected to the recovery catalog to successfully drop a stored script. Here is an example of using the **delete script** command:

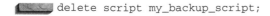

```
delete script my_backup_script;
```

Using Stored Scripts

Now that you have created some stored scripts, you probably want to use them. This is what the **execute script** command is for. Simply connect to the recovery catalog and use the **execute script** command within the confines of a **run** block, as shown in this example:

```
run {execute script my_backup_script;}
```

Printing Stored Scripts

If you want to print a copy of your stored script, you can use the **print script** command. Connect to the recovery catalog and run the **print script** command, as shown in this example:

```
RMAN> print script my_backup_script;

printing stored script: my_backup_script
{ backup database plus archivelog;}
```

You can also use the RC_STORED_SCRIPT_LINE recovery catalog view to display the contents of a stored script, as shown in this example:

```
select script_name, text from rc_stored_script_line
order by script_name, line;
SCRIPT_NAME      TEXT
--------------- ----------------------------------------
my_backup_script { backup database plus archivelog;}
```

RMAN Workshop: *Using RMAN Stored Scripts*

Workshop Notes

This workshop expects that you have an operational Oracle database (called recover), and that you are also using a separate Oracle database to store the recovery catalog in (called catalog).

Step 1. Connect to the target database and to the recovery catalog.

```
rman target rman_account/rman_password catalog rcat_user/rcat_password@catalog
```

Step 2. Create a stored script to back up the target database.

```
RMAN> create script my_backup_script
2> {backup database plus archivelog;}
created script my_backup_script
```

Step 3. Print out the stored script.

```
RMAN> print script my_backup_script;
printing stored script: my_backup_script
{backup database plus archivelog;}
```

Step 4. Execute the stored script to back up your database.

```
RMAN> run {execute script my_backup_script;}
```

Step 5. Delete the stored script

```
RMAN> delete script my_backup_script;
```

CHAPTER
14

RMAN Reporting

ecause everyone wants to know for sure that their databases have been backed up and are currently recoverable, RMAN comes with some good reporting tools. This chapter covers RMAN reporting in some depth. First, we look at the RMAN **list** command, followed by the RMAN **report** command. Each of these commands provides facilities for in-depth analysis of the database that you are using RMAN to back up and on those backups and are the primary ways of extracting information out of RMAN. You will find that lists and reports come in handy not only during recovery, but also when you want to see how RMAN is configured, and other administrative tasks (such as determining if a tablespace has been backed up).

The RMAN list Command

The RMAN **list** command is a method of querying either the database control file or the recovery catalog for historical information on backups. Lists provide an array of information, from lists of database incarnations to lists of backup sets and archive log backups. The bottom line is that if you want to know whether the database was backed up and when, then you want to generate a list. The format of lists tends initially to appear to be not very reader friendly. Once you have looked at a few lists, though, they seem a little easier to read. So, let's look at the **list** commands and how they can be interpreted.

Listing Incarnations

The **list incarnation** command provides you a list of each database incarnation for the target database. This list can be used to recover your database to a point in time before your last **resetlog** command was issued, if this is required (refer to Chapter 12 for more details on this operation). Here is an example of the **list incarnation** command output:

```
RMAN> list incarnation;
using target database controlfile instead of recovery catalog

List of Database Incarnations
DB Key  Inc Key DB Name  DB ID            CUR Reset SCN  Reset Time
------- ------- -------- ---------------- --- ---------- ----------
1       1       RECOVER  2539725638       NO  1          09-JUN-02
2       2       RECOVER  2539725638       NO  315881     24-JUN-02
3       3       RECOVER  2539725638       NO  316061     24-JUN-02
4       4       RECOVER  2539725638       YES 316908     25-JUN-02
```

In this listing, we find that our database has had four different incarnations, with each incarnation represented in each row of the report. Each individual incarnation has its own key (Database Inc Key), which we would use if we wanted to reset the database incarnation (refer to Chapter 12). We also get our database name and ID in this report. Next, the CUR column indicates whether the incarnation listed is the current incarnation. Finally, the Reset SCN and Reset Time columns basically indicate when the database incarnation was created (which is why the Reset SCN for the first entry is 1).

An important point to note is that the output generated with a recovery catalog and without a recovery catalog generally looks somewhat different. For example, this is the output of the **list incarnation** command while attached to a recovery catalog:

```
RMAN> list incarnation;

List of Database Incarnations
DB Key  Inc Key DB Name  DB ID            CUR Reset SCN  Reset Time
------- ------- -------- ---------------- --- ---------- ----------
59      67      RECOVER  2539725638       NO  1          09-JUN-02
59      68      RECOVER  2539725638       NO  315881     24-JUN-02
59      69      RECOVER  2539725638       NO  316061     24-JUN-02
59      60      RECOVER  2539725638       YES 316908     25-JUN-02
```

Note in this example that both the DB keys and the incarnation keys are different than those reported when using the control file. This leads to an important point: Many reports have keys that identify specific items in the reports. You will use these keys in other RMAN commands (such as the **reset database** command). Since the values of the keys change depending on whether or not you are connected to the recovery catalog, you need to be careful of which keys you need.

Listing Backups

The **list** command comes with a number of different options that allow you to report on the status of database backups and copies. In this section, we are going to look at several of these reports.

Summarizing Available Backups
Let's first look at a few ways of getting summary backup information. The **list** command provides a couple of options. The first option is the **list backup summary** report:

```
RMAN> list backup summary;

List of Backups
===============
```

```
Key TY LV S Device Type Completion Time #Pieces #Copies Tag
------- -- -- - ----------- --------------- ------- ------- ---------------
33  B  F  A DISK        14-JUL-02          1       1
35  B  A  A DISK        14-JUL-02          1       1       TAG20020714T202940
36  B  F  A DISK        14-JUL-02          1       1       TAG20020714T203012
37  B  F  A DISK        14-JUL-02          1       1       TAG20020714T203012
38  B  A  A DISK        14-JUL-02          1       1       TAG20020714T203754
39  B  F  A DISK        14-JUL-02          1       1
42  B  F  A SBT_TAPE    16-JUL-02          1       1       TAG20020716T155546
43  B  F  A SBT_TAPE    16-JUL-02          1       1
44  B  A  A DISK        16-JUL-02          1       1       TAG20020716T160403
45  B  A  A DISK        16-JUL-02          1       1       TAG20020716T160403
46  B  F  A DISK        16-JUL-02          1       1
47  B  F  A DISK        16-JUL-02          1       1
48  B  0  A DISK        16-JUL-02          1       1       TAG20020716T161048
49  B  0  A DISK        16-JUL-02          1       1       TAG20020716T161048
50  B  F  A DISK        16-JUL-02          1       1
51  B  1  A DISK        16-JUL-02          1       1       TAG20020716T161858
52  B  1  A DISK        16-JUL-02          1       1       TAG20020716T161858
53  B  F  A DISK        16-JUL-02          1       1
```

This report provides us with some nice summary information. The backup set key is listed in the Key column. The TY (type) and the LV columns indicate the type of backup listed (B = backup, F = full, A = archive log, and 0 and 1 = incremental backups). The S column indicates the status of the backup (Available, Unavailable, or Expired). The Device Type column let's us know whether the backup is a table or disk backup. We also have columns for the date of the backup (Completion Time), the number of pieces (#Pieces) or copies (#Copies) that the backup set consists of, and any tag that was assigned to the backup set (Tag).

Most of the **list** commands will accept the **summary** parameter at the end. For example:

```
list backup of database summary;
list expired backup of archivelog all summary;
list backup of tablespace users summary;
```

Listing Backups by Datafile

Another way to summarize backups is to use the **list backup by file** command to list each backup set and backup set piece. Here is an example of this report (we have removed some output to save a few trees):

```
RMAN> list backup by file;

List of Datafile Backups
========================
```

File	Key	TY	LV	S	Ckp SCN	Ckp Time	#Pieces	#Copies	Tag
1	52	B	1	A	468851	16-JUL-02	1	1	TAG20020716T161858
	49	B	0	A	468690	16-JUL-02	1	1	TAG20020716T161048
2	51	B	1	A	468848	16-JUL-02	1	1	TAG20020716T161858
	48	B	0	A	468680	16-JUL-02	1	1	TAG20020716T161048
3	52	B	1	A	468851	16-JUL-02	1	1	TAG20020716T161858
	49	B	0	A	468690	16-JUL-02	1	1	TAG20020716T161048
4	51	B	1	A	468848	16-JUL-02	1	1	TAG20020716T161858
	48	B	0	A	468680	16-JUL-02	1	1	TAG20020716T161048
5	51	B	1	A	468848	16-JUL-02	1	1	TAG20020716T161858
	48	B	0	A	468680	16-JUL-02	1	1	TAG20020716T161048

```
List of Archived Log Backups
=============================
```

Thrd	Seq	Low SCN	Low Time	BS Key	S	#Pieces	#Copies	Tag
1	10	403895	14-JUL-02	45	A	1	1	TAG20020716T160403
1	11	438568	15-JUL-02	45	A	1	1	TAG20020716T160403
1	12	466185	16-JUL-02	44	A	1	1	TAG20020716T160403

```
List of Controlfile Backups
============================
```

CF Ckp SCN	Ckp Time	BS Key	S	#Pieces	#Copies	Tag
468542	16-JUL-02	46	A	1	1	
468468	16-JUL-02	43	A	1	1	

```
List of SPFILE Backups
======================
```

Modification Time	BS Key	S	#Pieces	#Copies	Tag
26-JUN-02	39	A	1	1	
26-JUN-02	33	A	1	1	

This report summarizes each backup file that has been created by the type of backup (datafile backup, archive log backup, control file backup, and SPFILE backup) and then by datafile for the datafile backups. In this report, we get the date of the backup and the specific keys associated with the backup file. Depending on the type of backup, we get information that pertains to that type of backup.

Additional Backup Information

If you want as much information reported on your RMAN backups as you can get, then the **list backup** command is for you. It provides detailed information on the backups that you have taken, including backup sets, archived redo log backups, and control file/SPFILE backups. Let's look at an example of the results of the execution of the **list backup** command:

```
RMAN> list backup;

List of Backup Sets
===================
BS Key  Type LV Size        Device Type Elapsed Time Completion Time
------- ---- -- ----------  ----------- ------------ ----------------
33      Full   1M           DISK        00:00:06     14-JUL-02
        BP Key: 33   Status: AVAILABLE   Tag:
        Piece Name: D:\ORACLE\ORA912\DATABASE\C-2539725638-20020714-00
    SPFILE Included: Modification time: 26-JUN-02
```

This is the first backup set in our report. Note the backup set key of 33. The Type column tells us that it's a full backup, and the size is also included. We see that the backup went to disk, and that it took six seconds. Also, we see the time that the backup was completed. Further, we find that the associated backup piece key is identified (33) and that the backup is available. There is no tag associated with this backup, so that field is blank. Listed next is the piece name, which is the physical file that contains the actual backup. Finally, on the last line, we find that this is a control file/SPFILE backup by virtue of the **SPFILE Included** statement. Let's look at the next backup set in our report:

```
BS Key  Size        Device Type Elapsed Time Completion Time
------- ----------  ----------- ------------ --------------------
35      1K          DISK        00:00:15     14-JUL-02
        BP Key: 35   Status: AVAILABLE   Tag: TAG20020714T202940
        Piece Name: D:\BACKUP\RECOVER\BACKUP_1ADTIVLO_1_1

    List of Archived Logs in backup set 35
    Thrd Seq     Low SCN    Low Time  Next SCN   Next Time
    ---- ------- ---------- --------- ---------- ---------
    1    8       403640     14-JUL-02 403729     14-JUL-02
```

This backup set has a backup set key of 35. Most of the header information looks the same as the previous backup set except that this backup set piece has an actual tag assigned to it. However, this backup is an archive log backup, so in subsequent lines, RMAN provides a list of the archived redo logs backed up in the backup set. The thread and sequence number of the archive log are listed, along with the low SCN and time, and the next SCN and time. The low time/SCN and high time/SCN ranges allow you to determine when the archive log was created. So, let's move on to the next backup set.

```
BS Key  Type LV Size        Device Type Elapsed Time Completion Time
------- ---- -- ---------- ----------- ------------ ---------------
36      Full    368K         DISK        00:03:46     14-JUL-02
        BP Key: 36   Status: AVAILABLE   Tag: TAG20020714T203012
        Piece Name: D:\BACKUP\RECOVER\BACKUP_1BDTIVML_1_1
  List of Datafiles in backup set 36

  File LV Type Ckp SCN    Ckp Time  Name
  ---- -- ---- ---------- --------- -------------------------------------
  2       Full 403747     14-JUL-02
                  D:\ORACLE\ORADATA\RECOVER\RECOVER_UNDOTBS_01.DBF
  4       Full 403747     14-JUL-02 D:\ORACLE\ORADATA\RECOVER\TOOLS01.DBF
  5       Full 403747     14-JUL-02 D:\ORACLE\ORADATA\RECOVER\USERS01.DBF
```

This set is a full backup set as you can see in the Type column. Again, much of the header of this listing is the same as the previous ones. Later on down the listing we find the list of datafiles that are contained in this backup set. The next part of the report output is only slightly different, as it is for an incremental backup:

```
BS Key  Type LV Size        Device Type Elapsed Time Completion Time
------- ---- -- ---------- ----------- ------------ ---------------
48      Incr 0  368K         DISK        00:00:30     16-JUL-02
        BP Key: 46   Status: AVAILABLE   Tag: TAG20020716T161048
        Piece Name: D:\BACKUP\RECOVER\BACKUP_1QDTNP8O_1_1

  List of Datafiles in backup set 48
  File LV Type Ckp SCN    Ckp Time  Name
  ---- -- ---- ---------- --------- -------------------------------------
  2    0  Incr 468680     16-JUL-02 D:\ORACLE\ORADATA\RECOVER\RECOVER_UNDOTBS_01.DBF
  4    0  Incr 468680     16-JUL-02 D:\ORACLE\ORADATA\RECOVER\TOOLS01.DBF
  5    0  Incr 468680     16-JUL-02 D:\ORACLE\ORADATA\RECOVER\USERS01.DBF
```

As you can see, this last report snippet is almost the same as the previous snippet. The only differences are that **Incr** is used in the Type field to indicate that the backup is an incremental backup, and the LV (level) column shows the level of the incremental backup. If the incremental backup were a level 1 or level 2, then the LV column would show a number corresponding to the level of the incremental backup.

Listing Expired Backups

Using the **list backup** command will show you both available and expired backup sets. If you want to only see expired backups, then you can use the **expired** keyword, as shown in this example:

```
RMAN> list expired backup;

List of Backup Sets
===================
```

```
BS Key  Type LV Size        Device Type Elapsed Time Completion Time
------- ---- -- ----------  ----------- ------------ ---------------
98      Full 1M             DISK        00:00:06     15-JUN-02
        BP Key: 140   Status: EXPIRED   Tag:
        Piece Name: D:\BACKUP\ROBT_C-3395799962-20020615-16
  SPFILE Included: Modification time: 15-JUN-02


BS Key  Type LV Size        Device Type Elapsed Time Completion Time
------- ---- -- ----------  ----------- ------------ ---------------
99      Full 1M             DISK        00:00:04     15-JUN-02
        BP Key: 141   Status: EXPIRED   Tag:
        Piece Name: D:\BACKUP\ROBT_C-3395799962-20020615-17
  SPFILE Included: Modification time: 15-JUN-02


BS Key  Type LV Size
------- ---- -- ----------
100     Full 117M
  List of Datafiles in backup set 100

  File LV Type Ckp SCN   Ckp Time   Name
  ---- -- ---- --------- --------- --------------------------------------
  6       Full 1547860   15-JUN-02
D:\ORACLE\ORADATA\ROBT\ROBT_TEST_RECOVER_03.DBF
  7       Full 1547860   15-JUN-02
D:\ORACLE\ORADATA\ROBT\ROBT_TEST_RECOVER_01.DBF
  10      Full 1547860   15-JUN-02 D:\ORACLE\ORADATA\ROBT\ROBT_RBS_01.DBF
  11      Full 1547860   15-JUN-02
D:\ORACLE\ORADATA\ROBT\ROBT_TEST_TBS_01.DBF

  Backup Set Copy #1 of backup set 100
  Device Type Elapsed Time Completion Time Tag
  ----------- ------------ --------------- ------------------
  DISK        00:05:54     15-JUN-02       TAG20020615T163124

    List of Backup Pieces for backup set 100 Copy #1
    BP Key  Pc# Status      Piece Name
    ------- --- ----------- ----------------------------------
    142     1   EXPIRED     D:\BACKUP\ROBT\BACKUP_47DR3EF1_1_1

  Backup Set Copy #2 of backup set 100
  Device Type Elapsed Time Completion Time Tag
  ----------- ------------ --------------- ------------------
  DISK        00:05:54     15-JUN-02       TAG20020615T163124

    List of Backup Pieces for backup set 100 Copy #2
    BP Key  Pc# Status      Piece Name
    ------- --- ----------- ----------------------------------
    143     1   EXPIRED     D:\BACKUP\ROBT\BACKUP_47DR3EF1_1_2
```

Listing Backups by Tablespace Name and Datafile Number

The output of the **list backup of tablespace** or **list backup of datafile** command is very similar to the **list backup** output. These two **list backup** commands allow you to list output specific for a tablespace or a datafile, as shown in this example:

```
RMAN> list backup of tablespace users;

using target database controlfile instead of recovery catalog

List of Backup Sets
===================
BS Key  Type LV Size       Device Type Elapsed Time Completion Time
------- ---- -- ---------- ----------- ------------ ---------------
36      Full    64K          DISK        00:03:46    14-JUL-02
        BP Key: 36   Status: AVAILABLE   Tag: TAG20020714T203012
        Piece Name: D:\BACKUP\RECOVER\BACKUP_1BDTIVML_1_1

  List of Datafiles in backup set 36
  File LV Type Ckp SCN    Ckp Time  Name
  ---- -- ---- ---------- --------- ----
  5       Full 403747     14-JUL-02
D:\ORACLE\ORADATA\RECOVER\USERS01.DBF
```

In much the same way, you can list the backups of a specific datafile with the **list backup of datafile** command:

```
RMAN> list backup of datafile 3;

List of Backup Sets
===================

BS Key  Type LV Size       Device Type Elapsed Time Completion Time
------- ---- -- ---------- ----------- ------------ ---------------
37      Full    64K          DISK        00:06:36    14-JUL-02
        BP Key: 37   Status: AVAILABLE   Tag: TAG20020714T203012
        Piece Name: D:\BACKUP\RECOVER\BACKUP_1CDTIVMN_1_1
  List of Datafiles in backup set 37

  File LV Type Ckp SCN    Ckp Time  Name
  ---- -- ---- ---------- --------- ----
  3       Full 403761     14-JUL-02
D:\ORACLE\ORADATA\RECOVER\INDX01.DBF
```

Listing Archive Log Backups

Several options exist for listing archive log backups in RMAN. To obtain a complete summary of archive logs currently on disk (this does not mean that they have been backed up), the **list archivelog all** command is perfect, as shown here:

```
RMAN> list archivelog all;

List of Archived Log Copies
Key     Thrd Seq     S Low Time  Name
------- ---- -------  - --------  ----------------------------------------
14      1    13       A 16-JUL-02 D:\ORACLE\ADMIN\RECOVER\ARCH\ARC00013.001
15      1    14       A 17-JUL-02 D:\ORACLE\ADMIN\RECOVER\ARCH\ARC00014.001
```

Here we find a list of each archived redo log that Oracle has backed up, along with the thread number and the sequence number of that archived redo log. If we want a more detailed report, then we use the **list backup of archivelog all** report:

```
RMAN> list backup of archivelog all;

List of Backup Sets
===================
BS Key  Size         Device Type Elapsed Time Completion Time
------- -----------  ----------- ------------ ---------------
35      1K           DISK        00:00:15     14-JUL-02
        BP Key: 35   Status: EXPIRED   Tag: TAG20020714T202940
        Piece Name: D:\BACKUP\RECOVER\BACKUP_1ADTIVLO_1_1
   List of Archived Logs in backup set 35
   Thrd Seq     Low SCN    Low Time   Next SCN   Next Time
   ---- ------- ---------- ---------- ---------- ---------
   1    8       403640     14-JUL-02  403729     14-JUL-02

BS Key  Size         Device Type Elapsed Time Completion Time
------- -----------  ----------- ------------ ---------------
38      2K           DISK        00:00:10     14-JUL-02
        BP Key: 38   Status: AVAILABLE   Tag: TAG20020714T203754
        Piece Name: D:\BACKUP\RECOVER\BACKUP_1DDTJ057_1_1
   List of Archived Logs in backup set 38

   Thrd Seq     Low SCN    Low Time   Next SCN   Next Time
   ---- ------- ---------- ---------- ---------- ---------
   1    9       403729     14-JUL-02  403895     14-JUL-02
```

Note that the first archive log backup set in this report has an expired status, while the second has an AVAILABLE status. Thus, the second archived redo log backup set is available for RMAN recoveries while the first is not. If you want to look at expired backup sets only, add the **expired** keyword, **list expired backup of archivelog all**.

Listing Control File and SPFILE Backups

As you might expect, you can also list control file and SPFILE backups. The **list backup of controlfile** command provides you with a list of control file backups, and the **list backup of spfile** command provides output for SPFILE backups. Here is an example of each command and its results:

```
RMAN> list backup of controlfile;

List of Backup Sets
===================
BS Key  Type LV Size       Device Type Elapsed Time Completion Time
------- ---- -- ---------- ----------- ------------ ---------------
33      Full 1M            DISK        00:00:06     14-JUL-02
        BP Key: 33   Status: EXPIRED   Tag:
        Piece Name: D:\ORACLE\ORA912\DATABASE\C-2539725638-20020714-00
   Controlfile Included: Ckp SCN: 402892        Ckp time: 14-JUL-02

BS Key  Type LV Size       Device Type Elapsed Time Completion Time
------- ---- -- ---------- ----------- ------------ ---------------
39      Full 1M            DISK        00:00:15     14-JUL-02
        BP Key: 39   Status: AVAILABLE Tag:
        Piece Name: D:\ORACLE\ORA912\DATABASE\C-2539725638-20020714-01
    Controlfile Included: Ckp SCN: 403912       Ckp time: 14-JUL-02

RMAN> list backup of spfile;

List of Backup Sets
===================
BS Key  Type LV Size       Device Type Elapsed Time Completion Time
------- ---- -- ---------- ----------- ------------ ---------------
68      Full 0             DISK        00:00:09     18-JUL-02
        BP Key: 66   Status: AVAILABLE  Tag:
        Piece Name: D:\ORACLE\ORA912\DATABASE\C-2539725638-20020718-03
    SPFILE Included: Modification time: 26-JUN-02
```

Listing Copies

Just as you can use the **list** command to determine the status of backup sets, you can also use the **list** command to determine the status of database copies. You can generate a list of all copies with the **list copy** command:

```
RMAN> list copy;

List of Datafile Copies
Key     File S Completion Time Ckp SCN    Ckp Time        Name
------- ---- - --------------- ---------- --------------- ----------------
20      2    A 16-JUL-02       467894     16-JUL-02       D:\ORACLE\DATAFILE2.COPY
21      3    A 16-JUL-02       468574     16-JUL-02       D:\BACKUP\RECOVER\DATAFILE3.DBF
```

```
List of Controlfile Copies
Key       S Completion Time Ckp SCN   Ckp Time        Name
-------   - --------------- --------- --------------- --------------------
22        A 20-JUL-02         539680  19-JUL-02       D:\BACKUP\RECOVER_CTL_01.DBF

List of Archived Log Copies
Key       Thrd Seq     S Low Time  Name
-------   ---- ------- - --------- ----------------------------------------
24        1    21      A 18-JUL-02 D:\BACKUP\RECOVER\ARC00021.001
22        1    21      A 18-JUL-02 D:\ORACLE\ADMIN\RECOVER\ARCH\ARC00021.001
23        1    22      A 19-JUL-02 D:\ORACLE\ADMIN\RECOVER\ARCH\ARC00022.001
25        1    23      A 19-JUL-02 D:\ORACLE\ADMIN\RECOVER\ARCH\ARC00023.001
```

In addition to this summary list, you can create lists of individual datafile copies, archived redo logs, and control file copies. Let's look at those in some more detail for a moment.

Datafile Copies

Oracle allows you to generate a summary list of all datafile copies with the **list copy of database** command:

```
RMAN> list copy of database;

List of Datafile Copies
Key       File S Completion Time Ckp SCN   Ckp Time        Name
-------   ---- - --------------- --------- --------------- ----------------
20        2    A 16-JUL-02         467894  16-JUL-02       D:\ORACLE\DATAFILE2.COPY
21        3    A 16-JUL-02         468574  16-JUL-02       D:\BACKUP\RECOVER\DATAFILE3.DBF
```

In this output, we have two copies of datafiles that belong to our database, datafile2.copy and datafile3.dbf. While the actual name of the datafile or its assigned tablespace name is not listed, the file number is listed in the second column of the report. We could relate this file number to the associated tablespace by running the **report schema** command, which we discuss later in this chapter.

If you want to know whether you have a datafile copy of a tablespace or a datafile, you can use the **list copy of tablespace** or **list copy of datafile** command, as shown here:

```
RMAN> list copy of tablespace indx;

List of Datafile Copies
Key       File S Completion Time Ckp SCN   Ckp Time        Name
-------   ---- - --------------- --------- --------------- ----------------
21        3    A 16-JUL-02         468574  16-JUL-02       D:\BACKUP\RECOVER\DATAFILE3.DBF

RMAN> list copy of datafile 3;

List of Datafile Copies
Key       File S Completion Time Ckp SCN   Ckp Time        Name
-------   ---- - --------------- --------- --------------- ----------------
21        3    A 16-JUL-02         468574  16-JUL-02       D:\BACKUP\RECOVER\DATAFILE3.DBF
```

Archive Log Copies

If you want a list of archived redo log copies, you can use the **list copy of archivelog all** command:

```
RMAN> list copy of archivelog all;

List of Archived Log Copies
Key     Thrd Seq       S Low Time  Name
------- ---- -------   - --------- ----------------------------------------
24      1    21        A 18-JUL-02 D:\BACKUP\RECOVER\ARC00021.001
22      1    21        A 18-JUL-02 D:\ORACLE\ADMIN\RECOVER\ARCH\ARC00021.001
23      1    22        A 19-JUL-02 D:\ORACLE\ADMIN\RECOVER\ARCH\ARC00022.001
25      1    23        A 19-JUL-02 D:\ORACLE\ADMIN\RECOVER\ARCH\ARC00023.001
```

In this report, we find that there are three archived redo logs that RMAN is aware of. The latter two of these archive log records appear to be archived redo logs created in the normal archive log destination, and the first record is most likely a copy of an archive log made with the **copy archivelog** command.

You can also list copies of specific archived redo logs by time, sequence, or database SCN. Here are some examples of listing archived redo logs based on differing criteria:

```
RMAN> list copy of archivelog from sequence 22;

List of Archived Log Copies
Key     Thrd Seq       S Low Time  Name
------- ---- -------   - --------- ----------------------------------------
23      1    22        A 19-JUL-02 D:\ORACLE\ADMIN\RECOVER\ARCH\ARC00022.001
25      1    23        A 19-JUL-02 D:\ORACLE\ADMIN\RECOVER\ARCH\ARC00023.001

RMAN> list copy of archivelog from sequence 22 until sequence 23;

List of Archived Log Copies
Key     Thrd Seq       S Low Time  Name
------- ---- -------   - --------- ----------------------------------------
23      1    22        A 19-JUL-02 D:\ORACLE\ADMIN\RECOVER\ARCH\ARC00022.001
25      1    23        A 19-JUL-02 D:\ORACLE\ADMIN\RECOVER\ARCH\ARC00023.001
```

Control File Copies

Finally, RMAN can report on control file copies with the **list controlfile copy** command:

```
RMAN> list copy of controlfile;

List of Controlfile Copies
Key     S Completion Time Ckp SCN    Ckp Time        Name
------- - --------------- ---------- --------------- --------------------
22      A 20-JUL-02       539680     19-JUL-02       D:\BACKUP\RECOVER_CTL_01.DBF
```

The RMAN Report Command

The RMAN **report** command is used to determine the current recoverable state of your database and to provide certain information on database backups. In this section, we look at reports that tell you which datafiles have not been backed up in a specified period of time. We will also look at reports that tell you when specific tablespaces need to be backed up because of UNRECOVERABLE operations on datafiles. Finally, we will look at the use of the **report** command to report on database schemas and to report on obsolete database backups.

Reporting on Datafiles That Have Not Been Backed Up Recently

A question DBAs frequently ask themselves is, "When was the last time I backed up this tablespace?" RMAN provides some answers to that question with the **report need backup** command. For example, if you want to know what tablespaces have not been backed up in the last three days, you could issue the **report need backup days=3** command and find out. Here is an example of the output of just such a report:

```
RMAN> report need backup days=3;

Report of files whose recovery needs more than 3 days of archived logs
File Days  Name
---- -----  --------------------------------------------------------
4    2      D:\ORACLE\ORADATA\RECOVER\TOOLS01.DBF
5    2      D:\ORACLE\ORADATA\RECOVER\USERS01.DBF
```

From this report, it would appear that two datafiles will require application of more than three days' worth of archived redo to be able to recover them (which implies that these datafiles have not been backed up in the last three days). In this event, we might well want to back up the datafiles, or their associated tablespaces. We can also generate reports based on a given number of incrementals that would need to be applied, as shown in this example:

```
RMAN> report need backup incremental = 3;

Report of files that need more than 3 incrementals during recovery
File Incrementals Name
---- ------------ --------------------------------------------------------
1    4            D:\ORACLE\ORADATA\RECOVER\SYSTEM01.DBF
2    4            D:\ORACLE\ORADATA\RECOVER\RECOVER_UNDOTBS_01.DBF
3    4            D:\ORACLE\ORADATA\RECOVER\INDX01.DBF
4    4            D:\ORACLE\ORADATA\RECOVER\TOOLS01.DBF
5    4            D:\ORACLE\ORADATA\RECOVER\USERS01.DBF
```

In this example, several database datafiles will require four incrementals to be applied. This may well indicate that we need to perform a new backup on these datafiles at a higher incremental level, or even perform a new incremental base backup.

Reporting on Backup Redundancy or Recovery Window

We can use the **report need backup redundancy** command to determine which, if any, datafiles need to be backed up to meet our established backup redundancy policy. The following is an example of the use of this report. In this case, we want a list of all datafiles that do not have at least two different backups that can be used for recovery. These may be backup set backups or datafile copies.

```
RMAN> report need backup redundancy = 2;

Report of files with less than 2 redundant backups
File #bkps Name
---- ----- --------------------------------------------
1    1     D:\ORACLE\ORADATA\RECOVER\SYSTEM01.DBF
4    1     D:\ORACLE\ORADATA\RECOVER\TOOLS01.DBF
5    1     D:\ORACLE\ORADATA\RECOVER\USERS01.DBF
```

Likewise, we can establish a minimum recovery window for our backups and report on any datafiles whose backups are older than that recovery window. This is done with the **report need backup recovery window days** command:

```
RMAN> report need backup recovery window of 2 days;

Report of files whose recovery needs more than 2 days of archived logs
File Days  Name
---- ----- --------------------------------------------------------
1    4     D:\ORACLE\ORADATA\RECOVER\SYSTEM01.DBF
2    4     D:\ORACLE\ORADATA\RECOVER\RECOVER_UNDOTBS_01.DBF
3    4     D:\ORACLE\ORADATA\RECOVER\INDX01.DBF
4    4     D:\ORACLE\ORADATA\RECOVER\TOOLS01.DBF
5    4     D:\ORACLE\ORADATA\RECOVER\USERS01.DBF
```

In this case, several of our datafiles will require application of more than two days' worth of archived redo. So, if our recovery policy says we want backups where we only need to apply one day of redo, then we need to back up these datafiles.

Reporting on UNRECOVERABLE Operations on Datafiles

Unrecoverable operations on objects within tablespaces, and the datafiles that make up those tablespaces, lead to certain recoverability issues. For example, if a table is created using the Unrecoverable option and is subsequently loaded using the direct load path, then the tablespace will need to be backed up or else the data that was loaded will not be recoverable. It is for these circumstances that the **report unrecoverable** command is used, as shown here:

```
RMAN> report unrecoverable;
Report of files that need backup due to unrecoverable operations

File Type of Backup Required Name
---- --------------------- -----------------------------------
5    full or incremental   D:\ORACLE\ORADATA\RECOVER\USERS01.DBF
```

Reporting on the Database Schema

We are using the word "schema" here to mean the physical structure of the database. The schema includes the datafile name and number, the tablespaces they are assigned to, the size of the datafiles, and whether or not the datafiles contain rollback segments. This can be the current schema, or you can generate a report on the database schema at some past point in time. Here is an example of the execution of the **report schema** command:

```
RMAN> report schema;

Report of database schema
File K-bytes Tablespace RB segs Datafile Name
---- ------- ---------- ------- ----------------------------
1    174080  SYSTEM     ***     D:\ORACLE\ORADATA\RECOVER\SYSTEM01.DBF
2    10240   UNDOTBS    ***     D:\ORACLE\ORADATA\RECOVER\RECOVER_UNDOTBS_01.DBF
3    2048    INDX       ***     D:\ORACLE\ORADATA\RECOVER\INDX01.DBF
4    5120    TOOLS      ***     D:\ORACLE\ORADATA\RECOVER\TOOLS01.DBF
5    5120    USERS      ***     D:\ORACLE\ORADATA\RECOVER\USERS01.DBF
```

Reporting on Obsolete Backups

Backups are marked with an obsolete status if you are using a retention policy (which we discussed in Chapter 13). Here is an example of the execution of **report obsolete** with a retention policy set to redundancy 1.

```
RMAN> report obsolete;

RMAN retention policy will be applied to the command
RMAN retention policy is set to redundancy 1
```

```
Report of obsolete backups and copies

Type              Key Completion  Filename/Handle
----------------  --- ----------  -------------------------------------------
Backup Set         42 16-JUL-02
  Backup Piece     40 16-JUL-02   1kdtnoc4_1_1%
Backup Set         43 16-JUL-02
  Backup Piece     41 16-JUL-02   c-2539725638-20020716-00
Backup Set         56 18-JUL-02
  Backup Piece     54 18-JUL-02   D:\ORACLE\ORA912\DATABASE\C-2539725638-20020718-00
Backup Set         61 18-JUL-02
  Backup Piece     59 18-JUL-02   D:\ORACLE\ORA912\DATABASE\C-2539725638-20020718-01
Backup Set         66 18-JUL-02
  Backup Piece     64 18-JUL-02   D:\ORACLE\ORA912\DATABASE\C-2539725638-20020718-02
Backup Set         68 18-JUL-02
  Backup Piece     66 18-JUL-02   D:\ORACLE\ORA912\DATABASE\C-2539725638-20020718-03
Backup Set         69 19-JUL-02
  Backup Piece     67 19-JUL-02   D:\ORACLE\ORA912\DATABASE\C-2539725638-20020719-00
Backup Set         70 20-JUL-02
  Backup Piece     68 20-JUL-02   D:\ORACLE\ORA912\DATABASE\C-2539725638-20020720-00
Datafile Copy      20 16-JUL-02   D:\ORACLE\DATAFILE2.COPY
Datafile Copy      21 16-JUL-02   D:\BACKUP\RECOVER\DATAFILE3.DBF
Controlfile Copy   22 20-JUL-02   D:\BACKUP\RECOVER_CTL_01.DBF
Archive Log        24 19-JUL-02   D:\BACKUP\RECOVER\ARC00021.001
Archive Log        22 19-JUL-02   D:\ORACLE\ADMIN\RECOVER\ARCH\ARC00021.001
Archive Log        23 19-JUL-02   D:\ORACLE\ADMIN\RECOVER\ARCH\ARC00022.001
Archive Log        25 19-JUL-02   D:\ORACLE\ADMIN\RECOVER\ARCH\ARC00023.001
```

This report has several different backup sets, datafile copies, control file copies, and archive log copies that have been marked obsolete by Oracle. If you want to mark these backups as deleted, run the **delete obsolete** command, as shown in Chapter 13.

CHAPTER
15

Performance Tuning
RMAN Backup and
Recovery Operations

MAN actually works pretty well right out of the box, and you generally will find that it requires very little tuning. However, there are a number of other pieces that fit into the RMAN architectural puzzle. When all those pieces come together, you sometimes find that you need to tweak a setting here or there to get the best performance you can out of your backup processes. Generally, then, the RMAN tuning you end up having to do usually involves dealing with inefficiencies in the logical or physical database design, tuning of the Media Management Library (MML), or tuning RMAN and the MML layer to coexist better with the physical device that you are backing up to. In this chapter, we look at what you need to tune before you begin to tune RMAN itself. We then provide some tuning options for RMAN.

Before You Tune RMAN

If your RMAN backups take hours and hours to run, it's probably not RMAN's fault. More than likely, it's some issue with your database or with your MML. The last time you drove in rush hour traffic, did you think the slow movement was a problem with your car? Of course not. The problem was one of too many cars trying to move on a highway that lacked enough lanes. This is an example of a bandwidth problem, or a bottleneck. Cities attempt to solve their rush hour problem by expanding the highway system or perhaps by adding a subway, busses, or light rail.

The same kind of problem exists when it comes to tuning RMAN and your backup and recovery process. It's often not the fault of RMAN, although RMAN often gets blamed. More than likely, the problem is insufficient bandwidth of the system as a whole, and RMAN is just another car on the system's highway that contributes to the overall problem. In this chapter, we look at some ways of adding some high-speed, high-traffic lanes to your database system.

Frankly, much of this section is an exercise in tuning your Oracle database. The better your database performs, the better your RMAN backups will perform. Very large books have already been written on the subject, so we will just give a quick look at these issues. If you need more detailed information on Oracle database performance tuning, we suggest two very good Oracle Press books: *Oracle Performance Tuning 101* by Gaja Krishna Vaidyanatha (McGraw-Hill/Osborne, 2001), or the excellent *OCP Oracle9i Database: Performance Tuning Guide* by Charles Pack (McGraw-Hill/Osborne, 2002). Both provide an in-depth look at the Oracle database and performance tuning.

NOTE
We make some tuning recommendations in this chapter and in other places in this book. Make sure you test our recommendations on your system before you decide to fire and forget (meaning to make a change without checking that the change was positive). While certain configurations may work for us in our environments, you may find that they do not work as well for you.

RMAN Performance—What Can Be Achieved?

So, what is the level of RMAN performance that can be achieved with the currently available technology? Oracle Corporation, in its white paper "Oracle Recovery Manager: Performance Testing at Sun Customer Benchmark Center" (October 2001), available at technet.oracle.com, found that a backup or recovery rate of 1 terabyte (TB) per hour to tape was possible. As tape backup technology continues to improve, rates exceeding this will likely be possible.

Have the Right Hardware in Place

If you want high backup performance, then the first thing to look at is the backup hardware at your disposal. This consists of items such as tape drives, the associated infrastructure such as cabling, robotic tape interfaces, and any MML-layer software that you might choose to employ.

Backup media hardware will provide for you a given speed at which the device will read and write. Of course, the faster the device writes, the faster your backups. Also, the more devices you can back up to, the better your backup timing tests will be. This was clearly pointed out in Oracle's RMAN performance white paper mentioned in the preceding section. The doubling of the number of drives that RMAN could write to causes an almost linear improvement in performance of both backup and restore operations. The ability to parallelize your backups across multiple channels (or backup devices) is critical to quickly backing up a large Oracle database.

RMAN will benefit from parallel CPU resources, but the return diminishes much quicker with the addition of CPUs, as opposed to the addition of physical backup devices. The bottom line, then, is that having multiple backup devices will have a much greater positive impact on your backup and restore windows than adding CPUs will in most cases.

You will find that most backup devices are asynchronous rather than synchronous. An *asynchronous* device allows the backup server processes to issue I/O instructions without requiring the backup server processes to wait for the I/O to complete. An asynchronous operation, for example, allows the server process to issue a tape write instruction, and while that instruction is being performed, the process can proceed to fill memory buffers in preparation for the next write operation A *synchronous* device, on the other hand, would have to wait for the backup operation to complete before it could perform any other work. Thus, in our example, the synchronous process will have to wait for the tape I/O to complete before it can start filling memory buffers for the next operation. Thus, an asynchronous device is more efficient than a synchronous one.

Because asynchronous operations are preferred, you may want to know about a few of their parameters. First, the parameter BACKUP_TAPE_IO_SLAVES (which defaults to FALSE) will cause all tape I/O to be asynchronous in nature. We suggest you set this parameter to TRUE to enable asynchronous I/O to your tape devices (if that setting is supported). Once this parameter is established, you can define the size of the memory buffers that are used by using the **parms** parameter of the **allocate channel** command or **configure channel** command. You may also want to create a large pool when setting BACKUP_TAPE_IO_SLAVES to TRUE. This will help eliminate shared pool contention and memory allocation error issues that can accompany shared pool use when BACKUP_TAPE_IO_SLAVES is enabled. To determine how big to make your shared pool, LARGE_POOL_SIZE, Oracle suggests the following formula be used

(number of allocated channels) * (16MB + (4 * (BLKSIZE RMAN parameter value)))

The tape buffer size is established when the channel is configured. The default value is OS specific, but is generally 64KB. You can configure this value to be higher or lower by using the **allocate channel** command. For best performance, we suggest that you configure this value to 256KB or higher, as shown here:

```
allocate channel c1 device type sbt parms="blksize=262144,
ENV=(NB_ORA_CLASS=RMAN_db01)"
```

If you are backing up to disk, then you need to determine whether or not your OS supports asynchronous I/O (most do these days). If it does, then Oracle automatically uses that feature. If it does not, then Oracle provides the parameter **dbwr_io_slaves**, which, when set to a nonzero value, causes Oracle to simulate asynchronous I/O to disks by starting multiple DBWR processes.

For Oracle8i   The formula for setting LARGE_POOL_SIZE (for backup) is as follows:

LARGE_POOL_SIZE

> = (4 * (number of allocated channels) * (DB_BLOCK_SIZE) * (DB_DIRECT_IO_COUNT)
>
>   * (level of multiplexing) + (4 * (number of allocated channels) * (size of tape buffer)

For Oracle9i   The total size of disk buffers is limited to 16MB per channel. So, the Oracle9i formula for LARGE_POOL_SIZE for backup is as follows:

LARGE_POOL_SIZE

> = (number of allocated channels) * (16MB + (size of tape buffer))

NOTE
The size of a single tape buffer is defined by the RMAN channel parameter, BLKSIZE, and not *by 4 × the size of tape buffer.*

Tune the Database

A badly tuned database can have a significant negative impact on your backup timings. Certain database tuning issues can also have significant impact on your restore times. In this section, we briefly look at what some of these tuning issues are, including I/O tuning, memory tuning, and SQL tuning.

Tune I/O

Most DBAs understand the impact of I/O on basic database operations. Contention on a given disk drive for database resources (say, for example, the online redo log and a database datafile are on the same device) can cause significant system slowdowns. Just as poor I/O distribution can impact your database performance, it can also impact your backup and restore timings. This makes sense, because RMAN is going to be just another process (or, more likely, many processes due to parallel streams) that contends for I/O time on your devices.

Backing up is a read-intensive operation. If you have poor I/O distribution, not only will RMAN performance suffer, but other users will suffer as well, if not even worse, during the backup operation. Recovery may be somewhat easier if all of your recoveries are full database recoveries. However, if you are just recovering a datafile or a tablespace, while the database is open and in use, you may find that poor I/O distribution impacts your recovery window, and your users. The bottom line is that bad I/O distribution impacts not only your day-to-day database users, but also your backups and recoveries, causing them to take longer.

Much has been written on distribution of I/O on an Oracle database and how to do it properly. We suggest that you take a look at the Oracle white paper titled "Oracle Storage Configuration Made Easy" (Juan Loaiza, Oracle Corporation, available at technet.oracle.com). In this paper, Mr. Loaiza makes a compelling argument for an I/O distribution known as Stripe and Mirror Everything (SAME), discusses current disk speeds and feeds, and then demonstrates the logic of his SAME methodology. This methodology recommends that you stripe your data among the largest number of disks possible, and suggests this is a much better approach than striping across a few disks or using a parity disk approach, such as RAID-5 (mirroring is, of course, more expensive). Further, this paper recommends that a stripe size of about 1MB is generally optimal and demonstrates that such a configuration in Oracle's testing resulted in a 13 percent better read/write from the disk than nonstriped systems, with an associated loss in CPU overhead. This faster disk read/write will translate into faster backup timings.

Tune Memory Usage

Like any Oracle process, RMAN uses memory. When an RMAN operation is started, a buffer is allocated to the operation for RMAN to work out of. The size of the buffer allocated is dependent on a number of different factors, including the following:

- RMAN backup and recovery multiplexing effects

- The device type used

- The number of channels allocated during the operation

Each of these factors has an effect on how much memory RMAN will require. RMAN allocates memory buffers for operations. How it allocates these buffers depends on the type of device you are going to use. Let's look at the different buffer allocation methods in a bit more detail next.

Allocating Memory Buffers for Disk Devices   When backing up to disk devices, RMAN will allocate up to 16MB of memory. This memory is allocated based on the level of multiplexing (based on the **filesperset** setting). If the level of multiplexing is 4 or less, then RMAN will allocate 16 buffers of 1MB each. These 1MB buffers are divided among the number of datafiles to be backed up. So, if **filesperset** is set to 2, then each datafile will be allocated eight 1MB buffers.

If **filesperset** is between 5 and 8, then 512MB buffers are allocated and distributed evenly between the different datafiles. This way, no more than 16MB of buffers will be allocated. Finally, if the level of multiplexing is greater than 8, four buffers of 128MB will be allocated to each datafile, which amounts to 512KB per datafile.

Allocating Memory Buffers for SBT Devices   When backing up to an SBT device, RMAN allocates four buffers for each channel that is allocated. These buffers are 256KB in size generally, and thus the total memory allocated per channel is 1MB. This memory is generally allocated from the PGA, but if the **backup_tape_io_slaves** parameter is set to TRUE, then the SGA is used unless the large pool is allocated, in which case the large pool will be used. Thus, if you configure I/O slaves (and generally you should if you back up to SBT devices), then you should configure a large pool to reduce the overall memory requirements on the large pool.

Tune Your SQL

You might ask yourself what bad SQL running in your database has to do with performance tuning your backup and recovery timings. It's really quite simple. The negative performance impacts of poor SQL statement operations has an overall negative performance impact on your database and the system the database is on. Anything that has a negative impact on your database is likewise going to have a negative impact on your backup operations. Tune your SQL operations such that they reduce the overall number of I/Os required (logical and physical) and schedule your backups to occur during times of typical low system usage (if that is possible).

Tune Your Environment

Carefully consider your backup schedules, and ensure that they do not conflict with I/O-intensive database operations such as data loads or reports. Also, if you find your backups are taking too long, consider an incremental backup strategy and analyze your database to determine whether certain tablespaces might be made read-only so you don't have to continue to back them up often. Further, if you are running in ARCHIVELOG mode, you can consider staggering the backups of tablespaces on different days to reduce the overall timeframe of your backups (at the cost of somewhat longer recovery times, of course).

If you are running your database using Oracle Real Application Clusters, then RMAN can take advantage of the clustered environment to parallelize your RMAN operations (more information on this topic is provided in Chapter 18).

Tune Your Backup and Recovery Strategy

We already talked about tuning when you do your backups, but we also want to discuss tuning how you do your backups. If you have a large database, rather than just issuing a **backup database** command to back up the whole kit and caboodle, consider a more partitioned backup strategy. Consider backing up related datafiles that you are likely to restore together using individual **backup tablespace** or **backup datafile** commands, and assign those backups to one specific channel. Why do this? This reduces the need to swap tapes during recoveries and allows the recovery of related datafiles to occur as quickly as possible. Here is an example of such an operation:

```
RMAN> backup (tablespace tools channel 'ORA_DISK_1')
             (tablespace system, undotbs, users, testrbs, indx);
```

We might want to do this if we are backing up a read-only tablespace that we might later want to recover, or perhaps we have a tablespace that we seem to do frequent tablespace point-in-time recoveries (TSPITRs) on. These would be good candidates for such backup strategies.

Another issue to consider is the impact of your backup strategy on your recovery. One of the more painful problems with RMAN is that, depending on the platform (Unix is one example; the following three paragraphs do not apply to Oracle on Windows NT), if you restore an entire database with the **restore database** command, you must be careful to ensure that enough space is available for the restore. Everything is just fine as long as you have enough disk space, but consider for a moment a true disaster recovery situation where you do not have enough disk space in the right places. In this case, RMAN is going to spend perhaps an hour or more recovering your database. Once it runs out of disk space, you would assume that RMAN would just stop at that point, alert you to the lack of space problem, and then just stop the restore at that position. The truth, however, is a bit more painful.

Once the restore process fails, RMAN proceeds to remove every single file it restored in that restore session. Thus, if you spend two hours restoring all but one database datafile and then you run out of space during that restore, you are in deep trouble because RMAN is now going to remove all of those datafiles. This equates to a very unhappy DBA.

One solution to this problem is to restore specific tablespaces with different **restore** commands for each tablespace (or for a number of tablespaces). This allows you to restore your database datafiles in a bit more granular fashion, and the failure of one operation will not cause you to lose hours. Of course, if you use this type of operation, you will want to parallelize the restores and utilize multiple tape or disk devices to reduce contention and tape streaming issues. In this case, you need to run parallel RMAN sessions, each restoring its own set of tablespace data. Note that this type of restore operation is another reason why it's important to try to back up clusters of files that you will likely need to restore on the same channel. That way, you can stream the data off the tape quickly.

Note that some platforms, such as Windows NT, do check for available space before you actually start an RMAN database, datafile, or tablespace restore. In this case, the issue of running out of space, while still a problem, is not as much of a time waster.

Tuning RMAN

RMAN out of the box really works pretty well. Still, you can do a few things to tune it so that you get better performance, which is what this section is all about. First, we discuss the tuning options in RMAN itself. Then, we discuss some MML tuning issues.

Tuning RMAN Settings

There are a few ways to tune RMAN, which we discuss in this section. Tuning RMAN itself can involve tuning parallel operations and also configuring RMAN to multiplex (or not to multiplex, that is the question). This section also covers some things that you can do to actually tune down RMAN.

Parallel Channel Operations

Perhaps the biggest impact you can make when tuning your database backups is to parallelize them by using multiple RMAN channels. Typically, you configure a channel for each device you are going to back up to. Thus, if you will back up to three different disks, configure three different channels. You will see little or no benefit of paralleling backups on the same device, of course; so if you have a D drive and an E drive on your Windows NT system but both are just partitioned on the same disk, you will derive no benefit from paralleling backups to those two devices.

 NOTE
The memory buffering on tape systems may well make the allocation of additional channels worthwhile, so you should always do some timing tests to decide exactly how many channels you need to use on your system.

Paralleling backups is accomplished by allocating channels to the backup. Channels can have default values configured for them (along with the default degree of parallelization that will determine how many of the channels are used) with the **configure** command, discussed in Chapter 3. For example, if I had two tape devices that I was going to back up to, I'd likely configure two default channels and a default level of parallelization, as shown here:

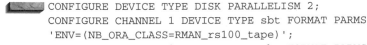
```
CONFIGURE DEVICE TYPE DISK PARALLELISM 2;
CONFIGURE CHANNEL 1 DEVICE TYPE sbt FORMAT PARMS
'ENV=(NB_ORA_CLASS=RMAN_rs100_tape)';
CONFIGURE CHANNEL 2 DEVICE TYPE sbt FORMAT PARMS
'ENV=(NB_ORA_CLASS=RMAN_rs100_tape)';
```

This would serve to ensure that each **backup** or **recover** command is automatically allocated two channels to parallelize the process.

Of course, depending on your device, you may well be able to run parallel streams to the device. The best thing to do is run several tests and determine from those tests the performance of a varying number of backup streams from both a backup and a recovery point of view. It may be that a different number of streams will be more efficient during your backup than during your recovery, and only testing will determine this.

We have already discussed the multiplexing of backups in RMAN and how to tune this feature. Tuning multiplexing can have significant performance impacts on your backups and recoveries. As we also discussed earlier, how you configure your multiplexing will impact the amount of memory that is allocated to the RMAN backup process. The more memory, the better, as long as you do not start to induce swapping back and forth to disk.

Also, properly configuring multiplexing can make streaming to tape devices more efficient. The more memory you can allocate to RMAN, the more data that can be streamed to your I/O devices. Finally, tape streaming is rarely an issue with newer-generation tape drives. Generally, they have a great deal of onboard buffer memory that is used to ensure that the tape is written to at a constant rate.

RMAN Multiplexing

Before we dive head first into performance considerations, we should take a moment to discuss multiplexing in RMAN. *Multiplexing* allows a single RMAN channel to parallelize the reading of database datafiles during the backup process and write the contents of those datafiles to the same backup set piece. Thus, one backup set piece may contain the contents of many different datafiles.

Note that the contents of a given datafile can reside in more than one backup set piece (which is evidenced by the fact that you can set **maxpiecesize** to a value smaller than that of any database datafile, but **maxsetsize** must be at least the size of the largest tablespace being backed up). However, in a given backup, a given datafile will only be backed up through one channel (or one backup set). Thus, if you allocate two channels (and, as a result, have two backup sets), and your database consists of one large datafile, the ability of RMAN to parallelize that datafile's backup will be limited to a great degree.

The level of RMAN's multiplexing is determined by the lesser of two RMAN parameters. The first is the **filesperset** parameter (established when you issue the **backup** command) and the second is the **maxopenfiles** parameter (established when the channel is allocated).

The **filesperset** parameter establishes how many datafiles should be included in each backup set. The number of datafiles in a given backup set will be some number less than or equivalent to **filesperset**. When you do a backup, RMAN will assign a default value for **filesperset** of either 64 or the number of input files divided by the number of allocated channels, whichever is less. You can use a nondefault value for **filesperset** by using the **filesperset** parameter of the **backup** command, as shown in this example:

```
backup database filesperset 4;
```

The **maxopenfiles** parameter establishes a limit on how many datafiles RMAN can read in parallel (the default is 8). You establish the **maxopenfiles** limit on a channel-by-channel basis. Here is an example of the use of **maxopenfiles**:

```
CONFIGURE CHANNEL 1 DEVICE TYPE DISK MAXOPENFILES 3 FORMAT
"d:\backup\recover\%U";
```

For example, if I created a backup set with **filesperset** set to 6 and **maxopenfiles** set to 3, RMAN would only be able to back up three datafiles in parallel at a time. The backup sets created would still contain at most six datafiles per backup set (assuming one channel is allocated and a degree of parallelism of 1), but only three datafiles would be written to the backup set at any time.

NOTE
*If you have your data striped on a large number of disks, you will not need to multiplex your backups, and you can set **maxopenfiles** to a value of 1. If you are striped across a smaller set of disks, consider setting **maxopenfiles** to a value between 4 and 8. If you do not stripe your data at all, **maxopenfiles** generally should be set to some value greater than 8.*

Multiplexing, and the establishment of the **filesperset** and **maxopenfiles** parameters, can have a significant impact on the performance of your backups (good and bad). Tuning RMAN multiplexing can decrease the overall time of your backups, as long as your system is capable of the parallel operations that occur during multiplexing. As with most things, too much of a good thing is too much, and certainly you can overparallelize your backups such that the system is overworked. In this case, you will quickly see the performance of your system diminish and your backup times increase quickly.

Multiplexing can also have an impact on tape operations. Since tape systems are streaming devices, it's important to keep the flow of data streaming to the device at a rate that allows it to continue to write without needing to pause. Generally, once a tape has a delay in the output data stream, the tape device will have to stop and reposition the write head before the next write can occur. This can result in significant delays in the overall performance of your backups. By setting **filesperset** high and **maxopenfiles** low, you can tune your backup so that it streams to your tape device as efficiently as possible. Beware, of course, of overdoing it and bogging down your system so much that the I/O channels or CPU can't keep up with the flow of data that RMAN is providing. As always, finding the proper balance takes some patient tuning and monitoring.

Tuning RMAN Down

Sometimes, you actually need to tune RMAN down. When you are backing up the database at the same time other operations are ongoing, RMAN can take up more system resources than you might otherwise prefer. The RMAN parameters **rate** and **readrate** can be used to throttle RMAN down, freeing system resources for other operations. Both the **rate** and **readrate** commands are set when allocating RMAN channels.

The **rate** command is used when backing up a database to limit the velocity at which data is written out to the backup pieces in terms of buffers per second. The **rate** parameter is set in units of buffers, not bytes (we discuss allocation and size of buffers later in this chapter).

The **readrate** parameter is used when restoring a database to limit the rate at which RMAN reads data from the backup pieces in terms of buffers per second. The **readrate** is specified in units of buffers, not bytes, so be careful when setting this parameter (we discuss allocation and size of buffers later in this chapter).

Neither the **rate** nor **readrate** command is used to improve performance, only to throttle it. RMAN will read and write at the maximum throughput level possible, by default.

Tune the MML Layer

Each component of RMAN may require some tuning effort, including the MML layer. Refer to Chapter 4 for general information on this topic, and then refer to Chapters 5 through 8 for more detailed information for your specific vendor MML configuration and tuning suggestions for that vendor.

You need to consider a number of things with regard to the MML backup devices. Most are going to be running in asynchronous mode, but if they do not, that may be a big cause of your problems. Also, sometimes DBAs will set the **rate** parameter when they allocate a channel for backups. This is generally something you do not want to do, because this will create an artificial performance bottleneck.

Also, some of the MML vendors provide various configurable parameters, such as a configurable buffer size, that you can configure in vendor-specific parameter files. Look into the tuning possibilities that these parameter files offer you.

There are other factors related to the MML layer, such as the supported transfer rate of the backup device you are using, compression, streaming, and the block size. You must analyze all of these factors in an overall effort to tune the performance of your RMAN backups.

Tuning Views You Can Use

Oracle provides a number of different views that you can use to monitor and tune RMAN performance. Using these views, you can determine how well the database, RMAN, and the MML are performing. You can also use these views to determine how long a backup or recovery process has taken and how much longer you can expect it to take. In this section, we look at these views and how you can best use them.

V$SESSION_LONGOPS and V$SESSION

The V$SESSION_LONGOPS view is useful during a backup or restore operation to determine how long the operation has taken and how much longer it is expected to take to complete. Join this view to the V$SESSION view for additional information about your RMAN backup or recovery sessions. Here is an example of a join between V$SESSION_LONGOPS and V$SESSION during a database backup:

```
SQL> select a.sid, a.serial#, a.program, b.opname, b.time_remaining
from v$session a, v$session_longops b
where a.sid=b.sid
and a.serial#=b.serial#
and a.program like '%RMAN%'
and time_remaining > 0;
 SID SERIAL# PROGRAM   USERNAME  OPNAME                   TIME_REMAINING
 ---- ------- --------- --------- -------------------- --------------------
   10       8 RMAN.EXE SYS RMAN: aggregate input                    1438
   14       3 RMAN.EXE SYS RMAN: full datafile backup               7390
```

In this example, we have an RMAN process running a backup. It has connected to the database as SID 14. The time remaining, 1054, is the expected time in seconds that this backup will take. You can thus determine how long your backup will take by looking at this report. Note that we also did a join to V$SESSION to get some additional information on our RMAN session, such as the username and the program name.

V$BACKUP_ASYNC_IO and V$BACKUP_SYNC_IO

The V$BACKUP_ASYNC_IO and V$BACKUP_SYNC_IO views contain detailed information on RMAN asynchronous and synchronous backup operations. These views are transitory in nature, and are cleared each time the database is shut down. These views contain a row for each asynchronous or synchronous backup or recovery operation. Perhaps the biggest benefit from this view is the EFFECTIVE_BYTES_PER_SECOND column in rows where the TYPE column is set to AGGREGATE. This column represents the rate at which the objects are being backed up or recovered in bytes per second. This number should be close to the listed read/write rate of your backup hardware. If the EFFECTIVE_BYTES_PER_SECOND column value is much lower than the rated speed of your backup hardware, then you should be looking for some sort of problem with your backup process. The problem could be caused by any number of things, from an overburdened CPU to a saturated network, or perhaps a configuration issue with the MML interface to your vendor's backup solution.

NOTE
*If you see data in V$BACKUP_SYNC_IO, this implies
that you are not doing asynchronous backups. If this
is the case, you need to investigate why your backups
are occurring in synchronous fashion.*

Here is an example of a query against V$BACKUP_ASYNC_IO and its results
after a database backup has been completed:

```
select device_type "Device", type, filename,
to_char(open_time, 'mm/dd/yyyy hh24:mi:ss') open,
to_char(close_time, 'mm/dd/yyyy hh24:mi:ss') close,
elapsed_time ET, effective_bytes_per_second EPS
from v$backup_async_io
where close_time > sysdate - 30
order by close_time desc;

device TYPE     FILENAME                        OPEN
------ -------- ------------------------------- -------------------
CLOSE                    ET         EPS
-------------------- ---------- ----------
DISK   OUTPUT   d:\backup\recover\5cdvfjvh_1_1  08/06/2002 20:24:43
08/06/2002 20:28:10    20700      566435

DISK   AGGREGATE                                08/06/2002 20:24:58
08/06/2002 20:28:09    19100      933288

DISK   INPUT    D:\ORACLE\ORADATA\RECOVER\SYSTEM 08/06/2002 20:24:58
01.DBF
08/06/2002 20:28:09    19100      933288

DISK   OUTPUT   d:\backup\recover\5bdvfjup_1_1  08/06/2002 20:24:18
08/06/2002 20:24:35    1700       24576

DISK   AGGREGATE                                08/06/2002 20:24:19
08/06/2002 20:24:34    1500      1118481

DISK   INPUT    D:\ORACLE\ORADATA\RECOVER\RECOV 08/06/2002 20:24:19
ER_UNDOTBS_01.DBF
08/06/2002 20:24:34    1500      699051

DISK   INPUT    D:\ORACLE\ORADATA\RECOVER\RECOV 08/06/2002 20:24:26
ER_TESTRBS_01.DBF
08/06/2002 20:24:33    700       748983
```

```
DISK    INPUT    D:\ORACLE\ORADATA\RECOVER\TOOLS  08/06/2002 20:24:27
02.DBF    08/06/2002 20:24:29      200     524288

DISK    OUTPUT   d:\backup\recover\5advfjug_1_1   08/06/2002 20:23:55
08/06/2002 20:24:13      1800      18204

DISK    AGGREGATE                                 08/06/2002 20:23:58
08/06/2002 20:24:11      1300      967916

DISK    INPUT    D:\ORACLE\ORADATA\RECOVER\USERS  08/06/2002 20:24:05
01.DBF
08/06/2002 20:24:11      600     873813

DISK    INPUT    D:\ORACLE\ORADATA\RECOVER\TOOLS  08/06/2002 20:23:58
01.DBF    08/06/2002 20:24:10      1200     436907

DISK    INPUT    D:\ORACLE\ORADATA\RECOVER\INDX0  08/06/2002 20:24:08
1.DBF
08/06/2002 20:24:09      100    2097152
```

In this case, we can see the effective transfer rate from the database to the backup set by RMAN. Further, we can see the name of the datafile that was backed up and the actual start and stop time of the backup itself.

Another way to measure the efficiency of your backup process is to use the V$BACKUP_ASYNC_IO view. This view has several columns of interest, which are listed and described in Table 15-1.

Column Name	Represents
IO_COUNT	The total number of I/O counts
READY	The number of asynchronous I/O calls for which a buffer was available immediately
SHORT_WAITS	The number of times that a buffer was requested and not available but became available after a nonblocking poll for I/O completion
LONG_WAITS	The number of times that a buffer was requested and not available and Oracle had to wait for the I/O device

TABLE 15-1. *V$BACKUP_ASYNC_IO Column Descriptions*

To determine whether there is an I/O problem, we can look at the ratio of I/Os to long waits (LONG_WAITS/IO_COUNTS), as shown in the following code segment:

```
select b.io_count, b.ready, b.short_waits, b.long_waits,
b.long_waits/b.io_count, b.filename
from v$backup_async_io b;

IO_COUNT      READY SHORT_WAITS LONG_WAITS B.LONG_WAITS/B.IO_COUNT
---------- ---------- ----------- ---------- -----------------------
FILENAME
----------------------------------------
         2          1           0          1          .5
D:\ORACLE\ADMIN\RECOVER\ARCH\ARC00052.001
         2          1           0          1          .5
D:\ORACLE\ADMIN\RECOVER\ARCH\ARC00046.001
         2          1           0          1          .5
D:\ORACLE\ADMIN\RECOVER\ARCH\ARC00051.001
         2          1           0          1          .5
D:\ORACLE\ADMIN\RECOVER\ARCH\ARC00050.001
       171        107          12         52          .304093567
D:\ORACLE\ORADATA\RECOVER\SYSTEM01.DBF
        11          8           2          1          .090909091
D:\ORACLE\ORADATA\RECOVER\RECOVER_UNDOTBS_01.DBF
         6          4           0          2          .333333333
D:\ORACLE\ORADATA\RECOVER\TOOLS01.DBF
         6          3           0          3          .5
D:\ORACLE\ORADATA\RECOVER\USERS01.DBF
         6          4           1          1          .166666667
D:\ORACLE\ORADATA\RECOVER\RECOVER_TESTRBS_01.DBF
         3          1           0          2          .666666667
D:\ORACLE\ORADATA\RECOVER\INDX01.DBF
         2          1           0          1          .5
D:\ORACLE\ORADATA\RECOVER\TOOLS02.DBF
```

The numbers returned by this query clearly indicate some sort of I/O bottleneck is causing grief (in this case, it's an overly taxed, single CPU).

PART
IV

RMAN: Beyond
Backup and Recovery

CHAPTER
16

Duplication: Cloning the Target Database

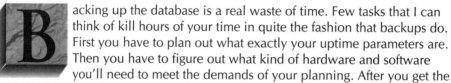acking up the database is a real waste of time. Few tasks that I can think of kill hours of your time in quite the fashion that backups do. First you have to plan out what exactly your uptime parameters are. Then you have to figure out what kind of hardware and software you'll need to meet the demands of your planning. After you get the hardware, then you have to test it all out, at which time you revise your plan to match reality. Then you actually back up the database, after which you have to maintain the backups. After a while, all the software changes and the hardware gets old, and we do it all over again. And all just so that maybe, just *maybe,* in case of the small chance that *something* might go wrong *sometime* in the future, you will be able to recover your data.

What a waste. But here you are: You're interested enough in your backup strategies not only to buy this book, but to make it all the way to Chapter 16. Because deep below the Sisyphusian labor of it all, we know it has to be done. Disasters happen. Mistakes happen. Hardware fails. Software has bugs. Nothing is secure except that we make it so through diligence and not a small touch of paranoia.

But backups are not all about pushing rocks up mountains, only to watch them roll back down. Instead, our database backups can be put to work. They can be used to restore the database to another system, or even just another disk on the same system, and then can be used to test out a new application, or test a migration to a new version of Oracle. We can then do load testing for performance reasons or try out a new hardware configuration. With clone databases at our disposal, we can leave little to chance and have an almost perfect grasp of what will happen if we change our production environment. And it only gets better. RMAN has integrated other elements of the Oracle RDBMS to make backups even more useful and effective. Now, RMAN can be used to create a standby database that can be kept up-to-date for disaster recovery. But we are getting ahead of ourselves.

RMAN helps you create clones via the **duplicate** command. This simple little command hides many levels of complexity that are worth knowing about before you begin to use it. In addition, a fair amount of prep work is required so that a duplication goes smoothly. But once understood, and after you've had a little time to practice, you'll find that database duplication is one of the real "killer apps" within the backup and recovery world.

RMAN Duplication: A Primer

The RMAN **duplicate** command is a simple command that hides a high level of complexity. If you've ever been through the process of restoring image copy backups of your database to another system, you know the amount of information that you have to keep track of: filenames, file locations, backup locations, archive log information, FTP processes, …there's plenty to do. RMAN has a straightforward command:

```
Duplicate target database to aux1;
```

This command prompts RMAN to perform the entire process of cloning your target database to another database. Granted, you have to do a little legwork first, but once you become familiar with the architecture, you'll see that the legwork is minimal and the payoff is huge.

Why Use RMAN Duplication?

Why is duplication necessary? An astute question. Why can't you just copy the control file to a new location, and run a restore and recovery? The answer is, you can! There is no reason that this won't work. However, if you use a recovery catalog, you will run into problems if you clone your database without using duplication. RMAN registers databases in the catalog based on the database ID (DBID), which is a number that identifies your database as unique, even if it has the same database name (the parameter DB_NAME in the init.ora) as another. If you don't use the **duplicate** command, you will have two databases with the same DBID. If you try to register your clone in the same catalog as your production system, you will get an error:

```
rman-20002: target database already registered in recovery catalog
```

This error can be a little misleading: You haven't registered the database! If you shrug your shoulders at this, and go ahead and try to back up your database, it will give you an even stranger error:

```
rman-20011: target database incarnation is not current
in recovery catalog
```

Perplexed, you go ahead and issue a **reset database**, as you think you should, and this works. You can now back up your database. Sweet. However, you have caused bigger problems. Now, you connect RMAN to your original, production server and try to back it up. But when you do, you get a hauntingly similar error:

```
rman-20011: target database incarnation is not current
in recovery catalog
```

This error is issued because RMAN considers your clone no more than a restored version of your production system, and so it now thinks the clone is the current incarnation of your production server, and it has no idea what your production server is. You can reset the incarnation back to the one that actually matches your production database, but you've essentially corrupted your catalog, and should unregister your database and reregister it in the catalog (refer to Chapter 3).

If you don't use a catalog, nonduplicated clones can wreak havoc, as well. Let's lay it out in an example. You clone your database to the same system as your primary database. You are using RMAN to back up both databases to tape, and because you aren't using a catalog, you have automatic control file backups turned on for both instances. One day, you lose a disk array, and your entire system goes belly up.

Both databases, and all their control files, are lost. "No problem," you think, "I've got control file autobackup turned on. I'll just use one of those to restore my systems."

But here's the stickler: The command **restore controlfile from autobackup** uses the database ID to track down the control file autobackup. Because both of your databases back up to the same tape, it may try to restore the control file from the wrong database, giving you the wrong files with the wrong data.

Obviously, both of these scenarios can be fixed, and they don't cause a loss of data. But they cause a loss of time. They can potentially extend your downtime past your agreement levels. In addition to these problems, using duplication in RMAN provides the power of the RMAN interface to keep things as simple as possible. And simple is good. Simple is wise.

The Duplication Architecture

Here's how duplication works. RMAN connects to your target database and the catalog, if you use one. This connection is necessary to gain access to the target database control file for details about where to locate backups. After you connect to the target, you must connect to your auxiliary instance. The auxiliary instance is the instance that will house your cloned database. Before duplication starts, you must have already built an init.ora file for the auxiliary instance and started it in **nomount** mode. This way, the memory segment has been initialized, and therefore RMAN can make a sysdba connection to it. The auxiliary instance does not have a control file yet (duplication will take care of that), so you cannot mount the auxiliary instance, even if you wanted to.

With these connections made, you can issue your **duplicate** command. It can look as simple as this:

```
Duplicate target database to aux1;
```

Or it can be complicated, depending on the variables involved:

```
run {
set until time = '08-JUL-2002:16:30:00';
duplicate target database to aux1
pfile=/u02/oracle/admin/aux1/pfile/init.ora
nofilenamecheck
device type sbt parms "env=(nb_ora_serv=rmsrv)"
logfile
'/u04/oracle/oradata/aux1/redo01.log' size 100m,
'/u05/oracle/oradata/aux1/redo02.log' size 100m,
'/u06/oracle/oradata/aux1/redo03.log' size 100m;}
```

The duplication process can be broken down into its distinct phases:

I. RMAN determines the nature and location of the backups.

2. RMAN allocates an auxiliary channel at the auxiliary instance.

3. RMAN restores the datafiles to the auxiliary instance.

4. RMAN builds a new auxiliary control file.

5. RMAN restores archive logs from backup (if necessary) and performs any necessary recovery.

6. RMAN resets the DBID for the auxiliary instance and opens the auxiliary database with **open resetlogs**.

First, RMAN sets any runtime parameters, such as an **until time** clause on the **duplicate** command. Then, based on these parameters, it checks the target database control file (or recovery catalog) for the appropriate backups. It then builds the RPCs for how to access the backups and which ones to access, but it does not execute the code at the target. Instead, RMAN creates a channel process at the auxiliary instance, referred to as the *auxiliary channel,* and to this channel RMAN passes the call to **dbms_backup_restore**. The auxiliary instance, then, accesses the backups and restores all necessary datafiles. Figure 16-1 illustrates how this takes place for both disk backups and tape backups.

Auxiliary Channel Configuration

For duplication to work, RMAN must allocate one or more channel processes at the auxiliary instance. In Oracle9i, you do not need to manually allocate an auxiliary channel at the time of duplication, since one will automatically be created using permanent configuration parameters stored in the target control file. The makeup of the auxiliary channel mainly comes from parameters you established for target channels: the default device type and the degree of parallelism both get set using the same persistent parameters that set the target channels. Therefore, if you are duplicating using backups taken to disk, you need not do anything to configure your auxiliary channels. However, if you are duplicating your database using backups taken to tape, you will need to configure your auxiliary channels to contain any media manager environment parameters that your target channels have. For example, the following code sets the default device type to tape and sets the default level of parallelism to two, and then configures two auxiliary channels with the correct parameters:

```
Configure default device type to sbt;
configure device type sbt parallelism 2;
configure auxiliary channel 1 device type sbt parms
= "env=(nb_ora_serv=mgtserv, nb_ora_class=oracle)";
configure auxiliary channel 2 device type sbt parms
= "env=(nb_ora_serv=mgtserv, nb_ora_class=oracle)";
```

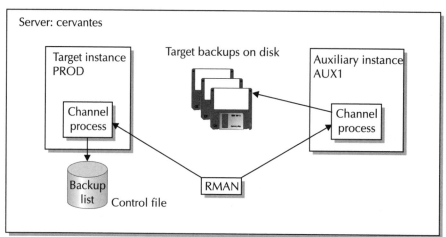

Duplication from Disk (same server)

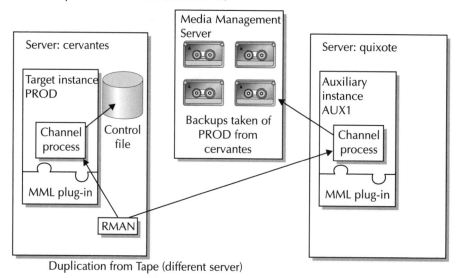

Duplication from Tape (different server)

FIGURE 16-1. *A bird's-eye view of duplication*

Restoring Datafiles to a Different File Location

After mounting the new control file, RMAN moves forward with the datafile restore. If you are duplicating your database to the same server that your target resides on, it is obviously necessary to change the location to which the files will be restored.

Even when restoring to a different server, differences in mount points and directory structures can require a new file location. The datafile restore step of the duplication process can be modified to point to a new file location in three ways. First, you can use the **configure** command to configure the auxname for any (or all) datafiles that need a new location. These configurations are stored in the target database control file.

```
Configure auxname for datafile 1 to '/u04/oradata/aux1/system01.dbf';
configure auxname for datafile 2 to '/u04/oradata/aux1/undo01.dbf';
...
```

Second, you can specify the new datafile names in a **run** command, as you would in previous versions:

```
Run {allocate channel c1 type 'sbt_tape';
set newname for datafile 1 to '/u04/oradata/aux1/system01.dbf';
set newname for datafile 2 to '/u04/oradata/aux1/undo01.dbf';
duplicate target database to aux1;}
```

Finally, you can use a parameter in your auxiliary database's init.ora file to set a new location for the files. The parameter is **db_file_name_convert**, and you pass it two strings: first, the old location of the file on the target; and second, the new location for the file in your auxiliary instance. You can do this in matched file pairs, like this:

```
db_file_name_convert=(
  '/u02/oradata/prod/system01.dbf', '/u02/oradata/aux1/system01.dbf',
  '/u03/oradata/prod/prd_data_01.dbf',
  '/u03/oradata/aux1/prd_data_01.dbf')
```

This is a simple string conversion parameter, so you can simply pass a single directory name to be changed. For instance, let's say you have your files spread over four mount points, but they all have prod in the directory structure, so that a select from V$datafile looks like this:

```
Select name from v$datafile;
----------------------------------------------------------
/u02/oradata/prod/system01.dbf
/u03/oradata/prod/prd_data_01.dbf
/u04/oradata/prod/indx_prd01.dbf
/u05/oradata/prod/temp01.dbf
```

Instead of pairing up each file, you can simply do the following:

```
db_file_name_convert=('prod' , 'aux1')
```

This works, as long as everything else about the file location is the same for your auxiliary database, such as the mount point.

Creating the New Control File

The new control file is created for the auxiliary instance after all the files have been restored. RMAN literally just issues a **create controlfile** command at the auxiliary instance, using the parameters you outlined in your **duplicate** command. After creating the control file, the auxiliary database is mounted. Now, RMAN performs a switch operation to switch to the new files. The switch is the means by which RMAN modifies the new control file at the auxiliary site to point to the new location of the datafiles.

Recovery and Archive Logs

After the files are restored and switched, it is time to perform recovery on the database, either to bring it to the current point in time or to bring it to the specified time in the **until time** clause. To perform recovery, RMAN needs access to the archive logs. If they have been backed up by RMAN, then RMAN can simply restore them from the backup location to the log_archive_dest specified in the init.ora of the auxiliary database. You can also manually move archive logs to the location required by the new instance, so that they are found on disk by RMAN and no restore is required. If you are duplicating to the same server as the target currently resides on, RMAN can find the archive logs in the log_archive_dest of the target.

Once restored, RMAN will perform the required amount of recovery. If you did not specify a point in time to end the recovery, RMAN will restore up to the last available archive log (as found in the view v$archived_log), and then stop. During duplication, RMAN cannot check the online redo log files for further recovery information. After it hits the end of the archive logs, it stops recovery. After recovery has completed, if RMAN restored any archive logs from backup, they are deleted.

Changing the Database ID

After media recovery is complete, the database is in a consistent state and it is time for RMAN to change the DBID of the new clone. RMAN has to wait until all other activity in the database has completed, as all operations to this point required the clone database to have the same DBID as the target. The archive logs would not apply to the clone during media recovery if the control file had a different DBID.

The process of changing the DBID is simple. RMAN has at its disposal a little procedure called **dbms_backup_restore.zerodbid( )**. With the database in a mounted state (not open), this package will go into the file headers and zero out the DBID in each file header. Then, RMAN shuts down the database and re-creates the auxiliary control file again. When the control file is rebuilt, Oracle checks the file headers for the DBID. When it does not find one, Oracle generates a new one and broadcasts it to every file header.

The zerodbid Procedure: Warning!

As you can imagine, a database that is shut down without a DBID in the file headers and with a control file that is being rebuilt is in a very vulnerable state. In the RMAN duplication process, however, elements that could go wrong are tightly controlled, so you don't have to worry too much. We point this out because it is possible to execute this package against any database to generate a new DBID. You just mount the database and run the following code:

```
Execute sys.dbms_backup_restore.zerodbid(0);
```

Then, you shut down the database and rebuild the control file using the **set** parameter:

```
Create controlfile SET database <db_name> resetlogs...
```

And voila! You have a new DBID. Seems simple enough, doesn't it?

Well, a lot can go wrong if you are trying to do this without the complete control over the environment that RMAN has during duplication. For instance, if you did not get a clean shutdown, and you need to perform media recovery before you can open resetlogs, you are out of luck. The archive logs have a different DBID. There is no way you will be able to open the database—it is stuck in an inconsistent state, and you cannot fix it. The same thing can happen if a file is accidentally left offline—it won't get the new DBID when you do an open resetlogs, and therefore you will not be able to bring it online. Ever. You will get the following error:

```
ORA-01190: control file or datafile <name> is from before
the last RESETLOGS
```

The moral of the story is to be very careful if you decide to use this procedure manually. There is a better way. In 9iR2, Oracle introduced a utility called DBNEWID, which is a safe and secure way of generating a new ID for a database without making a manual call to the **dbms_backup_restore** package. We talk about DBNEWID later in this chapter.

Log File Creation at the Auxiliary Site

When RMAN issues the final open resetlogs at the completion of the duplication process, it must build brand-new log files for the auxiliary database. This always happens when you issue a resetlogs, but with a **duplicate** command, you need to take into consideration what you want the new redo log files to look like. If you are duplicating to the same system as your target, at a minimum, you will have to rename your log files.

You can specify completely new redo log file definitions when you issue the **duplicate** command. Do this if you want to change the size, number, and/or location of the redo logs for the new database. This would look something like this:

```
Duplicate target database to aux1
pfile=/u02/oracle/admin/aux1/init.ora
logfile
'/u04/oracle/oradata/aux1/redo01.log' size 100m,
'/u05/oracle/oradata/aux1/redo02.log' size 100m,
'/u06/oracle/oradata/aux1/redo03.log' size 100m;
```

Alternatively, you can use the existing log file definitions from your target, and simply move them to a new location using the init.ora parameter **log_file_name_ convert**. This parameter acts exactly like **db_file_name_convert**, so you can convert the log files in coupled pairs, or you can simply use string conversion to change a single directory name.

```
log_file_name_convert=('/u02/oracle/oradata/redo01a.dbf',
'/u03/auxiliary/redo01a.dbf',…)
```

Duplication: Location Considerations

So far, we've completely glossed over one of the biggest stumbling blocks to understanding duplication. You must account for the location of your auxiliary instance in relation to the location of your target instance. Duplicating to the same server is very different from duplicating to a remote server. There are elements unique to each that you must understand before you proceed with duplication.

Duplication to the Same Server

You must tread lightly when duplicating to the same server, so that you don't walk all over your existing target database. If you were to simply make a copy of your target init.ora and then run the following code, you would run into a series of problems and errors:

```
Duplicate target database to aux1;
```

These errors would be related to the fact that you already have an instance running with the same name, and you have the same file locations for two databases.

Memory Considerations

Oracle references memory segments on the server based on the value of the init.ora parameter **db_name**. Therefore, Oracle cannot allow there to be two instances running on the same system with the same **db_name**. If you try to mount a second instance with the same name, you will get the following error:

```
ORA-01102: cannot mount database in EXCLUSIVE mode
```

Therefore, when duplicating to the same system, you need to change the **db_name** parameter in the auxiliary init.ora to be different from the database name of your target:

```
db_name='aux1'
instance_name='aux1'
```

File Location Considerations

Okay, you've squared away your memory problems, but you still have two databases that are trying to write to the same file locations. In fact, you have three different types of files that are all competing for the same name. If you don't account for file locations, duplication will fail at the step of trying to rebuild the control file:

```
RMAN-00571: ===========================================================
RMAN-00569: =============== ERROR MESSAGE STACK FOLLOWS ============
RMAN-00571: ===========================================================
RMAN-03002: failure of Duplicate Db command at 07/02/2002 13:52:14
RMAN-06136: ORACLE error from auxiliary database: ORA-01503: CREATE CONTROLFILE failed
ORA-00200: controlfile could not be created
ORA-00202: controlfile:
'/OraHome1/oradata/sun92/control01.ctl'
ORA-27086: skgfglk: unable to lock file - already in use
SVR4 Error: 11: Resource temporarily unavailable
```

This is good news for you, because otherwise you would have overwritten your production control file. You must change the auxiliary init.ora parameter **control_files** to point to a new location on disk, as this is the means by which RMAN determines where to restore the control files.

After we change the location of the control files, we must change the location of the datafiles. We talked about this previously: You can either use the **configure** command or the **db_file_name_convert** parameter, or use a run block, Oracle8i-style. If you fail to change the datafile locations when duplicating to the same server, you will get an error very similar to the previous control file error, telling you the files are currently in use and cannot be overwritten.

Finally, you must change the redo log file location. We talked about this previously, when we discussed the different steps that duplication walks through. You can use the **logfile** keyword as part of the **duplicate** command to build completely different redo files with different sizes, number of groups, and number of members. This option essentially rewrites the similar **logfile** parameter of the **create controlfile** stage of duplication. Alternatively, you can simply use the **log_file_name_ convert** parameter in the auxiliary init.ora file.

Same Server, Different ORACLE_HOME

It is common practice to clone the production database from its location to a different location on the same server, but have it be hosted by a different Oracle software installation. When you have a different ORACLE_HOME for the auxiliary instance, there are slightly different rules to conform to. All the rules about hosting on the same system apply as outlined previously. However, you must also consider the location of the backup pieces themselves. If you are duplicating from disk backups, this won't be a problem—just make sure you have your OS permissions worked out ahead of time. If you are duplicating from tape backups, however, you need to make sure that you have your MML file appropriately linked with the auxiliary ORACLE_ HOME the same way as it is linked in your target's ORACLE_HOME. Otherwise, your tape backups will be inaccessible by the auxiliary instance, and duplication will fail because the media manager will be inaccessible.

Duplication to a Remote Server

A successful duplication to an auxiliary instance on a different server from the target is no more or less complicated than duplication to the same server. It's just complicated in different ways.

Memory Considerations

Unlike duplication to the same server, you do not have to worry about the **db_name** parameter in the init.ora file. Because we are on a different server, Oracle has no hang-ups about the lock name used for memory.

Of course, it is good operational procedure to always be mindful of the **db_name** parameter during a duplication process, and cross-check all other instances running on the same server before beginning the duplication. That way, you have no unexpected errors down the road.

File Locations

Again, because we are on a new server, there is not quite the urgency to change any of the file location specifications for your auxiliary instance. There is not a database already running with the same files, so we can leave all file specifications the same as for the target instance, and thus avoid any possible errors in the configuration. Again, we can simplify much of this process when we are on a different system. If you do not change the location of the files, you must specify **nofilenamecheck** in the **duplicate** command. This tells duplication not to confirm that the filenames are different before performing restore. If this is not specified, RMAN will give you an error.

The one caveat to this simplicity is if the auxiliary host does not have the same file structure and mount point setup that the target host has. If you have different mount points or drive configurations, you still need to change your file specifications for the auxiliary instance so that RMAN can restore to a location that actually exists.

The Backup Location: Disk

The complicating factor for restoring to a different server comes from providing the auxiliary channel process access to backups that were taken at a different server. You must account for this whether you backed up to disk or to tape.

If you are duplicating from disk backups, your choices are limited. Remember that RMAN passes the calls to **dbms_backup_restore** to a channel process at the auxiliary instance, but it cannot take into account any file system differences. It must look for the backup pieces in the exact location and format that was recorded in the target database control file. For example, say you took a full database backup at your target system using the following command:

```
Backup database format= '/u04/backup/prod/%U';
```

This created your backup piece as a file called 01DSGVLT_1_1 in the directory /u04/backup/prod. This is recorded in the target control file. Then, during duplication, RMAN passes the **file restore** command to the auxiliary instance, and tells it to restore from /u04/backup/prod/01DSGVLT_1_1. That means that on your auxiliary instance, there must be a mount point named /u04, and there must be a directory named backup/prod, in which there resides a file called 01DSGVLT_1_1. If not, the duplication will fail with an error:

```
RMAN-03002: failure of Duplicate Db command at 07/02/2002 14:49:55
RMAN-03015: error occurred in stored script Memory Script
ORA-19505: failed to identify file "/u04/backup/prod/01dsgvlt_1_1"
ORA-27037: unable to obtain file status
SVR4 Error: 2: No such file or directory
Additional information: 3
```

There are three ways to make duplication from disk work. The first, and most straightforward, is to simply copy the backups from your target host to the auxiliary host and place them in the same location. Obviously, this involves a huge transfer of files across your network.

The second way to proceed is to NFS-mount the backup location on the target host from the auxiliary host. This will only work if you can mount the target location with the same mount point name as RMAN will use (in the preceding example, you would have to NFS mount /u04/backup/prod as /u04/backup/prod). For example, you would need to do the following from your auxiliary instance:

```
mount cervantes:/u04/backup/prod /u04/backup/prod
```

That way, from your auxiliary node, you should be able to do the following:

```
cd /u04/backup/prod
ls -l
touch testfile
ls -l
```

If for any reason you get an error when you try to change directories or when you try to touch a file, you will need to sort out your NFS and permissions issues before you proceed with duplication. Figure 16-2 illustrates the mounted file system approach to duplicating to a different server using disk backups.

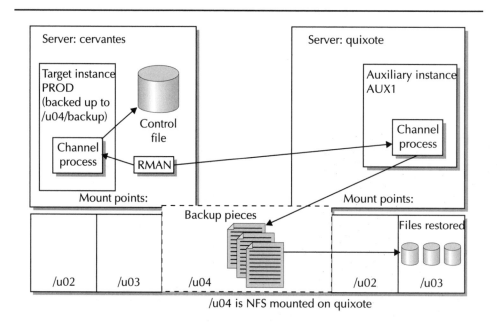

FIGURE 16-2. *Duplication to a different server using disk backups*

If you are on a Windows platform, instead of NFS, you will be mounting a network drive. The same rule applies: the drive specification must be the same on the auxiliary as it is on the target. So, if the backup was written to F:\backup, then you must be able to use F as a network drive, or duplication will fail. In addition, you will have to set up your auxiliary service (oracleserviceaux1) and your listener service (oracleOraHome92tnslistener) to log on as a domain administrator that has read/write privileges at both the auxiliary host and the target host. Otherwise, you will not be able to access the backups over the networked drive.

As you may have already noticed, it could be difficult to make a network file system operation be successful. If you have the same file systems on both the target and the auxiliary servers, you would not be able to use a straight NFS mount from the auxiliary to the target location of the backups on disk. Therefore, your only option would be to copy the backup pieces from one node to the other.

The source of these types of headaches, of course, is the fact that RMAN hard-codes the backup location when we back up to disk, and this location cannot be changed. However, in Oracle9i, there is one option that exists for us to change the backup location: the **backup backupset** command. With this command, we can back up a previous backup set that was on disk and move it to a different disk location.

This gives us considerable flexibility. Now, we can move the backup pieces from /u04/backup/prod to, say, /u06/backup/prod, which could then be NFS mounted from our auxiliary system. Or, from the target host, we could NFS mount a drive at the auxiliary host, and then use the **backup backupset** command to move the backups to the auxiliary host. For more on this command, refer to Chapter 8.

The Backup Location: Tape
By all estimations, duplicating to a remote server using tape backups is far less complicated or demanding than if your backups are on disk, because a tape backup does not have a location, per se, just a file handle. This file handle is all that RMAN knows or cares about; how that file handle relates to a location on a specific tape is completely controlled by the media manager. Therefore, all configuration that occurs for duplication from tape comes from media management configuration.

First, you must configure your MML file at the auxiliary site the same as at the target site. Because an auxiliary channel is doing the restore operations, it must be able to initialize the MML as outlined in Chapter 4. So, make sure you've linked your MML at the auxiliary site.

Next, you need to make sure that your Media Management Server is configured correctly. What this means is that your auxiliary node must be registered as a client in the same MM server that your target node is registered in and must have the necessary privileges to access the tapes for restore purposes. In particular, you must enable the auxiliary node to be able to restore backups that were taken from a different server. This functionality is usually disabled by default in most media management software, as it is a security hole to be able to restore files from one client to another. The steps that you should follow to enable clients to restore files from a different client are outlined in one of the four media management chapters (Chapters 5, 6, 7, and 8), depending on your software vendor.

After configuring your media management server, your final configuration step is to set up your auxiliary channels. As mentioned earlier, RMAN allocates one or more channels at the auxiliary instance to perform the restore and recovery steps of duplication. These channels are configured via the **configure** command, when you are connected to your target database from RMAN. The environment variables (parms) for the auxiliary channels must contain the usual MM environment control variables. In particular, it needs to specify the client from which the backups were taken. For instance, let's say your target node is named cervantes and your auxiliary node is quixote. Because you have been backing up from cervantes, this client name is encoded with your RMAN backups at the MM server. So, to be able to access these backups from the client quixote, you must specify from within RMAN that the client name is cervantes. Your auxiliary channel configuration command, then, would look something like this (given a NetBackup Media Management System):

```
RMAN> configure auxiliary channel 1 device type sbt parms
2> = "env=(nb_ora_serv=mgtserv, nb_ora_client=cervantes)";
new RMAN configuration parameters:
CONFIGURE AUXILIARY CHANNEL 1 DEVICE TYPE 'SBT_TAPE' PARMS
"env=(nb_ora_serv=mgtserv, nb_ora_client=cervantes)";
new RMAN configuration parameters are successfully stored
```

Then, when the auxiliary channel makes its **sbt( )** calls to the media management layer, it is telling the MM server to access backups that were taken using the client cervantes, instead of checking for backups made by quixote.

Duplication and the Network

Take a deep breath; we're almost through explaining all the intricacies of duplication, and are about to walk you through the steps themselves. There's one more area that you need to prepare prior to running a **duplicate** command from RMAN: the network. By network, we mostly mean configuring your Oracle Net files—tnsnames.ora and listener.ora. However, take this opportunity to consider your overall network as well—make sure the target node, auxiliary node, and media management server can all access each other okay, and that we have plenty of bandwidth.

From an Oracle perspective, we have to configure the Oracle Net files. If you remember from our discussion in Chapter 2, RMAN must make a sysdba connection to the target database. If you are connecting remotely, you have to configure a password file for the target node. In addition, you need a tns alias that uses dedicated instead of shared servers. For duplication, this still holds true, but you must also be able to connect to the auxiliary instance as sysdba using only dedicated servers.

This means that, no matter what, you're going to have to create a password file for either your target or your auxiliary machine. You may have been forgoing this step until now by always making a local connection to the target database. But you cannot simultaneously make a local connection to both the target and the auxiliary instances. So now, if you haven't already, it's time to build a password file.

RMAN Workshop: *Building a Password File*

Workshop Notes
On Unix platforms, the name of the password file must be orapw<*sid*>, where <*sid*> is the value of the ORACLE_SID to which the password is giving access. In the following exercise, the ORACLE_SID=prod. On Windows, the filename must be in the format pwd*sid*.ora. The locations given in this workshop must be used; the password file cannot be created anywhere else or it will be unusable.

Step 1.   You must edit the init.ora file and add the following parameter:

```
Remote_login_passwordfile=exclusive
```

Step 2.   Decide what your password will be, and then navigate to your ORACLE_HOME/dbs directory (ORACLE_HOME/database on Windows), and type

```
orapwd file=orapwprod password=<OraclE4ever>
```

Step 3.   Check that the file was created successfully, and then test it out by making a remote connection as sysdba.

After you have created your password file for your auxiliary instance, you need to configure the listener to route incoming connections to the auxiliary instance. As you may have already noticed, in Oracle9i Release 2, there is no need for a listener.ora file if you will only be connecting to open databases, because the database **pmon** process automatically registers the database with a running listener daemon on the system. So, you will often see that after a default 9iR2 installation, a listener is running, and it is listening for your database, even though you've done no configuration.

While this is excellent news, it does nothing for us in a duplication environment, because we must be able to make a remote connection to an auxiliary instance that is not open, only started (in nomount mode). Because it is not open, there is no pmon process to register the auxiliary instance with the listener, so the listener has no idea it exists. To get past this, you must set up an old-fashioned listener.ora file with a manual entry for the auxiliary database. We recommend using the GUI Net Manager utility to build this entry.

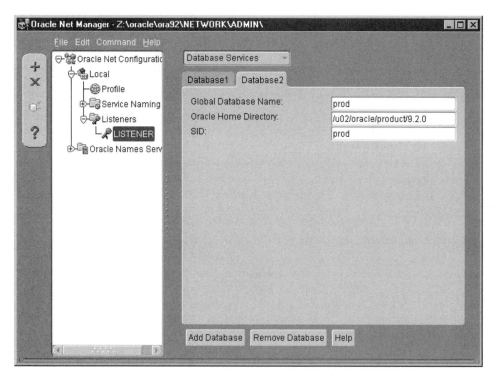

After you have configured the listener.ora at your auxiliary instance location, you must also build a tnsnames.ora entry at the site where you will be running RMAN from. This is the same as almost any other entry, except that when you build it, you must specify the auxiliary SID_NAME instead of the SERVICE_NAME. From the Net Manager, you fire up the Net Service Name Wizard. After you give the Net Service Name (Step 1), the protocol (Step 2), and then the hostname and port number (Step 3), you must change from Service Name to SID on page 4 of 5 of the Net Service Name Wizard. If you choose Service Name, the listener at the auxiliary site will try to find a service named aux1, but of course there is no service of that name. There is only a SID. Yeah, it's complicated. Do we have time to explain it exactly? Nah. Just take our word for it.

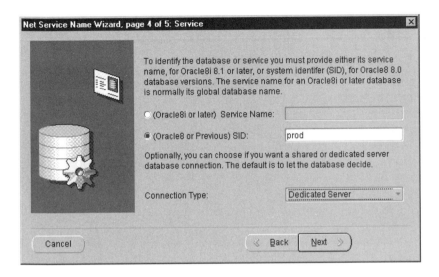

Duplication to the Same Server

Okay, so enough of the explanations, it's time to run through the duplication itself. First, we give a detailed step-by-step workshop for duplicating to the same server on which the target resides, using disk backups. Then, we give a brief explanation of what you would need to do the same thing with tape backups.

Setting an until Clause When Duplicating

There is a situation that you sometimes will encounter when performing duplication that requires you to specify an **until** clause. If you have ever used RMAN to restore your database using a backup control file, and you are now attempting to duplicate that database, you will be required to set an **until** clause. It is recommended to determine the most recent archive log available to duplication, and then use it as the ending point during duplication:

```
run { set until sequence n thread 1;
duplicate target database... }
```

Or, as a fix-all, you can set the scn to an impossibly high value:

```
set until scn  281474976710655;
```

RMAN Workshop: *Duplication to the Same Server Using Disk Backups*

Workshop Notes

Make sure that your OS has been configured to handle another Oracle instance, and that adequate memory and disk space exists. In the following example, our target database, sun92, has all of its datafiles, control files, and redo log files located at /OraHome1/oradata/prod. We will be setting the ORACLE_SID for the auxiliary instance to be aux1.

Step 1.   Build your auxiliary database directory structures:

```
mkdir /OraHome1/oradata/aux1
mkdir /OraHome1/oradata/aux1/arch
cd /OraHome1/admin
mkdir aux1
cd aux1
mkdir pfile bdump udump cdump
ls
```

Step 2.   Copy the target init.ora file to the auxiliary location. If your target database uses an spfile, you need to create a pfile from the spfile in order to capture parameters to move over.
   If you use an spfile at your target, enter the following:

```
Sql> connect /@sun92 as sysdba
create pfile='/OraHome1/admin/aux1/pfile/init.ora'
from spfile;
```

If you use an init.ora file at your target, enter the following:

```
cp /OraHome1/admin/sun92/pfile/init.ora
   /OraHome1/admin/aux1/pfile/init.ora
```

Step 3.   Make all necessary changes to your aux1 init.ora file:

```
Control_files=
   '/OraHome1/oradata/aux1/control01.dbf'
Background_dump_dest=/OraHome1/admin/bdump
user_dump_dest=/OraHome1/admin/udump
log_archive_dest_1=
   'location=/OraHome1/oradata/aux1/arch'
db_name='aux1'
instance_name='aux1'
```

```
remote_login_passwordfile=exclusive
db_file_name_convert=('sun92', 'aux1')
```

Step 4.   Build your aux1 password file. See the "Building a Password File" workshop earlier in this chapter.

Step 5.   Start the aux1 instance in nomount mode:

```
ORACLE_SID=aux1
export ORACLE_SID
sqlplus /nolog
sql>connect / as sysdba
sql>startup nomount
pfile=/OraHome1/admin/aux1/pfile/init.ora
```

Step 6.   Configure your network files for connection to aux1. After making any changes to your listener.ora file, be sure that you bounce your listener, or the change will not take effect.

```
lsnrctl
LSNRCTL>stop
LSNRCTL>start
```

The tnsnames.ora file should have an entry like this:

```
AUX1 =
  (DESCRIPTION =
    (ADDRESS_LIST =
      (ADDRESS = (PROTOCOL = TCP)(HOST = cervantes)(PORT = 1521))
    )
    (CONNECT_DATA =
      (SID = aux1)
      (SERVER = DEDICATED)
    )
  )
```

The listener.ora file should have an entry like this:

```
SID_LIST_LISTENER =
  (SID_LIST =
    (SID_DESC =
      (GLOBAL_DBNAME = aux1)
      (ORACLE_HOME = /OraHome1/)
      (SID_NAME = aux1)
    )
  )
```

Step 7.   From RMAN, connect to the target and auxiliary instance and run the **duplicate** command:

```
ORACLE_SID=sun92
export ORACLE_SID
rman
RMAN>connect target /
RMAN> connect auxiliary sys/password@aux1
RMAN>duplicate target datatabase to aux1
  pfile=/OraHome1/admin/aux1/pfile/init.ora
  logfile
  '/OraHome1/oradata/aux1/redo1.dbf' size 100m,
  '/OraHome1/oradata/aux1/redo2.dbf' size 100m,
  '/OraHome1/oradata/aux1/redo3.dbf' size 100m;
```

Using Tape Backups

If you were to perform the preceding exercises, but your backups were on tape, little would change. In fact, none of the code itself would change; you would simply insert an additional step prior to running the **duplicate** command itself. That step would be to configure your auxiliary channels to resemble the channels that the backups were taken with. In other words, do a **show** command:

```
RMAN> show channel;
RMAN configuration parameters are:
CONFIGURE CHANNEL 1 DEVICE TYPE 'SBT_TAPE' PARMS
"env=(nb_ora_serv=mgtserv)";
CONFIGURE CHANNEL 2 DEVICE TYPE 'SBT_TAPE' PARMS
"env=(nb_ora_serv=mgtserv)";
```

Then, simply create the auxiliary channels to match:

```
CONFIGURE AUXILIARY CHANNEL 1 DEVICE TYPE 'SBT_TAPE' PARMS
"env=(nb_ora_serv=mgtserv)";
CONFIGURE AUXILIARY CHANNEL 2 DEVICE TYPE 'SBT_TAPE' PARMS
"env=(nb_ora_serv=mgtserv)";
```

Duplication to a Remote Server

Duplication to a remote server has many of the same configuration steps as duplication to the same server. Particularly, if you are duplicating remotely but will use disk backups, the steps would be identical, although you could forgo all file-renaming steps. In addition, you would have to either copy your backups to the remote server or use NFS to mount the backups at the remote site. Covering NFS is outside the scope of this book, so we assume in the following workshop that you have the same file systems on both the target and auxiliary servers, and that you have copied the backups to the auxiliary system.

RMAN Workshop: *Duplication to a Remote Server Using Disk Backups*

Workshop Notes

This workshop assumes two servers: cervantes, the target, and quixote, the auxiliary. It assumes you have the same file system on both nodes and that you have copied your backups from cervantes to quixote. The most important thing to note here, versus duplication to the same server, is that we maintain the sun92 database SID throughout the process (instead of changing it to aux1).

Step 1. At quixote, build your auxiliary database directory structures:

```
mkdir /OraHome1/oradata/sun92
cd /OraHome1/admin
mkdir sun92
cd sun92
mkdir pfile bdump udump cdump
ls
```

Step 2. At cervantes, make a copy of the target init.ora file so that it can be moved to the auxiliary server. If your target database uses an spfile, you need to create a pfile from the spfile in order to capture parameters to move over.

   If you use an spfile at your target, enter the following:

```
Sql> connect /@sun92 as sysdba
create pfile='/OraHome1/admin/sun92/pfile/init.ora'
from spfile;
```

Step 3. Move the target init.ora file to the auxiliary site. From cervantes,

```
cd /OraHome1/admin/sun92/pfile
ftp Quixote.windba.com
username: oracle
password:
cd /OraHome1/admin/sun92/pfile
put init.ora
exit
```

Step 4.   Start the auxiliary instance in nomount mode at quixote:

```
ORACLE_SID=sun92
export ORACLE_SID
sqlplus /nolog
SQL>connect / as sysdba
SQL>startup nomount
pfile=/OraHome1/admin/sun92/pfile/init.ora
```

Step 5.   Configure the listener.ora at the auxiliary site (quixote):

```
SID_LIST_LISTENER =
  (SID_LIST =
    (SID_DESC =
      (GLOBAL_DBNAME = sun92)
      (ORACLE_HOME = /OraHome1/)
      (SID_NAME = sun92)
    )
  )
```

Step 6.   Configure the tnsnames.ora at the target site (cervantes):

```
sun92_aux =
  (DESCRIPTION =
    (ADDRESS_LIST =
      (ADDRESS = (PROTOCOL = TCP)(HOST = quixote)(PORT = 1521))
    )
    (CONNECT_DATA =
      (SID = sun92)
      (SERVER = DEDICATED)
    )
  )
```

Step 7.   From the target site, log in to the target database and switch the log file:

```
connect / as sysdba
alter system switch logfile
```

Step 8.   Move all archived logs from the archive destination on the target server to the archive destination on the auxiliary server. (This assumes you back up, then delete, all archive logs with RMAN, and therefore only have archive logs on the target that date back to the last archive log backup.) The following assumes you have a **log_archive_dest_n** parameter that points to /OraHome1/oradata/sun92/arch:

```
cd /OraHome1/oradata/sun92
tar -cvf arch.tar arch
gzip arch.tar
ftp Quixote.windba.com
username:oracle
password:
cd /OraHome1/oradata/sun92
bin
put arch.tar.gz
```

Exit from FTP, and then log in to quixote and unzip and untar the arch directory:

```
gunzip arch.tar.gz
tar -x arch.tar
cd arch
ls
```

Step 9.   From the target system (cervantes), run your **duplicate** command:

```
ORACLE_SID=sun92
export ORACLE_SID
rman
RMAN> connect target /
RMAN> connect auxiliary sys/password@sun92_aux
RMAN> sql 'alter system switch logfile';
RMAN> duplicate target datatabase to sun92
  nofilenamecheck
  pfile=/OraHome1/admin/sun92/pfile/init.ora
  logfile
  '/OraHome1/oradata/sun92/redo1.dbf' size 100m,
  '/OraHome1/oradata/sun92/redo2.dbf' size 100m,
  '/OraHome1/oradata/sun92/redo3.dbf' size 100m;
```

Using Tape Backups
for Remote Server Duplication

All the steps in the preceding exercise apply if you were to use tape backups instead of disk backups; again, the only difference is that you would also have to configure your auxiliary channels to reflect the needs of your media manager. In addition to specifying the media management server, and any classes or pools that you have for your regular channels, you also need to specify the target client name:

```
RMAN> configure auxiliary channel 1 device type sbt parms
2> = "env=(nb_ora_serv=mgtserv, nb_ora_client=cervantes)";
```

Incomplete Duplication:
Using the DBNEWID Utility

One of the most frustrating elements of performing duplication is that there is no "restartable duplication." In other words, if you make it through the step that restores all your files—arguably the longest step of the process—but there is failure, say, during the recovery, you must start the duplication process over again from scratch and restore all the files again. There is no way to correct the recovery process (by making missing archive logs available, for instance) and then pick back up where you left off.

In Oracle9*i* Release 2, this has been partially fixed by making available the DBNEWID utility, which will give your clone database a new DBID in a safe and controlled manner. This allows you, then, to do manual recovery against a duplicated database, prepare all the elements, and then run DBNEWID, which will complete the process started by duplication.

DBNEWID usage is simple. First, you must make sure you have a good backup taken prior to using this. Although it has a verification process, it is still possible to encounter unrecoverable errors during the changing of the DBID. After confirming a good backup, you need to get the database shut down in a consistent state and then brought back up to a mounted state:

```
shutdown immediate;
startup mount
```

Then, run the DBNEWID utility from the command line:

```
$ nid target=/
DBNEWID: Release 9.2.0.1.0 - Production
Copyright (c) 1995, 2002, Oracle Corporation.  All rights reserved.
Connected to database AUX1 (DBID=264335766)
Control Files in database:
    /OraHome1/oradata/aux1/control01.ctl
    /OraHome1/oradata/aux1/control02.ctl
    /OraHome1/oradata/aux1/control03.ctl

Change database ID of database AUX1? (Y/[N]) => y
Proceeding with operation
Changing database ID from 264335766 to 264335801
    Control File /OraHome1/oradata/aux1/control01.ctl - modified
    Control File /OraHome1/oradata/aux1/control02.ctl - modified
    Control File /OraHome1/oradata/aux1/control03.ctl - modified
    Datafile /OraHome1/oradata/aux1/system01.dbf - dbid changed
    Datafile /OraHome1/oradata/aux1/undotbs01.dbf - dbid changed
    Datafile /OraHome1/oradata/aux1/cwmlite01.dbf - dbid changed
    Datafile /OraHome1/oradata/aux1/drsys01.dbf - dbid changed
    Datafile /OraHome1/oradata/aux1/example01.dbf - dbid changed
```

```
Datafile /OraHome1/oradata/aux1/indx01.dbf - dbid changed
Datafile /OraHome1/oradata/aux1/odm01.dbf - dbid changed
Datafile /OraHome1/oradata/aux1/tools01.dbf - dbid changed
Datafile /OraHome1/oradata/aux1/users01.dbf - dbid changed
Datafile /OraHome1/oradata/aux1/xdb01.dbf - dbid changed
Control File /OraHome1/oradata/aux1/control01.ctl - dbid changed
Control File /OraHome1/oradata/aux1/control02.ctl - dbid changed
Control File /OraHome1/oradata/aux1/control03.ctl - dbid changed
```

```
Database ID for database AUX1 changed to 264335801.
All previous backups and archived redo logs for this database are
unusable.
Shut down database and open with RESETLOGS option.
Successfully changed database ID.
DBNEWID - Completed successfully.
```

After DBNEWID has completed, you must shut down and restart the database using **resetlogs**:

```
Shutdown immediate;
startup mount;
alter database open resetlogs;
```

For more information on using the DBNEWID utility, refer to the online documentation *Oracle9i Database Utilities Release 2 (9.2)*. This can be found at either metalink.oracle.com or technet.oracle.com.

Summary

In this chapter, we discussed the architecture behind the RMAN duplication process. Using duplication, we can produce clone databases from our RMAN backups to either the local system or a remote server. There are different configuration steps, depending on whether you will be duplicating locally or remotely. In addition, there are specific guidelines to follow if your backups are on disk or tape. We went through two RMAN Workshops that gave step-by-step instructions for duplication. We wrapped everything up with a brief discussion of the DBNEWID utility that comes with Oracle9i Release 2.

CHAPTER
17

RMAN and the
Standby Database

racle Standby Database has been an option bundled for free with the Oracle Database since Oracle7. It is an architectural feature that adds a little functionality to an operation that already take place on your system: the archival of every single change that happens on a database. The basic principle of the Standby Database is simply that because you are journaling every database change anyway, it makes sense to take a copy of your database, mount it, and apply those changes to the copy. Then, with a few minor tweaks, you can use that copy for disaster recovery. If the primary database is lost, you can activate your standby database, move your users over, and the life of your organization rolls on. Figure 17-1 shows an overview of the Standby Database architecture.

Since its initial inception as a disaster recovery solution, Oracle Standby Database has evolved into an even more powerful extension of your production database environment. The Standby Database now falls under a more general product heading of Data Guard, which combines the Standby Database architecture with a log broker and apply engine that gives a variety of different disaster recovery options. Data Guard can be configured to provide a guaranteed zero-data-loss disaster-protection solution, or it can be loosely used simply to keep a minimal data-loss solution available. In addition to Data Guard, the Standby Database can also be used to offload long-running queries from production environments.

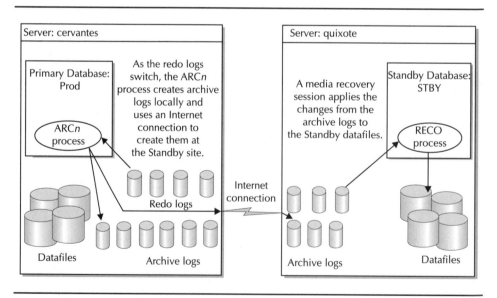

FIGURE 17-1. *The Standby Database overview*

RMAN has been integrated with the Standby Database to make a complete Oracle solution for disaster recovery and high availability. RMAN backups can be used to create the standby database, along with providing the initial recovery phase. Then, after you have created the standby database, RMAN can connect to the Standby and take backups that can be restored to the primary database. In this way, the resources used to perform a backup can be completely removed from your production environment.

Obviously, this book is about RMAN, and not standby databases. If you have more questions about Oracle Standby Database or Data Guard, please refer to the Oracle documentation on Data Guard. From here on out, we will assume you know the basics of Standby Database, and are ready to create one using RMAN.

RMAN and the Standby Database

Primarily, the relationship between RMAN and the standby database is a simple one: RMAN is used to create the standby database. If you are implementing a backup strategy that has RMAN doing all of your backups, you wouldn't really have any choice but to use RMAN, as the standby database must have primary database datafiles copied into place to begin with.

With the release of Oracle version 9.2, there are now two different kinds of standby databases: physical standby databases and logical standby databases. A physical standby database is nothing more than a copy of the primary database that is always in a state of media recovery. The Primary database ships its archive logs over via an Oracle Net connection, and they can be applied as they arrive, or you can manually apply them at set intervals. A physical standby database is never opened unless it is activated, at which point it becomes the primary database, and cannot be reverted.

A logical standby database behaves by slightly different rules. It uses new replication technology exclusive to version 9.2 that allows you to open the standby database and apply archive logs from the primary at the same time. It achieves this by converting the archive logs into logical DML statements that are executed on the standby while it is open, as opposed to using media recovery to apply those changes. Logical Standby Databases are one of the true killer apps of version 9.2, and we encourage you to explore what they can offer your shop.

RMAN backups cannot be used to create a logical Standby database, because the Primary database must be quiesced prior to taking a backup to be used for a logical standby. *Quiesced* refers to a database that is open, but all activity is frozen. RMAN cannot quiesce a database. Therefore, the rest of this chapter assumes you want to create and use a physical Standby database.

Requirements for Using RMAN for Standby Creation

Before RMAN can create the standby database, you have to walk through a few initial steps. These steps are identical to those outlined in the duplication process in Chapter 16:

1. Make all necessary changes in both the primary and standby database init.ora files.

2. Complete all necessary Net configuration.

3. Start the standby database in **nomount** mode.

The reason these steps are identical is that RMAN uses the **duplicate** command to create the standby, so all rules that apply to a duplication also apply to standby creation. This means that any file renaming issues are the same, the password file requirement is the same, and the particular way in which you have to configure the listener.ora and tnsnames.ora files is the same. If you're not sure what all of this means, review Chapter 16 on duplication prior to proceeding: everything from here on out is in addition to the duplication requirements and restrictions laid out in the previous chapter.

In addition to reviewing Chapter 16, you must also make a specific kind of control file backup. A regular control file backup is not used when we create a Standby database, because a standby database control file is different from a regular control file. It places more stringent conditions on applying archive logs during media recovery. A standby control file will also not allow a standby database to be opened with an **alter database open** command. Instead, you must activate a standby database (and thus make it the primary database) using **alter database activate standby database**.

To create a standby control file, you can use a SQL command:

```
Alter database create standby controlfile as
'/u04/backup/stby_cfile01.ctl';
```

If you create a standby control file in this fashion, you have to catalog it with RMAN before RMAN can use it in a **duplicate...for standby** operation:

```
RMAN>catalog controlfilecopy '/u04/backup/stby_cfile01.ctl';
```

Even simpler, you can use RMAN to create a standby control file. This way, you can create a copy on your tape device (if you use tape backups) using the **backup** command:

```
RMAN>  backup current controlfile for standby;
```

Once you have a standby control file ready, you can move forward with your standby creation using RMAN.

Finally, before we discuss the commands for creating your Standby, a little vocabulary lesson will come in handy. As you know from the previous chapter, the RMAN duplication process refers to two databases that must be connected to: the target database and the auxiliary database. The target is where the backups came from, and the auxiliary is the clone database being created from the target database backups.

In the language of the Standby Database architecture, you have two databases, as well: the Primary Database, which is your current production database, and the Standby Database, which is the unopened copy of the Primary Database that receives the archived redo logs from the Primary. When you are using RMAN to create a standby database, remember this: The target database is the primary database, and the auxiliary database is the standby database.

The duplicate...for standby Command

The **duplicate** command is utilized a little differently when you are using it for Standby creation. As we stated previously, all duplication rules apply, but we must add a few caveats and restrictions as well.

Memory Considerations

First of all, the **db_name** parameter in the init.ora file of the Standby database must match the **db_name** parameter of the Primary database. This is only marginally interesting news if you are creating your Standby Database on a different server, but it has important implications if you will be building the Standby on the same server as the Primary Database. Oracle uses the **db_name** to lock memory segments at the OS level, so if you try to mount two instances with the same **db_name**, you will get an error:

```
ORA-01102: Cannot mount database in exclusive mode
```

To get around this, you modify the init.ora file of the Standby Database and add the parameter **lock_name_space**. You set this to a value different from the **db_name**, and then Oracle uses this to lock memory segments without changing the **db_name**:

```
Lock_name_space='stby1'
```

Because the **db_name** must be the same, the **duplicate** command does not use the format **duplicate target database to <aux_name>**. This format was necessary to reset the database name in the new control file during duplication, but during standby creation, we don't create a new control file. Therefore, the command looks like this:

```
Duplicate target database for standby;
```

Log File Considerations

In addition to the missing **to** clause of the **duplicate** command, you cannot use the log file clause when creating a standby. The reason for this has everything to do with Standby Database options, such as the Standby Redo Logfile option that is available as part of a Data Guard solution. None of these options apply to the duplication process, but because of them, RMAN disallows the log file clause. Instead, if you are doing a straight Standby Database configuration, and you need to specify a different location for the log files, you need to use the **log_file_name_convert** parameter in your Standby init.ora file. This parameter acts exactly like **db_file_name_convert**, in that it is a simple string conversion and can be used to change a single directory name, or can be used in pairs to make multiple changes.

Datafile Considerations

If you will be creating your standby database to a different server than the primary database, you do not have to change anything about the datafile location, so long as the Standby Server has the same mount point and directory structure as the primary. As with regular duplication, if you will be using the same datafile locations on the standby that exist on the primary, you need to use the **nofilenamecheck** keyword in the **duplicate** command:

```
Duplicate target database for standby nofilenamecheck;
```

If you are creating the Standby Database on the same server as the Primary Database, you are required to change the file locations for the standby datafiles. You can do this in any of the same ways that you would with regular duplication: using the **configure auxname** command, using **set newname** in a **run** block, or using the **db_file_name_convert** parameter in the standby init.ora file.

Media Recovery Considerations

A standby database is never opened for read/write activity. It is mounted and placed in a state of media recovery, or it is opened in read-only mode and users are allowed to perform select statements only. Because of this peculiarity, the RMAN duplication performs a little differently than if you wanted to clone the database. First, it doesn't re-create the control file; it restores a standby control file. Second, it does not, by default, perform any media recovery on the datafiles after restoring them, and then it skips the steps that reset the DBID and open the database reset logs. So, when the **duplicate...for standby** completes, your standby is mounted but not open, and you will need to decide how to proceed with media recovery.

If you would like RMAN to perform the initial media recovery and apply archive logs that have been backed up by RMAN, you can use the keyword **dorecover** in your **duplicate** command:

Duplicate target database for standby dorecover;

Typically, you want to provide an **until** clause along with your **duplicate** command if you will be doing recovery, particularly if you are creating the standby at a remote site. If you are at a remote site, using **set until time** or **set until sequence** will enable you to make sure the recovery only attempts to use archive logs that are available at the other site. Of course, because we aren't setting the DBID or opening the clone, a failed media recovery session out of the **duplicate** command is no big deal: you can just pick back up manually where it left off.

RMAN Workshop: *Create a Standby Database Using RMAN*

We will now create a Standby database using RMAN.

Workshop Notes

This exercise creates a Standby Database on the same server as the Primary database. The ORACLE_SID for the Standby is stby, but the **db_name** will be the same as the Primary: sun92. We will use both the **db_file_name_convert** and **log_file_name_convert** parameters, and we will perform media recovery.

Step I.   Use RMAN to create a standby control file:

```
ORACLE_SID=sun92
export ORACLE_SID
rman
RMAN> connect target /
RMAN> backup current controlfile for standby
   format= '/space/backup/stby_cfile.%U';
```

You will need to specify a point in time after you created this standby control file, so perform a few log switches, and then record the last log sequence number from **V$archived_log**:

```
SQL> alter system switch logfile;
SQL> alter system switch logfile;
SQL> select sequence# from v$archived_log;
```

Step 2.   Build your standby database directory structures:

```
mkdir /space/oracle_user/OraHome1/oradata/stby
mkdir /space/oracle_user/OraHome1/oradata/stby/arch
cd /space/oracle_user/OraHome1/admin
```

```
mkdir stby
cd stby
mkdir pfile bdump udump cdump
ls
```

Step 3. Copy the target init.ora file to the auxiliary location. If your target database uses an spfile, you need to create a pfile from the spfile in order to capture parameters to move over.

If you use an spfile at your target, enter the following:

```
Sql> connect /@sun92 as sysdba
create pfile='/space/oracle_user/OraHome1/admin/aux1/pfile/init.ora'
from spfile;
```

If you use an init.ora file at your target, enter the following:

```
cp /space/oracle_user/OraHome1/admin/sun92/pfile/init.ora
   /space/oracle_user/OraHome1/admin/stby/pfile/init.ora
```

Step 4. Make all necessary changes to your stby init.ora file:

```
Control_files=
    '/space/oracle_user/OraHome1/oradata/stby/control01.dbf'
Background_dump_dest=/space/oracle_user/OraHome1/admin/stby/bdump
user_dump_dest=/space/oracle_user/OraHome1/admin/stby/udump
log_archive_dest_1=
    'location=/space/oracle_user/OraHome1/oradata/stby/arch'
standby_archive_dest=
    'location=/space/oracle_user/OraHome1/oradata/stby/arch'
lock_name_space='stby'
remote_login_passwordfile=exclusive
db_file_name_convert=('sun92', 'stby')
log_file_name_convert=('sun92', 'stby')
```

Step 5. Build your stby password file. See the password file workshop earlier in Chapter 16.

Step 6. Start the stby instance in **nomount** mode:

```
ORACLE_SID=stby
export ORACLE_SID
sqlplus /nolog
sql>connect / as sysdba
sql>startup nomount
pfile=/space/oracle_user/OraHome1/admin/stby/pfile/init.ora
```

Step 7.   Configure your network files for connection to stby. After making any changes to your listener.ora file, be sure that you bounce your listener or the change will not take effect:

```
lsnrctl
LSNRCTL>stop
LSNRCTL>start
```

The tnsnames.ora file should have an entry like this:

```
STBY =
  (DESCRIPTION =
    (ADDRESS_LIST =
      (ADDRESS = (PROTOCOL = TCP)(HOST = cervantes)(PORT = 1521))
    )
    (CONNECT_DATA =
      (SID = stby)
      (SERVER = DEDICATED)
    )
  )
```

The listener.ora file should have an entry like this:

```
SID_LIST_LISTENER =
  (SID_LIST =
    (SID_DESC =
      (GLOBAL_DBNAME = sun92)
      (ORACLE_HOME = /space/oracle_user/OraHome1/)
      (SID_NAME = stby)
    )
  )
```

Step 8.   From RMAN, connect to the target and auxiliary instance and run the **duplicate** command:

```
ORACLE_SID=sun92
export ORACLE_SID
rman
RMAN>connect target /
RMAN> connect auxiliary sys/password@stby
RMAN>run {
  set until sequence = 789 thread = 1;
  duplicate target database for standby
  dorecover;}
```

Taking Backups from the Standby Database

After creating your Standby Database, you can use it for a number of different purposes. Its primary reason for existence, of course, is to provide a disaster recovery solution for your production database. However, you can also suspend media recovery against the Standby, open it in read-only mode, and perform any number of data-mining operations that would suck too many resources away from your production system.

From the RMAN perspective, there is another excellent way to put the Standby Database to work. As you know from Chapter 15, there is a price to pay for running RMAN against your production database in terms of resources used. You utilize precious memory, CPU, and disk I/O resources when the backup is running. So, we recommend running your backups during the off-peak hours of your database. Sometimes, though, there are no off-peak hours. You could be a 24-hour operation, with constant database updates, or your database could be so large that backups are pretty much running around the clock.

If you have a physical standby database, you can take your production backups from the standby. These backups can then be restored to the primary database if the primary has a failure of some kind. Because the Standby has the same DBID and is always from the same incarnation, the RMAN datafile backups are interchangeable between the Standby database and the Primary database. The Standby is a true clone of the Primary.

The thing to understand about using the Standby to take production backups is that RMAN will connect to the Standby as the target database. Remember, up to this point, we've encouraged you to think of the Standby as the auxiliary database. But that only holds true for duplication operations. Once the Standby is established, you can connect to it as the target and perform backup commands. These backups can then be used for restore operations at the Primary database.

To use the Standby database in this fashion, you must have a recovery catalog set up. Without a recovery catalog, there is no way to propagate the records of the backups from the standby control file to the primary control file. With a recovery catalog, you resynchronize with the standby control file after a backup, so the records of the backup are put in the catalog. Then, you connect to the Primary database as the target, and make your catalog connection. To RMAN, the Primary and Standby are indistinguishable, so it accesses the same record set in the catalog when connected to either. Therefore, you can perform a resynchronization operation while connected to the primary, and it will refresh the primary control file with the records of backups taken while connected to the Standby.

Datafile Backups from the Standby Database

Backing up the datafiles from the Standby is the most common activity. To back up the datafiles, and then use them at the Primary database, you would do something like this:

1. From RMAN, connect to the standby database as the target, and connect to the recovery catalog:

```
RMAN> connect target sys/pswd@stby
RMAN> connect catalog rman/rman@rcat
```

2. Take your database backup. The catalog is automatically resynchronized after any **backup** command.

```
RMAN>backup database;
```

3. Exit RMAN and then start it again (this is the only way to disconnect from the target and catalog):

```
RMAN> exit
$ rman
```

4. Connect to your primary database as the target, and connect to the catalog:

```
RMAN> connect target sys/pswd@sun92
RMAN>resync catalog;
```

5. Perform a restore operation that utilizes backups taken from the Standby database:

```
RMAN> restore datafile 3;
RMAN> recover datafile 3;
```

Archive Log Backups from the Standby Database

Backing up the archive logs from the Standby is a somewhat trickier affair, because of how RMAN determines which archive logs need to be backed up: it checks the view **v$archived_log**. On the Primary Database, this view is incremented with each new archive log after it has been successfully created in the **log_archive_dest**. However, on the Standby Database, this view is updated only if your Standby is in managed recovery mode (where the archive logs are automatically applied at the Standby database). If your Standby is not in managed recovery mode, or due to your setup you will get archive log gaps at the Standby on a regular basis, it may be hard to get all the required archive logs backed up successfully from the Standby Database. In this case, we recommend using your Primary Database for its own archive log backups, and utilizing the Standby just for datafile backups.

Summary

In this chapter, we discussed the relationship that RMAN can have with the Standby Database architecture. Primarily, RMAN can be used to create the Standby Database using the **duplicate...for standby** command. We discussed the means by which you use the **duplicate** command to create the standby, and included an RMAN Workshop that walked through the steps of creating the Standby Database on the same server as the Primary Database. Then, we discussed how you could use an existing Standby Database to create backups using RMAN that could be restored to the Primary Database, as a means of offloading the work away from the production environment.

CHAPTER
18

RMAN and Real
Application Clusters

ll by itself, the architecture of Real Application Clusters (RAC) will confound all but the most alpha of database administrators. There's a trap door lying around every corner during the configuration of all the advanced failover and load-balancing features available. Adding clusters makes it even more confusing. Into this mix, you must consider how to back up and how to recover your clustered database.

Backing up a clustered database adds another layer of complexity to using RMAN. Sorry. We wish we had good news, but there's a reason we put this chapter near the end, right? It's not for the meek. Here, we discuss the unique backup and recovery challenges posed by the RAC-configured database and how to overcome them. We assume you're mostly familiar with RAC already, and thus we provide architectural explanation only to jog your overstuffed memory.

Throughout this chapter, we will use an example cluster database that has only two nodes: winrac1 and winrac2. These nodes share a disk array, which has raw partitions that are accessible by both nodes. Each node has an instance: prod1 on winrac1, and prod2 on winrac2. While we will limit our explanations to the most simple of RAC environments, a two-node cluster, be aware that nothing changes when you scale out to three, four, or more nodes. In our examples, you simply change the number from 2 to 3, and the number of channels from two to three, and so on. The more nodes you have, the more complex your backup/recovery strategies become, but the basic rules apply no matter the number of instances.

In Oracle9i Release 2, Oracle is introducing Cluster File System (CFS), which allows you to run a multinode cluster with a shared disk array that has been formatted with a file system, but is still accessible by all the nodes. Prior to CFS, the shared disk partitions had to be raw in order for them to be accessible by all instances. CFS provides a file system that enables multiple nodes to access its files simultaneously. In this chapter, we do not emphasize usage of CFS because, as of this writing, it has not been released yet and is still in a very early life-cycle stage. However, we do point out the situations in which it will make your life simpler in the future.

Real Application Clusters: Unique Backup Challenges

Before we dig any deeper, it's helpful to consider the architectural nature of the RAC cluster. Essentially, you have at least two different servers, each with its own memory and local disks, and each connected to a shared disk array. Oracle uses this hardware by creating two instances, one on each node, with their own SGA/PGA memory areas. Each instance has its own redo logs, but they exist on the shared disk and are accessible by the other nodes. All control files and datafiles are shared between the two instances, meaning there is only one database, with two threads accessing and updating the data simultaneously. Figure 18-1 provides an oversimplified look at RAC.

From the RMAN perspective, this architecture creates interesting challenges for taking backups. First of all, there are multiple instances running, but RMAN can connect to only a single node. This shouldn't pose any problems for backing up the datafiles, but we do have a problem when it comes to archive logs. Each instance is archiving its own redo logs to a local drive instead of the shared disks, so how do we get to those other archive logs? But let's start with the datafile backups.

Datafile Backups

Datafile backups in a RAC environment are pretty much the same as datafile backups in a single-node database: RMAN connects to a node and issues a **backup database** command. The memory that RMAN needs to perform the backup operation will be grabbed from that one node. If backing up to disk, the backups will be local to that node; if backing up to tape, that instance will have to be configured for integration with your MML.

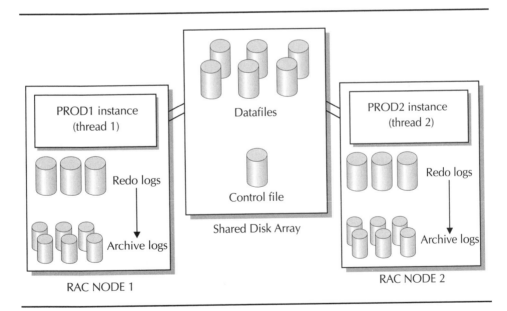

FIGURE 18-1. *RAC at its most basic*

The only problem with this scenario is that it puts quite a bit of load on a single node. This may be what you are after; if not, there is a better way. RMAN can connect to only a single node initially, but it can allocate channels at all of your nodes during an actual backup operation. The following shows an example of how this would be done:

```
Configure default device type sbt;
configure device type sbt parallelism 2;
configure channel 1 device type sbt
connect 'sys/password@prod1';
configure channel 2 device type sbt
connect 'sys/password@prod2';
backup database;
```

Then, you can run your backup and RMAN will spread the work between your two nodes. RAC datafiles sometimes have something known as *node affinity,* where a particular datafile is accessed faster from one node or the other. If this is the case for your cluster, RMAN knows about it, and will back up the datafile from the node where it can be read the fastest. If there is no node affinity on your system, RMAN just distributes the work across the two channels as it would any two channels used to parallelize a backup. Obviously, you could allocate two channels at each node, or three, or four....

Archive Log Backups

Archive log backups are far trickier than datafile backups because each node is responsible for its own archival, which means that each node has unshared files that only it can access. If we connect to only one node and issue a **backup archivelog all** command, RMAN will look in the control file and discover the listing for the archive logs from both nodes, but then, when it looks at the local node, it will only find the archive logs from that node and it will error out.

Of course, the question can be posed, "Why not write archive logs to a raw partition on the shared disk array?" The answer is that you could, if you don't mind

RMAN, RAC, and Net Connections

RAC comes with many extremely powerful load-balancing and failover features as part of the Net configuration. However, RMAN is a little too picky for these features. RMAN can connect to only one node, and cannot failover or be load balanced. Therefore, the Net aliases you use for the target connection and for the CONNECT clause of the channel allocation string must be configured to connect to a single node with a dedicated server.

the administrative nightmare. Think about it: with raw partitions, you can write only one file per partition, which means you would have to anticipate all of your archive log filenames and create symbolic links to a partition that exists for each archive log. Such a task is simply too labor intensive for even the most scheming Unix scripting mind among us. Of course, this won't be the case if you use CFS, because you can set up your **log_archive_dest** for each of your nodes to write to the same shared directory on a CFS drive. Then, your **archivelog backup** command can come from any node and will be able to back up all of the archive logs.

The other solution is to make sure that each node is archiving to a unique file location. For example, prod1 archives to a directory called /u04/prod1/arch, and prod2 archives to /u04/prod2/arch. Then, you can allocate channels at each node, as you did to load balance the datafile backups earlier and back up the archive logs.

```
Configure default device type sbt;
configure device type sbt parallelism 2;
configure channel 1 device type sbt
connect 'sys/password@prod1';
configure channel 2 device type sbt
connect 'sys/password@prod2';
backup archivelog all delete input;
```

RMAN has a feature known as *autolocate* that identifies which archive logs belong to which node and only attempts to back them up from that node. In this way, you don't have to specify in RMAN which logs you need backed up at which node—RMAN can figure it out for you.

Another option that would allow you to perform your archive log backup from a single node would be to NFS mount the archive log destination of the other node. For example, at the node winrac1, you have local archive logs located at /u04/prod1/arch. Then, on winrac1, you NFS mount the drive /u04/prod2/arch on winrac2 as /u04/prod2/arch. That way, when you run your archive log backups, RMAN checks the control file for the archive log locations, and it can find both locations while connected to only prod1. Figure 18-2 illustrates this methodology.

The only problem in the scenarios we've provided so far is that you are giving yourself a single point of failure for archive logs. If you archive your logs only to their respective nodes, and then you lose a node, you lose the archive logs from that node. That means that you may have to perform point-in-time recovery of the entire database to the point right before the node was lost.

A better strategy is to set up each node with a **log_archive_dest_2** parameter that writes to another node. One way to approach this task is to consider the NFS mount strategies already discussed in this chapter. Instead of just NFS mounting in read-only mode the archive destination of the other node, consider NFS mounting a drive on the other node with write access, and then setting that NFS mount as a second archive destination. Take our two-node RAC database for example. On

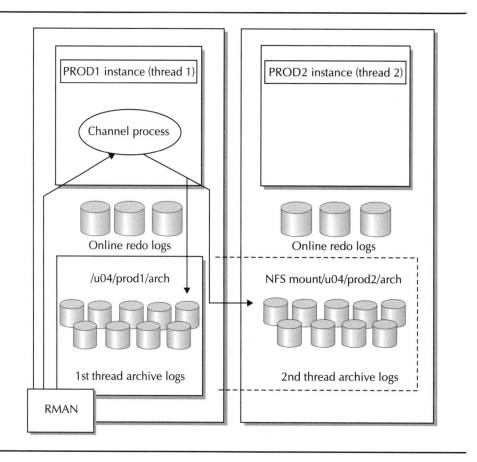

FIGURE 18-2. *Mounting the archive log destination*

winrac1, we could mount the shared directory /u04/prod2/arch from winrac2, and on winrac2, we could mount winrac1's /u04/prod1/arch directory. Then, we could set up the init.ora files for each node as shown in the following code:

```
Winrac1 init.ora file:
log_archive_dest_1='location=/u04/prod1/arch'
log_archive_dest_2='location=/u04/prod2/arch'
...
winrac2 init.ora file:
log_archive_dest_1='location=/u04/prod2/arch'
log_archive_dest_2='location=/u04/prod1/arch'
```

When set up like this, Oracle writes archive logs from each node to the archive destination of the other node. This gives us an elegant solution for backing up the archive logs from a single node and provides us with fault tolerance in case a node is lost.

RAC Recovery Challenges

Perhaps more confusing than getting the backups done is getting restore and recovery tasks taken care of in a RAC environment. Again, this is due to the complex nature of a database that has multiple instances. Multiple instances means multiple threads of archived redo logs, even though we have only a single set of datafiles. In addition, we have only one set of control files being shared between multiple instances, so even though actions are happening independently at each node, all database activity is being recorded in a single control file repository.

Restore Operations

When performing a restore from RMAN, we must point out again that RMAN can connect to only one node, but then can allocate channels at each node. This should sound pretty familiar by now; but that's not the tricky part. The part that hangs people up is keeping track of where files were backed up from.

File accessibility is the key to restore success on a RAC node. If you have been backing up to disk using channels allocated at each node, you must allocate the same channels at each node during a restore operation. No problem, you think, unless you've lost a node. If the node is down, your disk backups on that node are inaccessible, and restore operations will fail. The lesson is, if you're spending all this time and money on RAC so that you don't have a single point of failure, make sure you apply this philosophy to your backup and recovery strategy, as well. If you back up to disk, duplex the backup to more than one node. This might mean overriding the default autolocate feature, so that you can specify where exactly you want your backups to be backed up from. You do this by specifying the channel for datafile sets.

```
Configure default device type disk;
configure device type sbt parallelism 2;
configure channel 1 device type disk
connect 'sys/password@prod1';
configure channel 2 device type disk
connect 'sys/password@prod2';
backup (datafile 1,2,3,4,5 channel ORA_DISK_1)
       (datafile 6,7,8,9,10 channel ORA_DISK_2)   ;
# then switch the channels for the datafiles
backup (datafile 1,2,3,4,5 channel ORA_DISK_2)
       (datafile 6,7,8,9,10 channel ORA_DISK_1);
```

Media Management Considerations During a Restore

A better idea altogether is to stream your backups to tape—and use a centralized media management (MM) server to house your tape backups. If you have tape devices at each node and use them all for tape backup, you're increasing the degree of complexity unnecessarily. If you lose a node in your cluster, you then lose the MM catalog for all backups taken from that node. Chances are that your MM product has an automatic catalog backup, but then you have another restore to do, and where do you do it, and when? You need the catalogs at both of your other nodes for their backup information. So, you have a disaster that is fixable, but valuable minutes are racing by as you stick your nose in manuals, trying to figure it all out.

We prefer a centralized MM system, so that all three nodes can back up to tape devices that are all managed by the same MM server, and so there is a single MM catalog. That way, when a node is lost, you can simply specify the client name in your RMAN channel and do the restores to a different node. Which brings us to the most important point to remember when you use RMAN to restore your backup from tape: you must consider the node from which RMAN made the backup when doing the restore.

For example, in our two-node cluster, suppose that we have lost node winrac2, and that the disaster that took it out also corrupted some of our datafiles. We've been employing a backup strategy that allocated channels at both nodes to perform the backup, so our restore is going to have to allocate channels from both nodes. Oops! No chance of that, eh? Instead, we can allocate two kinds of channels at winrac1: normal tape channels and channels that specify the client as winrac2. It would look something like this:

```
Configure default device type sbt;
configure device type sbt parallelism 2;
configure channel 1 device type sbt
parms="env=(nb_ora_serv=rmsrv)";
configure channel 2 device type disk
parms="env=(nb_ora_serv=rmsrv, nb_ora_client=winrac2)";
restore datafile 5,12,13,18;
```

This is obviously a very simple example of what can be a complex headache. When all is said and done, we recommend a backup approach that takes datafile backups only from a single node in the cluster. If the size of your database prohibits such a simplistic approach, try to at least restrict RMAN to a small subset of your nodes. By doing so, you keep the complexity down when it comes time to perform restore operations.

Recovery Considerations After a Restore

After you get your files restored, it's time to perform media recovery by applying archive logs. Media recovery in a RAC environment has one rule that you must never forget: only one node can perform recovery. Burn it into your brain. This means that one node must have access to all the archive logs on disk. So, if you have been using an archive log strategy that has each node holding its own archive logs in a local disk, you must make that local disk available to the recovery node. You can do this via NFS, if you followed the guidelines specified in "Archive Log Backups," earlier in this chapter. You simply mount the archive log destination of the other node and issue your recover statement from within RMAN. If you're using CFS, this is not a problem and you can ignore archive log node affinity considerations.

The problem comes, again, when a node is lost. If a node is unavailable, then your recovery might be stuck if you have not been placing your archive logs in more than one destination. If you followed our advice earlier, though, you have been archiving your logs at each node to the archive destination of your other node. That way, you don't have to worry about the single-node recovery restriction, as both of your nodes have a copy of all archive logs.

If you have archive logs that you need to restore from RMAN backups, the same rules and guidelines apply to archive logs that apply to datafile restores. If you allocated channels at each node for the backup, then you need to do so for the restore. If you are missing a node, you have to allocate a channel that includes the client name for the media manager to find the proper backups (refer to the preceding section, "Media Management Considerations During a Restore"). In addition, you may have to restore the archive logs to a directory that exists locally if the **log_archive_dest** that existed on the missing node does not exist on the node doing the restore operation:

```
Restore archivelog like '%prod2%' to '/u04/prod1/arch%';
```

Advanced RMAN/RAC Topics

Once you have determined what your backup and recovery strategies will be for your RAC database, you can consider many of the same benefits that RMAN offers you in a single-node database environment: block corruption checking, null compression, and block media recovery. All of these benefits are yours in a RAC environment. In addition, advanced functionality such as database duplication exists as well. RMAN backups of RAC databases work for duplication and standby database creation, just as they would for a single-node system.

Duplication to a Single-Node System

If you administer a RAC cluster and aren't convinced yet that RMAN is the right tool for you, here's a little something to seal the deal: your RMAN backups of your RAC database can be used to create a clone of your RAC database on a single-node database. This gives you a copy of your production database without having to purchase and administer a second RAC cluster. Instead, you have a single-node database running on a cooked file system.

RMAN Workshop: *Duplicating a RAC Database to a Single-Node Database*

Workshop Notes

In this workshop, you will create a single-node clone of a two-node database. This can be done either to a new server or to a cooked file system on one of the nodes of the RAC cluster. In this example, you will be duplicating to a file system on one of the nodes in the RAC cluster. Because duplication must perform recovery, you must remember that a recovery session only has access to the node on which the recovery is being performed, so that node must have access to all the nodes' archive logs. This workshop assumes that you have NFS mounted the archive destination of each node on each other node, so that a full copy of each archive log stream is available at every node.

The two nodes of your cluster are opcbs01 and opcbs02, with instances of V92321 and V92322, respectively. You will be connecting to V92322 for all RMAN operations.

Step 1. Build your auxiliary database directory structures:

```
mkdir /u02/32bit/app/oracle/oradata/aux1
mkdir /u02/32bit/app/oracle/oradata/aux1/arch
cd /u02/32bit/app/oracle/admin
mkdir aux1
cd aux1
mkdir pfile bdump udump cdump
ls
```

Step 2. Copy the target init.ora file to the auxiliary location. If your target database uses an spfile, you need to create a pfile from the spfile to capture parameters to move over.

If you use an spfile at your target, enter the following:

```
Sql> connect / as sysdba
create pfile='/u02/32bit/app/oracle/admin/aux1/pfile/init.ora'
from spfile;
```

If you use an init.ora file at your target, enter the following:

```
cp /u02/32bit/app/oracle/admin/V92322/pfile/init.ora
   /u02/32bit/app/oracle/admin/aux1/pfile/init.ora
```

Step 3.   Make all necessary changes to your aux1 init.ora file:

```
Control_files=
   '/u02/32bit/app/oracle/oradata/aux1/control01.dbf'
core_dump_dest='/u02/32bit/app/oracle/admin/aux1/cdump'
Background_dump_dest='/u02/32bit/app/oracle/admin/aux1/bdump'
user_dump_dest=/u02/32bit/app/oracle/admin/aux1/udump
log_archive_dest_1=
   'location=/u02/32bit/app/oracle/oradata/aux1/arch'
db_name='aux1'
instance_name='aux1'
remote_login_passwordfile=exclusive
db_file_name_convert=
 ('/dev/vx/rdsk/usupport_dg', '/u02/32bit/app/oracle/oradata/aux1')
```

The following parameters can be removed entirely, including those that refer to the other instance:

```
cluster_database_instances=2
cluster_database=true
V92321.instance_name='V92321'
V92322.instance_name='V92322'
V92322.instance_number=2
V92321.instance_number=1
V92322.thread=2
V92321.thread=1
V92322.undo_tablespace='UNDOTBS2'
V92321.undo_tablespace='UNDOTBS1'
```

These can be replaced by just having the following:

```
undo_tablespace='UNDOTBS2'
```

Step 4.   Build your aux1 password file. Refer to the "Building a Password File" RMAN Workshop in Chapter 16.

Step 5.   Start the aux1 instance in **nomount** mode:

```
ORACLE_SID=aux1
export ORACLE_SID
sqlplus /nolog
sql>connect / as sysdba
```

```
sql>startup nomount
pfile=/u02/32bit/app/oracle/admin/aux1/pfile/init.ora
```

Step 6. Configure your network files for connection to aux1. After making any changes to your listener.ora file, be sure that you bounce your listener or the change will not take effect:

```
lsnrctl
LSNRCTL>stop
LSNRCTL>start
```

The tnsnames.ora file should have an entry like this:

```
AUX1 =
  (DESCRIPTION =
    (ADDRESS_LIST =
      (ADDRESS = (PROTOCOL = TCP)(HOST = opcbsol2)(PORT = 1526))
    )
    (CONNECT_DATA =
      (SID = aux1)
      (SERVER = DEDICATED)
    )
  )
```

The listener.ora file should have an entry like this:

```
 (SID_DESC =
    (GLOBAL_DBNAME = aux1)
    (ORACLE_HOME = /u02/32bit/app/oracle/product/9.2.0)
    (SID_NAME = aux1)
)
```

Step 7. From RMAN, connect to the target and auxiliary instance and run the **duplicate** command:

```
ORACLE_SID=V92322
export ORACLE_SID
rman
RMAN>connect target /
RMAN> connect auxiliary sys/password@aux1
RMAN>duplicate target database to aux1
  pfile=/u02/32bit/app/oracle/admin/aux1/pfile/init.ora
  logfile
  '/u02/32bit/app/oracle/oradata/aux1/redo1.dbf' size 100m,
  '/u02/32bit/app/oracle/oradata/aux1/redo2.dbf' size 100m,
  '/u02/32bit/app/oracle/oradata/aux1/redo3.dbf' size 100m;
```

The Single-Node Standby Database

Of course, if you can duplicate to a single node, then you can also use the **duplicate** command to create a standby database for your RAC cluster on a single node. Perhaps more than even straight duplication, this feature gives you an excellent cost-to-performance strategy for providing a disaster recovery solution for your RAC database. Instead of purchasing all the hardware and software necessary to have a complete second RAC system set up but unused for a standby database, you can create the standby on a single-node system. Obviously, it won't have the computing power or load-balancing features of the RAC database, but it gives a reasonable disaster solution so that you can hobble along until the RAC database is restored.

As with the duplication process, the secret lies in the **db_file_name_convert** parameter, which switches the file locations from raw devices to cooked devices. In addition, the single-node standby database can receive archive logs from each of the nodes in the RAC cluster and apply them in the correct chronological order.

RMAN Workshop: *Creating a Single-Node Standby Database from a RAC Database*

Workshop Notes
The single-node standby creation is nearly identical to that which you would perform against a non-clustered database. Most of the changes come from eliminating cluster-specific init.ora parameters for the standby database.

Step 1.   Use RMAN to create a standby control file:

```
ORACLE_SID=V92322
export ORACLE_SID
rman
RMAN> connect target /
RMAN> backup current controlfile for standby
  format= '/u02/backup/stby_cfile.%U';
```

You need to specify a point in time after you created this standby control file, so perform a few log switches, and then record the last log sequence number from v$archived_log. It doesn't matter which thread you choose, as the following command will force a log switch at all nodes:

```
SQL> alter system archivelog current;
SQL> select sequence# from v$archived_log;
```

Step 2. Build your standby database directory structures:

```
mkdir /u02/32bit/app/oracle/oradata/stby
mkdir /u02/32bit/app/oracle/oradata/stby/arch
cd /u02/32bit/app/oracle/admin
mkdir stby
cd stby
mkdir pfile bdump udump cdump
ls
```

Step 3. Copy the target init.ora file to the auxiliary location. If your target database uses an spfile, you need to create a pfile from the spfile to capture parameters to move over.

If you use an spfile at your target, enter the following:

```
Sql> connect / as sysdba
create pfile='/u02/32bit/app/oracle/admin/stby/pfile/init.ora'
from spfile;
```

If you use an init.ora file at your target, enter the following:

```
cp /u02/32bit/app/oracle/admin/V9232/pfile/init.ora
   /u02/32bit/app/oracle/admin/stby/pfile/init.ora
```

Step 4. Make all necessary changes to your stby init.ora file:

```
Control_files= '/u02/32bit/app/oracle/oradata/stby/control01.dbf'
Background_dump_dest=/u02/32bit/app/oracle/admin/stby/bdump
user_dump_dest=/u02/32bit/app/oracle/admin/stby/udump
log_archive_dest_1=
   'location=/u02/32bit/app/oracle/oradata/stby/arch'
standby_archive_dest=
   'location=/u02/32bit/app/oracle/oradata/stbyarch'
lock_name_space='stby'
remote_login_passwordfile=exclusive
db_file_name_convert=
 ('/dev/vx/rdsk/usupport_dg', '/u02/32bit/app/oracle/oradata/aux1')
log_file_name_convert=
 ('/dev/vx/rdsk/usupport_dg', '/u02/32bit/app/oracle/oradata/aux1')
```

The following parameters can be removed entirely, including those that refer to the other instance:

```
cluster_database_instances=2
cluster_database=true
V92321.instance_name='V92321'
```

```
V92322.instance_name='V92322'
V92322.instance_number=2
V92321.instance_number=1
V92322.thread=2
V92321.thread=1
V92322.undo_tablespace='UNDOTBS2'
V92321.undo_tablespace='UNDOTBS1'
```

These can be replaced by just having the following:

```
Instance_name='V92322'
undo_tablespace='UNDOTBS2'
```

Step 5. Build your stby password file. Refer to the "Building a Password File" RMAN Workshop in Chapter 16.

Step 6. Start the stby instance in **nomount** mode:

```
ORACLE_SID=stby
export ORACLE_SID
sqlplus /nolog
sql>connect / as sysdba
sql>startup nomount
pfile=/u02/32bit/app/oracle/admin/stby/pfile/init.ora
```

Step 7. Configure your network files for connection to stby. After making any changes to your listener.ora file, be sure that you bounce your listener or the change will not take effect:

```
lsnrctl
LSNRCTL>stop
LSNRCTL>start
```

The tnsames.ora file should have an entry like this:

```
STBY =
  (DESCRIPTION =
    (ADDRESS_LIST =
      (ADDRESS = (PROTOCOL = TCP)(HOST = opcbsol2)(PORT = 1521))
    )
    (CONNECT_DATA =
      (SID = stby)
      (SERVER = DEDICATED)
    )
  )
```

The listener.ora file should have an entry like this:

```
(SID_DESC =
  (GLOBAL_DBNAME = aux1)
  (ORACLE_HOME = /u02/32bit/app/oracle/product/9.2.0)
  (SID_NAME = aux1)
)
```

Step 8.   From RMAN, connect to the target and auxiliary instance and run the **duplicate** command:

```
ORACLE_SID=V92322
export ORACLE_SID
rman
RMAN>connect target /
RMAN> connect auxiliary sys/password@stby
RMAN>run {
  set until sequence = 43 thread = 1;
  duplicate target database for standby
  dorecover;}
```

Backing Up the Multinode RAC Database from a Single-Node Standby Database

Once you have created the single-node standby, you can take all of your backups from the standby, just as you would in a normal environment. This means that you can offload your production RAC backups from the RAC cluster itself to the node that is set up and running as a standby database. This takes the load off the cluster, gives you a disaster recovery solution, and gives you a simplified backup solution for archive logs because all the archive logs from all nodes will necessarily exist on the standby database.

Again, the secret is in **db_file_name_convert**. You are taking backups from the standby database that has the datafiles on a cooked file system, but even the standby control file knows the original location of the files (the raw system). So, when you go to restore a backup taken from the standby on the production RAC database, RMAN checks with the control file and finds the raw locations and places the files there.

In order for such a solution to work for you, you must use a recovery catalog. The recovery catalog acts as the transition agent for the metadata about the backups from the standby control file to the primary control file. After you take the backup from the standby, RMAN resynchronizes with the catalog, recording the backup metadata. Then, when you connect RMAN to the primary database and perform a manual resync, the backup metadata from the standby database control file is placed in the primary database control file records.

It is important to make sure that you connect to the standby database as the target database when performing backups from the standby. Then, you connect to the primary database as the target as well, to perform the resync. RMAN can tell the difference when it queries the target for a snapshot of the control file and sees that one has a standby control file flag and the primary has the current control file flag set. RMAN will not perform a full resync with anything but the current control file of the primary database.

Summary

In this chapter, we discussed the means by which RMAN interacts with databases in RAC clusters. We discussed how RMAN can allocate channels on each node for backup, but that recovery requires that all backups be accessible from a single node. We discussed the complications caused in archive log backups due to having multiple threads of redo being generated at different nodes. We concluded with examples for duplicating a RAC database to a single-node database, and for creating a single-node standby database from a RAC database.

CHAPTER
19

RMAN in the
Workplace:
Case Studies

e have covered a number of different topics in this book, and we are sure you have figured out that there are almost an infinite number of recovery combinations that you might be faced with. In this chapter, we provide numerous different case studies to help you review your knowledge of backup and recovery (see if you can figure out the solution before you read it). When you do come across these situations, these case studies may well help you avoid some mistakes that you might otherwise make when trying to recover your database. You can even use these case studies to practice performing recoveries so that you become an RMAN backup and recovery expert.

Before we get into the case studies, though, the following section provides a quick overview about facing the ultimate disaster, a real-life failure of your database.

Before the Recovery

Disaster has struck. Often when you are in a recovery situation, everyone is in a big rush to recover the database. Customers are calling, management is panicking, and your boss is looking at you for answers, all of which is making you nervous and wonder if your resume is up to date. When the real recovery situation occurs, stop. Take a few moments and collect yourself, and ask these questions:

1. What is the exact nature of the failure?

2. What are the recovery options available to me?

3. Might I need Oracle support?

4. Is there anyone else who can act as a second pair of eyes for me during this recovery?

Let's address each of these questions in detail.

What Is the Exact Nature of the Failure?

Back in the days when I was contracting, I was paged one night (on Halloween, no less!) because a server had failed, and once they got the server back up, none of the databases would come up. Before I received the page, the DBAs at this site had spent upward of eight hours trying to restart the 25 databases on that box. Most of the databases would not start. The DBAs had recovered a couple of the seemingly lost databases, yet even those databases still would not open. The DBAs called Oracle, and Oracle seemed unsure as to what the problem was. Finally, the DBAs paged me (while I was out trick-or-treating with my kids).

Within about 20 minutes after arriving at the office, I knew what the answer was. I didn't find the answer because I was smarter than all the other DBAs there (I wasn't, in fact). I found the answer for a couple of reasons. First, I approached the problem from a fresh perspective (after eight hours of problem solving, one's eyes tend to become burned and red!). Second, I looked to find the nature of the failure rather than just assuming the nature of the failure was a corrupted database.

What ended up being the problem, pretty clearly to a fresh pair of eyes, was a set of corrupted Oracle libraries. Once we recovered those libraries, all the databases came up quickly, without a problem. The moral of the story is that when you have a database that has crashed, or that will not open, do not assume that the cause is a corrupted datafile or a bad disk drive. Find out for sure what the problem is by investigative analysis. Good analysis may take a little longer to begin with, but generally it will prove valuable in the long run.

What Recovery Options Are Available?

Recovery situations can offer a number of different solutions. Again, back when I was a consultant, I had a customer who had a disk controller drive fail over a weekend, and the result was the loss of file systems on the box, including files belonging to an Oracle database in ARCHIVELOG mode. The DBA at the customer site went ahead and recovered the entire database (about 150GB), which took, as I recall, a couple of hours.

The following Monday, the DBA and I had a discussion about the recovery method he selected. The corrupted file systems actually impacted only about five actual database datafiles (the other file systems contained web server files that we were not concerned with). The total size of the impacted database datafiles was no more than 8 or 10GB. The DBA was pretty upset about having to come into the office and spend several hours, overall, recovering the database. When I asked the DBA why he hadn't just recovered the five datafiles instead of the entire database, he replied that it just had not occurred to him.

The moral of this story is that it's important to consider your recovery options. The type of recovery you do may make a big difference in how long it takes you to recover your database. Another moral of this story is to really become a backup and recovery expert. Part of the reason the DBA in this case had not considered datafile recovery, I think, is that he had never done such a recovery. When facing a stressful situation, people tend to not consider options they are not familiar with. So, we strongly suggest you set up a backup and recovery lab and practice recoveries until you can do it in your sleep.

Might Oracle Support Be Needed?

You might well be a backup and recovery expert, but even the experts need help from time to time. This is what Oracle support is there for. Even though I feel like I know something about backup and recovery, I ask myself if the failure looks to be something that I might need Oracle support for. Generally, if the failure is something odd, even if I think I can solve it on my own, I "prime" support by opening an ITar on the problem. That way, if I need help, I have already provided Oracle with the information they need (or at least some initial information) and have them primed to support me should I need it. If you are paying for Oracle support, use it now, don't wait for later.

Who Else Can Act as a Second Pair of Eyes During Recovery?

When I'm in a stressful situation, first of all it's nice to have someone share the stress with. Somehow I feel a bit more comfortable when someone is there just to talk things out with. Further, when you are working on a critical problem, mistakes can be costly. Having a second, experienced, pair of eyes there to support you as you recover your database is a great idea!

Recovery Case Studies

Now to the meat of the chapter, the recovery case studies. In this section, we provide you with a number of case studies, a list of which follows, in the order they appear:

1. Recovering from complete database loss in NOARCHIVELOG mode (with a recovery catalog)

2. Recovering from complete database loss in NOARCHIVELOG mode (without a recovery catalog)

3. Recovering from complete database loss in ARCHIVELOG mode (with a recovery catalog)

4. Recovering from complete database loss in ARCHIVELOG mode (without a recovery catalog)

5. Recovering from the loss of the SYSTEM tablespace

6. Recovering online from the loss of a datafile

7. Recovering from loss of an unarchived online redo log

8. Recovering through **resetlogs**

9. Using RMAN duplication to create a historical subset of the target database

10. Completing a failed duplication manually

11. Recovering from a tablespace dropped unintentionally

12. Re-creating the control file without losing backup metadata

13. Duplicating prior to **resetlogs**

In each of these case studies, we provide you with the following information:

- **The Scenario**   Outlines the environment for you.

- **The Problem**   Defines a problem that needs to be solved.

- **The Solution**   Outlines the solution for you, including RMAN output solving the problem.

Now, let's look at our case studies!

Case #1: Recovering from Complete Database Loss (NOARCHIVELOG Mode) with a Recovery Catalog

The Scenario
Thom is a new DBA at Unfortunate Company. Upon arriving at his new job, he finds that his databases are not backed up at all, and that they are all in NOARCHIVELOG mode. Because Thom's manager will not shell out the money for additional disk space for archived redo logs, Thom is forced to do offline backups, which he begins doing the first night he is on the job. Thom also has turned on autobackups of his control file, and has converted the database so that it is using an spfile. Finally, Thom has created a recovery catalog schema in a different database that is on a different database server.

The Problem
Unfortunate Company's cheap buying practices catch up to it in the few days following Thom's initial work, when the off-brand (cheap) disks that it has purchased all become corrupted due to a bad controller card. Thom's database is lost.

Thom's offline database backup strategy includes tape backups to a local tape drive. Once the hardware problems are solved, the system administrator quickly rebuilds the lost file systems, and Thom quickly gets the Oracle software installed. Now, Thom needs to get the database back up and running immediately.

The Solution

Thom's only recovery option in this case is to restore from the last offline backup, as demonstrated in Chapter 12. In this case, Thom's recovery catalog database was not lost (it was on another server), and his file systems are in place, so all he needs to do is recover the database. First, Thom needs to recover the database spfile, followed by the control file. Then, he needs to recover the database datafiles to the file systems.

The Solution Revealed   Based on the preceding considerations, Thom devises and implements the following recovery plan:

1. Restore a copy of the spfile. While you will be able to nomount the Oracle instance in many cases without a parameter file at all, to properly recover the database, Thom has to restore the correct spfile from backup. Because he doesn't have a control file yet, we cannot configure channels permanently. In this case, Thom has configured his autobackups of the control files to go to default disk locations. Thus, once Thom restored his Oracle software backups, he also restored the backup pieces to the autobackups of the control file. This makes the recovery of the spfile simple as a result:

   ```
   Rman target sys/password catalog rcat_user/rcat_password@catalogdb
   startup force nomount;
   restore spfile from autobackup;
   shutdown immediate;
   startup nomount;
   ```

2. Restore a copy of the control file. Using the same RMAN session as in Step 1, Thom can do this quite simply. After the restore operation, he mounts the database using the restored control file.

   ```
   Restore controlfile from autobackup;
   sql 'alter database mount';
   ```

3. Configure permanent channel parameters. Now that Thom has a control file restored, he can update the persistent parameters for channel allocation to include the name of the tape device his backup sets are on. This will allow him to proceed to restore the backup from tape and recover the database.

   ```
   Configure default device type to sbt;
    configure channel 1 device type sbt
    parms = "env=(nb_ora_serv=mgtserv, nb_ora_client=cervantes)";
   ```

4. Perform the restore and recovery:

   ```
   Restore database;
   recover database noredo;
   sql "alter database open resetlogs";
   ```

Case #2: Recovering from Complete Database Loss (NOARCHIVELOG Mode) Without a Recovery Catalog

The Scenario

Charles is the DBA of a development OLTP system. Because it is a development system, the decision was made to do RMAN offline backups and leave the database in NOARCHIVELOG mode. Charles did not decide to use a recovery catalog when doing his backups. Further, Charles has configured RMAN to back up the control file backups to disk by default, rather than to tape.

The Problem

Sevi, a developer, developed a piece of PL/SQL code designed to truncate specific tables in the database. However, due to a logic bug, the code managed to truncate all the tables in the schema, wiping out all test data.

The Solution

If there were a logical backup of the database, this would be the perfect time to use it. Unfortunately, there is no logical backup of the database, so Charles is left with performing an RMAN recovery. Since his database is in NOARCHIVELOG mode, Charles (the DBA) has only one recovery option in this case, which is to restore from the last offline backup (see Chapter 10). Because all the pieces to do recovery are in place (the RMAN disk backups, the Oracle software, and the file systems), all that needs to be done is to fire up RMAN and recover the database.

The Solution Revealed   Based on the preceding considerations, Charles devises and implements the following recovery plan:

1. Restore the control file. When doing a recovery from a cold backup, it is always a good idea to recover the control file associated with that backup (this prevents odd things from happening). In this case, Charles will be using the latest control file backup (since he doesn't back up the control file at other times). Since Charles uses the default location to create control file backup sets to, we don't need to allocate any channels. He does need to set the DBID of the system, since he is not using a recovery catalog before he can restore the control file. Once Charles restores the control file, he then mounts the database.

   ```
   rman target sys/password
   startup nomount
   ```

```
set dbid=2540040039;
Restore controlfile from autobackup;
sql 'alter database mount';
```

NOTE
The following table has RMAN backup and recovery information you might need later.

Name	Operating System	Location	Description
Titan	Solaris	http://www.fish.com/titan/	A collection of programs to help "titan" (that's "tighten") Solaris.
"Solaris Security FAQ"	Solaris	http://www.itworld.com/Comp/2377/security-faq/	A guide to help lock down Solaris.
"Armoring Solaris"	Solaris	http://www.enteract.com/~lspitz/armoring.html	How to armor the Solaris operating system. This article presents a systematic method to prepare for a firewall installation. Also included is a downloadable shell script that will armor your system.
"FreeBSD Security How-To"	FreeBSD	http://www.freebsd.org/~jkb/howto.html	While this How-To is FreeBSD specific, most of the material covered here will also apply to other Unix OSes (especially OpenBSD and NetBSD).
"Linux Administrator's Security Guide (LASG)" by Kurt Seifried	Linux	https://www.seifried.org/lasg/	One of the best papers on securing a Linux system.
"Watching Your Logs" by Lance Spitzner	General	http://www.enteract.com/~lspitz/swatch.html	How to plan and implement an automated filter for your logs utilizing swatch. Includes examples on configuration and implementation.
"UNIX Computer Security Checklist (Version 1.1)"	General	ftp://ftp.auscert.org.au/pub/auscert/papers/unix_security_checklist_1.1	A handy Unix security checklist.

Name	Operating System	Location	Description
"The Unix Secure Programming FAQ" by Peter Galvin	General	http://online.vsi.ru/library/ Programmer/UNIX_SEC _FAQ/secprog.html	Tips on security design principles, programming methods, and testing.
"CERT Intruder Detection Checklist"	General	http://www.cert.org/tech _tips/intruder_detection _checklist.html	A guide to looking for signs that your system may have been compromised.

2. The control file that Charles restored has the correct default persistent parameters already configured in it, so all he needs to do is perform the restore and recovery:

```
Restore database;
recover database noredo;
sql "alter database open resetlogs";
```

Case #3: Recovering from Complete Database Loss (ARCHIVELOG Mode) Without a Recovery Catalog

The Scenario
We meet Thom from Case #1 again. Thom's company finally has decided that putting the database in ARCHIVELOG mode seems like a good idea (Thom's boss thought it was his idea!). Unfortunately for Thom, due to budget restrictions, he was forced to use the space that was allocated to the recovery catalog to store archived redo logs. Thus, Thom no longer has a recovery catalog at his disposal.

The Problem
As if things have not been hard enough on Thom, we also find that Unfortunate Company is also an unfortunately located company. His server room, located in the basement like so many server rooms are, suffered the fate of a broken water main nearby. The entire room was flooded, and the server on which his database resides has been completely destroyed.

Thom's backup strategy has improved. It now includes tape backups to an offsite MM server. Also, he's sending his automated control file/SPFILE backups to tape rather than to disk. Again, he's salvaged a smaller server from the wreckage, which already has Oracle installed on the system, and now he needs to get the database back up and running immediately.

The Solution

Again, Thom has lost the current control file and the online redo logs for his database, so it's time to employ the point-in-time recovery skills discussed in Chapter 12. Thom still has control file autobackups turned on, so he can use them to get recovery started. In addition, he's restoring to a new server, so he wants to be aware of the challenges that restoring to a new server brings; there are media management, file system layout, and memory utilization considerations.

Media Management Considerations   Because he's restoring files to a new server, Thom must first make sure that the MML file has been properly set up for use on his emergency server. This means having the Media Management Client software and Oracle Plug-In installed prior to using RMAN for restore/recovery. Thom uses the SBTTEST utility—a good way to check to make sure that the media manager is accessible.

Next, Thom needs to configure his tape channels to specify the client name of the server that has been destroyed. As discussed in Chapter 4, he needs to specify the name of the client from which the backups were taken. In addition, he needs to ensure that the MM server has been configured to allow for backups to be restored from a different client to your emergency server.

File System Layout Considerations   Thom's new system has a different file system structure than his original server. The production database had files manually striped over six mount points: /u02, /u03, /u04, /u05, /u06, and /u07. His new server has only two mount points: /u02 and /u03. Fortunately, Thom employed directory structure standards across his enterprise, and all data directories are /oradata/prod/ on all mount points. In addition, he has a standard that always puts the ORACLE_HOME on the same mount point and directory structure on every server.

Memory Utilization Considerations   Thom's emergency server has less physical memory than his lost production server. This means he will have to significantly scale back the memory utilization for the time being in order to at least get the database up and operational.

The Solution Revealed   Based on the preceding considerations, Thom devises and implements the following recovery plan:

1. Determine the DBID of the target database. Thom can do this by looking at the file handle for his control file autobackup. He needs to be able to view the MM catalog to do so; even easier, Thom has every DBID for all his databases stored somewhere in a log—a notebook, a PDA, whatever. Whatever you decide to use, just make sure it's accessible in an emergency.

2. Restore a copy of the spfile. As you may remember, Thom will have to force an instance to be opened using a dummy spfile, and then restore the correct spfile from backup. Because Thom changed the default location for his control file/spfile autobackups to tape, he needs to manually configure the channel for this backup because he doesn't have a control file yet, and thus he cannot configure channels permanently. Instead, he has to imbed **channel allocation** commands in a **run** block, and then issue the **startup** command to start the database with the correct spfile.

```
Rman target /
set dbid=204062491;
startup force nomount;
run {
allocate channel tape_1 type sbt
parms='env=(nb_ora_serv=rmsrv, nb_ora_client=cervantes)';
restore spfile from autobackup;}
shutdown immediate;
startup nomount;
```

3. Make changes to the spfile. Thom must modify his spfile to take into account the new server configuration. This means changing memory utilization parameters and setting filename conversion parameters. Connect to the newly started instance from SQL*Plus and make the necessary changes.

```
Alter system set control_files= '/u02/oradata/prod/control01.dbf',
'/u03/oradata/prod/control02.dbf' scope=spfile;
alter system set db_file_name_convert= ('/u04' , '/u02' ,
'/u05' , '/u02' ,
'u06' , ' u03' ,
'u07' , 'u03') scope=spfile;
alter system set log_file_name_convert= ('/u04' , '/u02' ,
'/u05' , '/u02' ,
'u06' , ' u03' ,
'u07' , 'u03') scope=spfile;
alter system set log_archive_dest_1=
'location=/u02/oradata/prod/arch' scope=spfile;
alter system set db_cache_size=300m scope=spfile;
alter system set shared_pool_size=200m scope=spfile;
shutdown immediate;
startup nomount;
```

NOTE
*You could also choose to use the **set newname**
option here.*

4. Restore a copy of the control file. Using the same RMAN session as the preceding, Thom can do this quite simply (he's already set the DBID). Then mount the database using the restored control file.

```
run {
allocate channel tape_1 type sbt
parms='env=(nb_ora_serv=rmsrv, nb_ora_client=Cervantes)';
Restore controlfile from autobackup; }
sql 'alter database mount';
```

5. Configure permanent channel parameters. Now that Thom has a control file restored, he can update the persistent parameters for channel allocation to include the name of the lost server as the MM client. This serves two purposes: it allows RMAN to access the backups that were taken from the lost server, and RMAN will pass this client name to the MM server when any backups are taken from the new server. That way, when the lost server is rebuilt, any backups taken from this stopgap system will be accessible at the newly reconstructed production server.

```
Configure default device type to sbt;
configure device type sbt parallelism 2;
configure auxiliary channel 1 device type sbt parms
= "env=(nb_ora_serv=mgtserv, nb_ora_client=cervantes)";
configure auxiliary channel 2 device type sbt parms
= "env=(nb_ora_serv=mgtserv, nb_ora_cient=cervantes)";
```

6. Determine the last archive log for which there is a copy. Because Thom lost the entire server, he also lost any archive logs that had not yet been backed up by RMAN. So, he must query RMAN to determine what the last archive log is for which a backup exists:

```
List backup of archivelog from time = 'sysdate-7';
```

7. With the last log sequence number in hand, Thom performs his restore and recovery and opens the database:

```
Restore database;
recover database until sequence=<number>;
sql "alter database open resetlogs";
```

Case #4: Recovering from Complete Database Loss (ARCHIVELOG Mode) with a Recovery Catalog

The Scenario
Charles is taking over for Thom, because management recognized that Thom was a hero of a DBA and thus sent him and his wife to Hawaii for two weeks of R and R. Before he left, Thom's company added additional disk storage and decided that using the RMAN recovery catalog was probably a good idea.

Unfortunately for Charles, disaster seems to follow him around. At his last company, a huge electrical fire caused all sorts of mayhem, and this time it's gophers. Yes, gophers. Somewhere outside the computer room, a lone gopher ate through the power cable leading to the computer room. This resulted in an electrical fire and a halon release into the computer room. As a result of the electrical fire, the server and disks on which his database resides have been completely destroyed...again.

Charles reviews Thom's backup strategy. Again, Charles has salvaged a smaller server that survived the fiasco, which already has Oracle installed on the system, and now he needs to get the database back up and running immediately. Fortunately, the recovery catalog server is intact, so Charles can use it during the recovery.

The Solution
Again, Charles has lost the current control file and the online redo logs for his database, so it's time to employ the point-in-time recovery skills discussed in Chapter 12. The backup strategy still has control file autobackups turned on, so Charles can use them to get recovery started. In addition, he's restoring to a new server, so he wants to be aware of the challenges that restoring to a new server brings; there are media management, file system layout, and memory utilization considerations.

Media Management Considerations   Because Charles is restoring files to a new server, he must first make sure that the MML file has been properly set up for use on his emergency server. This means having the MM client software and Oracle plug-in installed prior to using RMAN for restore/recovery. Charles uses **sbttest** to check to make sure that the media manager is accessible.

Next, Charles needs to configure his tape channels to specify the client name of the server that has been destroyed. As discussed in Chapter 4, he needs to specify the name of the client from which the backups were taken. In addition, he needs to ensure that the MM server has been configured to allow for backups to be restored from a different client to your emergency server.

File System Layout   On Charles's new system, there is a different file system structure than on his original server. The production database had files manually striped over six mount points: /u02, /u03, /u04, /u05, /u06, and /u07. His new server has only two mount points: /u02 and /u03. Luckily, directory structure standards exist across his enterprise, and all data directories are /oradata/prod/ on all mount points. In addition, he has a standard that always puts the ORACLE_HOME on the same mount point and directory structure on every server.

Memory Considerations   Charles's emergency server has less physical memory than his lost production server. This means he has to significantly scale back the memory utilization for the time being in order to at least get the database up and operational.

The Solution Revealed   Based on the preceding considerations, Charles devises and implements the following recovery plan:

1. Get a copy of the spfile restored. First, Charles will nomount the database instance without a parameter file, since Oracle supports this. Then, he will restore the correct spfile from backup. Because he doesn't have a control file yet, he cannot configure channels permanently. Instead, he has to embed **channel allocation** commands in a **run** block, and then issue the **startup** command to start the database with the correct spfile. Since he has a recovery catalog, he doesn't need to set the machine ID as he did earlier.

```
Rman target / catalog rcat_user/rcat_password@catalog
startup force nomount;
run {
allocate channel tape_1 type sbt
parms='env=(nb_ora_serv=rmsrv, nb_ora_client=cervantes)';
restore spfile from autobackup;}
shutdown immediate;
startup nomount;
```

2. Make changes to the spfile. Charles must modify his spfile to take into account the new server configuration. This means changing memory utilization parameters and setting filename conversion parameters. Connect to the newly started instance from SQL*Plus and make the necessary changes.

```
Alter system set control_files=
'/u02/oradata/prod/control01.dbf',
'/u03/oradata/prod/control02.dbf' scope=spfile;
alter system set db_file_name_convert= ('/u04' , '/u02' ,
'/u05' , '/u02' ,
'u06' , ' u03' ,
'u07' , 'u03') scope=spfile;
alter system set log_file_name_convert= ('/u04' , '/u02' ,
```

```
'/u05' , '/u02' ,
'u06' , ' u03' ,
'u07' , 'u03') scope=spfile;
alter system set log_archive_dest_1=
'location=/u02/oradata/prod/arch' scope=spfile;
alter system set db_cache_size=300m scope=spfile;
alter system set shared_pool_size=200m scope=spfile;
shutdown immediate;
startup nomount;
```

3. Restore a copy of your control file. Using the same RMAN session, Charles can do this quite simply (he's already set the DBID). Then mount the database using the restored control file.

```
run {
allocate channel tape_1 type sbt
parms='env=(nb_ora_serv=rmsrv, nb_ora_client=Cervantes)';
Restore controlfile from autobackup; }
sql 'alter database mount';
```

4. Configure permanent channel parameters. Now that Charles has a control file restored, he can update the persistent parameters for channel allocation to include the name of the lost server as the MM client. This serves two purposes: it allows RMAN to access the backups that were taken from the lost server, and RMAN will pass this client name to the MM server when any backups are taken from the new server. That way, when the lost server is rebuilt, any backups taken from this stopgap system will be accessible at the newly reconstructed production server.

```
Configure default device type to sbt;
configure device type sbt parallelism 2;
configure auxiliary channel 1 device type sbt parms
= "env=(nb_ora_serv=mgtserv, nb_ora_client=cervantes)";
configure auxiliary channel 2 device type sbt parms
= "env=(nb_ora_serv=mgtserv, nb_ora_cient=cervantes)";
```

5. Determine the last archive log for which there is a copy. Because Charles lost the entire server, he also lost any archive logs that had not yet been backed up by RMAN. So, he must query RMAN to determine what the last archive log is for which a backup exists:

```
List backup of archivelog from time = 'sysdate-7';
```

6. With the last log sequence number in hand, Charles performs his restore and recovery and opens the database:

```
Restore database;
recover database until sequence=<number>;
sql "alter database open resetlogs";
```

Case #5: Recovering from the Loss of the SYSTEM Tablespace

The Scenario

Nancy, an awesome DBA, is in charge of a large database installation. She shut down her database so the system administrators of her Unix system could do some file system maintenance. Unfortunately, during the maintenance operation, the system administrators at her company managed to drop a file system her database is sitting on. They have since restored the file system, but none of the files from her database are on it, so she must recover them. Nancy lost all datafiles from the following tablespaces: USERS, SYSTEM, and INDEX.

The Solution

Fortunately for Nancy, this is not a complete loss of her system. Her online redo logs and control file are all intact. Because she has to recover the SYSTEM tablespace, she has to do her recovery with the database closed, not open. Otherwise, the recovery is a pretty easy one.

The Solution Revealed   Based on the preceding considerations, Nancy devises and implements the following recovery plan:

1. Restore the database:

```
Rman target / catalog rcat_user/rcat_password@catalog
startup force mount;
restore tablespace users, system, index;
recover tablespace users, system, index;
alter database open;
```

Case #6: Recovering Online from the Loss of a Datafile or Tablespace

The Scenario

Yang was working on his database the other day when a power surge caused a media failure. Unfortunately for Yang, he lost one file system. This file system contained the following:

- All the datafiles for a tablespace called WORKING_DATA
- One datafile for a tablespace called HISTORICAL_DATA

Several other tablespaces in this database are not related to the tablespace he is recovering, so Yang needs to do this recovery with the database up and running.

The Solution
Yang will restore the WORKING_DATA TABLESPACE and the lone datafile missing from the historical_data tablespace via RMAN. He first will take offline the tablespace and datafile, so others may continue to work.

The Solution Revealed   Based on the preceding considerations, Yang devises and implements the following recovery plan:

1. Take offline the WORKING_DATA TABLESPACE:

   ```
   sql "alter tablespace working_data offline";
   ```

2. Take offline the historical_data datafile needed to recover (Yang has already queried the V$DATAFILE view to determine that it is datafile 13):

   ```
   sql "alter database datafile 13 offline";
   ```

3. Restore and recover the tablespace and datafile using RMAN, and then bring them online:

   ```
   restore tablespace working_data;
   restore datafile 13;
   recover tablespace working_data;
   recover datafile 13;
   sql "alter tablespace working_data online";
   sql "alter database datafile 13 online";
   ```

> **NOTE**
> *If either tablespace contains active rollback segments, this recovery case may not work. In the event of the loss of active rollback segment tablespaces, you may well be required to do an offline recovery of that tablespace or datafile.*

Case #7: Recovering from Loss of an Unarchived Online Redo Log

The Scenario
Today is not Bill's day. A large thunderstorm is raging outside, and Bill has forgotten that his car's soft top is down. To make Bill's day worse, a strike of lightening hits

the data center and fries several disk drives that Bill's database calls home. Once the hardware is repaired, Bill is horrified to find that he has lost all of his online redo logs, in addition to some of his datafiles. Fortunately, his control file is intact.

The Solution
Bill needs to restore his database using incomplete recovery. Since the online redo logs are not available, Bill has to accept that there will be some data loss as a result of the recovery.

The Solution Revealed   Based on the preceding considerations, Bill devises and implements the following recovery plan:

I. Determine the last archive log for which there is a copy. Because Bill has to do incomplete recovery, he must query RMAN to determine what the last archive log is for which a backup exists:

```
startup mount;
List backup of archivelog from time = 'sysdate-7';
```

The output will look something like the following output—note the log sequence number (log sequence number 3, in bold at the bottom of the report). Since this is the oldest backed up archived redo log, this is as far as Bill can recover to.

```
List of Backup Sets
===================
BS Key  Size         Device Type Elapsed Time Completion Time
------- ----------   ----------- ------------ ---------------
216     48K          DISK        00:00:03     16-AUG-02
        BP Key: 247    Status: AVAILABLE    Tag: TAG20020816T095848
        Piece Name: D:\BACKUP\RECOVER\75E08R2P_1_1

  List of Archived Logs in backup set 216
  Thrd Seq    Low SCN     Low Time   Next SCN    Next Time
  ---- ------- ---------- ---------- ---------- ---------
  1    2       1271924     16-AUG-02 1272223     16-AUG-02

BS Key  Size         Device Type Elapsed Time Completion Time
------- ----------   ----------- ------------ ---------------
218     2K           DISK        00:00:02     16-AUG-02
        BP Key: 249    Status: AVAILABLE    Tag: TAG20020816T100344
        Piece Name: D:\BACKUP\RECOVER\77E08RC1_1_1

  List of Archived Logs in backup set 218
  Thrd **Seq**    Low SCN     Low Time   Next SCN    Next Time
  ---- **-------** ---------- ---------- ---------- ---------
  1    **3**       1272223     16-AUG-02 1272321     16-AUG-02
```

2. With the last log sequence number in hand, perform the restore and recovery and open the database. Bill first restores the database using the **until sequence** parameter. This ensures that all database datafiles will be restored to a point in time no later than log sequence 3. Also note the use of the **force** parameter, which ensures that all datafiles are restored. Recall that one of the requirements for point-in-time recovery is that all database datafiles must be restored to the same consistent point in time. Thus, it's important to restore all datafiles to at least a point in time prior to the point in time Bill wants to recover to.

```
Restore database until sequence=4 thread=1 force;
```

3. Recover the database until sequence 4 (since the **until sequence** recovers up to but not including the listed sequence number, Bill added one number to the last sequence number, and thus gets 4):

```
recover database until sequence=4 thread=1;
```

4. Manually back up the control file for the database before opening the database with the **resetlogs** command. This provides Bill with some protection should disaster strike between the time he opens the database with the **resetlogs** command and the time he is able to back up his database (as shown next in Case #8).

```
shutdown immediate;
quit;
d:\> copy d:\oracle\oradata\recover\control01.ctl
d:\backup\recover\special\control01.ctl.083102
rman target sys/robert
startup mount;
```

NOTE
*You may find that you have some archived redo logs that belong to the old instance you just recovered that are not yet backed up. At this point, it's a good idea to manually back them up in case you need them later (such as might be the case with recovery through **resetlogs**). Note that RMAN will not be able to back up these archived redo logs after you open the database using the **resetlogs** command.*

5. Open the database:

```
sql "alter database open resetlogs";
```

NOTE
If Bill's database had been shut down normally (via **shutdown normal,** **immediate,** *or* **transactional)** *before the online redo logs were lost, he may well have been able to open the database without needing to recover it.*

Case #8: Recovering Through resetlogs

The Scenario

Bill spent all night doing his recovery and he called in Tim to monitor the restore and finish the database recovery. Once the recovery was done, Tim was supposed to back up the database. One problem is that the business requirement demanded that the database be open and available during the backup.

Tim came in and finished the recovery. Following that, he opened the database using the **resetlogs** command (as previously described in Case #7). Following the business requirements, Tim began the backup, but allowed users access to the database. Unfortunately, on this troubled day, a power surge hit Tim's system and again the disk drives of Tim's database were damaged. After another hardware repair, Tim finds that several datafiles were lost. To make matters worse, he has no complete backup of these datafiles since he issued the **resetlogs** command.

CAUTION
This specific case is, without a doubt, one of the most difficult, troublesome, and risky types of recovery. It is very dependent on everything being just right and on the nature of the previous recovery. If you open any database using the **resetlogs** *command, it is strongly advised that you take a backup of that database immediately and do not depend on this recovery method to save you.*

The Solution

Tim is about to show what a seasoned DBA he is by performing a point-in-time recovery though **resetlogs**. Tim has practiced this type of restore before, but he also knows that this recovery situation is risky.

The Solution Revealed   Based on the preceding considerations, Tim devises and implements the following recovery plan:

1. Mount the database and use RMAN to determine the SCN at the point of the creation of the new database incarnation. This SCN represents the SCN Tim will begin the first recovery to. If you have the current control file, you can use RMAN to easily determine what the last SCN of the previous incarnation was. After Tim lists the database incarnations and determines the SCN he needs to recover to, he shuts down the database again.

```
rman target sys/robert
startup mount
 list incarnation;
RMAN> list incarnation;
using target database controlfile instead of recovery catalog
List of Database Incarnations
DB Key  Inc Key DB Name  DB ID              CUR Reset SCN  Reset Time
-------  ------- --------  ----------------  --- ----------  ----------
1       1       RECOVER  2539725638         NO  1           09-JUN-02
2       2       RECOVER  2539725638         NO  315881      24-JUN-02
3       3       RECOVER  2539725638         NO  316061      24-JUN-02
4       4       RECOVER  2539725638         NO  316908      25-JUN-02
5       5       RECOVER  2539725638         NO  1251881     16-AUG-02
6       6       RECOVER  2539725638         YES 1272237     17-AUG-02
shutdown abort;
```

In this case, Tim takes the reset SCN for the current incarnation and subtracts 1 from it, which represents the last SCN of the previous incarnation. In this example, Tim is restoring to SCN 1272236 (taking the current incarnation reset SCN and subtracting 1 from it).

This information is also available in the form of a control file dump. You can either dump the current control file, or mount the database with the control file backed up in Case# 7 and then dump the control file contents from SQL*Plus, as shown here:

```
SQL> alter session set events 'immediate trace name controlf level 10';
```

This results in a trace file being put in the location defined by the **user_dump_dest** parameter. In the trace file, you will find this line:

```
Resetlogs scn: 0x0000.0004d5ec Resetlogs Timestamp  06/25/2002 16:31:55
```

Convert the Resetlogs SCN to a decimal number (in this case, this equates to SCN 316908) and subtract 1 from that number to determine the SCN you need to recover to. Write this number down because you will need it.

2. Make a backup of the current database control file, and back up one member of each of the current online redo logs:

```
D:\> copy d:\oracle\oradata\recover\control01.ctl
D:\backup\recover\special\control01.ctl.curr
```

```
D:\> copy d:\oracle\oradata\recover\redo01.log
D:\backup\recover\special\redo01.log
D:\> copy d:\oracle\oradata\recover\redo02.log
D:\backup\recover\special\redo02.log
D:\> copy d:\oracle\oradata\recover\redo03.log
D:\backup\recover\special\redo03.log
```

3. Restore the control file that Bill backed up in Case# 7 to each control file location:

```
C:\>copy d:\backup\recover\special\control01.ctl.083102
D:\oracle\oradata\recover\control01.ctl
C:\>copy d:\backup\recover\special\control01.ctl.083102
D:\oracle\oradata\recover\control02.ctl
C:\>copy d:\backup\recover\special\control01.ctl.083102
D:\oracle\oradata\recover\control03.ctl
```

4. Determine the log sequence numbers to recover to, using the **list backup archivelog all** command:

```
RMAN> list backup of archivelog all;
List of Backup Sets
===================
BS Key  Size        Device Type Elapsed Time Completion Time
------- ----------  ----------- ------------ ---------------
230     79K         DISK          00:00:03     17-AUG-02
        BP Key: 261    Status: AVAILABLE   Tag: TAG20020817T174916
        Piece Name: D:\BACKUP\RECOVER\7KE0CB0T_1_1
  List of Archived Logs in backup set 230
  Thrd Seq    Low SCN    Low Time   Next SCN   Next Time
  ---- -----  ---------- ---------- ---------- ---------
  1    1      1313085    17-AUG-02 1217907    17-AUG-02
BS Key  Size        Device Type Elapsed Time Completion Time
------- ----------  ----------- ------------ ---------------
232     2K          DISK          00:00:02     17-AUG-02
        BP Key: 263    Status: AVAILABLE   Tag: TAG20020817T175406
        Piece Name: D:\BACKUP\RECOVER\7ME0CB9V_1_1
  List of Archived Logs in backup set 232
  Thrd Seq    Low SCN    Low Time   Next SCN   Next Time
  ---- -----  ---------- ---------- ---------- ---------
  1    2      1317907    17-AUG-02 1272236    17-AUG-02
```

In this case, Tim needs to restore to log sequence 2 (which is highlighted). The next SCN setting on log sequence number 2 is the same as the one Tim wants to recover to.

5. Restore and recover the database to the log sequence number:

```
rman target sys/robert
startup mount
restore database until logseq 2 thread 1;
recover database until logseq 2 thread 1;
shutdown
```

6. Mount the database. Before Tim can finish the recovery, he needs to create a new control file. Once that's done, he can complete the recovery.

```
rman target sys/robert
startup force nomount;
set dbid=2540040039;
Restore controlfile from autobackup;
alter database mount;
recover database;
alter database open resetlogs;
```

Case #9: Completing a Failed Duplication Manually

The Scenario

Tim decided to use RMAN duplication to create a clone of his production database on a different server. He ran the **duplicate** command, and the datafiles were successfully restored to the new server. The database is very large, and this file restore process took six hours to complete. However, Tim forgot to move the archive logs over to the auxiliary server for media recovery, so the duplication failed. This means that the cloned database is not fully recovered, and it does not have a new DBID.

The Solution

Tim isn't worried, though, and he certainly isn't going to take another six hours to perform the file restore. As described in Chapter 16, Tim can manually perform the media recovery and then use the DBNEWID utility on the clone database to create a new DBID and finish the duplication process without RMAN's assistance.

The Solution Revealed   Based on the solution he decided upon, Tim will implement the following action plan to complete his failed duplication:

1. Move the archive logs from the production to the auxiliary site. The recommended approach was described in Chapter 16, in which **tar** and **gzip** were used to compress the archive destination directory into a single

file, and then FTP was used to move that single compressed file from the production server to the auxiliary server.

```
cd /space/oracle_user/OraHome1/oradata/sun92
tar -cvf arch.tar arch
gzip arch.tar
```

2. Use FTP to move the arch.tar file to the auxiliary system, and then enter the following:

```
cd /space/oracle_user/OraHome1/oradata/sun92
gunzip arch.tar.gz
tar -xvf arch.tar
```

3. Perform manual recovery on the database. Tim needs to note the sequence number of the last archive log available on his target database, and then set the recovery to stop at that sequence number. The %s variable in the LOG_ARCHIVE_FORMAt signifies the sequence number and will be in the archive log name. Tim will perform manual recovery from SQL*Plus, connecting locally to his auxiliary database (at the auxiliary site).

```
ORACLE_SID=aux1
export ORACLE_SID
Sqlplus /nolog
SQL> connect / as sysdba
SQL> recover database using backup controlfile until sequence 11 thread 1;
```

4. Use DBNEWID to create a new DBID for the clone database. Tim's auxiliary database has been mounted, but it has not yet been opened. This is the right state to use DBNEWID. If you are unsure of the database state, you can go ahead and remount it without doing any harm.

```
SQL> Shutdown immediate;
SQL> startup mount;
SQL> exit
$ nid target=/
$ sqlplus /nolog
SQL> connect / as sysdba
SQL> Shutdown immediate;
SQL> startup mount;
SQL> alter database open resetlogs;
```

Case #10: Using RMAN Duplication to Create a Historical Subset of the Target Database

The Scenario

Svetlana is a DBA at an online toy-train reseller. Her production database is under heavy load, with constant updates, inserts, and deletes. Over time, she has noticed that performance is starting to trail off for data-mining operations against certain inventory-tracking tables. She suspects foul play from the Cost-Based Optimizer, thinking that the Explain Plan might be changing in an adverse way. To test things out, she is looking for a way to get a historical snapshot of a subset of production tables. She's considered duplication in the past, but doesn't have enough room on any server to clone the entire production database.

The Solution

Svetlana can use the new Oracle9i Release 2 feature of being able to specify tablespaces to skip during duplication. In this way, she can include only tablespaces that are part of the subset that she needs to test. In addition to skipping tablespaces, she can now specify an **until** clause in the **duplication** command itself to set the historical point in time that she would like to test against.

The Solution Revealed   Chapter 16 has excellent workshops for performing duplication. For Svetlana to have success with her point-in-time duplication subset, she needs to do all the same duplication footwork described in Chapter 16 prior to performing the duplication. Svetlana will be duplicating to the same server that runs her target database, so she needs to make sure that she has her file renaming strategy worked out. Then, she needs to get an auxiliary database started in NOMOUNT mode. After that, she runs her duplication code.

```
$ rman log=/space/backup/pitrdup.out
connect target /
connect auxiliary sys/password@aux1
duplicate target database to aux1
 pfile=/space/oracle_user/OraHome1/admin/aux1/pfile/init.ora
 skip tablespace 'CWMLITE' , 'USERS' , 'ODM' , 'TOOLS'
 until sequence = 11 thread = 1
 logfile
 '/space/oracle_user/OraHome1/oradata/aux1/redo01.dbf' size 5m,
 '/space/oracle_user/OraHome1/oradata/aux1/redo02.dbf' size 5m,
 '/space/oracle_user/OraHome1/oradata/aux1/redo03.dbf' size 5m;
```

The outcome would look something like the following RMAN log. This output has been truncated to save space; we've left the highlights that show what RMAN is doing to get rid of unneeded tablespaces. Remember that when you set an **until sequence** clause in RMAN, the sequence you specify is not included as part of the recover set. So, in Svetlana's code, she has archive logs through sequence 10, but not sequence number 11.

```
Recovery Manager: Release 9.2.0.1.0 - Production
Copyright (c) 1995, 2002, Oracle Corporation.  All rights reserved.
connected to target database: SUN92 (DBID=204062491)
connected to auxiliary database: aux1 (not mounted)
```

```
Starting Duplicate Db at 09-JUL-02
using target database controlfile instead of recovery catalog
allocated channel: ORA_AUX_DISK_1
channel ORA_AUX_DISK_1: sid=14 devtype=DISK
Datafile 3 skipped by request
Datafile 7 skipped by request
Datafile 8 skipped by request
Datafile 9 skipped by request
printing stored script: Memory Script
{   set until scn  1122792;
    set newname for datafile  1 to
 "/space/oracle_user/OraHome1/oradata/aux1/system01.dbf";
...
    set newname for datafile  10 to
 "/space/oracle_user/OraHome1/oradata/aux1/xdb01.dbf";
    restore
    check readonly
    clone database
    skip tablespace  USERS, TOOLS, ODM, CWMLITE   ;
}
executing script: Memory Script
executing command: SET until clause
executing command: SET NEWNAME
...
Starting recover at 09-JUL-02
datafile 3 not processed because file is offline
datafile 7 not processed because file is offline
datafile 8 not processed because file is offline
datafile 9 not processed because file is offline
starting media recovery
...
media recovery complete
Finished recover at 09-JUL-02
...
{   Alter clone database open resetlogs;}
executing script: Memory Script
database opened
printing stored script: Memory Script
{# drop offline and skipped tablespaces
sql clone "drop tablespace  USERS including contents";
# drop offline and skipped tablespaces
sql clone "drop tablespace  TOOLS including contents";
# drop offline and skipped tablespaces
sql clone "drop tablespace  ODM including contents";
# drop offline and skipped tablespaces
sql clone "drop tablespace  CWMLITE including contents";}
executing script: Memory Script
sql statement: drop tablespace  USERS including contents
sql statement: drop tablespace  TOOLS including content
```

```
sql statement: drop tablespace  ODM including contents
sql statement: drop tablespace  CWMLITE including contents
Finished Duplicate Db at 09-JUL-02
Recovery Manager complete.
```

Case #11: Tablespace Dropped Unintentionally

The Scenario
Martin is the senior DBA in a midsize IT department. He has three less-seasoned DBAs that work for him. On a request, he created an Enterprise Manager user for one of the junior DBAs, Scott, so that Scott could mind the shop while Martin took a well-deserved vacation. Soon thereafter, Martin received a call from Scott, saying that one of the production tablespaces "disappeared from his EM view" and he can't figure out why. At the same time, Martin's beeper goes off: the users can't access some of the application pages anymore. With a sickening feeling, Martin checks his database, and finds that a tablespace has been dropped.

It's already been over an hour of the busiest time of day, and rolling back the entire database is not an option. He can't perform TSPITR, because the tablespace was dropped (one of the TSPITR restrictions).

The Solution
After reviewing his options, Martin decides that he can create space on his server to perform a point-in-time duplication with just the dropped tablespace and its index tablespace, and skip all the other tablespaces. After the duplication completes, he can use Transportable Tablespaces to move the dropped tablespace back into his production environment.

The Solution Revealed   As you may have already guessed, Martin's solution will be the same one used by Svetlana in Case #10. The RMAN **duplicate** command will be employed, with a **skip tablespace** clause excluding all tablespaces but the dropped one (and any with dependent objects). For a blow-by-blow description, refer to Case #10. The **until time** or **until sequence** clause that Martin uses will reflect the time before Scott dropped the tablespace.

After duplication is complete, Martin will use Oracle's Transportable Tablespace feature to move the tablespace from his clone database to the production database. Transportable Tablespaces is a feature that is built into Oracle8i and higher that utilizes built-in DBMS packages and the export/import utility to move metadata about a tablespace from one database to another. By using this methodology, Martin's production database sees no downtime, and his tablespace is back up to the point in time prior to it being dropped.

Transportable Tablespaces is a topic beyond the scope of this book, but you can find details about it in most DBA handbooks published by Oracle Press.

Case #12: Re-Creating the Control File Without Losing Backup Metadata

The Scenario

Tracey needs to re-create her database control file. She had thought of everything when she put her new Human Resources database into production—it was configured, tuned, and set to scale up as data was added. She had her backup strategy in place with RMAN, taking nightly backups. However, she had not planned on employing Oracle's Real Application Clusters (RAC) software, and thus she set MAXINSTANCES to 1 when she created her database. She needs to employ RAC now, which requires her to change this value. The only way for her to change this value is to rebuild the control file. However, if she does that, she knows that she will lose all her backup metadata, which is also unacceptable.

The Solution

Tracey does not use a recovery catalog for RMAN backups; if she had, re-creating the control file wouldn't be a problem. In fact, that is the solution to her dilemma: she will create a temporary recovery catalog, synchronize her control file with the catalog, and then rebuild the control file. After she rebuilds the control file, she can connect to her catalog and resynchronize again, and all the data will be placed back in her new control file. After that, she can remove the recovery catalog.

The Solution Revealed   Based on her solution, Tracey will implement the following action plan:

1. Create the user that will own the recovery catalog. Because the recovery catalog is only temporary, she can ignore convention and create the recovery catalog in the target database itself. This way, she avoids any added complexity.

   ```
   Create user rman_temp identified by rman_temp
   default tablespace users
   temporary tablespace temp;
   User created.
   grant connect, resource, recovery_catalog_owner to rman_temp;
   Grant succeeded.
   ```

2. Connect to the target and the recovery catalog, and create the catalog and register the target. Because the target and the recovery catalog are both local, RMAN can connect to both without specifying a tnsalias. The act of registering the target database in the catalog performs a resync, so a manual **resync** command is not required.

```
$ rman
RMAN> connect target /
connected to target database: PROD (DBID=4172407992)
RMAN> connect catalog rman_temp/rman_temp;
connected to recovery catalog database
recovery catalog is not installed
RMAN> create catalog;
recovery catalog created
RMAN> register database;
database registered in recovery catalog
starting full resync of recovery catalog
full resync complete
```

3. Shut down the target database and rebuild the control file. We won't go into depth here, but generally this is done by issuing an **alter database backup controlfile to trace** command, and then modifying the trace file into a SQL script and executing it against the target database. After doing so, Tracey will need to open the database.

4. Connect RMAN to the target and the catalog again, and resynchronize. When the catalog recognizes the **db_name** and DBID of the target, it will check its own records and compare them to the target database control file. When it find no records in the control file, it will update them.

```
RMAN> resync catalog;
starting full resync of recovery catalog
full resync complete
```

5. Remove the temporary recovery catalog. The easiest way to do this is simply to drop the catalog owner from SQL*Plus.

```
SQL> connect / as sysdba
Connected.
SQL> drop user rman_temp cascade;
User dropped.
```

Case #13: Duplication Prior to a resetlogs

The Scenario

Kevin runs an application development shop that customizes data access tools for his corporation. A few days ago, he introduced a new application version into production after rigorous testing. However, after introduction, the application began modifying the wrong rows on certain update statements. This wasn't caught until today, but the effect was widespread and catastrophic: the entire production database had to be restored to the point in time prior to the introduction of the new application.

The challenge to Kevin now is to try and determine what happened when the new application began interacting with his production database.

The Solution
Kevin needs to perform a point-in-time duplication. However, the production database has been opened with **resetlogs**, so, by default, all backups prior to **resetlogs** are unavailable. To get access to them, Kevin has to use the following commands:

```
List incarnation of database;
Reset database to incarnation <key>;
```

Remember that to use previous incarnations for restore operations, you must have a recovery catalog. However, you cannot use duplication when the target database is not the current incarnation.

To get past this restriction, Kevin has to build a "fake" production database with a control file restored from prior to the **resetlogs**. After doing the restore for this database, he will have to use the DBNEWID utility to change the DBID to differentiate it from his real production database.

If this looks to you like an old-fashioned "clone" operation, you're right. The **duplicate** command fails us if we need to create clones before a **resetlogs**. Therefore, we use RMAN to create a clone, and then we can change the DBID to ensure uniqueness.

The Solution Revealed   Based on the preceding solution, Kevin implements the following action plan:

1. Build a temporary recovery catalog. Kevin's backup strategy did not include the use of a recovery catalog. However, to take advantage of RMAN's database incarnations, a catalog is required. Even if he had a catalog that he used for his enterprise, in this case, a temporary catalog provides him with the certainty that there won't be multiple databases with the same **db_name** registered. He will be connecting to the fake target database in **nomount** mode, and thus there is no DBID available to identify the database, only the **db_name** in the init.ora file. If the catalog has more than one database registered with the same **db_name**, then he will get an ambiguous database error.

   As in Case #12, the temporary recovery catalog can be built in the production database if necessary. Nothing that Kevin does from here on out will reference the actual production database, so it's a prime candidate for the catalog. Refer to Case #12 for more details on the temporary recovery catalog.

2. Build an init.ora file for the fake target instance. Two changes need to be made to this init.ora file: change the location specified by any location parameters, and then set the parameter **lock_name_space**. Kevin will stage all files related to the fake target to the directory /space/fake. Then, he will also have to change his datafile and log file locations for the clone. Unfortunately, using the init.ora parameters **db_file_name_convert** and **log_file_name_convert** won't cut it for this operation. Kevin will have to set new filenames in his RMAN **run** command during restore.

Kevin uses an spfile, so he creates his init.ora file like this:

```
Sql> connect /@sun92 as sysdba
create pfile='/space/fake/init.ora'
from spfile;
```

3. Make all necessary changes to the fake init.ora file. This includes removing the parameter **remote_login_passwordfile**—this simply isn't necessary for Kevin's purposes here.

```
Control_files=
    '/space/fake/control01.dbf'
Background_dump_dest=/space/fake
user_dump_dest=/space/fake
core_dump_dest=/space/fake
log_archive_dest_1=
    'location=/space/fake'
lock_name_space='fake'
# remote_login_passwordfile=exclusive
```

4. Start the fake instance in **nomount** mode:

```
ORACLE_SID=fake
export ORACLE_SID
sqlplus /nolog
connect / as sysdba
startup nomount pfile=/space/fake/init.ora
```

5. Connect RMAN to the fake instance and the temporary catalog. Take a look at the database incarnations.

```
$ rman target /
Recovery Manager: Release 9.2.0.1.0 - Production
connected to target database: sun92 (not mounted)
RMAN> connect catalog rman/rman@sun92
connected to recovery catalog database
RMAN> list incarnation of database;
```

```
List of Database Incarnations
DB Key  Inc Key DB Name  DB ID               CUR Reset SCN  Reset Time
-------  ------- --------  ----------------    --- ---------- ----------
1        14      SUN92     204062491           NO  155402     24-JUN-02
1        2       SUN92     204062491           NO  1679107    10-JUL-02
1        84      SUN92     204062491           YES 1699329    10-JUL-02
```

6. Based on the incarnation information, reset the database incarnation:

```
RMAN> reset database to incarnation 2;
database reset to incarnation 2 in recovery catalog
```

7. Restore a copy of the control file, and then mount the restored control file. The location that Kevin restores this control file to is immaterial. He will be using this as the control file for his "fake" target database, so there's no need to build an entire Oracle file structure for this fake database. Its lifespan is short. Kevin is placing all files in /space/fake.

```
RMAN> restore controlfile to '/space/fake/control01.ctl';
Starting restore at 10-JUL-02
allocated channel: ORA_DISK_1
channel ORA_DISK_1: sid=13 devtype=DISK
channel ORA_DISK_1: starting datafile backupset restore
channel ORA_DISK_1: restoring controlfile
output filename=/space/fake/control01.ctl
channel ORA_DISK_1: restored backup piece 1
piece handle=/space/backup/c-204062491-20020710-00 tag=null params=NULL
channel ORA_DISK_1: restore complete
Finished restore at 10-JUL-02
RMAN> alter database mount;
database mounted
```

8. Restore the database to the new fake location, and perform media recovery. The **restore** command is a little tricky here; because Kevin can't use the **duplicate** command, he won't be able to let RMAN take care of all the details related to changing the filenames for his datafiles. Therefore, Kevin resorts to "old-school" RMAN commands to change the file locations for restore, and then switches to those new files and performs media recovery.

```
run {
set newname for datafile 1 to '/space/fake/system01.dbf';
set newname for datafile 2 to '/space/fake/undotbs01.dbf';
set newname for datafile 3 to '/space/fake/cmwlite01.dbf';
set newname for datafile 4 to '/space/fake/drsys01.dbf';
set newname for datafile 5 to '/space/fake/example01.dbf';
set newname for datafile 6 to '/space/fake/indx01.dbf';
set newname for datafile 7 to '/space/fake/odm01.dbf';
set newname for datafile 8 to '/space/fake/tools01.dbf';
```

```
set newname for datafile 9 to '/space/fake/users01.dbf';
set newname for datafile 10 to '/space/fake/xdb01.dbf';
restore database;
switch datafile all;
recover database until sequence 4 thread 1;}
```

9. Change the online redo log file locations, and open the database. Again,
   Kevin is performing a manual clone process, so he can't specify new log file
   locations from within RMAN. Instead, he must go to SQL*Plus and change
   the file locations manually.

```
SQL> select member from v$logfile;
MEMBER
--------------------------------------------------
/space/oracle_user/OraHome1/oradata/sun92/redo03.log
/space/oracle_user/OraHome1/oradata/sun92/redo02.log
/space/oracle_user/OraHome1/oradata/sun92/redo01.log

SQL> alter database rename file
'/space/oracle_user/OraHome1/oradata/sun92/redo03.log' to
'/space/fake/redo03.log';
Database altered.

SQL> alter database rename file
'/space/oracle_user/OraHome1/oradata/sun92/redo02.log' to '/space/fake/redo02.log';
Database altered.

SQL>  alter database rename file
'/space/oracle_user/OraHome1/oradata/sun92/redo01.log' to
'/space/fake/redo01.log';
Database altered.

  SQL> select member from v$logfile;
MEMBER
----------------------
/space/fake/redo03.log
/space/fake/redo02.log
/space/fake/redo01.log

SQL> alter database open resetlogs;
Database altered.
```

NOTE
*Instead of doing the manual switching of data
files and log files, Kevin could have modified the
clone init.ora with the **db_file_name_convert and
log_file_name_convert** parameters. However, poor
Kevin was forced by the authors to do the manual
work to illustrate a point. Poor guy.*

10. Use DBNEWID to change the DBID for the clone database. To ensure uniqueness, Kevin finalizes his fake database by creating a new DBID. While Kevin knows this is not exactly critical, there is good reason to be able to distinguish between the production database and the fake database to perform this operation. The two databases have too much in common for his own comfort level.

```
SQL> shutdown immediate;
Database closed.
Database dismounted.
ORACLE instance shut down.
SQL> startup mount pfile=/space/fake/init.ora
ORACLE instance started.
Database mounted.
SQL> exit
$ nid target=/
DBNEWID: Release 9.2.0.1.0 - Production
Copyright (c) 1995, 2002, Oracle Corporation.  All rights reserved.
Connected to database SUN92 (DBID=204062491)
Control Files in database:
    /space/fake/control01.ctl
Change database ID of database SUN92? (Y/[N]) => y
Proceeding with operation
Changing database ID from 204062491 to 205524989
    Control File /space/fake/control01.ctl - modified
    Datafile /space/fake/system01.dbf - dbid changed
...
    Datafile /space/fake/xdb01.dbf - dbid changed
    Control File /space/fake/control01.ctl - dbid changed
Database ID for database SUN92 changed to 205524989.
All previous backups and archived redo logs for this database are unusable.
Shut down database and open with RESETLOGS option.
Successfully changed database ID.
DBNEWID - Completed successfully.
SQL> connect / as sysdba
Connected.
SQL> shutdown immediate;
ORA-01109: database not open
Database dismounted.
ORACLE instance shut down.
SQL> startup mount pfile=/space/fake/init.ora
ORACLE instance started.
Database mounted.
SQL> alter database open resetlogs;
Database altered.
```

Kevin now has a copy of his production database, cloned prior to the **resetlogs**. He can then run application tests to see what may be causing the corruption. Because the new clone has its own DBID, he can use RMAN to make backups of it—that way, if it gets corrupted again, he can restore it from its own backups, instead of going through the headache of cloning from production again.

Summary

We hope you found these case studies helpful. We have done our best to provide you with a number of different circumstances that might come your way, and provide solutions you can practice on a test system so that you will be ready to implement them in real life, should occasion arise. This is also the last chapter in this book on RMAN. We had a ball putting it together, and we hope that you find it useful. Thanks for buying it, and do please let us know if you found it to be helpful, and provide any suggestions for the next revision!

PART
V

Appendixes

APPENDIX
A

RMAN Syntax
Reference Guide

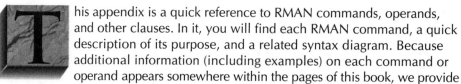

his appendix is a quick reference to RMAN commands, operands, and other clauses. In it, you will find each RMAN command, a quick description of its purpose, and a related syntax diagram. Because additional information (including examples) on each command or operand appears somewhere within the pages of this book, we provide chapter references in this appendix for each command to help you find the additional command detail you might need. It is our hope that this part of your book will become dog-eared and heavily used!

High-Level RMAN Command Set Syntax

RMAN has a number of high-level commands. This diagram provides an overview of those commands.

Syntax Diagram

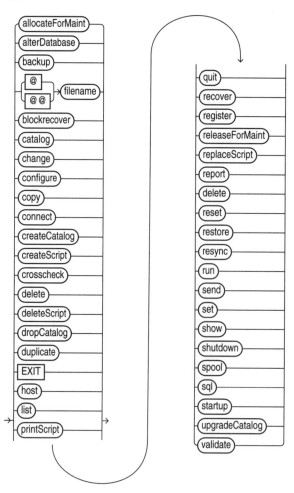

@ and @@ Commands

The @ and @@ commands allow you to execute RMAN commands that are stored in external operating system files (command files). You can use these commands at the command line, from the RMAN prompt, or within the confines of a **run** block. The @ command causes RMAN to look for the script in the current working directory. The @@ command is the same as the @ command except when contained in a script, in which case the @@ command causes RMAN to look in the directory that the running script is in for the next command file to execute.

Syntax Diagram

Chapter Reference

Chapter 13 contains additional information on the use of these commands and an example.

Example

 @c:\oracle\rman\runbackup.cmd

allocate channel Command

The **allocate channel** command allows you to manually allocate an RMAN channel. A channel represents a connection between RMAN and a database instance, and at least one channel must be allocated for any RMAN backup or restore operation.

Syntax Diagram

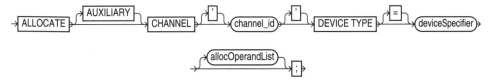

Chapter References

This command is referenced in almost every chapter in this book. Chapter 9 contains detail information on RMAN channel configuration. Chapter 3 contains detailed information on configuring default channels for use with RMAN.

Example

```
allocate channel c1 device type disk format 'd:\backup\robt\robt_%U';
```

allocate channel for maintenance Command

This command needs to be used to allocate channels (as opposed to use of the **allocate channel** command) before you use the **change**, **crosscheck**, or **delete** commands. If you have default channels configured, they will be allocated using this method, and you will not need to do anything further.

Syntax Diagram

Chapter Reference

In Oracle9i, due to default parameters, there is no reference to manually allocating a maintenance channel in Chapter 13. This can be used to override the manual maintenance channel if necessary. It is required for maintenance operations in Oracle8i.

Example

```
allocate channel for maintenance device type sbt;
```

allocOperandList Subclause

This subclause is used with the **allocate channel**, **allocate channel for maintenance**, and **configure** commands. It is used to specify various channel-related control information, such as the format of the backup set pieces, the maximum piece size, and other related information.

Syntax Diagram

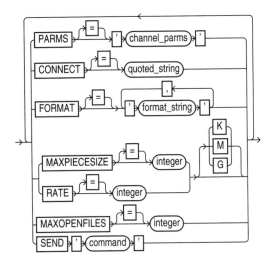

Chapter References
Use of this subclause is demonstrated in several chapters, including Chapters 3, 10, 11, 12 and 13.

Example

```
ALLOCATE CHANNEL c1 DEVICE TYPE sbt PARMS="SBT_LIBRARY=?/lib/mm_lib2.so"
connect 'backup_mgr/nodepassword@node1' rate=2m;
```

alter database Command

The **alter database** command provides an interface that allows RMAN to alter the state of the target database and operates just like the same command in SQL*Plus. You can use this command to mount the database or to open the database normally or with the **resetlogs** option.

Syntax Diagram

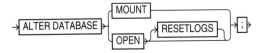

Chapter References
This command is demonstrated in Chapters 9 and 12.

Example

 `alter database open resetlogs;`

archivelogRecordSpecifier Subclause

The **archivelogRecordSpecifier** subclause is used to define one characteristic of
a single archived redo log (or, optionally, a range of archived redo logs files) that
you wish to back up, restore, recover, or use for maintenance operations. These
characteristics may be based on time, SCN, or log sequence number.

Syntax Diagram

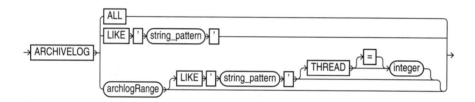

archLogRange Parameter Syntax

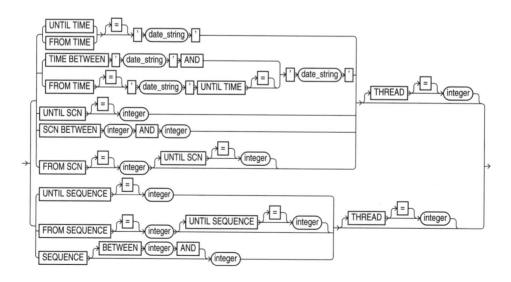

Chapter Reference
This subclause is covered in Chapter 12.

Example

```
backup archivelog sequence between 2211 and 2266 thread 1 delete input;
restore archivelog from time 'sysdate - 1';
```

backup Command

The **backup** command is used to back up your database (online or offline), a specific tablespace or datafile, or a specific set of tablespaces or datafiles. Additionally, the **backup** command allows you to back up database archived redo logs, control files, and server parameter files. Furthermore, the **backup** command can be used to create datafile or control file copies or to back up existing RMAN backup sets.

Syntax Diagram

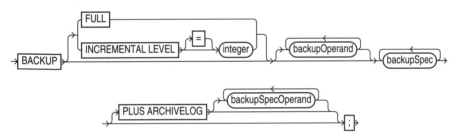

backupSpec Parameter Syntax

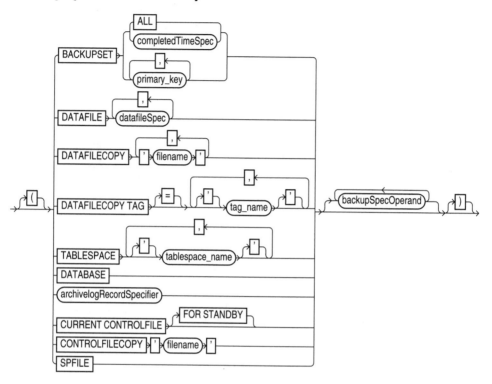

backupOperand Parameter Syntax

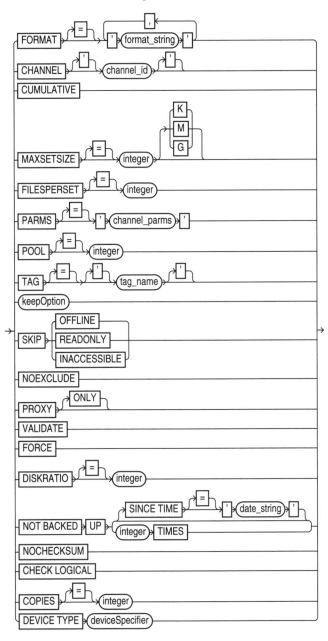

backupSpecOperand Parameter Syntax

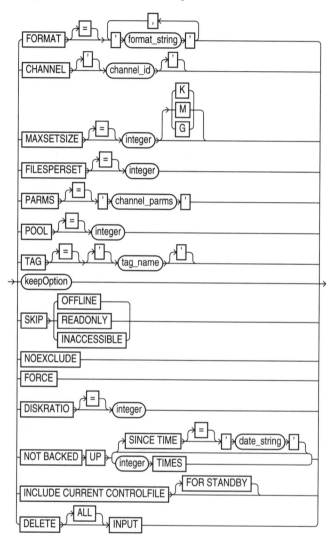

Chapter Reference
This command is covered in detail in Chapter 9.

Example

```
backup database plus archivelog delete input;
backup tablespace users, system;
backup datafile 1,2,3;
backup archivelog all;
```

blockrecover Command

The **blockrecover** command allows you to recover an individual data block or set of data blocks within a datafile.

Syntax Diagram

bmrBlockSpec Parameter Syntax

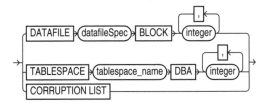

bmrOption Parameter Syntax

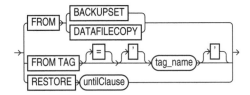

Chapter Reference
This command is covered in Chapter 12.

Example

```
BLOCKRECOVER DATAFILE 19 BLOCK 44,66,127;
```

catalog Command

The **catalog** command enables you to perform several functions, including the following:

- Add metadata about a user-managed datafile, control file, or archived log copy to the recovery catalog and control file.

- Record a datafile copy as a level 0 backup in the RMAN repository. This allows you to use that datafile copy as part of an incremental backup strategy.

- Record the existence of user-managed copies (datafile, control file, or archive logs) of Oracle Release 8.0 or later databases created before RMAN was installed.

- Record the existence of the last user-managed datafile copies made after the final shutdown in Oracle version 7 and before running the migration utility.

Once you have cataloged a backup file in RMAN, it can then be used by RMAN to recover your database.

Syntax Diagram

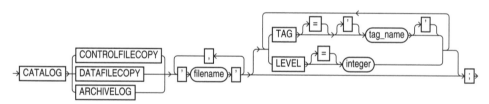

Chapter Reference

Chapter 13 contains more information on the use of this command.

Example

```
CATALOG DATAFILECOPY 'd:\oracle\backup\system01.bak',
'd:\oracle\backup\users01.bak' LEVEL 0;
```

change Command

The **change** command is used to modify the status of backups, copies, or archived redo logs in RMAN to a status of either AVAILABLE or UNAVAILABLE. You can also use the **change** command to alter the status of backups, copies, or archived redo logs to DELETED, which indicates that the backup, copy, or archived redo log is to be permanently removed from the RMAN repository. Generally, the **crosscheck** and **delete expired** commands are used for these purposes rather than the **change** command.

Finally, the **change** command can be used to modify or exempt a backup or copies from the current default retention.

Syntax Diagram

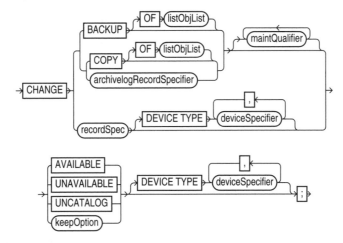

Chapter Reference
Chapter 13 contains a discussion on the use of the **change** command with regard to the retention policy. This book uses the **crosscheck** and **delete expired** commands in lieu of the **change** command for catalog maintenance operations.

Example

```
CHANGE BACKUP TAG 'gold_copy_database_bkup' KEEP FOREVER NOLOGS;
```

Command-Line Parameters
The RMAN executable has several command-line parameters that you can use. These parameters allow you to connect to the target database, the recovery catalog, or an auxiliary instance, run command scripts, or perform other activities.

Syntax Diagram

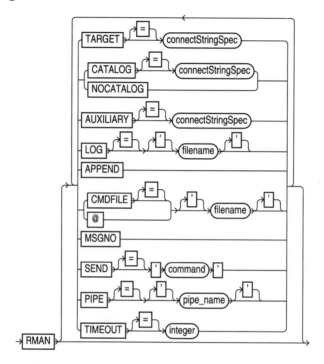

Chapter Reference
Chapter 3 contains information on the command-line interface to RMAN.

completedTimeSpec Subclause

The **completedTimeSpec** subclause is used to specify when a backup or copy completed.

Syntax Diagram

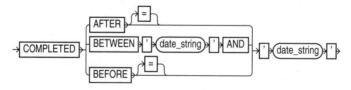

Chapter References
This subclause is used in several chapters throughout the book, including Chapter 13.

Example

 `crosscheck backup of database completed between 'sysdate' and 'sysdate-30';`

configure Command
The **configure** command is used to configure default RMAN configuration settings for such things as channels, the default retention policy, and backup optimization.

Syntax Diagram

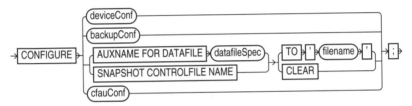

deviceConf Parameter Syntax

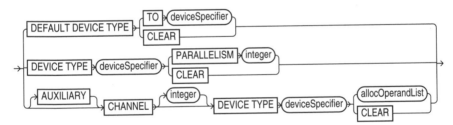

backupConf Parameter Syntax

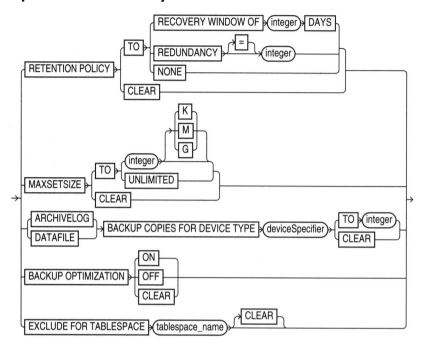

cfauConf Parameter Syntax

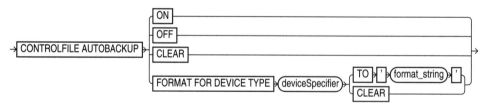

Chapter Reference

Chapter 3 covers the **configure** command in great detail.

Example

```
configure exclude for tablespace exclude_me;
configure device type disk parallelism 2;
configure device type disk clear;
configure device type sbt parallelism 2;
configure default device type to sbt;
```

```
configure channel 1 device type sbt connect 'sys/robert@test1'
  parms 'env=(nsr_server=bktest1)';
configure channel 2 device type sbt connect 'sys/robert@test2'
  parms env=(nsr_server=bktest2)';
```

connect Command

The **connect** command is used to connect to the target database, the recovery catalog, or the auxiliary instance from within RMAN (as opposed to doing so from the RMAN command line).

Syntax Diagram

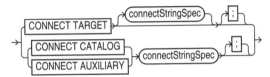

Chapter References

Examples of this command may be found in almost every chapter of this book.

Example

 connect target sys/robert@maindb

connectStringSpec Subclause

This subclause is the text string consisting of the username, password, and net8 service name, that is used to connect to a given database instance.

Syntax Diagram

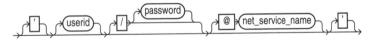

Chapter References

Examples of this command may be found in almost every chapter of this book.

Example

 connect target **sys/robert@maindb**

copy Command

The **copy** command is used to create an image copy of a datafile (database or another copy), archived redo log, or a control file (current or another copy). Copies are always written to disk.

Syntax Diagram

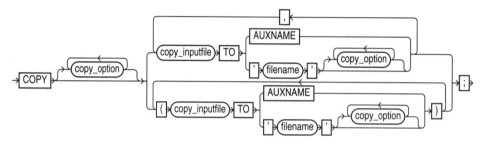

copy_option Parameter Syntax

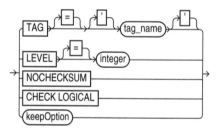

copy_inputfile Parameter Syntax

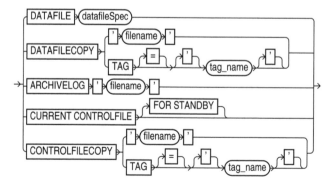

Chapter Reference
The **copy** command is covered in Chapter 9 in detail.

Example

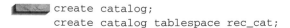

```
copy datafile 3 to 'd:\backup\datafilecopy\users01.dbf.bak';
copy datafile 'd:\oracle\oradata\users01.dbf' to
'd:\backup\datafilecopy\users01.dbf.bak';
```

create catalog Command
The **create catalog** command is used to create the recovery catalog.

Syntax Diagram

Chapter Reference
The **create catalog** command and creation of the recovery catalog in general are covered in Chapter 3.

Example

```
create catalog;
create catalog tablespace rec_cat;
```

create script Command
The **create script** command allows you to create a stored command script within RMAN. You must have a recovery catalog to use this command.

Syntax Diagram

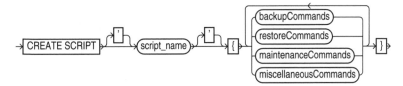

Chapter Reference

The **create script** command is covered in Chapter 13.

Example

```
CREATE SCRIPT backup_db
{ BACKUP DATABASE PLUS ARCHIVELOG DELETE INPUT; }
```

crosscheck Command

The **crosscheck** command is used to compare existing backup sets and backup set pieces with the contents of the recovery catalog or control file. Any backup set piece found to be missing is marked as EXPIRED and will be unavailable for any backup operation. Any backup set piece that had been previously marked as EXPIRED will be marked as AVAILABLE.

Syntax Diagram

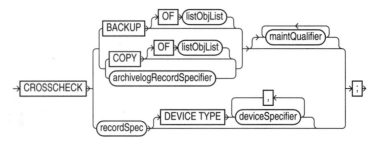

Chapter Reference

The **crosscheck** command is covered in Chapter 13.

Example

```
crosscheck backup;
crosscheck backup completed between 'sysdate-30' and 'sysdate-60';
crosscheck archivelog all;
crosscheck archivelog time between 'sysdate' and 'sysdate - 30';
```

datafileSpec Subclause

The **datafileSpec** subclause specifies a datafile by filename or absolute file number. It is used by several commands including the **backup**, **restore**, and **recover** commands.

Syntax Diagram

Chapter References

Chapter 9 includes several examples of the use of this subclause, as do Chapters 10 and 12.

Example

```
backup datafile 1,2,3;
backup datafile 'd:\oracle\oradata\system01.dbf';
restore datafile 1,2,3;
recover datafile 1,2,3;
```

delete Command

The **delete** command is used to mark expired(generally missing physical components) or obsolete (through retention policy) backup set pieces as DELETED. Once a backup is marked as DELETED, it cannot be recovered through the RMAN interface (though the **dbms_backup_restore** package can still be used to manually recover the backup set pieces in an emergency).

Syntax Diagram

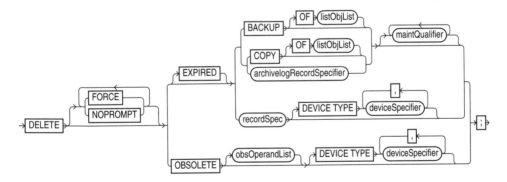

Chapter Reference

Chapter 13 contains coverage of the **delete** command.

Example

```
delete expired backup;
delete expired archivelog;
```

delete script Command

The **delete script** command allows you to delete an existing RMAN script stored in the recovery catalog.

Syntax Diagram

Chapter Reference

Chapter 13 contains more information on the **delete script** command.

Example

```
delete script revenge;
```

DeviceSpecifier Subclause

The **DeviceSpecifier** subclause is used to specify the type of storage for a backup or copy. Valid device specifiers are **disk** for disk devices and **sbt** for MML devices.

Syntax Diagram

Chapter References

Use of the **DeviceSpecifier** clause can be found in almost every chapter of this book.

Example

```
ALLOCATE CHANNEL FOR MAINTENANCE DEVICE TYPE sbt;
```

drop catalog Command

The **drop catalog** command is used to remove the recovery catalog schema objects from the recovery catalog. Note that it does not drop the recovery catalog schema owner or any other objects that may have been created within the schema of that owner that do not belong to RMAN. Also note that after issuing the command once, RMAN will require that you issue the command a second time before it performs the operation.

Syntax Diagram

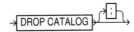

Chapter Reference

Chapter 3 contains information on the **drop catalog** command.

Example

```
drop catalog;
```

duplicate Command

The **duplicate** command is used to create either a duplicate database (with a new DBID) or a standby database (with the same DBID) using RMAN backups of a given target database.

Syntax Diagram

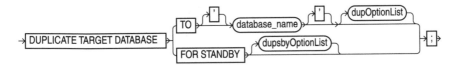

dupOptionList Parameter Syntax

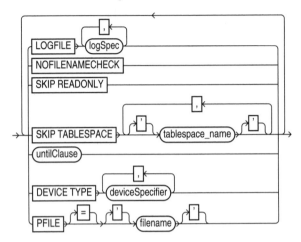

logSpec Parameter Syntax

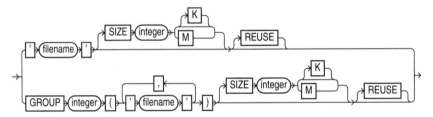

dupsbyOptionList Parameter Syntax

Chapter References

Chapters 16 and 17 provide more detail on this command.

Example

```
duplicate target database to newdb
    until time 'sysdate-5'
    pfile = $oracle_home/dbs/initnewdb.ora
```

```
logfile
  group 1 ('?/oradata/newdb/redo01a.log',
           '?/oradata/newdb/redo01b.log') size 200k,
  group 2 ('?/oradata/newdb/redo02a.log',
           '?/oradata/newdb/redo02b.log') size 200k
  group 3 ('?/oradata/newdb/redo03a.log',
           '?/oradata/newdb/redo03b.log') size 200k reuse;
```

execute Command

The **execute** command allows you to run a stored command script from the
RMAN prompt.

Syntax Diagram

Chapter Reference

Chapter 13 provides more detail on this command.

Example

run {execute my_script}

exit Command

The **exit** command causes you to exit the current RMAN session.

host Command

The **host** command is used to execute operating system commands from the
RMAN prompt.

Syntax Diagram

Chapter Reference

This command is referenced in examples in Chapter 13 in this book.

Example

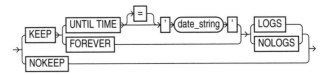

```
host 'dir';
host 'copy d:\oracle\oradata\recover\*.* d:\backup\recover\*.*';
```

KeepOption Subclause

The **KeepOption** subclause is used to modify the retention status of a given backup or copy. It can be used to define an alternate retention time criteria (given a valid date/time string) or no retention criteria at all (using the **nokeep** parameter), or to keep the backup forever (**keep forever**).

Syntax Diagram

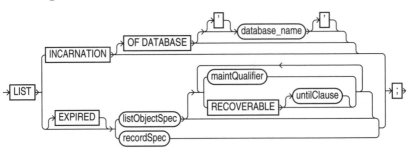

Chapter Reference

Chapter 13 contains information and examples on the use of this subclause.

list Command

The **list** command provides information on RMAN backups, including backup sets, image copies, and proxy copies. For example, the **list** command can be used to list available or expired backups that might be available for a restore and recovery operation, database incarnations, or the status of specific backups based on a number of criteria, including tag, completion time, and device.

Syntax Diagram

listObjectSpec Parameter Syntax

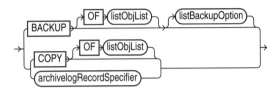

listBackupOption Parameter Syntax

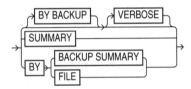

Chapter Reference

Chapter 14 contains information and examples on the use of the **list** command.

Example

```
list backup;
list backup of datafile 1,2,3;
list backup summary;
```

ListObjList Subclause

This subclause is used to define the object being referenced by the **change**, **crosscheck**, **delete**, and **list** commands.

Syntax Diagram

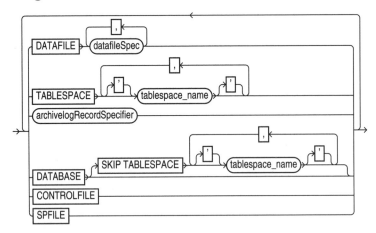

Chapter Reference

Chapter 14 contains information and examples on the use of this subclause.

Example

```
list backup of database;
list backup of datafile 1,2,3;
list backup of tablespace users;
```

maintQualifier Subclause

The **maintQualifier** subclause is used to specify database files and archived redo
logs when using the **crosscheck**, **delete**, or **crosscheck** commands.

Syntax Diagram

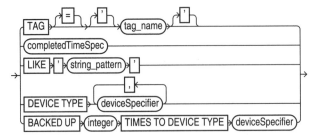

Chapter References

This command is referenced in examples in several chapters in this book, primarily in Chapter 13.

Example

```
delete archivelog all backed up 2 times to device type disk;
delete backup tag='Tuesday';
```

opsOperandList Subclause

This subclause is used to define retention criteria to mark a backup or copy as obsolete or to list or report on such a backup.

Syntax Diagram

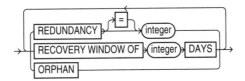

Chapter Reference

Chapter 14 contains information and examples on the use of this subclause.

Example

```
delete obsolete recovery window of 14 days;
delete redundancy 3;
```

print script Command

The **print script** command causes RMAN to output a listing of a specific stored script.

Syntax Diagram

Chapter Reference

Chapter 13 provides more detail on this command.

Example

 `print script ali_baba;`

quit Command

The **quit** command causes the recovery manager session to end.

Syntax Diagram

recordspec Subclause

The **recordspec** subclause is used in the **change**, **crosscheck**, **delete**, and **list** commands to define which objects those commands should address.

Syntax Diagram

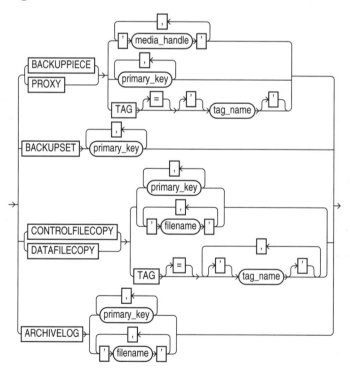

Chapter References

The **recordspec** subclause is demonstrated in several chapters in this book, including Chapter 14.

Example

 `crosscheck backuppiece tag='gold copy';`

recover Command

The **recover** command is used to recover a database, tablespace, or datafile. It is typically used after one or more datafiles belonging to a database have been recovered from backup media via the **restore** command. The **recover** command causes all needed archived redo logs to be extracted from RMAN backups and applies that redo to the object being recovered.

Syntax Diagram

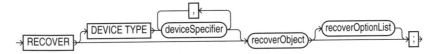

recoverObject Parameter Syntax

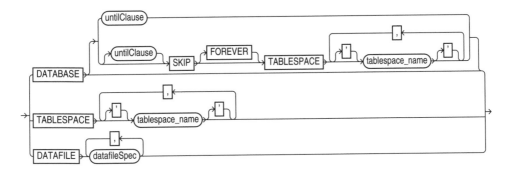

recoverOptionList Parameter Syntax

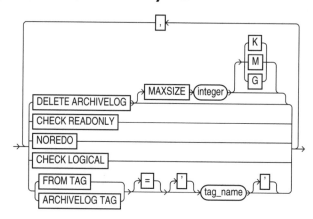

Chapter References
Chapters 10 and 12 deal with the **recover** command in great detail.

Example

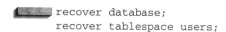
```
recover database;
recover tablespace users;
```

register Command

The **register** command is used to register a database with an existing recovery catalog.

Syntax Diagram

Chapter Reference
The **register** command is covered in Chapter 3.

Example

```
register database
```

release channel Command

The **release channel** command is used to release channels allocated with the **allocate channel** command. Generally, channels are released automatically by RMAN, so this command is rarely actually needed in practice. The **release channel** usage is constant for both regular channels and maintenance channels.

Syntax Diagram

releaseForMaint Parameter Syntax

(To be used for channels created for maintenance operations)

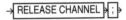

Example

```
allocate channel sbt_ch1 device type sbt;
release channel sbt_ch1;
allocate channel for maintenance device type disk;
release channel;
```

replace script Command

The **replace script** command is used to replace command scripts stored in the recovery catalog.

Syntax Diagram

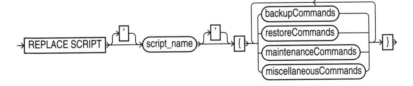

Chapter Reference

Chapter 13 provides more detail on this command.

Example

```
REPLACE SCRIPT backup_full
{
    BACKUP DEVICE TYPE sbt DATABASE PLUS ARCHIVELOG;
}
```

report Command

The **report** command is used to analyze the RMAN metadata contained in the recovery catalog or the database control file. The output from the **report** command can be used to determine the backup/recovery status of the database and its component parts.

Syntax Diagram

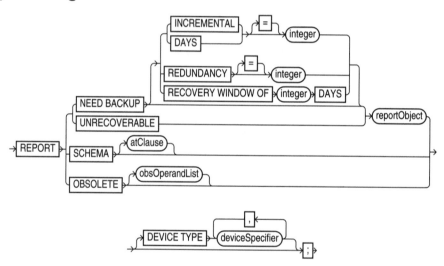

reportObject Parameter Syntax

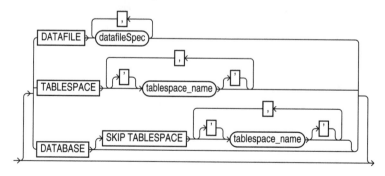

atClause Parameter Syntax

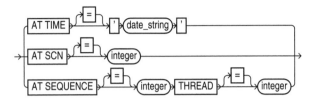

Chapter Reference

Chapter 14 provides more detail on this command.

Example

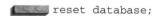
```
report need backup days=3;
report unrecoverable;
report obsolete;
```

reset database Command

The **reset database** command is used to do the following:

- Indicate that a manual **resetlogs** operation has been executed and a new database incarnation should be recorded in the recovery catalog.

- To reset the database to a previous database incarnation in order to restore the database to a point prior to the issuing of a **resetlogs** command.

Syntax Diagram

Chapter Reference

Chapter 12 provides more detail on this command.

Example

```
reset database;
```

restore Command

The **restore** command is used to restore the database, tablespaces, datafiles, control files, archived redo logs, and SPFILES from the backup media, in preparation for a recovery operation.

Syntax Diagram

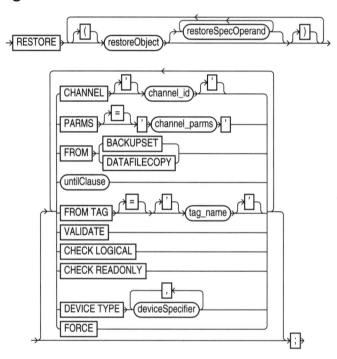

restoreObject Parameter Syntax

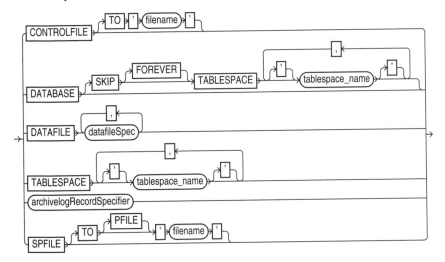

restoreSpecOperand Parameter Syntax

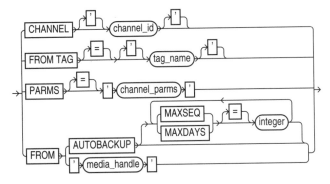

Chapter References
Chapters 10 and 12 provide more details on this command.

Example

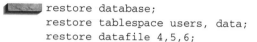
```
restore database;
restore tablespace users, data;
restore datafile 4,5,6;
```

resync Command

The **resync** command is used to resynchronize the recovery catalog with the database control file. Optionally, the recovery catalog can be resynchronized from a snapshot control file.

Syntax Diagram

Chapter Reference

The **resync** command is explained in Chapter 13.

Example

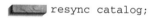
```
resync catalog;
```

run Command

The **run** command is used to compile and execute one or more RMAN commands within the confines of the braces of the **run** block. Operationally, the **run** command is followed by an open bracket, and then one or more RMAN commands. The **run** command is then completed through the use of a close bracket, at which time the block of commands will be compiled and executed immediately.

Syntax Diagram

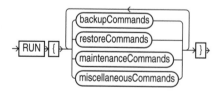

Chapter References

The **run** command is demonstrated in many chapters throughout the book.

Example

```
RUN {
  SQL "ALTER TABLESPACE data_2001 OFFLINE IMMEDIATE";
  RESTORE TABLESPACE data_2001;
  RECOVER TABLESPACE data_2001;
  SQL "ALTER TABLESPACE data_2001 ONLINE";
}
```

send Command

The **send** command is used to send a vendor-specific string to one or more channels. Because these strings are vendor specific, they should be documented in your vendor-supplied media management layer (MML) documentation.

Syntax Diagram

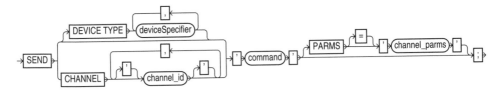

Chapter References

See Chapters 4 through 8 for more information on the MML layer and the valid vendor strings.

Example

RMAN> SEND 'ENV=serv_bck01';

set Command

The **set** command configures RMAN settings for the current RMAN session (that is, the settings are not persistent). The **set** command comes in two different flavors. The first set of commands (**set_run_option**) are only valid within the confines of a **run** block. The second set of commands (**set_rman_option**) are for use at the RMAN prompt and not within the confines of a **run** command.

Syntax Diagram

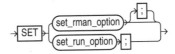

set_rman_option Parameter Syntax

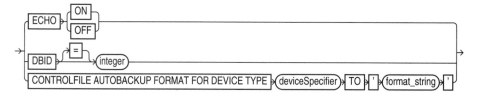

set_run_option Parameter Syntax

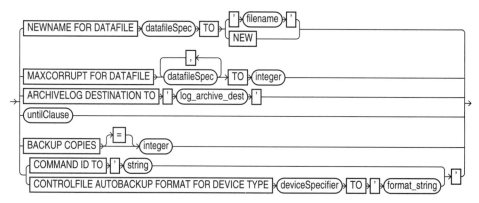

Chapter Reference
Chapter 9 provides more details on this command.

Example

```
SET DBID 222534855;
RUN {
   SET UNTIL TIME '12/25/2002 12:00:00';
   SET CONTROLFILE AUTOBACKUP FORMAT FOR DEVICE TYPE DISK;
   RESTORE CONTROLFILE FROM AUTOBACKUP MAXSEQ 100;
}
```

show Command

The **show** command is used to display the current persistent configuration settings.

Syntax Diagram

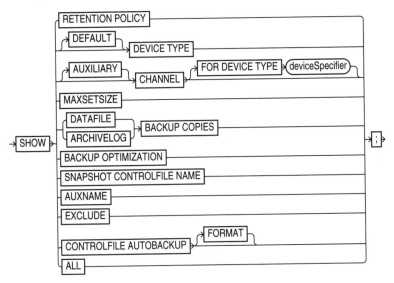

Chapter Reference
This command is demonstrated in Chapter 3.

Example

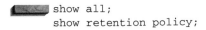
```
show all;
show retention policy;
```

shutdown Command

The **shutdown** command is used to shut down the database. This command does not cause the RMAN session to terminate.

Syntax Diagram

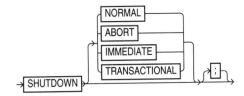

Chapter References

This command is demonstrated in several chapters in the book, including Chapters 10 and 12.

Example

```
shutdown;
shutdown immediate;
shutdown transactional;
```

spool Command

The **spool** command defines a log file that RMAN will spool output to. RMAN will overwrite an existing spool file, or append to it if the **append** option is used.

Syntax Diagram

Example

```
Spool log to '/tmp/df2log.f';
```

```
backup datafile 2;
```

Chapter Reference

The **spool** command is not used in our book.

SQL Command

The **sql** command is used to execute SQL statements in the target database from the RMAN prompt.

Syntax Diagram

Chapter References

This command is demonstrated in several chapters, such as Chapter 12.

Example

```
sql "alter tablespace users offline immediate";
sql "alter tablespace data_2001 add datafile
''d:\oracle\oradata\recover\recover_data_2001_01.dbf'' size 100m;"
```

startup Command

The **startup** command is used to start the instance of, mount, or open the target database.

Syntax Diagram

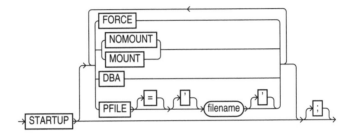

Chapter References

This command is demonstrated in several chapters, such as Chapter 9.

Example

```
startup nomount;
startup;
```

switch Command

The **switch** command causes an RMAN datafile copy to become the current database datafile. This command is often used if the database datafiles need to be restored to a location other than their original location.

Syntax Diagram

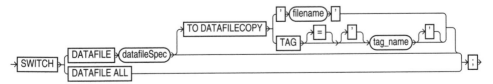

Chapter Reference

See Chapter 10 for more information on the use of this command.

Example

```
run
{
set newname for datafile 'd:\oracle\oradata\recover\system01.dbf' to
'e:\oracle\oradata\recover\system01.dbf';
restore datafile 1;
switch datafile all;
recover datafile 1;
alter database open resetlogs;
}
```

untilClause Subcommand

The **untilClause** subcommand defines an upper limit that applies to the related operation. The limit can be defined by time, SCN, or log sequence number.

Syntax Diagram

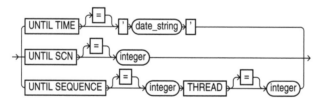

Chapter References

Chapter 11 contains examples of the use of this subcommand, as do several other chapters.

Example

```
BACKUP ARCHIVELOG FROM TIME 'SYSDATE-31' UNTIL TIME 'SYSDATE-14';
RESTORE DATABASE UNTIL TIME "TO_DATE('09/20/00','MM/DD/YY')";
```

upgrade catalog Command

The **upgrade catalog** command is used to upgrade a recovery catalog from an older version to a newer version of RMAN.

Syntax Diagram

Chapter Reference

Chapter 13 contains information on the **upgrade catalog** command.

Example

upgrade catalog;

validate Command

The **validate** command is used to check and validate that a given backup set can be restored. All the pieces of the backup set will be scanned by RMAN during the operation.

Syntax Diagram

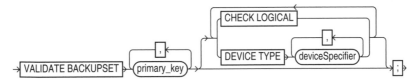

Chapter Reference

Chapter 13 contains information on the **upgrade catalog** command.

Example

validate backup set 1203;

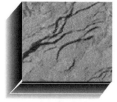

APPENDIX B

Exploring the Recovery Catalog

he recovery catalog provides a series of views that can be used to explore the metadata being produced by your RMAN backup strategy. These views have base tables that are populated when you register your database, and then on any subsequent **resync** command from the catalog. The naming convention for these is RC_*; for example, RC_BACKUP_SET or RC_BACKUP_REDOLOG.

In Oracle9*i*, the recovery catalog has grown more and more redundant as many of the views that were unique to it in the past have been incorporated into tables in the target database control file. This means there is now a corresponding V$view for every RC_* view in the catalog. For instance, if the recovery catalog table is RC_BACKUP_SET, the V$view would be V$BACKUP_SET. The only difference will be a primary key column in the catalog that does not exist in the V$view.

This appendix provides a list of the critical RC_* views in the catalog, along with brief explanations. It is beyond the scope of this book to give a complete rundown of each column in each view; the Oracle-provided documentation does this excellently. Instead, we give a brief explanation of what the view might mean to you and how you might use it. We've left out all views that deal with proxy copies, as these are not covered in this book, and views that deal with stored scripts are also absent.

Having access to the RC_* views is a critical tool when setting up and refining a backup strategy; no doubt you will also want access prior to any restore and recovery operation. It is extremely useful to put together a series of scripts that you can run on demand, or even schedule a report output on a regular basis. Here, we provide an example of a few catalog queries that may prove useful to you during backup and recovery operations.

It is worth noting that some of the examples in this appendix select against the V$view of the target database, while others refer to the RC_* views in the catalog. If you are making selections against the catalog, and you have more than one database registered, you will always need to delimit your query based on the DBID or the DB_NAME (if it's unique within the catalog). Otherwise, you will get information for more than one database, which won't be that useful unless you are trying to gather enterprise-wide information.

RC_ARCHIVED_LOG (V$ARCHIVED_LOG)

The archive log history in V$ARCHIVED_LOG will be one of the most heavily utilized views you have at your disposal. Due to the confusing nature of backing up archive logs and restoring them for recovery purposes, having access to their metadata is critical. Bear in mind that RC_ARCHIVED_LOG does not hold information about any backups you have of your archive logs (see RC_BACKUP_REDOLOG for that); it holds only information about all archive logs that have been generated by the target. Because archive logs are constantly being generated, whereas catalog resynchronizations are relatively less frequent, you will find yourself most often at

V$ARCHIVED_LOG over the catalog version of this view. The kind of code that would give you the most out of this view would look something like this:

```
column name format a50
column completion_time format a25
alter session set nls_date_format= 'DD-MON-YYYY:HH24:MI:SS';
select name, sequence#, deleted, status, completion_time
from v$archived_log;
```

RC_BACKUP_CONTROLFILE (V$BACKUP_DATAFILE)

This view provides information about backups you have taken of your control file. This does not include control file copies; there is a different view for copies that have been made with the **copy** command or cataloged with the **catalog** command. This view is an excellent source to reference if control file restore operations are behaving strangely, particularly if you are trying to duplicate for standby database creation.

It is worth noting that the V$view that corresponds to this view is V$BACKUP_DATAFILE. To review control file copies in V$BACKUP_DATAFILE, you would look at records with a file number of 0—this represents the control file:

```
SELECT FILE#, CREATION_TIME, RESETLOGS_TIME, BLOCKS,
BLOCK_SIZE, CONTROLFILE_TYPE FROM V$BACKUP_DATAFILE
WHERE FILE#=0;
```

The following query would give you information about all the control file backups for the database PROD90, with the completion time, status, type of control file (B for a normal backup and S for a Standby control file backup), and date of the autobackup (this will be null if you do not have the control file autobackup configured):

```
column completion_time format a25
column autobackup_date format a25
alter session set nls_date_format= 'DD-MON-YYYY:HH24:MI:SS';
select db_name, status, completion_time, controlfile_type,
autobackup_date from rc_backup_controlfile
where db_name= 'PROD90';
```

RC_BACKUP_CORRUPTION (V$BACKUP_CORRUPTION)

This view lists the corruption that exists in datafile backups. To tolerate corruption, the value of MAXCORRUPT must be set to a nonzero value, which indicates how many corrupt blocks RMAN will back up before it throws an error and aborts. The corrupt blocks are not discarded, but rather are backed up as is.

Do not confuse this view with RC_DATABASE_BLOCK_CORRUPTION (described later in this appendix), which lists blocks that are corrupt in the database based on the last **backup** operation (or **backup validate** operation).

RC_BACKUP_CORRUPTION lists blocks that are corrupt in the backup, not in the database itself.

The following code provides a list of corrupt blocks, with block number, file number, backup piece in which the corruption exists, and the type of corruption for the database PROD90:

```
select db_name, piece#, file#, block#, blocks, corruption_type
from rc_backup_corruption where db_name='PROD90';
```

RC_BACKUP_DATAFILE (V$BACKUP_DATAFILE)

This view has extensive information about datafiles that exist in backup sets. If you are interested in viewing specific information about datafiles that have been backed up, then you should use this view.

RC_BACKUP_PIECE (V$BACKUP_PIECE)

Reference this view for information about specific backup pieces that have been created during normal backup operations. Remember that a backup set contains more than one backup piece, and that the backup piece is the physical file that corresponds to the logical unit of the backup set.

RC_BACKUP_REDOLOG (V$BACKUP_REDOLOG)

The name of this view is something of a misnomer: RMAN cannot back up online redo logs; it can back up only archived redo logs, which are most often simply referred to as archive logs. This view lists archive logs that exist in backup sets. There is a record for each archive log that has been backed up; if the same archive log is backed up twice, there will be two records.

The following query provides information for a particular range of archive logs, with backup set information, the status of the backup set, and the completion time:

```
alter session set nls_date_format= 'DD-MON-YYYY:HH24:MI:SS';
select db_name, bs_key, sequence#, thread#, first_change#, status
from rc_backup_redolog;
```

RC_BACKUP_SET (V$BACKUP_SET)

Information in this view refers to each logical backup set. You have to specify which type of backup set you would like to review: full backups, incremental backups, or archive log backups.

RC_BACKUP_SPFILE (V$BACKUP_SPFILE)

In this view, you will find information on SPFILE backups that exist in backup sets.

RC_CONTROLFILE_COPY (V$DATAFILE_COPY)

Like RC_BACKUP_CONTROLFILE, the corresponding view here, V$DATAFILE_COPY also includes information about control files, encoded as file number 0. In the catalog, this view contains control file copy information for control files created with the **copy** command or cataloged with the **catalog** command.

RC_COPY_CORRUPTION (V$COPY_CORRUPTION)

This view is the same as RC_BACKUP_CORRUPTION, except it reports blocks that are corrupt in copies instead of in backup sets. The **select** statement, then, would omit a **piece#** but would otherwise be identical.

```
select db_name, file#, block#, blocks, corruption_type
from rc_COPY_corruption where db_name='PROD90';
```

RC_DATABASE (V$DATABASE)

This view contains basic information about each database registered in the catalog: the database name, ID, current incarnation number, and last RESETLOGS time and SCN.

RC_DATABASE_BLOCK_CORRUPTION (V$DATABASE_BLOCK_CORRUPTION)

In this view, we find the corruption list that is populated when a **backup** or **backup validate** operation discovers corrupt blocks. Remember that these are the actual corrupt blocks in the database, not in the backups or copies themselves. This view is refreshed on each backup operation to reflect current corruption (if any). V$DATABASE_BLOCK_CORRUPTION is the view used during block media recovery when you specify **blockrecover corruption list**, and is therefore the one that you will most often be referencing. The following **select** statement will provide a list of important information about the corrupt blocks.

```
Select file#, block#, corruption_type
from v$database_block_corruption;
```

RC_DATABASE_INCARNATION (V$DATABASE_INCARNATION)

This view contains a record for each incarnation of each database registered in the catalog. The most important information here is the RESETLOGS information, which by definition defines each incarnation. There is a corresponding V$view, V$DATABASE_INCARNATION, but do not be fooled: If you want to be able to use database incarnations to restore backups prior to resetlogs, you will need a catalog. The following statement will pull key information from the view for all databases.

```
select dbid, name, dbinc_key, resetlogs_time, current_incarnation
from rc_database_incarnation
where name= 'PROD';
```

RC_DATAFILE (V$DATAFILE)

This view exists so that the catalog has access to the same schematic information as the control file about the location and specifics of each datafile in the database. V$DATAFILE is much more likely to be used when you want to look at your datafile information; however, in a recovery situation, this view can be extremely helpful if a current control file is not available. It also contains tablespace information in addition to datafile information, and in that way resembles the fixed view DBA_DATA_FILES. In addition, this view contains permanent configuration information for the commands **configure exclude** and **configure auxname**. Here is a common SQL statement used against RC_DATAFILE:

```
SQL> select db_name, ts#, tablespace_name, file#, name,
bytes, included_in_database_backup, aux_name
from rc_datafile
where db_name='PROD';
```

RC_DATAFILE_COPY (V$DATAFILE_COPY)

In this view, we find metadata about datafile copies created by the **copy** command or OS copies that have been registered with the **catalog** command.

RC_LOG_HISTORY (V$LOG_HISTORY)

V$LOG_HISTORY is the view that contains historical information about online redo logs, such as when they switched and what the SCN was at the switch. This is a little redundant with V$ARCHIVED_LOG, but V$LOG_HISTORY does not concern itself with any current files, just the historical log switching information.

RC_OFFLINE_RANGE (V$OFFLINE_RANGE)

Offline ranges set the parameters for when a datafile went offline or read-only, and when it came back to read/write mode (if ever). It is important for RMAN to know this about a file when doing backups as well as restores. From a recoverability standpoint, it is critical to have the entire time range when a file was offline, or online.

RC_REDO_LOG (VLOG, VLOGFILE)

From a schematic point of view, this is the same for RMAN as knowing the information in V$DATAFILE—on rebuilds, it will need to know where the online redo log files are located. This view is a combination of both V$LOG and V$LOGFILE, so that thread and group membership is available alongside the name of each log.

RC_REDO_THREAD (V$THREAD)

Thread information is really only important in Real Applications Cluster (RAC) environments, where there is more than a single thread of redo being generated at once. This view lists a record for each separate thread in the current database incarnation, along with the status of the thread and its redo stream.

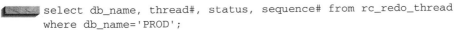

```
select db_name, thread#, status, sequence# from rc_redo_thread
where db_name='PROD';
```

RC_RESYNC

This view provides information for each catalog resync operation that occurs. Obviously, there is no corresponding V#view for this one. This view can be used to determine if any of your enterprise databases need a resync, or to troubleshoot possible resynchronization problems.

```
SQL> select db_name, controlfile_time, controlfile_sequence#,
resync_type, resync_time
from rc_resync where db_name='PROD817';
```

RC_RMAN_CONFIGURATION (V$RMAN_CONFIGURATION)

This view is equivalent to a **show all** command, giving the name and value for each configuration parameter that is set for each of your target databases. It is worth noting that three configuration parameters are not stored here: **configure exclude** information is found in RC_TABLESPACE (V$TABLESPACE), **configure auxname** information is found with RC_DATAFILE (V$DATAFILE), and **configure snapshot controlfile** information is only found in the target database control file (there is no catalog equivalent).

It also is worth noting that RC_RMAN_CONFIGURATION does not have a DB_NAME column, so you have to use the primary key db_key value from RC_DATABASE to get the values for the appropriate database registered in your catalog.

```
SQL> select name, value from rc_rman_configuration where db_key=134;
```

RC_TABLESPACE (V$TABLESPACE)

Tablespace information is included in this view. There is a real benefit here, compared to V$TABLESPACE—historical information about dropped tablespaces is kept in the catalog. Therefore, you can use this view to look back and see when a tablespace was dropped. In addition, this view contains the information recorded for any **configure exclude** commands.

APPENDIX
C

Oracle8*i* Syntactical Differences

f you are committed to a fully functional and fully packaged solution for backup and recovery, and therefore feel committed to the availability of your database, then I have only one piece of advice for you: make the move to Oracle9i. The RMAN product and its integration with the database is so much more highly evolved, using Oracle9i is almost like working with a different product than Oracle8i.

Am I overstating things? Maybe a little. But there are a hundred good reasons to leave Oracle8i in the rear-view mirror, and if you need an excuse to upgrade, RMAN can be that excuse. Its features are more robust, and it's easier to use, easier to maintain, and just more refined in general.

Heaven help you if you are stuck in Oracle8.0.x and you are considering RMAN, or even actively using it. I shudder to think.

Okay, so maybe you can't make the move just yet. These things happen; we understand. Besides, if you have never worked with RMAN in Oracle8i, you simply can't appreciate how nice it has become in Oracle9i. This appendix will guide you through the primary differences between RMAN in Oracle8i and RMAN in Oracle9i. This is not an exhaustive, line-by-line comparison—we simply don't have the time or the space. But we cover the primary differences that may confuse you if you're using this book as an RMAN guide but don't have any Oracle9i target databases.

Error Stack Differences

RMAN in Oracle9i really cleaned up its act. Literally. In Oracle8i, every time you see a line of text returned, an RMAN "error" number accompanies it. This not only is visually mystifying, but also makes it difficult to find which error exactly is the source of the problem. For instance, in both Oracle8i and Oracle9i, we attempted to allocate a tape channel when no media management product had been installed. Note the error stack differences:

In Oracle8i:

```
RMAN-03022: compiling command: allocate
RMAN-03023: executing command: allocate
RMAN-00571: ===========================================================
RMAN-00569: =============== ERROR MESSAGE STACK FOLLOWS =============
RMAN-00571: ===========================================================
RMAN-03007: retryable error occurred during
            execution of command: allocate
RMAN-07004: unhandled exception during command execution on channel x
RMAN-10035: exception raised in RPC: ORA-19554: error allocating
            device, device type: SBT_TAPE, device name:
```

```
ORA-19557: device error, device type: SBT_TAPE, device name:
ORA-27000: skgfqsbi: failed to initialize storage subsystem (SBT) layer
ORA-19511: SBT error = 4110, errno = 0,
          BACKUP_DIR environment variable is not set
RMAN-10031: ORA-19624 occurred during call to
DBMS_BACKUP_RESTORE.DEVICEALLOCATE
```

And in Oracle9i:

```
using target database controlfile instead of recovery catalog
RMAN-00571: ===========================================================
RMAN-00569: =============== ERROR MESSAGE STACK FOLLOWS =============
RMAN-00571: ===========================================================
RMAN-03009: failure of allocate command on x channel
            at 08/17/2002 23:29:36
ORA-19554: error allocating device, device type: SBT_TAPE, device name:
ORA-27211: Failed to load Media Management Library
```

Notice that even the channel allocation message has an RMAN "error" number in Oracle8i. Get used to it, because every line of output from RMAN has a number in Oracle8i. Don't worry, you'll see plenty of errors and, after a while, you'll get used to it, like that guy watching the falling green symbols in *The Matrix*. Also note that the error messages in Oracle9i, in general, give you a better understanding of the underlying cause. Did I mention it's a good idea to upgrade?

Permanent Configuration Parameters (or the lack thereof)

One of the primary usability advantages in Oracle9i is the existence of permanent configuration parameters stored in the control file and used to establish channels and whatnot every time you request a backup or recovery operation. These simply do not exist in Oracle8i. In Oracle 8.0, if you simply type the command **backup database** at the RMAN prompt, you get a syntax error:

```
RMAN-00571: ===========================================================
RMAN-00569: =============== ERROR MESSAGE STACK FOLLOWS =============
RMAN-00571: ===========================================================
RMAN-00558: error encountered while parsing input commands
RMAN-01005: syntax error: found "backup": expecting one of:
"allocate, alter, beginline, catalog ...
RMAN-01007: at line 1 column 1 file: standard input
```

Instead, you would need to construct a full **run** block with the entire command in it. That means you have to allocate the channel and then issue the **backup** command, like this:

```
Run {
allocate channel c1 type 'sbt_tape'
parms = "env= (nb_ora_serv=rm-wgt, nb_ora_client=Cervantes)";
allocate channel c2 type 'sbt_tape'
parms = "env= (nb_ora_serv=rm-wgt, nb_ora_client=Cervantes)";
backup
filesperset=4
database format =  'FULL_%U.BAK';
backup archivelog all delete input; }
```

You would do this every time. As you might imagine, storing scripts is extremely popular in version Oracle8i. Otherwise, there's just too much room for error each and every time you type your code.

The Automatic Log Switch after Backup

After every full backup of the database, but prior to the backup of your archive logs, you should write into your target database a SQL statement that performs a log switch, or a manual archival of the current log. In Oracle9i, there is an automatic archival of the current redo log before any archive log backup; this allows any subsequent backup of the archive logs to contain a full copy of all redo necessary to restore the datafile backups.

The point of this log switching after the database backup, but before the archive log backup, is to establish a logical working "full" backup. By "full" we mean a self-contained set of all data necessary to restore the database and open it. A commonly used guideline in most backup and recovery strategies is that when a backup is taken, that particular backup is complete—without any previous or subsequent backups, the database could be restored and opened using any one particular backup. This makes sense, and RMAN supports this natively in Oracle9i.

However, in Oracle8i, the archive log backup runs after the datafile backup, and backs up all archive logs that appear in the V$ARCHIVED_LOG view. However, this archive log backup, taken immediately after the datafile backup, does not contain the redo that was generated during the datafile backup itself. And when you are taking hot backups, the redo that gets generated during the backup is required for the backup to be recovered to a consistent point and opened. But Oracle8i RMAN does not back up the necessary redo until the next scheduled backup operation takes place. Therefore, if you have a system failure between backups, your last backup may not be good enough because it does not include necessary redo log backups.

To avoid this, you would modify the backup script in the preceding section like this:

```
Run {
allocate channel c1 type 'sbt_tape'
parms = "env= (nb_ora_serv=rm-wgt, nb_ora_client=Cervantes)";
allocate channel c2 type 'sbt_tape'
parms = "env= (nb_ora_serv=rm-wgt, nb_ora_client=Cervantes)";
backup
filesperset=4
database format =   'FULL_%U.BAK';
sql 'alter system archive log current';
backup archivelog all delete input; }
```

Differences in V$ARCHIVED_LOG View

The view V$ARCHIVED_LOG has changed between Oracle version 8i and version 9i. In Oracle9i, the more descriptive column STATUS exists, which gives the status of the archive log based on RMAN operations: available, deleted, unavailable, or expired (A, D, U, and X, respectively). In Oracle8i, no such column exists; you simply have the DELETED column, with a value of YES or NO. Any operation by RMAN that physically deletes the file marks it as deleted. In addition, any maintenance command that checks the OS and fails to find an archive log marks it as deleted.

Channel Allocation for Maintenance Commands

The lack of permanent configuration parameters also has an effect on maintenance commands, such as **crosscheck** and **report**. These commands cannot run in Oracle8i unless you first allocate a channel for maintenance. A maintenance channel (a delete channel in Oracle8i) is allocated outside a **run** block and remains allocated until you manually release it. For instance,

```
RMAN> allocate channel for maintenance type disk;

RMAN-03022: compiling command: allocate
RMAN-03023: executing command: allocate
RMAN-08030: allocated channel: delete
RMAN-08500: channel delete: sid=13 devtype=DISK
```

```
RMAN> crosscheck backup of database;

RMAN-03022: compiling command: XCHECK
RMAN-03023: executing command: XCHECK
...
RMAN> release channel;

RMAN-03022: compiling command: release
RMAN-03023: executing command: release
RMAN-08031: released channel: delete
```

Block Media Recovery

There is no block media recovery in Oracle8i. This means the smallest unit of
granularity for you to restore is the datafile, meaning that a block corruption can
be very costly for uptime. Have we properly encouraged you to upgrade yet?

The Importance
of the Recovery Catalog

In Oracle8i, the recovery catalog has a far more prominent role in activities than in
Oracle9i. In fact, there's a list of operations that require the catalog in Oracle8i that
can be done without one in Oracle9i. Here's a list of catalog-only commands in
Oracle8i:

- **change (available | unavailable | backupset | crosscheck** | and so forth)
- **configure compatible**
- **create | delete | replace | print script**
- **crosscheck backup**
- **delete expired backup**
- **list incarnation**
- **report schema at time**
- **reset database**
- **resync catalog**
- **set auxname**

Running in NOCATALOG Mode

Oracle8i assumes that you will be using a recovery catalog at all times. So, if you don't connect to a catalog prior to running a command, you get an error:

```
RMAN-06172: not connected to recovery catalog database
```

To get past this error, you have to either connect to a catalog or explicitly tell RMAN that you are connecting in NOCATALOG mode. You cannot do this after starting RMAN already—you have to tell it when you start, like this:

```
$>rman target / nocatalog
```

No Control File Autobackup

Oracle8i does not come equipped with a complete loss solution such as the control file autobackup that exists in Oracle9i. This means that if you run in NOCATALOG mode in Oracle8i, you have a single point of failure with your control file. If you lose all copies of your control file, your RMAN backups are worthless, even though they contain copies of the control file. But without the control file, the backups are inaccessible. Although we mentioned in Chapter 12 that you can make explicit calls to **dbms_backup_restore** to get access to control files in RMAN backups without a current control file, this is by no means a supported or smart approach. Instead, if you're running without a catalog, make explicit copies of the control file outside of RMAN using the following command:

```
alter database backup controlfile to '/u02/backup/cfilebkup.ctl';
```

Then get these copies moved off the target database server. Put them on your laptop, your workstation, your other servers, and under your pillow. This is your safety net.

Retention Policies in Oracle8i

You have only one retention policy choice in Oracle8i: redundancy. The recovery window was introduced in Oracle9i. So, you need to run reports based on a level of redundancy. If you have a time-based business rule for backup retention, you just have to count how many backups you have scheduled in that timeframe and then use that number for your policy.

In addition, there is no command **delete obsolete** in Oracle8i. This means that you have to manually compile a list of backups that are obsolete with a **report**

obsolete command, and then manually remove them with a **change** command. This would look something like the following:

```
report obsolete redundancy = 10 device type 'sbt_tape';
```

From this, you would compile a list of backup set primary key numbers. Then, you would use the **change** command to remove them:

```
allocate channel for maintenance type 'sbt_tape' parms <MML info>;
change backupset <key, key, key, etc.> delete;
release channel;
```

Duplication

Duplication in Oracle8i is, in many ways, similar to that in Oracle9i, except that you have to build your **run** block instead of using permanent configuration settings. In particular, this means you have to allocate auxiliary channels manually. For instance, consider the **duplicate** command we used in the RMAN Workshop "Duplication to the Same Server, Using Disk Backups" in Chapter 16. You would modify it like this:

```
Run {
allocate channel c1 type disk;
allocate auxiliary channel aux1 type disk;
duplicate target database to aux1
  pfile=/space/oracle_user/OraHome1/admin/aux1/pfile/init.ora
  logfile
  '/space/oracle_user/OraHome1/oradata/aux1/redo1.dbf' size 100m,
  '/space/oracle_user/OraHome1/oradata/aux1/redo2.dbf' size 100m,
  '/space/oracle_user/OraHome1/oradata/aux1/redo3.dbf' size 100m; }
```

In addition, you cannot use the **configure auxname** command to rename files prior to running your **duplicate** command. Instead, in Oracle8i, you use **set auxname** within the **run** block itself, like this:

```
Run {
set auxname for datafile 1 to '/u02/dup_data/system01.dbf';
set auxname for datafile 2 to '/u02/dup_data/undo01.dbf';
…
allocate channel c1 type disk;
allocate auxiliary channel aux1 type disk;
duplicate target database to aux1… }
```

Remember that using the **set auxname** command in Oracle8i requires the use of a recovery catalog.

There is a difference in the parameters **db_file_name_convert and log_file_ name_convert** between Oracle versions 8i and 9i. In Oracle9i, you can place text strings in pairs, so that the following

```
db_file_name_convert=('sun92', 'aux1', '/u02' , '/u03')
```

would convert every instance of the string 'sun92' to the string 'aux1', and 'u02' to 'u03' in each datafile in which the first strings were found. In Oracle8i, there can only be a single matched pair: you can only convert 'sun92' to 'aux1'. This means that every datafile in your database must have at least some character string in common, or you cannot use the _file_name_convert parameters.

A final note on duplication. The **duplicate** command was not introduced until version 8.1.5, so if you are in Oracle8.0.*x*, you have to use manual conversion methods to create a clone database. In addition, the ability to create a standby database using the **duplicate...for standby** command was not introduced until version 8.1.7.

APPENDIX
D

Setting Up an RMAN Test Environment

est environments are tricky, and every shop has its own concept of what testing is required, and at what level, for application design, quality assurance, version control, and so forth. Obviously, a short appendix in a backup and recovery book won't be able to address an entire test environment. But if you have this book in hand, and you are looking to implement a backup strategy that includes RMAN, we encourage you to set up an environment that is safe for testing the exercises in this book.

A test environment for backup and recovery is different from other testing environments. First of all, you have to be able to remove datafiles, or even the entire database, on a whim, without having to clear it with other users. In other words, you need your own database. If you begin testing RMAN functionality on a shared database, pretty soon you'll either start getting angry phone calls from other users or find yourself locked out of the machine by the SA. A backup and recovery test environment is simply too volatile to share. Think about it from the other end: You're busy testing a backup yourself, when suddenly the backup aborts because someone started removing datafiles in order to test their own restore and recovery.

On the other hand, you need to test your strategies in an environment that most closely matches that of your production databases. Therefore, you can't always run in isolation, because you might need to tune your backup on a large production-grade server that has the same kind of load as production.

What we suggest, then, is that you approach RMAN backup and recovery testing as a two-tier investigation. First, get comfortable with the functionality and behavior in the isolation of a small test server. Second, take the lessons you've learned and schedule time on a larger, production-grade database server to test. This way, you can schedule time on a test box for a backup/recovery test outage, and not spend that valuable time trying to learn lessons that could have been figured out on your workstation.

So, what does this approach look like more specifically? The answer is provided in this appendix.

The Test Box

The first-level test machine for RMAN functionality doesn't need to be a supercomputer. In fact, think of the first level of testing as just a rehearsal—you're reading through your lines, getting the placement right, and talking through the steps with the other actors and the director.

Matching Your Production Environment

If possible, your RMAN testing should take place on the same operating system that you run in production. This is a rather humorous thing to say, I know: who has a single OS in their environment anymore? Anyway, if you will be backing up only Solaris servers, it makes sense to invest a little money in a Sun workstation. That way, you can begin production environment matching as soon as possible.

Going Cheap

It's not that critical to have your first wave of testing done on the same OS as your production environment. RMAN acts the same on all platforms, and the exercises in this book will work on all platforms. So, if you're in the market for an RMAN test box, we have only two words: go cheap. Buy a commodity-priced computer that runs Windows or Linux. Find a refurbished box out on eBay or something. Don't spend a lot of time or energy trying to get a souped-up box with all the bells and whistles.

Processor Speed

Don't worry about processor speeds at this level. Even if you monitor for performance at this level, the data is meaningless when compared to your production environment. Instead, spend money on other resources: mainly, disk space and memory.

Memory

You need enough memory to run three Oracle instances simultaneously, along with your media management software. If you will be testing with Enterprise Manager or some other management software package, factor that in as well. We suggest, at a minimum, 512MB of memory, but really, you should have 1GB of memory. Otherwise, you'll start swapping and slow things down considerably.

Disk Space

Disks are cheap, and you don't need some SCSI disk or anything, just space. Speed, again, is not important at this level. Go buy an 80GB hard drive from a local computer store, and that should be sufficient. You're doing concept testing at this level, so you can control the sizes of databases to keep things under control. But keep in mind that you're going to have more than one database, and you will also be backing up to disk (most likely), so you need space for RMAN backup pieces, as well. So load up on disk space if you can.

The Oracle Configuration

After you get your test box up and running, you need to think about your Oracle installation and configuration. This step depends on what exactly you need to test. Will you be backing up multiple versions of Oracle? Will you be using Enterprise Manager?

Multiple Homes

If you will be testing out multiple versions, be sure to install them in chronological order from oldest to newest; for example, install Oracle version 8.1.7 before 9.0.1, and 9.0.1 before 9.2.0. Before you get very far, patch Oracle to the latest level. There are always RMAN bugs getting fixed, so it makes sense to be at the most patched level.

Creating Databases

Obviously, you need at least one database created in each ORACLE_HOME that you have installed. These databases may be default databases created during Oracle installation, but an even better scenario would be to use databases that are configured somewhat like production databases. Obviously, from a size perspective, that may not be possible, but you can scale datafile sizes down while keeping the same number of datafiles and tablespaces.

In addition, try scaling down the memory utilization of these test boxes to be as low as possible. You won't actually be doing that much processing, so you don't need a lot of buffer cache available. The smaller you keep the System Global Area (SGA), the better off your little test box will be.

You also need a recovery catalog database that is separate from the target databases that you are using for testing. We always recommend that your recovery catalog database be the most recent version, so put this in a 9.2 home. In a pinch, this can also be used as a target, but try to keep your recovery catalog database out of the mix of databases that you blow away and rebuild. It just makes life easier.

Oracle Enterprise Manager

If you plan to use Enterprise Manager, make sure there is enough memory to do so. There is a memory cost of about 300MB for having the OMS and Agent up and running on a box. We encourage you to give this product a run-through, and not just for RMAN utilization. You'll find at least a few tools that will become indispensable.

The one caveat to testing with EM is that the Agent can only operate successfully on computers that have a fixed IP address that is registered in a DNS server. If your test box isn't capable of this, EM won't work for you. That being said, you can cheat, but it's kind of messy. Essentially, on any box that you want an Agent to run on, you must be able to do an **nslookup** on both the hostname and the IP address. So even if you have a dynamic address, you can always use the dynamic address's hostname if necessary.

Media Management Considerations

If you have the ability, you should install a version of the media management client that you will be using in production. Then, install the Oracle plug-in and do the backups to tape the same as you would in production. This gives you the best ability to anticipate what to expect when you implement your strategy in your enterprise.

If you can't get access to the media management product that is used for your enterprise, we suggest installing the free Legato Single Server Version (LSSV) that comes with Oracle9i Release 2. Even if you don't have a local tape drive on your test box, LSSV can be configured to fake a tape drive on disk, so that you become accustomed to configuring RMAN for tape writes.

To set up LSSV to write to a fake tape drive, you must manually configure the device in the Networker Administrator. We discussed the setup of LSSV on Windows in Chapter 4. After following those setup steps, do the following:

1. Open Networker Administrator and double-click your computer in the Server list.

2. From the options on the right, choose Devices. A new window will appear, and if you have no tape devices, nothing will be underneath your computer name.

3. Leaving Networker Administrator open, go to Windows Explorer and navigate to a folder where you want your *fake* tape to be located. Create an empty text file called simply **volume**.

4. Go back to Networker Administrator, right-click your computer name, and choose Create.

5. In the Create Device dialog box, name the new volume file in the Name list box, and then choose Optical from the Media Type drop-down list box.

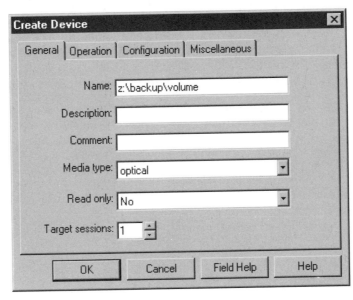

6. Click OK. You will see the path and name of your text file appear under your computer name.

7. Right-click on your new tape device and choose Operations | Label. Leave all the defaults, and just click OK.

Your tape device will show an animation of it being mounted, and then will have a READY status. You can now back up to tape.

The RMAN Configuration

Now that you have your system set up with Oracle installed and databases built, the following are a few hints on the testing process itself:

■ *Have a cold backup that remains untouched.* Before you do any RMAN testing, shut down your database and take a cold OS copy backup and place it in a folder that doesn't get touched. This is your last line of defense if you completely mess everything up during your RMAN testing.

■ *Switch your redo logs a lot.* One of the biggest mistakes that are made with RMAN testing is that the timeframe between the backup and restore is unrealistically short. Confusion sets in because there is no space between the completion time of the backup and the "until time" of the restore operation. So, after any backup, make sure you switch the log file three or four times, just to put a little "distance" between operations.

■ *Leave your catalog database alone.* You will be tempted to use the database that houses your catalog as a target and perform some tests with it. That is fine—that's why it's called a test environment. But you can seriously undermine your testing if you foul up your catalog. Do yourself a favor and leave the catalog database to its own devices. And export your catalog schema with a user-level export before any new test session begins.

■ *Keep up with catalog maintenance.* This may be your test environment, but you will be creating a lot of backups over time, and you have a limited amount of space on your little test box. Take the opportunity to test out using retention policies, and get rid of old backups.

■ *Remove clones as soon as possible.* Attack of the clones! If you're using the **duplicate** command, you can end up with a number of different instances running and taking up precious memory and disk space. Hey, it's a clone, and you're in a test environment—get rid of it as soon as you make it.

■ *Leave a clone file system in place.* You don't need to go through the steps of building the file system and the init.ora file for your duplicate database every time you want to test the **duplicate** or **duplicate...for standby** command. Leave the file system and supporting files in place, and use the same db_name and SID. On Windows, be sure to leave the Oracleservice<SID> in place in the Services control panel.

■ *Don't get attached.* Sometimes, you need to just blow everything away and start over from scratch, particularly if you don't have good maintenance habits. Eventually, your database will get to the point that it has had tablespaces dropped, had re-created, dropped, and forgotten files placed in the wrong directory, had archive logs stored all over the place—basically a rambling mess. Don't worry. That's why they call it testing. Don't get too wrapped up in the environment you have, just whack everything and start over from the cold backup you took prior to testing.

That's about it. You'll surely find some of your own valuable lessons after you've done a bit of testing. After going through the conceptual learning on your small test box, take the scripts you've built and the knowledge you've gained and schedule some time on a production-grade system to make sure everything is going to scale up to your enterprise. You'll be glad you took the time to find out before you went live. Happy trails!

Index

M

N

S

INTERNATIONAL CONTACT INFORMATION

AUSTRALIA
McGraw-Hill Book Company Australia Pty. Ltd.
TEL +61-2-9900-1800
FAX +61-2-9878-8881
http://www.mcgraw-hill.com.au
books-it_sydney@mcgraw-hill.com

CANADA
McGraw-Hill Ryerson Ltd.
TEL +905-430-5000
FAX +905-430-5020
http://www.mcgraw-hill.ca

GREECE, MIDDLE EAST, & AFRICA
(Excluding South Africa)
McGraw-Hill Hellas
TEL +30-1-656-0990-3-4
FAX +30-1-654-5525

MEXICO (Also serving Latin America)
McGraw-Hill Interamericana Editores S.A. de C.V.
TEL +525-117-1583
FAX +525-117-1589
http://www.mcgraw-hill.com.mx
fernando_castellanos@mcgraw-hill.com

SINGAPORE (Serving Asia)
McGraw-Hill Book Company
TEL +65-863-1580
FAX +65-862-3354
http://www.mcgraw-hill.com.sg
mghasia@mcgraw-hill.com

SOUTH AFRICA
McGraw-Hill South Africa
TEL +27-11-622-7512
FAX +27-11-622-9045
robyn_swanepoel@mcgraw-hill.com

SPAIN
McGraw-Hill/Interamericana de España, S.A.U.
TEL +34-91-180-3000
FAX +34-91-372-8513
http://www.mcgraw-hill.es
professional@mcgraw-hill.es

UNITED KINGDOM, NORTHERN,
EASTERN, & CENTRAL EUROPE
McGraw-Hill Education Europe
TEL +44-1-628-502500
FAX +44-1-628-770224
http://www.mcgraw-hill.co.uk
computing_neurope@mcgraw-hill.com

ALL OTHER INQUIRIES Contact:
Osborne/McGraw-Hill
TEL +1-510-549-6600
FAX +1-510-883-7600
http://www.osborne.com
omg_international@mcgraw-hill.com

GET YOUR FREE SUBSCRIPTION
TO ORACLE MAGAZINE

Oracle Magazine is essential gear for today's information technology professionals. Stay informed and increase your productivity with every issue of *Oracle Magazine.* Inside each free bimonthly issue you'll get:

- Up-to-date information on Oracle Database, E-Business Suite applications, Web development, and database technology and business trends
- Third-party news and announcements
- Technical articles on Oracle Products and operating environments
- Development and administration tips
- Real-world customer stories

IF THERE ARE OTHER ORACLE USERS AT YOUR LOCATION WHO WOULD LIKE TO RECEIVE THEIR OWN SUBSCRIPTION TO ORACLE MAGAZINE, PLEASE PHOTOCOPY THIS FORM AND PASS IT ALONG.

Three easy ways to subscribe:

① Web
Visit our Web site at www.oracle.com/oraclemagazine. You'll find a subscription form there, plus much more!

② Fax
Complete the questionnaire on the back of this card and fax the questionnaire side only to +1.847.647.9735.

③ Mail
Complete the questionnaire on the back of this card and mail it to P.O. Box 1263, Skokie, IL 60076-8263

Oracle Publishing

FREE SUBSCRIPTION

○ Yes, please send me a FREE subscription to *Oracle Magazine*   ○ **NO**

To receive a free subscription to *Oracle Magazine*, you must fill out the entire card, sign it, and date it (incomplete cards cannot be processed or acknowledged). You can also fax your application to +1.847.647.9735.
Or subscribe at our Web site at www.oracle.com/oraclemagazine/

○ From time to time, Oracle Publishing allows our partners exclusive access to our e-mail addresses for special promotions and announcements. To be included in this program, please check this box.

signature (required)   date

X

○ Oracle Publishing allows sharing of our mailing list with selected third parties. If you prefer your mailing address not to be included in this program, please check here. If at any time you would like to be removed from this mailing list, please contact Customer Service at +1.847.647.9630 or send an e-mail to oracle@halldata.com.

name   title

company   e-mail address

street/p.o. box

city/state/zip or postal code   telephone

country   fax

YOU MUST ANSWER ALL NINE QUESTIONS BELOW.

① WHAT IS THE PRIMARY BUSINESS ACTIVITY OF YOUR FIRM AT THIS LOCATION? (check one only)

- □ 01 Application Service Provider
- □ 02 Communications
- □ 03 Consulting, Training
- □ 04 Data Processing
- □ 05 Education
- □ 06 Engineering
- □ 07 Financial Services
- □ 08 Government (federal, local, state, other)
- □ 09 Government (military)
- □ 10 Health Care
- □ 11 Manufacturing (aerospace, defense)
- □ 12 Manufacturing (computer hardware)
- □ 13 Manufacturing (noncomputer)
- □ 14 Research & Development
- □ 15 Retailing, Wholesaling, Distribution
- □ 16 Software Development
- □ 17 Systems Integration, VAR, VAD, OEM
- □ 18 Transportation
- □ 19 Utilities (electric, gas, sanitation)
- □ 98 Other Business and Services

② WHICH OF THE FOLLOWING BEST DESCRIBES YOUR PRIMARY JOB FUNCTION? (check one only)

Corporate Management/Staff
- □ 01 Executive Management (President, Chair, CEO, CFO, Owner, Partner, Principal)
- □ 02 Finance/Administrative Management (VP/Director/ Manager/Controller, Purchasing, Administration)
- □ 03 Sales/Marketing Management (VP/Director/Manager)
- □ 04 Computer Systems/Operations Management (CIO/VP/Director/ Manager MIS, Operations)

IS/IT Staff
- □ 05 Systems Development/ Programming Management
- □ 06 Systems Development/ Programming Staff
- □ 07 Consulting
- □ 08 DBA/Systems Administrator
- □ 09 Education/Training
- □ 10 Technical Support Director/Manager
- □ 11 Other Technical Management/Staff
- □ 98 Other

③ WHAT IS YOUR CURRENT PRIMARY OPERATING PLATFORM? (select all that apply)

- □ 01 Digital Equipment UNIX
- □ 02 Digital Equipment VAX VMS
- □ 03 HP UNIX
- □ 04 IBM AIX

- □ 05 IBM UNIX
- □ 06 Java
- □ 07 Linux
- □ 08 Macintosh
- □ 09 MS-DOS
- □ 10 MVS
- □ 11 NetWare
- □ 12 Network Computing
- □ 13 OpenVMS
- □ 14 SCO UNIX
- □ 15 Sequent DYNIX/ptx
- □ 16 Sun Solaris/SunOS
- □ 17 SVR4
- □ 18 UnixWare
- □ 19 Windows
- □ 20 Windows NT
- □ 21 Other UNIX
- □ 98 Other
- □ 99 None of the above

④ DO YOU EVALUATE, SPECIFY, RECOMMEND, OR AUTHORIZE THE PURCHASE OF ANY OF THE FOLLOWING? (check all that apply)

- □ 01 Hardware
- □ 02 Software
- □ 03 Application Development Tools
- □ 04 Database Products
- □ 05 Internet or Intranet Products
- □ 99 None of the above

⑤ IN YOUR JOB, DO YOU USE OR PLAN TO PURCHASE ANY OF THE FOLLOWING PRODUCTS? (check all that apply)

Software
- □ 01 Business Graphics
- □ 02 CAD/CAE/CAM
- □ 03 CASE
- □ 04 Communications
- □ 05 Database Management
- □ 06 File Management
- □ 07 Finance
- □ 08 Java
- □ 09 Materials Resource Planning
- □ 10 Multimedia Authoring
- □ 11 Networking
- □ 12 Office Automation
- □ 13 Order Entry/Inventory Control
- □ 14 Programming
- □ 15 Project Management
- □ 16 Scientific and Engineering
- □ 17 Spreadsheets
- □ 18 Systems Management
- □ 19 Workflow

Hardware
- □ 20 Macintosh
- □ 21 Mainframe
- □ 22 Massively Parallel Processing

- □ 23 Minicomputer
- □ 24 PC
- □ 25 Network Computer
- □ 26 Symmetric Multiprocessing
- □ 27 Workstation

Peripherals
- □ 28 Bridges/Routers/Hubs/Gateways
- □ 29 CD-ROM Drives
- □ 30 Disk Drives/Subsystems
- □ 31 Modems
- □ 32 Tape Drives/Subsystems
- □ 33 Video Boards/Multimedia

Services
- □ 34 Application Service Provider
- □ 35 Consulting
- □ 36 Education/Training
- □ 37 Maintenance
- □ 38 Online Database Services
- □ 39 Support
- □ 40 Technology-Based Training
- □ 98 Other
- □ 99 None of the above

⑥ WHAT ORACLE PRODUCTS ARE IN USE AT YOUR SITE? (check all that apply)

Software
- □ 01 Oracle9i
- □ 02 Oracle9i Lite
- □ 03 Oracle8
- □ 04 Oracle8i
- □ 05 Oracle8i Lite
- □ 06 Oracle7
- □ 07 Oracle9i Application Server
- □ 08 Oracle9i Application Server Wireless
- □ 09 Oracle Data Mart Suites
- □ 10 Oracle Internet Commerce Server
- □ 11 Oracle interMedia
- □ 12 Oracle Lite
- □ 13 Oracle Payment Server
- □ 14 Oracle Video Server
- □ 15 Oracle Rdb

Tools
- □ 16 Oracle Darwin
- □ 17 Oracle Designer
- □ 18 Oracle Developer
- □ 19 Oracle Discoverer
- □ 20 Oracle Express
- □ 21 Oracle JDeveloper
- □ 22 Oracle Reports
- □ 23 Oracle Portal
- □ 24 Oracle Warehouse Builder
- □ 25 Oracle Workflow

Oracle E-Business Suite
- □ 26 Oracle Advanced Planning/Scheduling
- □ 27 Oracle Business Intelligence
- □ 28 Oracle E-Commerce
- □ 29 Oracle Exchange
- □ 30 Oracle Financials

- □ 31 Oracle Human Resources
- □ 32 Oracle Interaction Center
- □ 33 Oracle Internet Procurement
- □ 34 Oracle Manufacturing
- □ 35 Oracle Marketing
- □ 36 Oracle Order Management
- □ 37 Oracle Professional Services Automation
- □ 38 Oracle Projects
- □ 39 Oracle Sales
- □ 40 Oracle Service
- □ 41 Oracle Small Business Suite
- □ 42 Oracle Supply Chain Management
- □ 43 Oracle Travel Management
- □ 44 Oracle Treasury

Oracle Services
- □ 45 Oracle.com Online Services
- □ 46 Oracle Consulting
- □ 47 Oracle Education
- □ 48 Oracle Support
- □ 98 ther
- □ 99 None of the above

⑦ WHAT OTHER DATABASE PRODUCTS ARE IN USE AT YOUR SITE? (check all that apply)

- □ 01 Access
- □ 02 Baan
- □ 03 dbase
- □ 04 Gupta
- □ 05 BM DB2
- □ 06 Informix
- □ 07 Ingres
- □ 08 Microsoft Access
- □ 09 Microsoft SQL Server
- □ 10 PeopleSoft
- □ 11 Progress
- □ 12 SAP
- □ 13 Sybase
- □ 14 VSAM
- □ 98 Other
- □ 99 None of the above

⑧ DURING THE NEXT 12 MONTHS, HOW MUCH DO YOU ANTICIPATE YOUR ORGANIZATION WILL SPEND ON COMPUTER HARDWARE, SOFTWARE, PERIPHERALS, AND SERVICES FOR YOUR LOCATION? (check only one)

- □ 01 Less than $10,000
- □ 02 $10,000 to $49,999
- □ 03 $50,000 to $99,999
- □ 04 $100,000 to $499,999
- □ 05 $500,000 to $999,999
- □ 06 $1,000,000 and over

⑨ WHAT IS YOUR COMPANY'S YEARLY SALES REVENUE? (please choose one)

- □ 01 $500, 000, 000 and above
- □ 02 $100, 000, 000 to $500, 000, 000
- □ 03 $50, 000, 000 to $100, 000, 000
- □ 04 $5, 000, 000 to $50, 000, 000
- □ 05 $1, 000, 000 to $5, 000, 000

123101